THE SECOND CHURCH

Writings from the Greco-Roman World Supplement Series

John T. Fitzgerald, Editor

Number 1

The Second Church
Popular Christianity A.D. 200–400

THE SECOND CHURCH
Popular Christianity A.D. 200–400

Ramsay MacMullen

Society of Biblical Literature
Atlanta

The Second Church:
Popular Christianity A.D. 200–400

Copyright © 2009 by the Society of Biblical Literature

All rights reserved. No part of this work may be reproduced or transmitted in any form or by any means, electronic or mechanical, including photocopying and recording, or by means of any information storage or retrieval system, except as may be expressly permitted by the 1976 Copyright Act or in writing from the publisher. Requests for permission should be addressed in writing to the Rights and Permissions Office, Society of Biblical Literature, 825 Houston Mill Road, Atlanta, GA 30329 USA.

Library of Congress Cataloging-in-Publication Data

MacMullen, Ramsay, 1928–
  The second church : popular Christianity, A.D. 200–400 / by Ramsay MacMullen.
      p. cm. — (Writings from the Greco-Roman world supplement series ; no. 1)
  Includes bibliographical references and index.
  ISBN: 978-1-58983-403-3 (pbk. : alk. paper)
  ISBN: 978-1-58983-404-0 (electronic library copy)
  1. Church history—Primitive and early church, ca. 30–600. I. Title.
  BR165.M235 2009b
  270.1—dc22   2009001214

17 16 15 14 13 12 11 10 09   5 4 3 2 1
Printed in the United States of America on acid-free, recycled paper
conforming to ANSI/NISO Z39.48-1992 (R1997) and ISO 9706:1994
standards for paper permanence.

Contents

Figures — vii
Credits — viii
Preface — ix

1. The Eastern Empire — 1

2. Greece and the Balkans — 33

3. North Africa — 51

4. Italy and the Northwest — 69

5. Conclusions — 95

Abbreviations — 115
Appendix: Churches Built before 400 — 117
Notes — 143
Bibliography of Works Cited — 177
Index — 205

Figures

1.1: The eastern provinces (inset, northern Syria)	1
1.2: The house-church in Dura-Europos	2
1.3: Dura-Europos, the baptistery	4
1.4: How they would look at a service	5
1.5: The Tyre basilica, reconstructed	11
1.6: The laity fitted into the Anastasis church at Jerusalem	13
1.7: Antioch in Pisidia, the fourth-century basilica	16
1.8: The Kharab Shems church a century ago	18
1.9: The Kharab Shems church, ground plan	18
1.10: Jeradé (north Syrian) church interior	19
1.11: A funerary picnic on a tombstone in Konya (Turkey)	24
1.12: Antioch in John Chrysostom's time	27
1.13: St. Babylas martyr church at Kaoussié	28
2.1: The Greek provinces and lower Danube	35
2.2: Trieste's martyr church	36
2.3: Three phases in worship at Philippi	38
2.4: Mosaics of the "Paul basilica" under the Octagon	39
2.5: Air-view of Manastirine cemetery	41
2.6: The excavation results in Manastirine	42
2.7: Martyr-memorial services (ca. 375)	43
2.8: A mensa from Ephesus	45
2.9: St. Demeter's crypt at Thessalonica	47
2.10a: The Kapljuc basilica	48
2.10b: Chancel-reconstruction	48
3.1: The North African provinces	52
3.2: Basilicas of Sitifis, "A" at right, "B" at left	54
3.3a: Plan of St. Salsa's chapel	56
3.3b: Reconstruction of St. Salsa's chapel	57
3.4: The *area* adjoining the "Alexander chapel", Tipasa	60
3.5: The cult of the family's dead at Tipasa	61
3.6: St. Salsa cemetery, basilica, and chapel	64
3.7: The cathedral at Theveste (Tebessa)	66
3.8: The entry-court and grand stairway, Tebessa	67

4.1: Catacomb gallery, six *loculi* on each side	70
4.2: Selected church sites pre-400	71
4.3: A *cubiculum* with an *arcosolium* to the rear	73
4.4: A *refrigerium* (the Vibia tomb)	75
4.5: A *refrigerium* (SS. Marcellino e Pietro catacomb)	75
4.6: Isola Sacra *mausolea*	78
4.7: Isola Sacra *mausoleum* and built mensa	79
4.8: St. Peter's plus "the Six"	81
4.9: A corner of the "Anonima della via Ardeatina"	83
4.10: A feast day in S. Sebastiano	84
4.11: St. Peter's façade (the Pola casket)	88
4.12: Italy and beyond	90
4.13: Felix' cult center in Nola	92
5.1: "Cyprian's memoria" at Carthage	99
5.2: Frend's idea of the place of Christianity	103

Credits

Figs. 1.4, 2.7, 3.5, and 4.10 (the "renderings") by Wladek Prosol; the maps (figs. 1.1, 2.1, 3.1, 4.2, and 4.12) by Stacey Maples in the Yale University Library; and several drawings by Sam Kirby. Figs. 1.2–3, courtesy of Yale University Art Gallery; 1.7, Courtesy Turkish Historical Socety, Ankara; 1.8, courtesy Department of Art and Archaeology, Princeton University; fig. 1.10, Saarbrucker Druckerei und Verlag; 1.11, courtesy of Dr. M. Sahin; 2.4, courtesy of Dr. Charalambos Bakirtzis; 2.5, Photo Arheoloski Muzej, Split, and its exhibit *Salona Christiana* (1994); 3.4, courtesy Comité des travaux historiques et scientifiques (Leschi 1957, 378); 3.6, courtesy Ministère de l'Information et de la Culture, Beaux-Arts et Antiquités, Algeria (Christern 1968, 199 fig. 4); 3.7, courtesy Office National de gestion et d'exploitation des biens culturels protégés, Algeria (Christern 1976, Tafel 2a); 3.8, Gerd Schneider in Christern (1976) fig. 12 and Franz Steiner Verlag, Stuttgart; 4.3, Research Services and Collections, Sterling Memorial Library, Yale University; 4.4–5, courtesy General Collection, Beinecke Rare Book and Manuscript Library, Yale University (Wilpert 1903, Tav. 132 and 157); 4.6, courtesy Professor Paul Zanker; 4.9, Deutsches Archäologisches Institut Archiv; 4.11, courtesy Biblioteca di Archeologia e Storia dell'Arte, Rome; 5.1, courtesy Professor Liliane Ennabli (Ennabli 1975, 13); 5.2, courtesy Darton, Longman, and Todd Ltd., London (Frend 1984, map D)

Preface

The two centuries indicated in the title have, at about mid-point, one date inevitably given first mention and most emphasis: the year 312. This, for anyone interested in early Christian history, must have special meaning; for it was then that Constantine, ruler over the western half of the Roman Empire, declared himself a believer, moved by a vision he had had of a cross in the sky. Before, there had been cruel persecutions; after, only the so-called Peace of the Church. It was announced jointly by Constantine and his colleague to the east, in an Edict of Milan of 313.

With what result? The endless variety of non-Christian beliefs among populations that we call Gallic, Iberian, Punic, Syriac, Coptic, Lycaonian, Berber, Macedonian, and so forth, not to mention the Greeks and Romans—populations which of course thought of themselves and the divinities they addressed simply as "us" and "ours"—all continued in their lives undisturbed, for a time. There was no such thing as a State religion to make them over by force; nor did Constantine or his new ecclesiastical advisers want any martyrs. The stick and carrot, however, could be applied by the convert emperor as he pleased, without challenge; they could be given publicity and erratically enforced almost from the first year of the Peace, to induce the growth and ascendancy of Christendom, and an end to all alternatives. A new world could be sensed, about to be born and to change everything.

The point of change interests us. Of course. How could it not? No one can look at it without wanting to see it a little more distinctly; and nothing will serve us better for the purpose than the mind's eye. I depend on this always. I assume the same instrument of vision is what anyone would use, not just historians—the mind's eye, its focus drawn back to see the object in a broad setting, and then again pressed forward on the object to see it in some detail. Imagination, so used, becomes a zoom lens, turned at first on the catacombs, then on the basilicas.

These two elements can dramatize the story: first, those miles and miles of tunnels under the modern city and suburbs of Rome, in which it was once imagined that the Christians had to sustain their faith clandestinely, until, with the converted Constantine enthroned in their very midst, they could emerge to freedom of worship in the open air. They might do so, then, in the vast assembly halls the emperor built for them, sparkling with rare marbles and mosaics, in the capital at first and then throughout the ancient world. Almost overnight his co-religionists gained in wealth, prominence, numbers and influence.

The symbolism of their rise from underground to such pomp and publicity has something wonderfully fulfilling about it—something almost theatrical. And we cannot only imagine but with our own eyes see and wander about today in both catacombs and basilicas, asking and answering our own questions. Ancient history is rarely so accommodating.

Even the people, the living people can be restored to these settings, to make them complete, by a sort of disciplined evocation; and if this succeeds it may not only satisfy our natural curiosity about our fellow creatures, but, further, explain certain puzzling points of development and history in early Christendom.

Just here, however, I see the first of three obstacles to that so-perfect evocation: first, that Rome is not enough. Rome even with all Italy added is not the whole story, nor anywhere near.

For, if we pull back to a view that takes in the ancient world as a whole, it is obvious that the third-to-fourth-century changes affected Christians everywhere, of whom the great majority could be found in the southeastern quarter of the Mediterranean world. Here, not in Rome and Italy, Christianity had begun; from here it spread. The impulse was ever from the Greek-speaking East, westward.

In its course we can see the familiar caricature of muscular Romans on display, set over those so-mental Greeks. Romans were distrustful of fancy thinking and too-ready speech (unless it could justify itself in an election or a court-case). They preferred orders to arguments—in contrast, the Greeks, a people in love with their own words, loving new ideas. So Christendom in the period of expansion with which I am concerned gives us the amazing Origen and Gregory the Wonderworker, and Clement of Alexandria; Eusebius father of ecclesiastical history; Athanasius whom nothing kept from battle, who, so to speak, brought in the ascetic Anthony from the desert and placed him before an enormous audience as the exemplar of a new piety; then, in the second half of the fourth century, a number of other names even more familiar, men of rare eloquence, notably the two Gregory's, Basil, John Chrysostom in Antioch and Constantinople—all these, Greek-speaking. By contrast, in the Latin West, the heroes of an equal fame are far fewer: only Tertullian and Cyprian and, after the mid-fourth century, Ambrose and Jerome (Augustine belonging rather more to the next century).

It is a sign of its eastern origins, too, that Christian services were celebrated in Greek by the Roman *ecclesia* (this, a Greek word transliterated into Latin). Such was still the practice in the mid-fourth century, when a good proportion of the people buried in the catacombs were still using Greek as their native language. Centuries of immigration, including forced displacement as slaves, had had a profound effect on the great capital of the ancient world. Among other signs of its operations was religion, including post-Pauline Christianity, which had spread slowly, not so much by evangelism as by people themselves moving about, bringing the comfort of their traditions with them and seeking out their like, to make stronger cultural communities wherever they settled. Even further west than Rome, in the 160s and 170s, Irenaeus in southern France is a case in point, Greek-speaking, as are the Christians in the Rhone Valley that he wrote about or, in the next century, others to the north, in the Danube provinces.

I must warn of a second obstacle, if not to evocation, then to the accuracy of it; for, without any special intent, advances in our knowledge of third- and fourth-century Christendom have falsely favored Rome's western, Latin provinces. These are too much seen as the areas "where the action is," or was. Such is the common perception. But why should not Antioch be the focus of study, or Constantinople, Alexandria, Ephesus or Carthage? Explanation lies in a mere accident. The lucky western nations through their preponderant riches and population have for centuries controlled their own perceptions of the past, and everyone else's, too. We are of course more interested in our own most direct inheritance than in anyone else's. Yet "our" perception of what is natural today quite misrepresents the asymmetries of long ago.

It was inevitable. Nowhere in the eastern half of the Mediterranean world is, or in recent centuries has there ever been, such wealth as the Vatican by itself alone commands, today, for the exploration of early Christian history. Where but in Italy might Antonio Bosio's lifelong explorations of the catacombs find support and publication in 1632, when all the lands off to the east were still under Ottoman rule? It was Bosio's great work that came into the hands of the eleven-year-old Giovanni Battista de Rossi, to serve him as guide and inspiration in his own prodigious labors of a lifetime, similarly, over the course of the next century, to reveal the extent and story of the Christians underground.

Western interest in Christendom of the central or eastern provinces did eventually develop, but slowly. It was almost by afterthought, through archeological exploration, preeminently by the Germans in Turkey, the French in Syria, the British in Egypt. Dura in Iraq, site of the one and only certain so-called "house-church", was noticed first by Capt. M. C. Murphy of the British army, whereupon an American expert was called in for a first inspection, and serious digging undertaken in due course by French experts with Americans added to the team (but also a Dane, Harald Ingholt, and a Russian, the great Michael Rostovtzeff).

Rostovtzeff had had to complain about the fate of his early writings on ancient history: "They're in Russian, they're not read"; and his complaint had to be in Latin, to be half-understood! On early Christian architecture (of prime importance for my own subject here) no survey is better than Orlandos'; but it's in Greek; so it is never mentioned.[1] Quite naturally. We of western European languages don't handle either Russian or Greek. "We" shouldn't be expected to. But the point is, an accident of the modern world distorts and obscures "our" understanding of the ancient world; and what has been disregarded and so lost through centuries of inattention is, unluckily, now gone forever. Only, some attempt at the correction of the record ought to be made before our focus fixes finally upon that better-known drama in Italy.

A third obstacle to an understanding of what happened in and as a result of 312 is a matter of numbers: the great names acknowledged above, like Origen, and those not so great but still known to us through their writings or the mentions of them as heroes of one sort or another—all these together count as no more than a hundredth of one per cent of the Christian population at any given moment. It is not to discount their influence, then, that we may fairly ask: How may we catch some glimpse of the great mass of Christians, the commonality?

Answer must be chiefly sought underground; for Christians as a population are best known to us not by the written word, except occasionally inscribed. Instead, it is only by excavation, and not only of the catacombs, that their lives and behavior can be drawn up for our inspection. Literary evidence can only represent that upper stratum among the Christian population who controlled the written record, almost every one a bishop, from among whom later centuries would make choice of the most perfect thinkers and stylists, to preserve them to the present, where this was at all possible. So the cream rose to the top; the privileged and elite spoke for all. All Christians must be perceived as the elite happened to mention them, much or little; or as the elite happened to see them, more or less accurately, or not.

How might the written record be tested and perhaps corrected? The answer: only by what might be found in the earth, long lived on and, one might say, lived *over*, and thus covered up and preserved to the present day.

My focus here must therefore be on archeology and the still tangible signs of human behavior. They invite the action of the mind's eye, to make plain their use. They are, in the first place, built structures, whether tombs or houses or places of assembly; but they may also be quite little things that someone may notice, like a shelf, or a hole in the ground the size of a bucket, or a hole or a slot in a stone at a particular place evidently for a particular purpose, or bits of a cooking pot still with the signs of charring on them. Such use of the mind's eye may be quite revealing of little common truths. What may emerge may be some reality never mentioned by the great names. It couldn't possibly interest Origen and his like.

They liked to speak of religious practice as it should be. Theirs was a sometimes theoretical, often normative view; and it is well known to us today, indeed it overwhelms us, in thousands of surviving sermons, hundreds of canons published through church councils, and in an always active exchange of correspondence among bishops filled with opinions about what the world ought to be like. What the bishops didn't see, however, we ourselves can and ought to see, with an effort. What they saw but were not interested in or chose to ignore, purposefully, we can recognize as actual practice, differing from exalted norms, differing in social strata, differing according to time and region as Christian habits changed—all, reality.

Paul-Albert Février spoke with insistence about "realité historique" and "réalisme" in opposition, or at least as an essential supplement, to written texts. Among archeologists devoted to the evocation of Christians' life long ago, he was one of the very best, and a good teacher to anyone interested in the Christian past.[2]

Such are the various possibilities or contentions that I have in mind in the pages that follow, appealing to the reader's eye. A quarter-century has passed since I began to wonder if something could not be done with all the surviving reality—all that is known and indeed familiar—in the period chosen here for my focus;[3] and I hope its familiarity may not diminish its remarkable character.

1
The Eastern Empire

1. Dura-Europos

"Europeans" they still called themselves in the Greek language, four and a half centuries after the founding of their city by Alexander's men; but by then, they were also "Dureni" in the local lingo, living in "Dura".[1] There they were at a north-south and east-west crossroads perched on a high bank above the Euphrates, a frontier city and therefore a garrison city in Roman times, walled; within the walls, something over 50 hectares, say, 125 acres, with a population of 6,000 to 8,000.

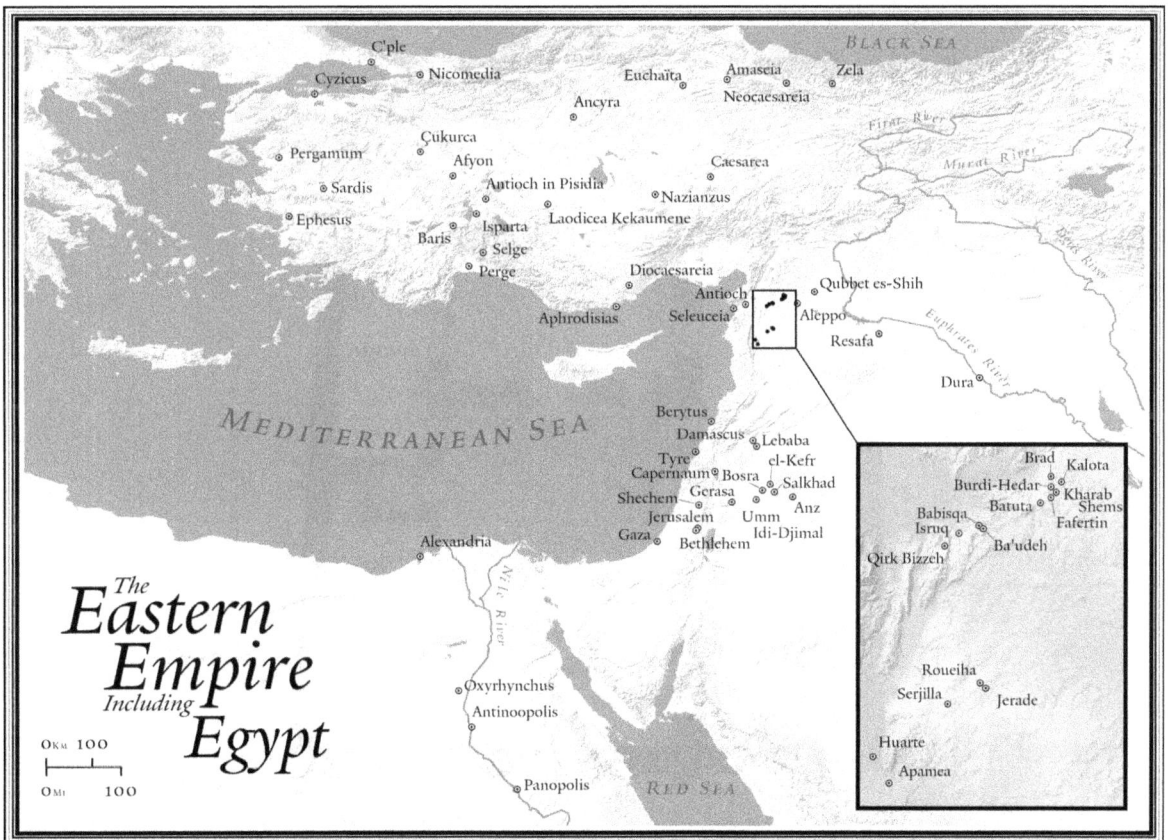

Fig. 1.1: The eastern provinces (inset, northern Syria)
(locations appearing in the appendix)

Their city was besieged in 256/7 and parts near the wall were filled in to strengthen it against the attackers; and then, after its capture, the whole was covered at last by the blown sands. Nothing was known of it until a chance discovery by soldiers in the wake of WWI. The whole site still awaits such awakening and study as Pompeii has received; yet a number of small areas have been carefully excavated, some of them recently. They reveal various dwellings, public areas, troop stations, commercial premises, sanctuaries; they reveal a private house in which a large hall was equipped with an altar against one wall, a built bench running around all four sides, and other arrangements to turn it into a place of traditional religious assembly;[2] and another house of many rooms in which, similarly, Christians held their meetings.

To use a private house for religious instruction and worship—that is a recourse familiar to us in Paul's letters and other sources describing the earliest Christians. What in fact could be more natural? Surely no religious group looked on askance, let alone a group that was occasionally persecuted, could ever expect to enjoy an open dedicated structure in the city for its services. So the tourist even today in Amsterdam can see the upper rooms where in the seventeenth century Roman Catholics had to meet in secret—as in the later eighteenth century the strange followers of Emanuel Swedenborg met in a house in Manhattan (my great-great-grandfather's) there to establish the New Jerusalem in the New World. No doubt there are a thousand examples in a thousand cities of such most ordinary arrangements, the only ones possible for small religious minorities.

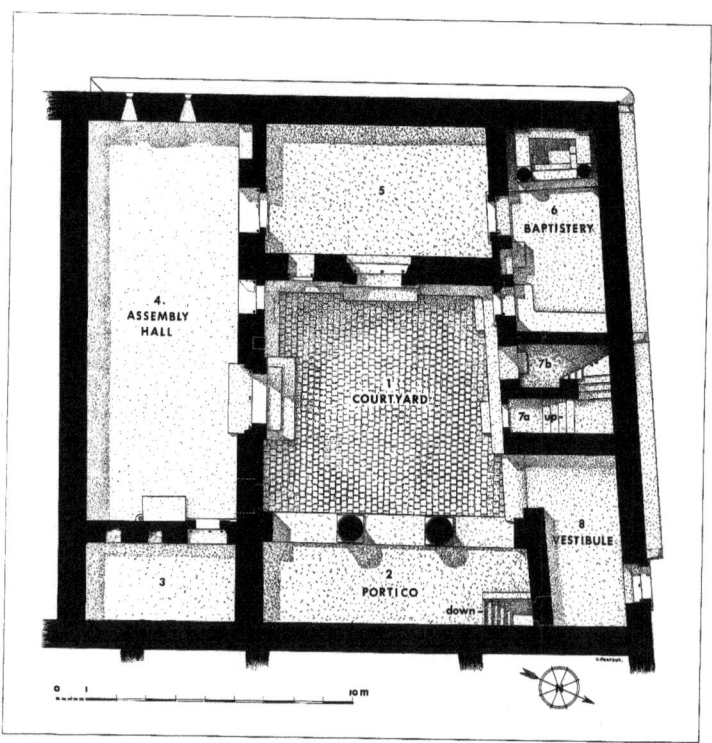

Fig. 1.2: The house-church in Dura-Europos

Ordinary they may be. Nevertheless, they are interesting, intensely so in Dura, because here we have the only clear and uncontested example of what are sometimes called "house-churches" resulting from the adaptation of some certain space for worship within private or commercial premises. The plan revealed by excavation is often shown (fig. 1.2). Here, in one of the city's typical two-story buildings in a residential section, a big meeting room was made out of two smaller ones by knocking out an intervening wall and so producing a space of roughly 12 x 5 m (Room 4). At its east end was a low dais. In an adjoining courtyard, around parts of two walls, ran a few meters of bench for people waiting or attending a dinner. Beyond the courtyard was an entrance to what could only be a baptistery (Room 6), identified by another built bench around its east and part of its north wall, and by its adjoining tile-lined basin—but best of all by the frescoes on its walls with biblical scenes. These drew on both New and Old Testaments, those of the Old perhaps fitting with the presence and infusions of a Jewish community and synagogue elsewhere in the city. Dura held many immigrant groups. The baptismal basin was dignified by a pair of steps going up to it, and a pair of columns setting off the entrance.[3] All together, baptistery, assembly hall and court each communicated with Room 5. This latter was meant for anyone aspiring to full entry into the assembly, that is, catechumens. Here is where "European" Christianity began, at least, if we had to specify a known built structure.

Something can be learned about the actors and the activities here from the evidence itself; and something more from other sources.

In that first category of data is the lack of any pipe into or out of the baptismal basin, from which it must follow that the ritual involved the sprinkling of the holy water, not immersion. There are also conclusions suggested by the amount of seating space in the several smaller rooms and courtyard, enough for one or two dozen persons but not more, and in the assembly hall, too. Here, the excavator responsible for the final report, Carl Kraeling, imagined everyone on mats on the floor. Such, there may have been; but analogies from other sites and common sense, too, require chairs and benches as well that will have been of wood, therefore destroyed by time, for the older and more respected members of the group, including the clergy. Once such comforts are in place, next, the two sexes must be separated by a safe space between them; more space must be left around the front part of the hall where the dais and priest and altar table would be dishonored by too close crowding. Thus what seems to measure more than 90 square meters can never have held more than seventy-five persons, if so many. The congregation, in sum, amounted to less than one per cent among all the "Europeans" of the day, after twenty years or more of existence in the city.

But is this right? The figure prompts the question, Is Dura representative of the region it lies in? Or are the apparent proportions of the converted within the whole body of residents quite false? Was there in fact some day or season of year when every Christian in Dura could be expected to be present? If the answer is yes, at Eastertide, then was it in the assembly hall and perhaps the courtyard as well? If so, the attendance would indeed be very small. Perhaps, however, the assembly hall was never meant for festal occasions. Easter would instead find the Christians in larger numbers gathered in a cemetery outside the walls, where no excavation has been carried out. I defer these questions until a later page.

Fig. 1.3: Dura-Europos, the baptistery

Room 5 can be identified as a place where those who wished to become full members underwent their initiation. To this they could enter from a neutral area, the court. Next beyond it lay the baptistery. The rites of initiation are known to have emphasized the everyday infestation of the unbaptized by demons, against whom the exorcists were directed. An early church manual, of a sort that needs explanation a little later, mentions a "shrine for those to be cleansed", a *katechumenion* in common use;[4] and Kraeling points to the exorcism room at Gerasa in Syria and the action of exorcists by blowing into the catechumen's mouth. Quite predictably, then, the necessary special purity of Room 5 was assured by having all its three doorways marked by apotropaic devices, as Kraeling points out; just as whole houses in Egypt at the time and later might have "Ammon lives here" painted over the front door, or "Here lives Hercules" on the lintel to protect all within. Most common would be the simple sign of safety, an ankh; eventually, a cross, or "Jesus Christ lives here".[5] Such prudent practices are attested in various eastern provinces, not only the Syria of Dura.

Catechumens may be pictured entering from the court, then, a group of men or a group of women. They would notice the special protection for the entrances to Room 5, and therein they would huddle into themselves as much as they could, respectfully, fearfully, the way anyone would wish to do who was about to be preached at (which is what "catechumen" means)— knowing also they were to be cleansed of demons. Some among them would have heard of the process. Very alarming it was, when the possessed foamed at the mouth, flailed around, shrieked. Or was it the demon that shrieked? People had seen, or knew someone else who had seen, the evil ones themselves in flight from such powerful rites. The words employed for exorcism were by themselves terrifying. In any case, the dualism between God and the Powers of evil was brought home to the catechumens even in the specially exorcized bread that they must be served at church suppers. They were not to join the confirmed at those times.[6]

The baptistery walls suggest what form their instruction took. Here they could see and profit from paintings on all sides, each chosen for its usefulness in the teaching of some lesson. Of course, most of the display is now lost: for instance, in two scenes of five women, only small parts of most figures survive. Much of what is left leads only to more questions and differing interpretations. One thing is clear, however: that Dura's Christianity was of its own sort. It constituted a sect, one characterized by "a special doctrine of Salvation, less through obedience to the Law than through mystical communication with the divine, a communication with God through Christ as intermediary, seen as the savior who guards Christians against Evil, against the demons and the stars".[7] Christianity was thus a living faith, which meant, alive with variety. Of this fact, centuries both past and to come were the demonstration, in a hundred ways.

To show it in life, a reconstruction helps: the sexes separated with men to the right as one entered, in eastern fashion; the priest presiding with a wooden table behind him, standing as I suppose though it is possible that he had a chair to himself; and his clergy seated to one side, honored women, virgins or widows, to the other side. Other rooms would be in use, since the uninitiated couldn't attend the full synaxary, the regular service with welcome, prayers, readings, hymns, sermon, and the Eucharist.

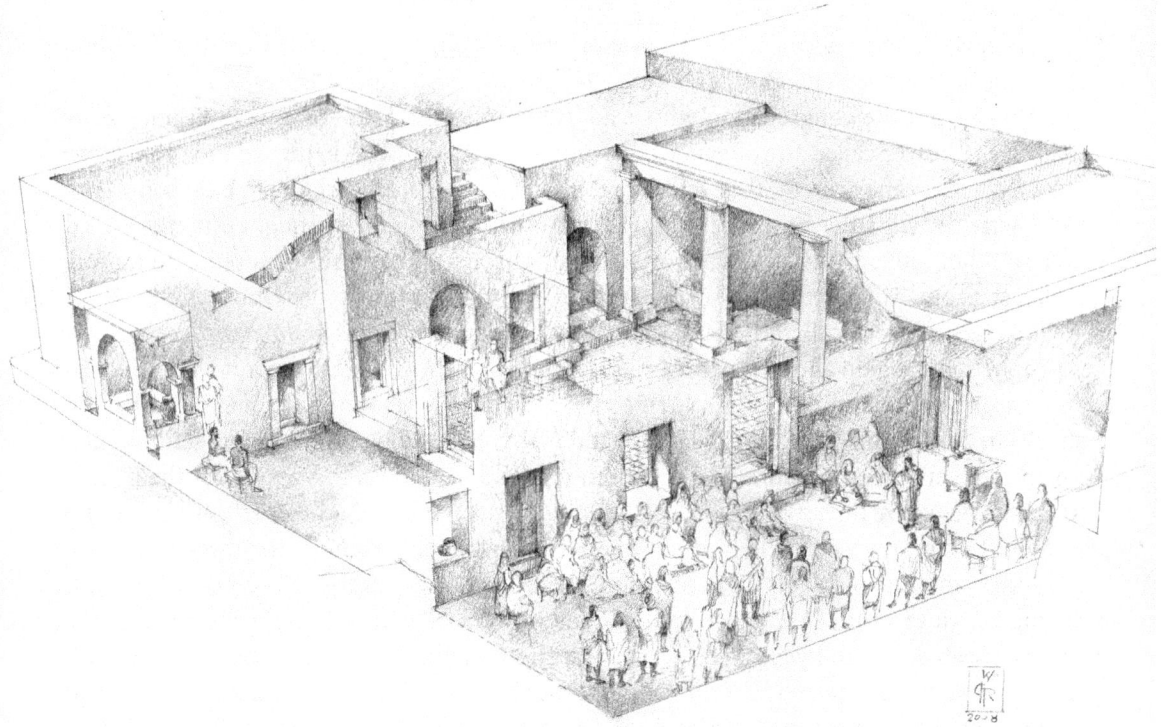

Fig. 1.4: How they would look at a service

Latin, Syriac, Aramaic and Palmyrene were all spoken in Dura, though Greek prevailed. The mix of origins showed in the way of life of the population, itself very mixed. It is safe to say that the group drawn to the Christian house would wear a variety of clothes matching their accents. A good many of the men would have let their beards grow, in proper fashion.[8] Beyond that, and the modesty of their numbers and their arrangements for worship, there is little that can be added to a picture of them. But they existed; their house and its paintings and so forth can all be touched, today.

Beyond the first category of evidence, which is the tangible drawn out of the earth, there is a second: the written. The tangible invites interpretation from this second; and indeed there does exist and did circulate, surely by the opening of the third century when a congregation had formed in Dura, surviving short descriptions of church services in eastern settings, along with several manuals of church administration, ready to be used to explain the working rooms of the sort seen in fig. 1.2.

From the A.D. 150s and Nablus (the ancient Neapolis in Palestine), Justin describes simple rites deriving more or less naturally from the Jewish, though with some obvious change in the choice of Readings and the addition of the Eucharist. The meeting-day, as Justin says, gathered everyone from city or country.[9] They listened to selections from both Testaments, followed by instruction from the priest, "the person presiding"; whereupon "we all rise together" (and had been seated previously) to pray standing up; next, the bringing in of bread and wine mixed with water, introduced by the priest's prayers and blessings delivered "as forcefully as he is able", with "Amens" from his listeners; after which, the bread and wine were then distributed. It is the Eucharist. There is no reason to think this was not the procedure at Dura in Room 4, the assembly hall.

From this same region, whether Syria or Palestine or Egypt and from about the same date or a little earlier, emerges "The Teaching", the *Didache*.[10] It provides a further detail, that those from the congregation who read out of the Old Testament were to offer their thanks, the prayer called the *anaphora*, "in any way they wished," being, so to speak, amateurs. Not everyone present, then and there or later, elsewhere, would be in easy command of his letters. No matter—a collection of sacred writings would be brought out and placed on a stand or table, with reverence, for his use; but the feel of the services remained informal, just as one would expect in such a point of assembly as Room 4 at Dura.

In a later manual called the *Didascalia*, that is, the *Instructions of the Apostles* originating in the same region and of the third century (whether the first or the second half), advice about seating at common meals is spelt out. Here again they sound informal or perhaps it should be said, human: "If there isn't in fact a place" to seat one of the congregation's "distinguished gentlemen", *honorabiliores*, whom it would be natural but wrong for the bishop to acknowledge by interrupting the service, then let someone of a brotherly spirit "get up and give him his own seat, and himself, stand. Or if, while the younger members are seated, an older man or woman gets up to offer him their place, then do you, Deacon, look around among the younger to see who is youngest, man or woman, and make her get up and let the other be seated who did yield her seat; for you should make her last and least who did not stand and yield her seat, so that they may be taught to yield to others who are older. And if a poor man or woman turns up, and elderly as well, and there's no place, do you, Bishop, make a place for such folk with all friendliness, *ex toto corde*, even if you have to sit on the floor, yourself."[11] So it is expected, as we here learn incidentally, that there will be chairs or benches but sometimes not enough for everybody; and age and social position are a concern in sorting people out, for more or less honor.

No different from the world known to parable (Lk 14.8f.): "When you are invited by someone to a wedding, don't seat yourself at the top couch where someone of better position than yourself may be asked by him to sit; and the person who invited both of you may say, 'Give way to this man'; and at that point you start to seat yourself at the very lowest place, quite ashamed."

The same *Didascalia* also directs that the clergy should sit toward the east end of the meeting place. This is where men belong; and next after the clergy, the laity who are men, and next, the laity who are women. Women, as Clement of Alexandria adds, ought to cover their heads entirely so that no lock of hair at all appears. Tight control over the appearance of women at a place of worship we can see in the temples of Greek tradition, earlier; and still tighter, control over the contacts between the sexes in the rural parts of third-century Syria, in Christian instructions.[12] But the instructions may perhaps reflect only small gatherings in small quarters such as we see at Dura.[13] In larger quarters, later, the space would more naturally be divided not crosswise in the nave, with women to the rear, but lengthwise in the fashion familiar to us, once we have church plans, with their rectangular shape and most often with aisles on either side. Where that is the case, the greater honor of the right hand, where Christ sits with God, and of the male sex generally, was never in dispute. As to the practice of facing east for prayer, prescribed by the *Didascalia*, at Dura this would mean toward the altar, since Room 4 was "oriented".

The congregation cannot be captured in a still photo; rather, in cinematic form, since they participated actively. In Egypt but with knowledge of Syria where he came from, Clement describes the usual manner of prayer, where he is speaking meditatively as well as descriptively, and says that it amounts to a conversation with God; and as such, we may speak sub-vocally, offering our wish as a murmur even though with the force of a shout; and (recalling the term so common in traditional thanks to the Greek gods, who are termed "listening", *epekoos*) God hears even this; so it is that we raise our faces and our hands to the heavens, and set our feet in motion as a last augmentation of our voice.[14] Swaying and dancing in prayer is a thing that will be seen more than once in the pages that follow.

Besides the *Didache* and *Didascalia*, another ancient manual is the *Apostolic Tradition* of about the same date as the *Didascalia*: that is, the third century.[15] It was first compiled in Greek, but the language proves nothing: Greek was the language of the church in Rome, and from Rome this third manual seems to have originated. Perhaps it was composed by one Hippolytus; but his identity is not certain.[16] In time the value of the text was seen and it was translated into many languages including two dialects of Coptic, and Syriac, Arabic, Aramaic, not to mention Latin.

It may be called on to give us a picture of the Dura courtyard provided with such a good stretch of benches along two walls. Surely their purpose was the weekly evening meal, "the love" as it was called (in Greek, *agape*; in later Latin, *cena dominica*, "the Lord's Meal"). Communal dining was the natural practice in religious communities of every faith throughout the empire, each according to its own style. Its signs appear in various sanctuaries at Dura. It was certainly well known to eastern churches. Paul had described it (I Cor. 8.10); Pliny

(*Ep.* 10.96) observed it among Christians in the early second century when he was serving as special governor in the Pontus region; and it is mentioned in the same period by Ignatius of Antioch. In the mid-third century, when the Dura church was active, Origen provides a view into Syrian church suppers, accused of being a bit too lavish.[17] Toward the turn of the third century, too, in Alexandria, a priest entrusted with the education in his church could speak of the proper manners and restraint at festival dinners, such as might be taught anywhere in Syria, too, declaring, "If you want to sing and praise God to the music of the cithara or the lyre, no blame attaches to it"; for we may recall the example of David.[18] Finally, from the *Apostolic Tradition*, we learn who it was that provided the food for these meals, what manners were enforced, and what other rules were good. But the details it seems best to defer until they can be fitted into their proper place, namely, the Rome community; for, regardless of its percolation through many late manuals, there is surely some risk in assuming that this body of instruction was at home in Dura.

The risk lies in assuming a degree of uniformity in Christian practices that isn't clear until somewhat later. To reason from the *Apostolic Tradition*, to Dura, we would have to know a great deal more than we do about that obscure subject (only obscure because never studied!): power across all parts of the church. Just how was this power, which is influence, to be earned? Who could claim to have it, judged by what criteria? Thus, how was it that the customs of one church were adopted, more or less completely, by some other, and at what point in time did the liturgy of some whole region conform to a single model, a single manual? The materials for an answer to these questions are not lacking, but this is not the place to go into them. Enough to say, only, that the mechanisms by which the acknowledged right to command, once gained, could be applied to larger and larger communities, were little developed. Written exchanges among churches, and far more important, face-to-face exchanges in intra- or inter-provincial meetings of heads of communities, still in the third century remained relatively ineffectual. Of course they were later to play a remarkable role.[19]

To finish with Dura, I return only to the questions about numbers and proportions that I raised on an earlier page. At issue was the degree of Christianizing in the eastern provinces in the third century, the period of Dura's congregation and their meeting-place, measured against their apparently small numbers, and the possibility that in fact those numbers inside the meeting hall were by no means the whole story.

The literary evidence for the share of Christians in the general population has been a thousand times parsed, and very widely but reluctantly discarded as quite unreliable; and then, parsed again, for salvage; and so forth. I offer a view of the problem in the area which is now Turkey, in a very long note. There, I choose to focus on inscriptions, the closest we can get to anything quantifiable. They show, in a few eastern regions, tiny clusters of converts expressing themselves quite openly, before the great persecution of A.D. 303 and the years immediately following, while other towns and territories give no sign of the church's presence at all.[20] In general, epigraphy will not support any statement of prevailing conversion pre-Constantine. The conclusion, like the evidence it flows from, is very particular and, even so, open to question; but it is at least *hard* evidence. We can touch it. I confess, I like this, and I therefore look for it where I can.

To supplement inscriptions it might be expected that ruined churches from the earliest times might survive in the eastern empire, not like Dura, but in good enough shape to be at least approximately dated. This is not so. Yet literary evidence does tell us something about the cities in which organized Christian groups existed, meaning "churches" in the sense of people, not bricks.[21] Between these two senses of the word, Clement of Alexandria draws a distinction, as if built sanctuaries, *hiera*, indeed existed. No doubt they did by his time, toward the end of the second century. Not until the 260s, however, is the Greek word *ekklesiai*, like the word "churches", used to mean both Christian communities and their physical structures;[22] and it is only now that the latter are first mentioned explicitly, by Porphyry. The setting is Syrian cities, and he describes Christian buildings as quite splendid. One such in Antioch, Eusebius too describes as showy; he mentions another in his home town of Caesarea.[23] Then, by the end of the century, a grand one existed in the capital city of the whole East at that time, Nicomedia; others unspecified, elsewhere also. All were razed in the great persecutions.[24] Such scattered testimonies entitle us, as it seems to me, to picture at least a dozen of the larger eastern cities equipped with some building especially for Christian worship, compared with which, Dura's little assembly hall was quite in scale—that is, comparing 6,000 or 8,000 (Dura's total population) with the 50,000 or 100,000 or even more citizens to be found in Nicomedia or Antioch, Tyre or Ephesus.

But the room inside the Dura hall, or inside big churches in big cities, can't have defined the whole Christian population; for, in a number of references, we are told of another common space where any number could meet: the cemeteries.

Throughout the ancient world, by every city of which we know the customs, the dead were not allowed within the walls. They would pollute, their presence would invite some disaster. Only gods and heroes were allowed in and, of course honored as they deserved at the very center, on some height, some acropolis or capitol. Still, in law, any mortal burial in its proper place, suburban, was space set apart and sacred; therefore, space fit for worship.

Most likely from the 80s, we hear of altars for divine worship placed directly above the resting place of the persecution's victims (Rev. 6.9). The mention here was meant to be intelligible to readers generally in western Asia Minor.[25] At Smyrna in the suburbs a few generations later the Christian population annually celebrated the martyrdom of Polycarp, as we happen to know. They did so obviously at some fixed, revered place—some shrine. Again, toward the mid-third century, we are told of the practice by Origen. A Bible passage (Mt 24.12) reminds him of the word *agape*; and from this he goes on in his own words to speak of those who had given their lives for their faith. He and his listeners, the catechumens, would reassemble in their *synagogai* from their visits to the burial grounds where, amidst the relics of the martyrs, they had been strengthened and inspired.[26] There, as we can see, there would have been room for more than could be fitted within a single house-church or even several (and Origen's words indicate more than one such in his city, Alexandria). Church manuals of the same third century and the fourth as well add confirmation and details about the celebration of the Eucharist at gatherings in the cemeteries. There would be readings and chants both for the martyrs and the beloved dead—thus, the most encompassing service to honor all of "those who are asleep." As to any Christian community's property rights, inside or outside the walls of any city and so to include both house-churches and burials areas, these were to be affirmed by an emperor a decade later, in a good mood.[27]

And later still, in the wake of the early fourth-century persecutions, eastern bishops were informed that they could reclaim "the so-called sleeping places", which is what the evidently still-novel term *koimeteria* meant, literally. Then other edicts in renewed persecutions forbade the use of cemeteries for meetings.[28] This last evidence is especially useful since it is official. Under persecution by other Christians, the faithful forbidden inside their cities still sought safety for worship in the cemeteries, this, in the mid-fourth century.[29]

So, in the little-noticed open spaces outside a city's walls, services were possible that no house-church could provide. It is true that remains of such eastern cemeteries from pre-Constantinian times have yet to be found, for study; likely conjecture cannot be tested.[30] Specifically about Dura's burial grounds, we know nothing. Yet in the light of evidence which I come to in due course, I cannot believe that Dura's Christians did not often meet at some communal graveyard along the road leading out of town; I would be surprised if such a meeting did not sometimes assemble numbers larger than could ever fit inside the rooms looked at, above; therefore, surprised if the share of Christians in the general population did not surpass that one per cent or less, hazarded above. To say more would take me even beyond hazard.

2. Peacetime

The "Peace of the Church" that followed upon the Edict of Milan in 313, though it was very briefly interrupted twice thereafter, remade the world in the most dramatic ways and with the most visible effect. For one thing, the places associated with Jesus' birth, crucifixion, and resurrection, all were honored by Constantine with memorial sanctuaries of great splendor. They were to enjoy a long life and fame. But an earlier, less well known venture by a local bishop gave to Tyre a church rapturously described by Eusebius, so that its plan can be easily reconstructed.[31] This is just what the mind's eye requires.

Even in its airy form—mere words of a high-rhetoric sort translated by us into their stone original—the appearance of the church is clear. We are invited to approach it as a tourist might. We enter first the wooden precinct wall that surrounded the whole and kept out *hoi polloi*, declaring as it did, here are holy things, let the uninitiated stand back. Within that guardian circuit, comes next a square courtyard surrounded by porticoes along its inner sides, with a large fountain in the open center, this, to serve for libations and refreshment of the waiting crowds. Anyone about to go into the church itself might want to wash the dust of his journey from his hands and feet. From there in the courtyard, three grand portals opened into the basilica itself, the central of them being huge and bronze and carven in a way that would remind us today of the Doors of Paradise in Florence.

Inside, the church had two pairs of side aisles defined along their inner side by a row of columns which in turn supported a further height of wall, and clerestory lighting at that upper level. The window-openings were decorated with elaborate wooden lattice-work where later centuries would have stained glass. On both sides, the outer aisles of the pair were reserved for those who were undergoing instruction, the catechumens separated by sex, right and left.

Next, protruding about a quarter of the way into the nave, a chancel with a wooden screen defining it and the area within which only the clergy might enter. The intent was to set them apart from the laity, in the fashion of the Temple in Jerusalem; and their space was raised by a couple of steps above the level of the nave as a reminder of their eminence.

They enjoyed the honor of built benches in two pairs on either side of the apse, with a bench in addition that followed the curve of the apse and surrounded the throne, a moveable wooden one, I suppose, reserved for the bishop—one of those "towering thrones" that Eusebius mentions, "to honor the presiding priest". Before him was the altar. For lay persons there was "a huge number of thrones and seats and benches" in the nave.[32]

This church, the first or oldest known to us in the least detail, was begun in 313 and dedicated in 315. To judge from the ample dimensions of its circuit walls and outbuildings, and the prior treatment of the ruins on the site as a dump, it must have been located in the suburbs where land was at a discount. Its bishop Paulinus, the admired friend of Eusebius, evidently had the very best connections through which such a large project could be funded and by whose help, incidentally and quite illegally, he could rise to the still more glorious see of Antioch, a decade later. Still, in 313, to save costs and as the usual thing where remodeling was to be undertaken, no doubt he made use of the foundations of what had been destroyed in the persecutions. Consequently, the basic plan, the plan of the nave at the very least, would have been resurrected from that of the original construction dating to the latter part of the third century.[33]

This copying, to us, must seem entirely natural; to Paulinus, equally. What he needed was a structure big enough to hold some predictable number of people, all attending to what would be said by the person or persons presiding; therefore, a rectangular shape, and a curved, cupped end for acoustic purposes, and perhaps a raised area before it so that every-

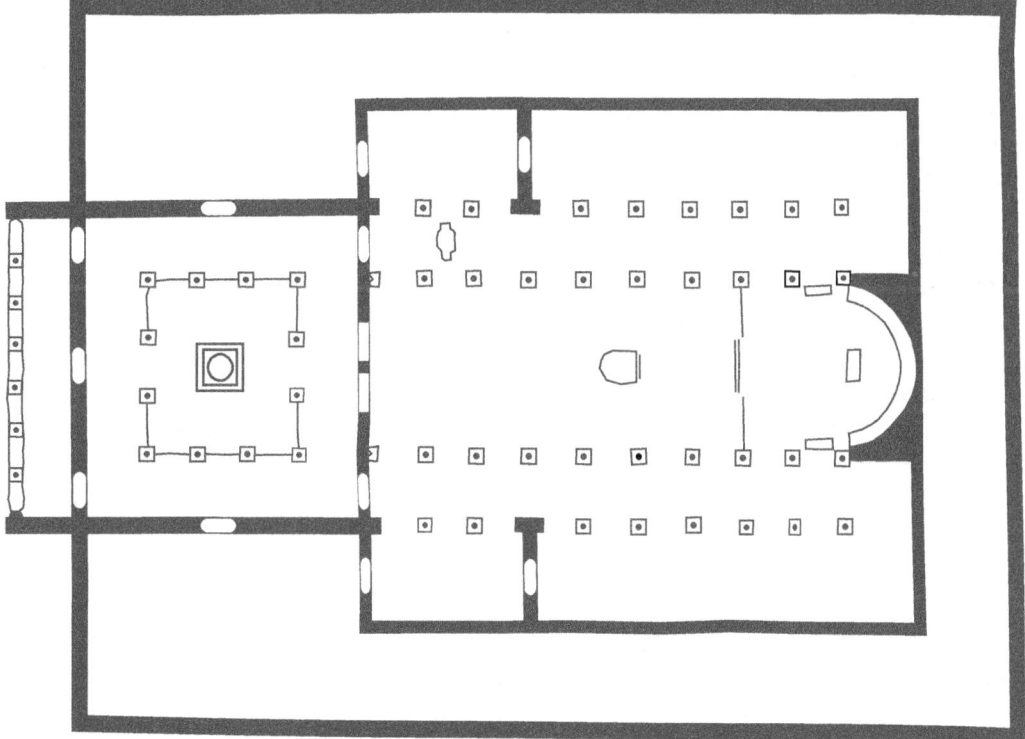

Fig. 1.5: The Tyre basilica, reconstructed

one could see and hear the important person sitting there. Serving these common needs, most cities of the empire had exactly what any church leader would have in mind, namely a basilica as a model, used for many public purposes; and more than one church in the period subsequently originated in a civil basilica, with quite minimal changes.[34]

Before looking more closely at the internal features of the Paulinus church, something more obvious invites comment: the ubiquity of the plan. It was commonsensical; it suggested itself and so can be found absolutely everywhere; but it must also have been recommended and spread through the sharing of experience among bishops. After 313, provincial and then regional councils became increasingly the routine, proving very useful. Bishops and their accompanying deacons, readers, and exorcists could talk about what they were doing and what their problems were. It was not all theology, by any means.[35] In consequence the favored architectural models spread about to every province, and with what seems to me remarkably little departure or variation (though small departures could have large liturgical implications, and thus, theological implications also).

These exciting developments unfolded quite abruptly. In the appendix, I can point to only five eastern churches of a third-century date, though unspecified ones are mentioned in literary sources (above, at notes 23f.). In the short period 313–325, however, there are no less than 22 and more than 18 in the next quarter-century, compared with only some seven or eight in the third quarter and nine or ten in the rest of the fourth century. Where the possible dating has to be looser, I have assigned a half-credit to the two quarter-centuries relevant. The resulting figures bring out in a striking fashion just how sudden was the effect of the Edict of 313.

For fifteen or so sites, an estimate of capacity is possible, in very rough terms. The totals in the appendix range from a maximum of 800 persons in attendance for two at Jerusalem, to a mere 40 at a semi-rural church. Estimates can only be approximate. A square meter would be needed for each member of a crowd not jammed uncomfortably together as they might be in a subway, today; space was always left between the sexes, except, I suppose, for the married and their slaves, if they had any; and an increasing space was reserved also to the clergy, not only where they might be at a given moment, but wherever their duties might require them at different points in the service. The matter will become clearer on a later page with discussion of chancels, soleas, and ambones.

One warning may be needed: the ambiguity in the word *church*, *ekklesia*, which has been pointed out. It invites misunderstanding. A city, a town, indeed a village might have a bishop, known from the subscriber-lists of councils; and from this fact one might infer that he preached from a cathedral—some structure of dignity and size. But anything of this sort was obviously unknown in the earlier generations of Christendom, and in the third century was still rare; nor can it be taken for granted in the fourth century. In trying to guess the size of the Christian population in a given quarter-century, it is thus far safer to look at the archeological evidence than at the written.

And when this is done, puzzling questions arise. Take Antioch. Here was one of the empire's largest half-dozen cities which its preacher priest John, "the Golden-mouth", in the 370s credited with a population of 200,000, exclusive of slaves and children. We are to accept, thus, a total around a quarter-million. Half of these, if John judged truly, were good Christians affiliated with its principal church.[36] Of this great structure, initiated by Con-

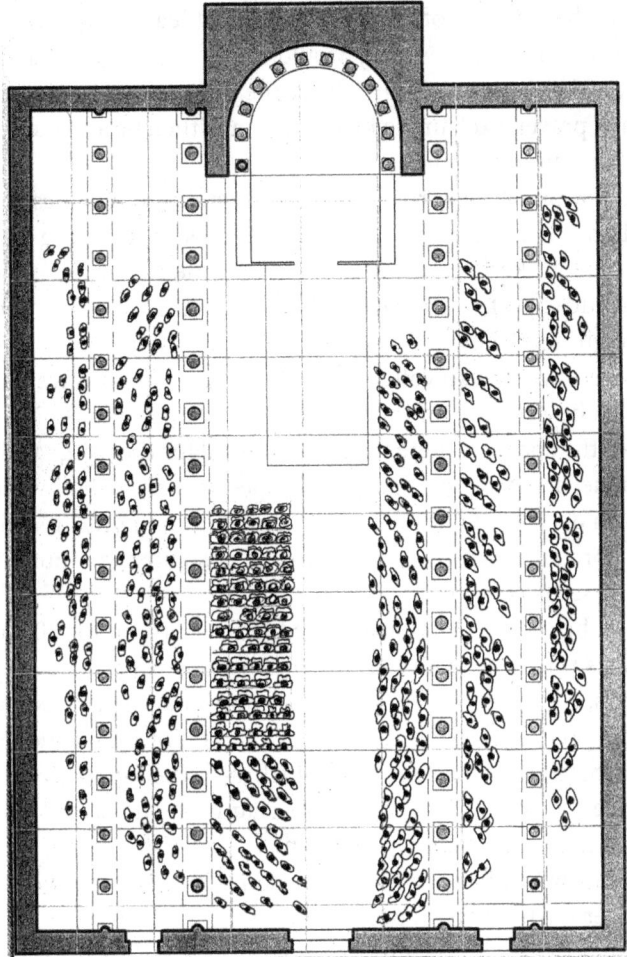

Fig. 1.6: The laity fitted into the Anastasis church at Jerusalem

stantine himself, no tangible trace remains today, nor of whatever others may have existed, counted by John as heretical. Suppose, however—what is most unlikely—that his church equaled in size the gift of Constantine to Jerusalem, the largest known to us in the east, the so-called Anastasis. There would then be room for 500 persons to hear John preach.

Or is this not a good estimate? How is it to be calculated, anyway? If the floor of the Anastasis is marked off in five-meter squares, used to suggest how and where some persons might be seated but where most must be ready to stand for two hours or more; if they are drawn to scale; and if some central part of the main aisle leading up to the apse is left clear, as it really should be for the entrance of the clergy—what attendance would there be room for? The answer is, just 500 if my drawing is to be believed, or some 600 at the very most.

In the outer aisles on either side would be the catechumens, men and women separately. They, like those casually attending and the faithful (the *fideles* in Latin definition, admitted to the Eucharist) would arrange themselves in a way to avoid having their sight of the nave blocked; for nobody wants to stare at a column for two hours.[37] They cannot be imagined within only a few inches of each other, either; we must leave them some room for action. For, during the service, as we know, they would kneel, sit, rise to their feet, extend themselves full length on the floor, chant, give back the proper words in responses, raise their hands above them in prayer, exchange a kiss. They must then be assigned a full square meter in my drawing, as a minimum.

In the nave, often or perhaps routinely, there would be benches for the "more honorable". This would allow closer crowding; thus, let us say, requiring only two-thirds of a square meter per person. Perhaps the seated were in the majority, in which case another fifty or so must be added to the imagined audience. There may have been upper galleries for still more, though not many.[38] But we have to take account of the clerical procession up the middle of the nave, the so-called Triumph, and the mid-nave pulpit, the ambo, of which mention must be deferred for the moment. Still more unoccupied space must be left around the apron of the chancel where the area reserved for the clergy would be marked out by some mosaic-panel arrangement on the floor, perhaps enforced by a low wooden fence or stone barrier with decorated panels. So it is shown in the *DACL* reconstruction which I accept. By all these probabilities, then, I arrive at an absolute maximum attendance of 600, so far short of our first expectations.

In the appendix, below, the Anastasis is credited with room for 800, not 600. But there in those regional lists throughout, in order to anticipate any possible skepticism about the capacity of churches, I give estimates which are more than generous, even the double of what I think are the probable figures. Whatever the total of John's audience, whether 500, 600 or 800, the mismatch is a true stumbling block, a *skandalon* in biblical terms. It cannot be accepted—between the numbers Chrysostom claims for either the believers or the whole city, and a church to hold 1 per cent or 2 per cent!

What is to be done with this figure, when we come to turn it into a living picture of worship? Let me consider it from several points of view.

We should begin by cutting down the total of the city to the estimate of 150,000 offered by another contemporary and a resident, Libanius. Then, too, we should ask the obvious question whether it was common for people who could certainly call themselves Christians, to attend services more than once a year, or on a couple of high holy days at most. Like other bishops, Chrysostom complains of too-rare attendance. The complaint is hardly unexpected.

Additionally, however, he makes clear that, when he looked about him, he saw and therefore addressed, or characterized in some fashion, a very small minority of his co-religionists. They are the cream of society. The fact is clear in many passages: as, when he urges them to the Eucharist and uses a homely metaphor to recommend the invitation. He compares their just-completed prayers and hymns, to purifying preparations, "just as you see our slaves sponging our tables in preparation for our dinner guests." The picture he shares with his audience is one of wealth taken for granted. The same emerges from the sermons of other eastern bishops of the time, when they are tested: Basil, Asterius of Amaseia, Gregory of Nazianzus.[39] "We ourselves dwell in splendid mansions adorned with marble of every sort," says Gregory, going on to describe every feature of luxury that "we" enjoy, who are of his class and of his listeners'. He and the others use the second person plural in connection with all sorts of tell-tale particulars indicating just what those persons were like, who are directly before their eyes. They are only rarely women, and never slaves or children; they have some education or may be reproached for having, or for recalling for Bible-study, too little of what every child ought to be a master of. And they all have some domestic staff, sometimes even their children have slaves. It is "the extremest poverty" to have only one. Too much luxury is their problem, too many fine things about them, which are often reproached.

In contrast to "we" and "you" of this rank and style of life, there are "those", the others who are not present and who are sometimes referred to with scornful snobbery: lowly bureaucrats, petty retailers, peddlers, artisans, laborers, rustics—in short, 95 per cent of the population. Outside the church doors, beggars hung about in crowds just as beggars had always crowded the temples, and still did, looking for handouts, especially a day's food that their ill-fortune would not grant them otherwise.[40]

Certainly in small towns, or on great religious days in great cities when every sort of person would attend, a sermon's message might well be more inclusive. I return to these gatherings, below. If an ever-wider sampling of surviving sermons is made in search of the missing women and working people, these will be found even in daily services, very occasionally. The *proportion* of reference to them nevertheless remains the same, that is, quite insignificant. For the student today who would see early Christendom in some anachronistic light, as equally welcoming to all, the plain facts are thus rather uncomfortable and are accordingly resisted.[41]

It is unwelcome, too, that members of the church were more exactly sorted out into their right place, as it was defined by the authorities, reaching beyond the mere separation of men and women at services, to control the precedence and privileges of various groups among them. Women were assigned to particular cadres as those who would never marry, with their special place to sit or stand; and then behind them, those of an advanced age who were past marriage or widowed; and then the ladies married to *honorabiliores*. All these entered the church by a less decorated and ample doorway than men, kissing its jamb, and they would be segregated in the less honored side aisle or perhaps to the rear of the nave, as is clear at least for Syrian churches; or they would be put up in a second-floor gallery under the care of a eunuch, as was the practice in Constantinople. Veiled, additionally they must select a costume as little attractive as possible; and they must keep still. So Paul had advised the Corinthians; he is quoted of course by later bishops, among them, Chrysostom. As to their joining in the hymns and chants, never! Only prostitutes and female entertainers sang. From behind high wooden partitions in his church, women could not look over to see the men.[42]

Once, in Dura's simple setting, there had been no great gulf between laity and clergy, so far as we can guess, and certainly no great physical distance at worship. A century later, a bishop had become a high and mighty figure, lodged in his own palace, commanding all sorts of benefits and powers;[43] and the clergy beneath him were also set apart, invisibly, through the general respect for their condition. He is "the King" upon his entrance, his deacons are "the Angels."[44] Visibly, also, these various ranks could be distinguished at the start of each day, for the first service offered to pilgrims, in an atrium, a courtyard, narthex, or some open space in front of the church, in the dark. Cockcrow would have given the signal for all to forgather, as the pious Egeria toward the end of the century often noted in her diary (just as cockcrow could still be heard in pre-car days, a half-century ago in less traveled eastern areas, along with donkey-braying and dogs' barking to announce false dawn). Everyone awaited the bishop. He would be the last to arrive, the first to enter the church and with him in his train, all his inferiors. They swept past the laity, who next might then enter, everyone in an assigned place, everyone in due order, men and women alike, knowing their place.

As to the expression of all this architecturally, and so in the archeological record: "Presbyters shall not enter before the bishop but shall be seated on the platform, the *bema*, after he is seated." So says a canon of a council meeting at Laodicea.[45] The curved bench for presbyters around the apse, the *synthronon*, can be seen plainly in the Tyre church, as was noted above; and for the bishop in their midst, there was what Eusebius calls "a lofty throne for the honoring of the presiding one".[46] It would be, I suppose, a wooden affair with two or three of steps before it; or sometimes a built stone chair. The bema itself, the whole raised platform on which all the clergy sat for some of the service, occupied a third of the nave, sometimes more or sometimes less, and was surrounded by a screen or partition on its left and right sides a meter or two in height, of various degrees of elaboration. Along its front edge rose a much higher ornamental partition to mark off the most holy area from the nave, accented by what came to be called the triumphal arch, the *fastigium* in Latin. Its doorways could be closed by curtains, on which no expense of pure silk and gold thread was spared.[47]

To this elevated and half-secret, half-revealed sanctum only the ministrants were admitted; and they approached it in a way that brought out its great importance. For, led by their bishop, the priests, the deacons and lectors entered the church in a formal parade that began each service, attended to the rear by choirboys singing, with candles and incense. They proceeded slowly up the nave to their appointed places along the ancient equivalent of a red carpet, that is, a strip of mosaic floor marked off and bearing the name in Greek, *solaia* (Lat. *solea*). An example could have been seen at Tyre at the very beginning of the Peace (above, fig. 1.5); or again later in the century, a more intrusive one at Antioch in the basilica running the entire length of the laity space.

But this Antioch (fig. 1.7) is not Chrysostom's city; rather, the much smaller Pisidian town of the same name, in the western suburbs of which lay the building in question; and in fact this solea cannot be seen any longer. Here was a basilica excavated in the 1920s and somehow

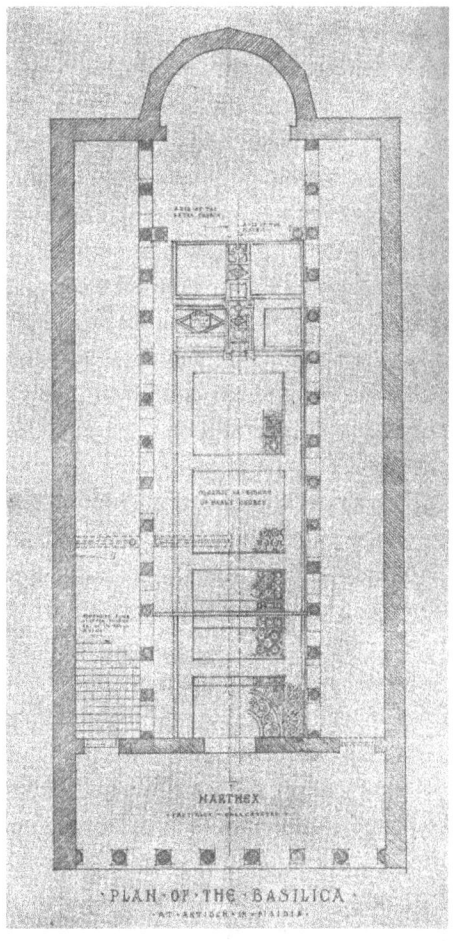

Fig. 1.7: Antioch in Pisidia, the fourth-century basilica

lost. Lost! a whole church—like many dozens of Eastern sites and buildings to say nothing of individual inscriptions and works of art known to travelers of that and a previous generation, but in the first half of the last century noted as once seen and studied but now vanished, or damaged. The plaint recurs again and again in scholarly reports of the sites. For the structure in Pisidian Antioch we thus have only a drawing to preserve the record of its walls, its column-bases, its solea defined by a low barrier, some of the mosaic panels and the inscriptions contained in these latter, running down the solea. They serve to date the work to the period of Chrysostom's preaching in the other Antioch, the Great.[48]

The passageway marked out on the floor might terminate in a preaching- and singing-place at mid-nave. This was known as the ambo (a word apparently derived from the Greek, "to mount").[49] By 371 it was familiar enough to be mentioned in the legislation of an eastern church council. Except in a region of northern Syria, it was a high pulpit, a wooden thing with steps leading up so that a preacher could be better heard; and it was placed to one or another side of the nave in churches after the mid-fourth century. From such an elevation Chrysostom himself took up the practice of speaking, toward the end of his career in Constantinople. It worked far better than the slightly raised throne from which otherwise bishops would deliver their sermons, sitting down.

In northern Syria, however, ambones of another sort can be seen in more than thirty among many scores of little rural churches still surviving, or at least once surviving in the past century so as to be surveyed and photographed. These internal structures are shaped like the letter C with rather long arms, rising in mid-nave above the laity. They measure three to five meters across—thus, big enough to hold on their built benches five or ten persons, who would be the clergy, of course. The one at Kharab Shems is one of the best known because the whole church it is in is so well preserved—the photogenic star of all the sites in this region.

I show the ground plan as well (fig. 1.9), noting the length of the aisles (18 m) and the width across aisles and nave together (12.5 m). Allowing for an ambo, the chancel, columns, and passageway to the door left clear for the entrance of the clergy, fifty or sixty of the laity might have crowded in. However, at nearby Kalota and Fafertin the ambo is so close to the door, one cannot suppose that any audience at all was meant to stand in front of it; and the regional practice, perhaps here as elsewhere in the east, in fact placed everyone in the aisles, leaving the nave, like the chancel, entirely to the clergy for their comings and goings. During the readings from scripture the priest would stand in the ambo at a lectern, provisions for which are sometimes evident; as also, shelves for texts to be stored, and, later, a little throne not for an officiant but for the Bible itself to be accommodated honorifically.[50]

Converts to Christianity brought with them the ancestral custom of facing east in the moment of prayer, and this, with a quotation also from the Psalms, explains the orientation of eastern churches, so that there might be no disrespect shown to the altar in the apse or chancel. The question comes up, then, whether priests faced the altar in prayer or turned their backs on it so as to lead the laity, or again, whether they addressed the backs of those whom they were leading if the ambo in which they stood was placed far down the nave, near the entrance.[51] Must they not face the altar?—regardless of whether it was placed at the edge of the chancel, almost in the laity space, or far back in the apse, close to the curved wall there?[52] These and other details about the service I must leave to the specialists to debate.

Fig. 1.8: The Kharab Shems church a century ago

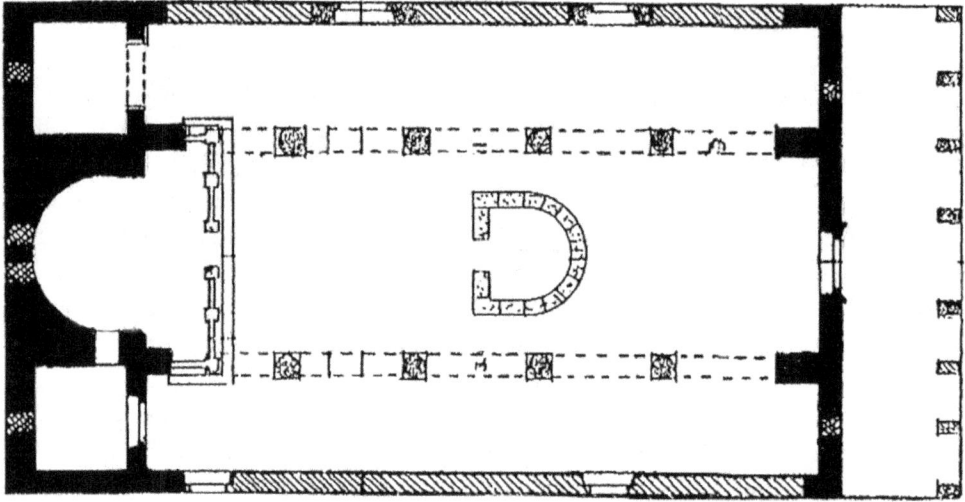

Fig. 1.9: The Kharab Shems church, ground plan

What percentage the total attendance might have represented within the village of Kharab Shems and its territory can be roughly estimated from the archeology of the region. Northern Syria like the eastern provinces generally in the later Empire was enjoying a good level of prosperity. This is reflected in the farmers' houses, none of them very grand but

THE EASTERN EMPIRE   19

most of them of a comfortable size.⁵³ They suggest some density of population, from which the churches evidently drew only a very small portion for worship: 50 or 75 at the most, at such parish churches as Kharab Shems, out of two or three thousand residents round about; therefore, some 5 per cent.

The architecture of the region presents a variety of plans and uses in unique detail. Had construction been in wood, nothing at all would have survived to modern times, whereas in fact not only places of worship here but of commerce and residence as well were stone-built, of local necessity, therefore imperishable. True, the stones have been freely robbed across the centuries; but what time has erased in one site can be supplied from another. Thus a reconstruction is possible, shown here axonometrically (fig. 1.10). We could be looking at

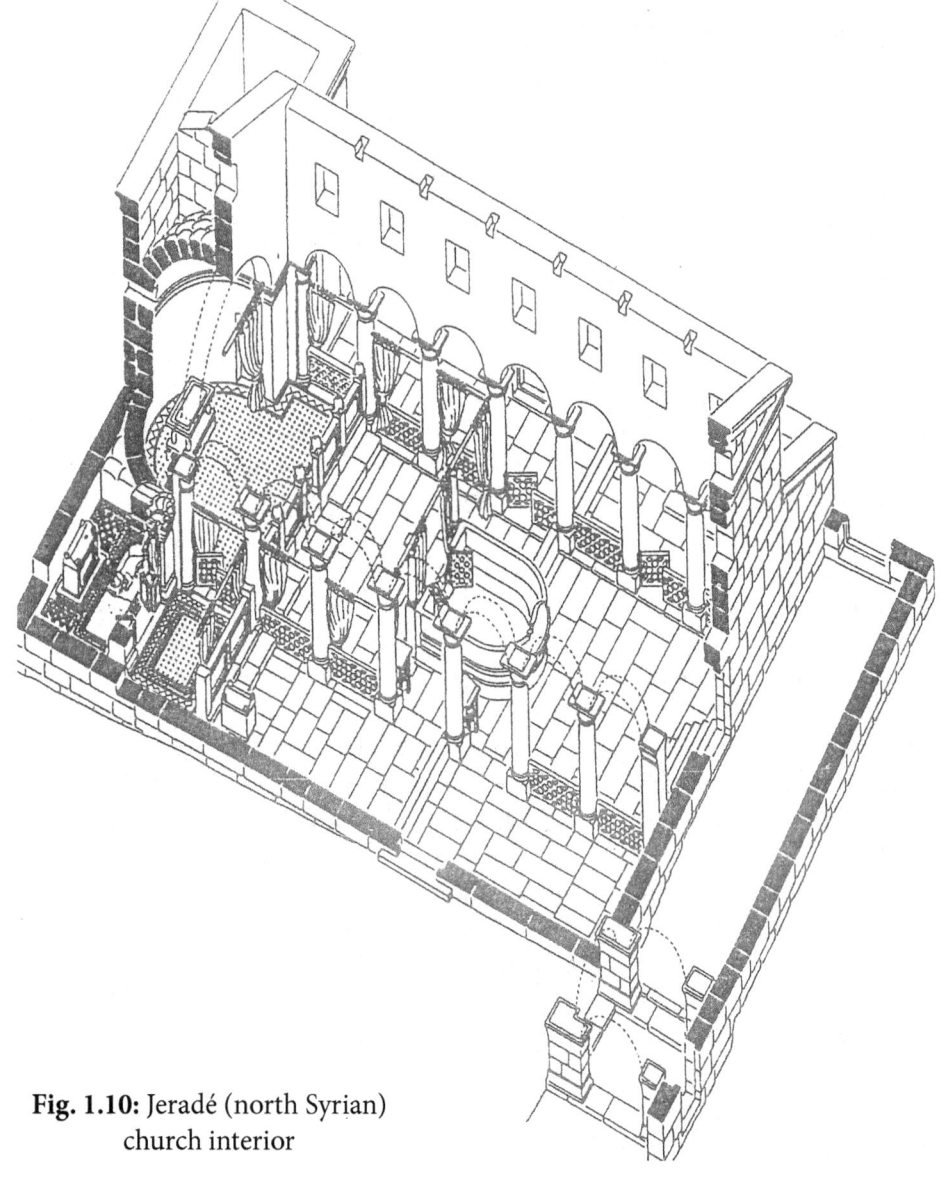

Fig. 1.10: Jeradé (north Syrian) church interior

Kharab Shems or Brad, Burdj Hedar or Kalota, all roughly the same in their ground plan and dimensions.

What is interesting about the reconstruction is the elaborate articulation it puts on display—the degree to which space has been chopped up by barriers and allocations—even here in the back-country.[54] Compare this with the scene in fig. 1.4. Though the two are separated by no more than a century, the difference is remarkable. At Jeradé just as was the rule in better known churches, described earlier, a certain part we may be sure was set aside for women catechumens, another for men catechumens, some other for ordinary worshippers (male) and ditto (female), with the least obvious corners for slaves if any had been brought along. They would be told where they should stand. Half of the whole interior was evidently out of bounds to the laity altogether, fenced off and super-sacred behind a screen at the edge of the chancel to control what was visible, and when. Here was the reserve of the priesthood, involved in their ever more complicated and dramatic rituals.[55]

As to that Jeradé priesthood—little educated, not in full command of their letters, speaking Syriac more easily than Greek, and in sum, in the eyes of the likes of John Chrysostom, bearded boors and bumpkins—they were in the eyes of their own neighbors much to be honored. Certainly they were God's representatives; but they also counted among the community's most substantial property owners. In just the same way, in larger centers, bishops would now be drawn from among the families of municipal senators, every one of them a substantial landholder. To set themselves above and apart from others was the natural thing for them to do in the planning of a church, great or small, just as their non-clerical friends and kinsmen, seated before them at services in their Sunday best clothes, would on other days expect to assert their own privileges and priority in other, secular settings.

On all such folk, churches had to depend financially. True, they might occasionally get help from other benefactors. We have el-Kefr, built by a great government official in 392. He did so not *ex officio*, for there was no such thing as a state church in the Roman Empire. No, his gift was from the rents of his properties, just as emperors themselves built and endowed churches in the east out of their crown estates, whether they were Constantine or Valens. More representative than the el-Kefr church is the one at Brad, offered as a prayer by a well-known builder of the region, Julianus, in 402, with various elements of the structure bearing inscriptions to commemorate other donors from within the congregation over the space of three years of construction: here an arched doorway, there another, just as the component parts of a university today bear the names of donors in some prominent position.[56] The little building at Qirqbizze may be mentioned, too, formed out of a part of an estate house, large by local standards, at some point in the second quarter of the fourth century, to which a triumphal arch was added by mid-century and an ambo a half-century after that. Construction from the beginning was in the owner's hands. And far more often, indeed the general rule, was the patronage by the clergy themselves: for instance, at Babisqa in the 390s, where the priest who helped with construction costs was also one of the local Haves; or at Qubbet es-Shih, Lebaba or Fafertin.

Thus in the early generations of the Peace we can see the churches coming into the possession and control—the very ownership—of local elites.

Nothing that did not have about it a certain formality, a sense of place and decorum and up-and-down, could have pleased the elite. It was this that found expression in the preacher's sermons; this, that inspired such built forms as can be found even in northern Syria: complicated, chopped-up structures like that shown in the illustration above (fig. 1.10).

And the role of social position in the church's growth may be illustrated further by evidence sought beyond little places like Kharab Shems. In Antioch, John Chrysostom knew the realities of his world and spoke accordingly, to the rich, to share their riches with the church. So he exhorts them,

> There are many that own villages and estates, yet they care nothing [about the promotion of the church] and they say nothing. Instead, for building a bath-house, and how much costs are rising, and how grand halls and mansions should be constructed, they have attention to spare—but not for the cultivation of people's souls, ... that all should be Christians. How, tell me, is a peasant to be Christian, seeing yourself so indifferent to your own salvation? Can you not give some sign, and so persuade him?—with the powers that you possess, of love for your fellow man, of care for dependents, of mildness and entreaty and all the rest. There are indeed many who make forums and baths buildings—but hardly churches! Anything but that! Yet I adjure you, I beg you, I ask you as a favor or rather, I propose it as a law, that no one should be in the possession of an estate that lacks a church. Don't tell me there is one nearby, right in the district; that the expense would be great and without any return. If you have anything to spare for the poor, now, spend it on that instead. It's better done there than here. Support an instructor for them or a deacon or a team of clergy.... It serves the cause of peace among your peasants; the priest will be revered and contribute to the security of the estate. There will be prayers for you non-stop, hymns and services for you, and offerings for you every Sunday.... Consider how you will have a treasure in return laid up for you for the day of the Second Coming, if you raise a place of worship to God.[57]

We see the audience in its usual proportions, very wealthy and therefore inevitably not very many, and of course, bound to exert some control over their church's creation. All the facts fit together: liturgy, architecture, numbers.

A great landowner of Cappadocia put up a church on his properties in the 370s. He was the bishop, father of Gregory of Nazianzus. We have seen in Pisidian Antioch how bishop, lector and a layman all recorded their names on pavement mosaics of the city's chief church, as its builders. They too were obviously persons of wealth; so too the bishop Arcadius, Basil's friend who built a cemetery church, and other bishops in Laodicea Combusta and Baris, known from inscriptions. Away in Egypt a decade or two earlier, and in a large number of Syrian instances recorded later, beyond the period I have chosen, the rich gave and gave again.[58]

But really they had no choice. Evergetism (as it is beginning to be known from the Greek word) had been for many centuries accepted as the great engine of civilization. It was accepted not only by the general public but by the wealthy, too. According to its terms, they must share their wealth with their community, and with no grudging hand, because their community was thought to have some sort of right to a share in their wealth: a right which must be acknowledged "generously", even "lavishly", *philotimos*, as the word meant in Chrysostom's day. Of course the beneficiaries must repay their benefactors. They must give voice to their admiration. No one understood this better than Chrysostom himself, describing in wonderful words the precious moment in a public assembly and the emotions that must overwhelm a great donor when he was applauded, "reveling in his heart's desire like a person drunk with vainglory."[59] It was to claim that reward, in the mosaics on the floor of the Pisidian basilica, that those who provided this or that adornment of the building had their names immortalized in commemorative inscriptions.

We may imagine the initiatory ceremonies, the encaenia of a new church, such as that at which Eusebius delivered the opening address. The church was Tyre's, as we have seen, where the very emperor himself had gratified his co-religionists with his most enormous patronage. Its every sign was on display in as spectacular a fashion as could be imagined, witness the rapturous descriptions from the orator. He cannot say too much about the size, the beauties and proportions of his bishop friend Paulinus' new show-piece. From that moment on, evergetism toward the Syrian Christian community must be the most glorious thing one could possibly think of. And not many years after the Tyre encaenia, in the celebration of the Nicene council, still more bishops by the hundreds were invited to the palace to dine with the emperor. To *dine* with him! The compliment was absolutely dizzying. With any one of those hundreds, thereafter, who among the local elite would not have cared to dine, himself? To join such a man's church, too, must be the right thing, the right first step. Benefactions would inevitably follow.

3. Suburbs

So, as I put it, the elite *owned* the churches they attended. That was how it worked out. But in the imposing edifices which the elite had built, it could not be very comfortable for the non-elite to join in worship. Around Kharab Shems, for example, where Syriac was so much spoken, the farming population would, I suppose, include many who simply could not follow the service. And the sermons, too: it is not surprising that the undistinguished many, the unimportant 95 per cent of the population, were not drawn to instruction about the need for restraint in their dining habits or in their use of cosmetics; or on the obligation to give to the poor (themselves!). Nor was it pleasant to be referred to slightingly, or ignored.

And that figure of 95 per cent, now: it does invite reflection. It was examined in the light of John Chrysostom's principal church; it can be examined also in the light of the fifty-odd other eastern sites of which there is some record, and among which, some are of known dimensions. They could handle a congregation of fifty, perhaps a hundred and fifty persons, rarely three or four hundred. The percentage which these represent within the probable population around them is very small.

By so early a date as 325, Alexandria and its suburbs could boast of some two dozen churches. Their number sounds respectable; but it must be set against a total of a quarter million or more in the city, for whom there would thus be room at worship for only 1 or 2 per cent.[60] We know also of the three or four tiny towns in what is now central Turkey, almost totally Christian in the third or first half of the fourth century. Their significance has been discussed (n. 20, above); it was by no means enough to define the region as a whole. Clearly we do not have in archeology, still less in written sources, anything like a full picture of the Christian presence in the eastern provinces. Nevertheless, the contrast between the small-town or urban populace at large, and the fifty or the few hundreds, or at most, the thousand in attendance at services in the largest basilicas of the largest cities, still at the end of the fourth century, is very striking. As I said earlier, in biblical terms it is a *skandalon*, a stumbling block.

Certainly there might occasionally be a greater attendance than there was room for in a church, and so some were left outside; but the mention of any such thing happening hardly ever appears in the very large volume of surviving fourth-century sermons. On the night before Easter Sunday in Antioch, bishops of the early fourth century held a vigil in the suburbs, not because of the need for more space; rather, because of the congregation getting out of hand in the dark and violating the dignity of the church. So, at least, we may gather from John Chrysostom's words that bring the scene to the mind's eye: "Shall we come to the very altar," he protests, "with clamor and commotion? For I see many in the gloaming clamorous and shouting, shoving each other, jumping about, exchanging insults. What are you about, man?—when the priest is standing in front of the altar, stretching up his hands to the heavens?"[61] On other less important holy days than Lent, and in the wake of earthquakes and similar moments of public distress, preachers describe large crowds; yet not too large all to fit inside.[62]

Those in the hierarchy who were responsible for determining the size of a new construction thus seem to have made sensible estimates. In time, if the need for space increased because of the fuller conversion of their world, a second or third church could to be added. Such a need is hardly detectible in the period of my choice.

The mismatch that appears so puzzling to me can perhaps be addressed by looking beyond churches and their differing liturgy, whatever it may have been, region by region, century by century. The key may be those gatherings just referred to, of Christians out-of-doors. Indeed, the crowds attending were sometimes more numerous in open settings than could fit within any house-church or basilica. Jean Bernardi suggested as much, long ago, though without saying just how they were accommodated.[63] The answer, if it can be discerned, would show just where and how the 95 per cent expressed their own Christianity.

In earlier times and into the third century, the custom of church suppers, *agapai*, had reached out to some parts of the congregation, beyond house-church walls, it is not clear just how much (it is mentioned quite prominently in the manuals of both eastern and western origin, and flowed into the Eucharist in ways not well understood). It appears to be this tradition which Eusebius speaks of, as adjunct to services honoring the local martyrs: *symposia*, that is, parties accompanied by singing to the harp, *psalteria*, "as an offering of thanks to the men," the martyrs, where there would be "many, too, that express their charity to persons in need, refugees and the penniless".[64] The setting would be a cemetery. A generation later, bishops meeting in Laodicea (west-central Turkey, today) took up the subject and agreed to ban such "loves" as they were called, assembled in churches where people laid out their dining-couches on the floor; and a little later still, John Chrysostom describes the feeding of three thousand widows and virgins and indigents in the dining halls, the *triklinia*, built close up to his church outside the city.[65]

Triklinia are easily pictured—no doubt just like those attached to Syrian and other eastern temples for pilgrims and local worshippers. Endowments for these and other sorts of mention are ubiquitous in written evidence from all over the east: from Palmyra or Ephesus or Oxyrhynchus in Egypt. There were, for instance, dozens of dining rooms attached to the Demeter- and Kore-temple at Corinth, brought to light by excavation. Thanks to these we can almost see the Christians sharing such feasts, for of course the people arranging to use the rooms and to invite guests sometimes included Christians. Paul didn't approve (I Cor 8.10ff.); it was still a problem in the third century.[66] Sources of the period show the Christians looking over their shoulders at their neighbors' sacred meals, with which they were familiar. There would naturally be some copying, too—the newer Christian custom from the traditional. The latter was sometimes too jovial to be taken as a model, the good times were too good for the tastes of the clergy.[67] Chrysostom's admonition to the press of worshippers before the altar, just quoted, is a proof.

Anyone familiar only with the religious scene in the West today, and unable to imagine anything much different, will suppose that there was nothing of worship in the drinking and eating that went on in temple rooms; that the guests at the dining couches gave never a thought to the superhuman being, invisible and benignant, in their midst, no more than an American family might at Thanksgiving or an English one sitting down to the Christmas goose. Yet we have a devotee of Sarapis speaking in public about his faith, that is, his "conviction of things not seen" in the familiar biblical definition which is also my definition in these pages; and he describes how "men keenly share a vivid feeling of oneness when they summon him to their hearth and set him at their head as guest and diner—... the fulfilling participant in all cult associations, who ranks as leader of the toasts among them whenever they assemble."[68] The text is not unique, by any means, though the sources are in general reluctant to reveal people's inner thoughts and feelings in their everyday lives, including their religious lives. We thus know as little or as much of the temple as we do of the *agapai* where the guests needed constant reminding that they were not to drink too much, not to gorge, and in short, to treat the occasion respectfully. It was, after all, meant to be an act of worship.

Fig. 1.11: A funerary picnic on a tombstone in Konya (Turkey)

Dining rooms were, even more than in temples and church precincts, a common feature in cemeteries. In these, the dead could be lovingly recalled in family picnics at burial sites. Grave-stones show us the funerary or memorial meal with women seated, the men recumbent on dining couches in the usual way. The sarcophagi of the deceased had holes and pipes to carry libations to them, making them participants. They still lived, in a way; indeed, "the dead are nourished by our libations and whatever we bring to their tombs, and if they have no friends or kinfolk left on earth above, they must go unfed and famished".[69] True, the evidence for these private practices throughout the eastern provinces is almost all epigraphic or archeological; but it is none the less satisfactory. We have, for example, from the south of modern Turkey, a representative scene of the celebration (fig. 1.11) as a family of modest means might commission it; and if more should be needed to bring the scene before the mind's eye, I offer some help below (fig. 2.8). From a little beyond the boundaries of my subject, toward the mid-fifth century, we have an immigrant from Lycia to Greece described as "cognizant of the rites due to the departed; for he neglected none of the dates when they are habitually honored, but each year, on certain fixed days, he made the rounds ... and in a particular spot propitiated the souls of his ancestors."[70]

The written testimonies cited above are all non-Christian; but then, almost no eastern cemeteries have survived for study where we could expect such confirming signs as do tell us about the Christians of other regions of the empire. Silence in the east is just that—not a proof that they knew nothing of what was familiar elsewhere. In better documented centuries such practices are in fact found among Christians up to the very present; and it is hard to explain them except as remains of an unbroken tradition from remote times.

And furthermore, we have the witness of a church manual of John Chrysostom's days in Antioch, representative of practices widely accepted in the region. Surely this is as much as is needed for the period that interests me. It prescribes the good manners that Christians are to show "at memorial dinners for the deceased."[71] If, incidentally, they needed to be reminded how to behave, they must be of the same class as the family shown in the Konya relief and as that rough crowd rebuked by Chrysostom.

Good manners, however, had something serious about them; for it was after all the spirits of the departed that one addressed, it was their company that was invoked and enjoyed. In short, the moment was religious. That seems to me the most likely reason why, sometimes and in some places, Christians didn't want their loved ones interred too close to non-believers. The rites mustn't be mixed up. In Phrygia, therefore, in the mid-third century, a man commissioned a tomb for himself in which, as he specified, "no one is to be buried except one of my family who is a believer."[72]

There were honors and mourning to be shown to the ordinary dead, still more to the extraordinary. From the first century on, in the east, those who had given their lives for their faith were seen in a particular light, as in some sense or degree superhuman; and so in the cemeteries they received special veneration from a much wider circle than their family. The fact is first attested at the time of the book of Revelation; other testimonies of the second and third centuries were referred to earlier (at n. 25). In the fourth century, built facilities for picnics or meals in homage to them, inviting their help, are mentioned by Eusebius and in Basil's letters.

In confirmation we have archeological evidence within the frame of which we can see the Christians at worship.[73] The most interesting piece may be the underground burial chamber, the hypogeum, in Huarté village, a morning's walk from Apamea. Here, chopped out of the rock, are a small room and a big room (11 x 3.5 m), the two containing seven sarcophagi. One is in a human shape. Into its carved mouth at one end a hole was drilled with a metal tube lining it, this to receive libations; a second hole allowed their recovery. A second sarcophagus was also equipped with a hole, but only one. Both sarcophagi were given a position of honor in the big room, and the rest, as close by as was possible. Near the entrance were a lot of broken vessels for cooking, eating and drinking. The excavator supposes, very reasonably, that the honored pair received veneration and the tribute of feasts brought to their door—thus a mingling of family memorial rites with veneration for two extraordinary persons, who were most likely ascetics famous in the neighborhood.

These ritual visits and meals were a common practice at Huarté before the end of the fourth century. Then a small basilica was built over the hypogeum; or rather, the basilica's narthex, the west-end porch, was built over it. Next to this, a slightly larger basilica went up at the same time. Local custom had thus taken on dimensions that required a formal place of worship. Evidently there were crowds. The world had a new cult-center for a saint, or for two saints.

It was far from the first, of course. In the history of the subject, Constantine had played his usual role as master-impresario, "bringing to Constantinople the holy remains of Andrew, Luke, and Timothy" (the report is Jerome's; the date in the 330s).[74] We can be sure these precious relics were treated with signal respect, though what size or elaboration may have been given to their shrines, there is no surviving stone to tell. Many other martyr-shrines like them elsewhere must be assumed; some dozens could be instanced in the fifth century, beyond the reach of my study. But an example that does belong commemorates Saint Babylas on the edge of Antioch, as it once was (the river has changed its bed).[75]

Babylas' story is one of many chapters, told by the historian Sozomen. While serving as the city's bishop, the saint fell victim to Decius' persecution. A century later his bones were rescued from their too-humble cemetery on the road south, by Constantine's nephew. It was his hope that they might, through their sanctity, cleanse and sanctify the delightful dubious Daphne—Daphne, lying a few miles further along the same road. It was well known to Sozomen, who describes it as

> the famous suburb of Antioch, which plumed itself on its crowded groves of cypress and, among them, the variety of planting. In the shade of the trees, at different seasons, grew every species of the most sweet-smelling flowers that the earth affords.... But it was thought to be a bad thing to walk about here. The setting and nature of the place was well suited to a relaxation of conduct.... Anyone who frequented Daphne without a lover at his side was considered an ignorant boor.[76]

The saint's relics, then, were given a home and a mission here. The site chosen was the precincts of a pagan temple (as was often the case with Christian shrines).[77] But in Daphne of all places! When the apostate emperor Julian, ten years later, demanded their removal,

> the Christians, getting together, dragged the sarcophagus several miles along to a point within the city bounds where it is today, and so gives its name to the site. Men and women, it is said, and youths and maidens, the old people and little children, dragged the coffin, urging each other on and singing hymns the whole way.

Once more to the cemetery a half-kilometer beyond the river and so, almost at the city's door, in what is now the village of Kaoussié, Babylas had returned; and eventually, in the 380s, a shrine for him was built there by the bishop Meletius of those years, with four wings, each about 25 x 11 m (fig. 1.13). Here Meletius was to be buried in the stone coffin right under the altar, himself on top of the saint; here, John Chrysostom duly preached over the saint's remains. Here too, other heroes had been interred over the centuries, including particular bishops. The relics of the great Ignatius had been brought back from Rome; buried here was the young woman Drosis whose exploits Chrysostom recalled on her feast day;

also a certain Julian. Where they rested is described as a "house", a built structure which must mean a walled precinct, filled with coffins and carven tombs.[78]

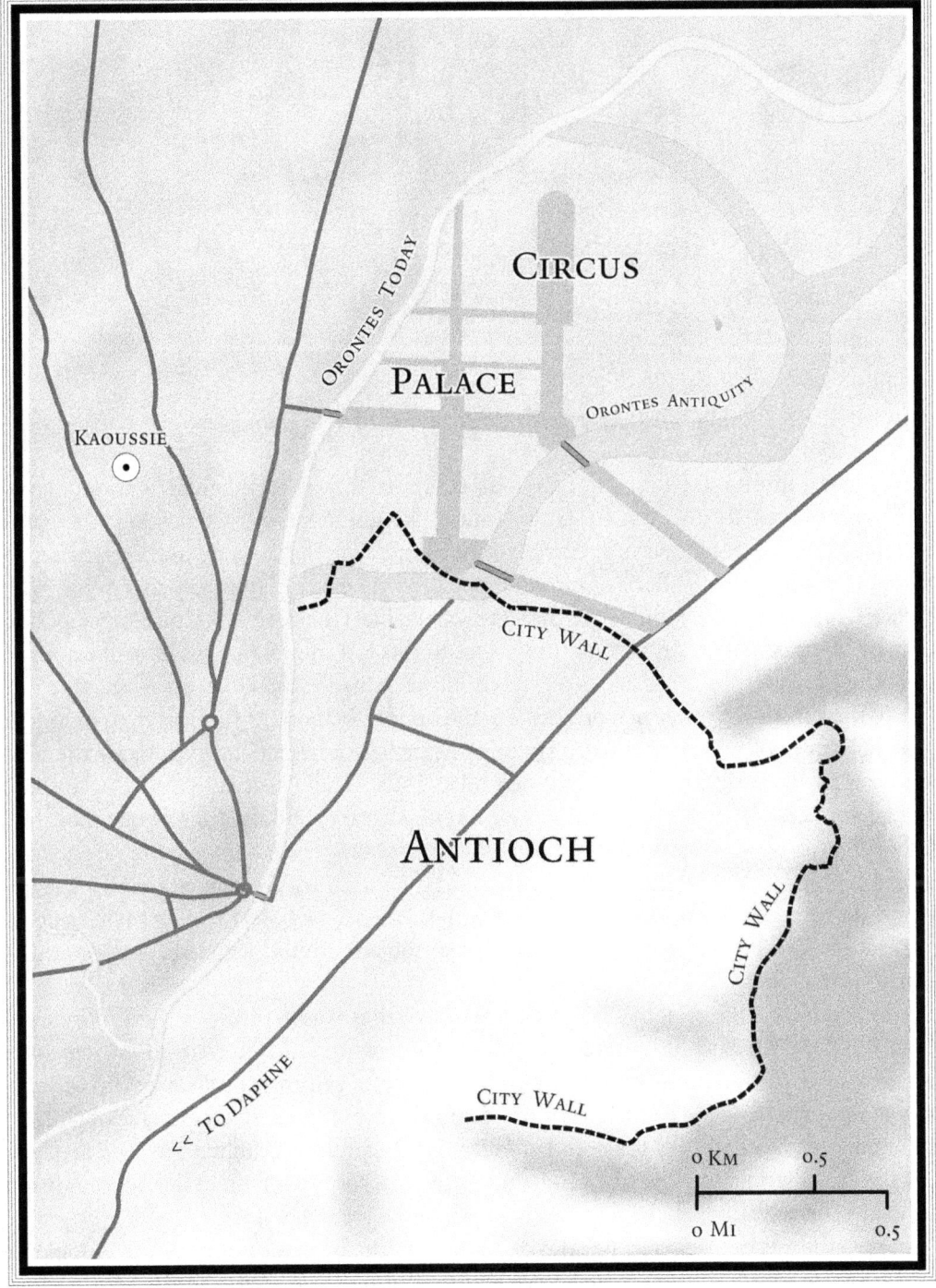

Fig. 1.12: Antioch in John Chrysostom's time

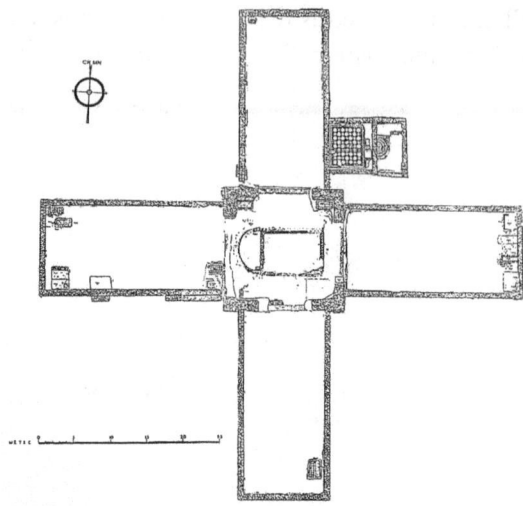

Fig. 1.13: Saint Babylas martyr church at Kaoussié

In many martyr-shrines, the plan was centralized, not rectangular. Variants could be octagonal like the one at Antioch, or round like Euphemia's at Chalcedon (the grand example, a *tholos*, described in the appendix); round also, the rotunda at the Anastasis. If round, it might have a gallery or circumambulatory encircling it; or cruciform but with, perhaps, one arm of the four longer than the others, like Constantine's Constantinopolitan Church of the Apostles.[79] It is something close to this last model that we have at Kaoussié. Here the excavator, Jean Lassus, noticed burials both inside and close up against the outside of the shrine, for other persons besides the builder-bishop. At the center, to dignify it, rose a platform of which only some six or eight inches of height survive, where the bishop's throne would sit. There is in addition a baptistery and a sacristy; hence, necessarily, regular services. A patch of surviving floor mosaic declares, "In the time of our most holy bishop Flavian [381–404] and the most venerable manager, *oikonomos*, the priest Eusebius, the priest Dorys fulfilled both his vow and the mosaic of this wing, *exedra*." The text is repeated on the floor of three of the four wings. And as a whole, the plan invites a focus on what lies in their midst, toward which all may look or around which all may process as tourist-worshippers.[80]

To receive burial near the saint's or any holy relics was a precious thing. Privileged space was controlled by the hierarchy, naturally. Those who could afford to contribute to the building costs of a memorial church did so in the hope of gaining this favor, as did Meletius here at Kaoussié, along with the clergy succeeding him; but likewise the parents of Gregory of Nyssa in the church they built, and at Huarté and Laodicea Combusta as we have seen, and Brad and Serjilla and elsewhere—all, testifying to a common faith in the saints as insurers of aid and salvation, all from the second half of the fourth century.[81]

From this period we have, besides or actually in the brief biographies and eulogies of saints, a glimpse of those holy beings in action, through wall paintings at their shrines. There was no need to wait for Giotto; there were his predecessors widely at work in eastern churches, so say Asterius of Amaseia in Cappadocia and Gregory of Nyssa. So says

Basil, too. At an anniversary festival he concludes the display of his eloquence with an appeal to masters of another art, weaving in allusions to martyrdom as an athletic contest, an *agon*:

> Come to me now, all you most famous illustrators of great struggles! Glorify with your arts the ravaged form of the leader [that is, the locally acclaimed martyr Gordius]. Make brilliant the crowned victor with the colors of your skill! For I would depart, vanquished by you, through the representation of the martyr's heroic accomplishments.... Let the demons cry out, even now and every day smitten by you.[82]

And so forth—but useful to show the wide diffusion of illustrative art in service to worship, and the use of a flow of scenes like a comic strip; further, and most obvious, showing the common wish truly to *see* the heroes of the faith. Their powers and wonderful answers to prayer were celebrated, too, in word-pictures—John Chrysostom at a saint's day moment reminding his listeners (who hardly needed to be told), "Take up any person demon-possessed and raving and bring him to that holy tomb where rest the relics of the martyr [Julian], and you will see them en masse take flight and quit the field."[83]

This faith in the mighty powers of their martyred heroes helps to explain the large and sometimes unruly crowds that attended the saints' anniversaries, imitative of the celebrations that families held for their dead but on a far larger scale. The Greek term is the same for both: "remembrance" (*mneia*). It is used by the assembled bishops of the Laodicean council (can. 51) in the 360s; and for Latin readers, the term *refrigerium*, "funerary banquet" of either sort, is also used. All the routines and rites were the same, even the general distribution of food; and every martyr, every saint, had his own day.

Many details can be drawn from the eulogies such as the occasion required, delivered by Gregory of Nazianzus, or Basil, or Chrysostom, filled out from Gregory of Nyssa's poems and from slightly later sources. First would come the so-called "all-night", as people arrived at the spot for the dawn's commencement. Incense, candles and lamps were lit in the usual gestures of acclaim and celebration for the night and the daytime as well, equally in traditional or Christian fashion. Then followed the day of observation or even a week (so those present knew that they should bring their food and drink); and during this time, relics in reliquaries could be paraded about and religious trinkets bought from dealers. General participation in the form of singing and dancing was expected, with instrumental accompaniment.[84]

Both men and women danced; and they did so sometimes in groups as choruses or sometimes in place, as I understand references to the moving of one's feet in the rhythm of the service. Since dancing, however, was seen as likely to lead to sex, or at least to thoughts of that, priests and bishops sometimes spoke against it in terms of disgust not to say horror: Basil was one but there were others also.[85] At open-air worship, as due warnings declared, shameless women in abandoned gestures fling off their veils, loosen their hair, trail their dresses (whatever that means), laugh aloud, scatter their inviting glances at the crowds, challenge the glances of men. Men were watching, yes, but beware! The martyr being honored was there, watching, too.

The more ascetic among the clergy saw all this in a very dark light. One of them thinking back on his eastern years—a certain Vigilantius much esteemed by Jerome, and then angrily attacked by him—spoke out against the Christian practices of the east that he had lived among in the 390s. They were nothing but idolatry. If he meant to say that they represented the non-Christian traditions of gesture and behavior in religious services, with very little change, then he was right. Gesture and behavior were indeed very much what non-Christians had been used to think of, across the centuries, as the proper and most acceptable language in which to address a superhuman being: by music, that is, both instrumental and choral, and by joyful expressions of every sort, and by the sharing of food and drink in humble, loving fellowship. Let those Beings addressed only show their love in return! The word *philanthropia,* gods' love for man, was quite at home in pagan tradition; likewise the cherishing of relics and offering of incense and many, many other things, too.[86]

There was of course a danger here. "We see almost a pagan's rituals," said Vigilantius, "introduced into the churches under the guise of religion: tons of candles in broad daylight, and pinches of dust in little treasured vessels and wrapped in linen, kissed in worshipful fashion. Men offer great honors of this kind to the blessed martyrs whom they think to illuminate by cheap candles."

To which Jerome replies, "Who ever adored the martyrs (*adoravit*)?" His point was a good one only so long as it wasn't examined. True, in Jerome's world and language, "adoration" or "worship" must be reserved for a "god", and among superhuman beings there was but one such worthy of the name. All the rest were mere *daimones*: Zeus, Artemis, Belial, it made no difference, all "demons". If, however, adoring meant the rendering of homage and subservience regardless of the quality of Being addressed, then there was only the one tradition shared among all faiths of the time. The tradition was, to repeat, a language; it could be used in any conversation with the divine; but Jerome and the crowds at church festivals didn't understand each other.

He goes on, "I don't deny that all of us who believe in Christ have originated in idolatrous error; for we were not born Christians, but *re*-born. But because we once venerated idols, *colebamus*, must we now not venerate God?—lest we seem to revere Him with the same honors as the idols? What used to be done for idols is therefore detestable? This [that we do] is rather done for the martyrs and should therefore be welcomed. For, too, throughout all the churches of the east, apart from any relics, during the reading of scripture the lamps are lit though the sun be already shining, not to dispel the dark but to make manifest our happiness, *laetitia*."[87]

The tension explored by Vigilantius between what he observed in the popular address to the martyrs, and what he and many in the church thought suitably restrained, provoked Jerome, I suppose, because he half-agreed with his former friend; hence the defensive violence of his protest. Hence the admission, too, that all of "us" were recent converts, though he need not have included himself and many others. He would excuse them all for acting only "through ignorance and the simple-mindedness of the laity of this world, or most likely religious women, of whom we must say (Rom. 10.2.), 'I grant them their zeal for God but they are ill-informed'" (§7).

It is easy to sense serious differences between the leadership like Jerome and those many others, the 95 per cent as I called them earlier, who clustered round the martyrs and gave such enormous vitality to this element in the church's development. They expressed themselves in the only way they could imagine; and the leadership must allow it, and apologize for it, and blame it in the usual terms (exactly those used by Celsus once, to ridicule Christians), as something you would see only among uneducated dolts and women.

That the 95 per cent were obviously and inevitably different from the leadership appears also in reproaches directed against their bad manners. At the great gatherings they shoved each other and shouted insults, as Chrysostom protested. They were shabbily dressed and they knew it, comparing themselves to the rich folk around them.[88] They spoke bad Greek, or none at all. No bishop or priest could talk to them with the same confidence that he felt in his own church. They were of another church, to some uncertain degree. Their difference expressed itself even, and most seriously, in worship itself.

They were more at home with Powers of a size and purport they could approach without terror—that shivering terror which was proper for communicants at the Eucharist, as Chrysostom and others had told them. Instead, the many wanted help in their daily lives, where it was daily needed, not in the Hereafter. It was this scale of supplication that governed the most of their traditional faith. It must still be satisfied by the new. We may be sure of this. Testimonies to their needs and expectations within that older faith are indeed enough and more than enough for our understanding. I speak of the eastern provinces up to the edge of the fourth century, when religious inscriptions become less full and candid. For the Latin-speaking provinces, in a later chapter, there is a little help of a different sort.[89] In general, however, and particularly after the mid-third century, the minds of the many must be read not from what they said but from what they did. That is, from our seeing.

Church leaders lived among their social equals in cities, even if many of them depended on rents from their rural properties. In the fourth century they were increasingly set apart from the urban working poor or indigent; their way of life was different, naturally; and differences were especially marked between themselves and the rural population. Jean Bernardi long ago detected and rightly reckoned the breadth and significance of the gulf that separated them, to be seen in the corpus of sermons surviving from Basil and others in the east.[90] He was right that the rural population gigantically outnumbered the urban—by a factor, let us say, of eight or ten (the figure obviously depends on one's definition of "city" as opposed to "village"). There is also clearly detectible a tone of address and choice of what to speak about in the homiletic corpus which favored the urban and shut out the rural, while at the same time making no allowance for Syriac or rural dialect among the preacher's listeners. Beyond these important points, however, the sermons help us to see the Christians of the sort attracted to the great festivals, always with an unusual attendance (above, n. 62) but most markedly at saints'-day celebrations. How they behaved was something simply not seen among the classes represented at church on an ordinary Sunday.

In trying to imagine who these crowds were, I return to that mismatch in numbers which seemed to me so perplexing, and therefore so well worth an attempt at an explanation. Christendom in the latter years of the fourth century had won its wars; it was, in the view of all modern accounts, triumphant. Must that not mean, then, vastly greater crowds than the few scores or hundreds inside the churches? Must they not be found in an alternative "church", one that drew forth from the city to the suburbs, and drew into the suburbs from the surrounding villages, estates, and farms, another population that was, nevertheless, Christian? And do not the martyr-shrines give a tangible form to the explanation?

Converts were simply of a different order from those who had built and taken over the churches; of a different order, looking for different rewards from their faith.

I offer these suggestions to be tested by evidence from other regions of the empire, and then to be discussed all together in the conclusions.

2

GREECE AND THE BALKANS

For anyone leaving the east, the first stop would of course be Byzantium, simply because it was *there*, it was on the way, and then in time, because it was Constantinople, the capital where everything met or happened.

The transformation of this city through the prodigious ambition of the first Christian emperor could be seen in a hundred ways. Prominent among them, you would expect the expression of his faith. The bishop Eusebius, his adviser (at times) and his admirer (always), was in a position to follow what Constantine did and to remember it all later with due reverence and orotundity; but about the emperor's record in Constantinopolitan construction he limits himself to the mention of "many houses of prayer", many chapels "through which he honored the martyrs' memory and consecrated his own city to the God of martyrs". There seems to have been nothing grand except the Church of the Apostles, directly under the altar of which the emperor gave orders for his own eventual burial in the manner of saint-in-chief—and this, he certainly thought he was! His body was removed to a more suitable resting place a few decades later.[1]

However, from the late, sometimes puzzling written sources that supplement Eusebius, and from some very limited excavation, there is reason to believe that Constantine before his death in 337 had laid plans also for a really proper church. In his son's reign, primacy within it, or at least within the Christian community, soon became the object of a fierce struggle between two parties. Armed guards tried to install the emperor's favored candidate. They turned their swords against a crowd obstructing them even in sacred precincts. In the resulting stampede and violence, many lost their lives. So the ecclesiastical historian Socrates Scholasticus tells us, quoting the number from some earlier source: 3,150 dead, lying there to be counted. He goes on to add that the emperor at about this time "founded the Great Church which is today" (in the earlier fifth century) "called Sophia."[2]

From this account we learn something about the more or less credible number of the city's Christians. The order of their magnitude is what we might expect. We learn also that there was more than one large church from the 340s on, as congregations grew; for the slaughter then was not in the Great Church. This latter, so named from the start, was only in the process of construction. The use of it, however, could have begun many years before its completion, just as a contemporary had seen happening in half-finished churches in both eastern and western cities.[3]

We learn later that the Great Church was close to the palace; it faced east and was aligned with the hippodrome, therefore evidently conceived as part of the conventional palace complex for the ruler. It held martyrs' relics brought from Antioch; it had an ambo in mid-nave. And it was over-all racetrack-shaped, like a very elongated letter U. Since, as will appear in chapter 4, such a plan was a favorite of Constantine, there is no reason to doubt what we are told.[4] More about this great building, we cannot say for sure.

It is idle to guess at its size. It suffered terribly from fire in 404, and wasn't re-made until 415. Was it then re-made in a serious way, according to a substantially different plan and dimensions? Or simply repaired? For my purposes it is enough to imagine the structure as it looked in 360 at its consecration, when it was certainly smaller than the area occupied by the fifth-century building and different over-all, too, in its ground-plan: not Hagia Sophia as we know it today. It seems to have been about the right size for the city at the time: a city, that is, with something over 100,000 residents. Much building went on around it, however, in the decades to follow, so that an official census of Constantinopolitan churches in 425 could count fourteen. This was after a recent reign noted for generous involvement in church affairs; so, at my cut-off moment in the year 400, perhaps there were only ten or a dozen serving a population now of 150,000. If these churches on average could accommodate an attendance of 400 at the most, then 2.5 to 3 per cent of the citizens would find a place at worship.[5] The interest in the estimate, however wobbly the figure may appear, may be left until my last chapter.

The hugeness of the existing Hagia Sophia is fixed in our minds. We can see it. We suppose that it truly represents, and so we can also see, the Christians in it and around it. But the context of country and economy in which it rose, on the western side of the Bosphorus, could never support anything on such a scale in such a capital. Only the lands to the east could do that through their tribute of immigrants and commerce and cash. To the west, things were entirely different.

What had once been the world of Pericles and Philip was not impoverished, but yet small-scale, out of the stream of history or in the stream only to its great cost.[6] Of the known churches (eleven as I have shown them in the appendix), none would hold more than a few hundred persons; most, far fewer. None was early, the majority dating only to the last quarter of the fourth century. Thessalonica was a large center, with ancient Christian roots, yet no detectible place of worship at all before 450. In Crete, there are enough early churches, true enough, but hardly a one before this same date.[7] The archeology on the island is representative of every part looked at in this chapter; and adding the testimony of inscriptions hardly helps.[8]

We may think we know more. Saint Paul's letters to cities around the shores of Greece, and other apostles' visits elsewhere in the book of Acts, all give to Christianity in this area a false familiarity. In fact, however, the Christian evidence on the ground is at first, nothing; thereafter, in the third and fourth centuries, very little and patchy. Internal documents in the form that might best be hoped for, as sermons, don't exist.

There may or may not be an equivalent of Dura, that is, a house-church to show the first seeds of faith implanted in a special place of meeting. A tiny chapel (5 x 4 m) in a villa a day's walk down the coast from Porec (Parentum), datable to the early 300s, is a sort of approximation to Dura; but it served only the purposes of the owner and his people; and its scale is a problem. Indeed in this period the Christian communities of Porec itself, or of the somewhat larger Trieste or Pola, could be counted only in the tens, not the hundreds of persons.[9] Certainly there were converts in this period. However few, they must be thought of as having some room where they got together, in whatever town; but unless its internal features can be known, we haven't gained very much. At the most we have been helped to see how straggling and inconsequential the church was in the early days, before the Peace of 313, so far as archeology can inform us. The picture is quite in accord with what we can see in the next century, too.

Trieste's Christian community, however, deserves a moment of attention. Its first known building for worship lay out of town, in the suburban cemetery: an unroofed little walled enclosure some seven by four meters in size as a memorial to a victim of the persecutions. His name now can at best be conjectured (Justus). To his resting place below ground, early in the Peace, two more were added by persons seeking the blessing of nearness to him, and adjoining the enclosure a roofed one was now built, twice as large, with an altar in its midst and a mosaic floor down the middle of which the design indicated a solea, a path with a raised edge to define it. Here would enter the presiding priest, all the other officiants, and then the congregation along either side on anniversary occasions. By the end of the fourth century the original enclosure was given its own altar, a mensa in the terminology of the day, above the coffin with its relics. Finally, in the fifth century, the east wall of the original little enclosure was taken down so as to open this side to an apse; the other three walls also

Fig. 2.1: The Greek provinces and lower Danube
(locations appearing in the appendix)

Fig. 2.2: Trieste's martyr church

were replaced by delicate columns, and the space they enclosed, made into a chancel. The martyrium had become a most respectable basilica, thanks to funding by wealthy members of the clergy and laity. Progress of a saint's cult can thus be followed across several generations, at first only with the liberty to show itself, and then in successive phases with more and more ambition.[10] The same progress can be traced in other places to be touched on a little later.

Intermediate between these little towns—Trieste, Pola, Porec, Iader—and the great Constantinople, there lie two other sites of a middling size: Philippi and Salona. Each holds its own interest.

And first, Philippi. A century of excavation has opened up a view of a suburban church.[11] It lay to the east about a kilometer from the walls, facing on the highway. Its plan shows a familiar basilical form with an ambo at mid-nave and another up in the chancel; in the apse was a curving built bench for all the clergy, with three levels to distinguish their ranks.

Beneath the site of the altar was a reliquary crypt with a hole in it through which libations could be poured. Something under two hundred persons could be accommodated for worship, and perhaps more in galleries. Under its floor in the position of honor, in the northeast corner (the right hand corner as one faced west, in the Latin fashion), was the *koimeterion* of Paul the presbyter, styled "the healer of the Philippians" and threatening anyone who intruded on his resting place; "for this is the single grave of a high priest". The building is conveniently called after him (and not to be confused with the basilica of Paul, described below). In the corresponding corner to the southeast two more presbyters were buried, with coins of the period 337–361; and burials in the other two corners held one more presbyter and an imperial official, with a second imperial official just outside the north aisle under a small service room. Time has erased the names and titles of a half-dozen other tombs that were admitted to the church, no doubt all secular or clerical big-wigs.[12]

The provision for ranks and privileges in the structure of the church are characteristic of the time. Illustration can be found in the larger basilicas inside Philippi (called A and B by the unadventurous excavators, with A dated no earlier than 400, perhaps decades later, while B is later still), where the space between the columns along the side aisles is filled by a screen high enough to prevent any view into the nave at all; so whoever stood or sat on the wrong side was taught his place.[13] This evidence, however, takes me beyond my chosen period of study.

The presbyter-Paul church may have been close to a cemetery. There is no obvious sign that it was built to serve memorial purposes. Still, those purposes appear in burials elsewhere around the city. They are notable for a festival custom brought in by Italian settlers: the very pleasant "Roses" of no fixed date in May—simply whenever the flower bloomed—to be enjoyed in company with those loved ones that were lost. Wherever Rome had sent out its colonizers, the Roses settled in with them; families or burial-club members gathered their bouquets and brought them to the graveside, there to sit down and eat and drink and remember; and it was from Philippi that the custom seems to have spread further into eastern lands. In any case, there it is well established for the inscription-experts to bring it to life. Their texts speak of funds provided in wills for the purchase of wine, or often for the purchase of a little plot where vines could be planted and their crop harvested for the celebration.[14] A sum of money would be specified in stone. Let all who passed and all the community take notice, "after my death, they shall offer to me or to the Parentalia" ("Ancestors Day," which was the other name for the Rosalia). John Chrysostom had reminded his listeners of the root of the word "cemetery", "the sleeping place". There, the dead could still be reached. The banquet at their bedside is shown on funerary reliefs here just as in sites further east (fig. 1.11).[15] But few stones survive to tell us more at Philippi beyond the troubles of the mid-200s, and there is no proof that the Rosalia continued among the Christian converts in this city, however clearly this was the case elsewhere.

Instead, preserved by a rare chance, we have a painted sign of Chrysostom's time over the entrance to a Philippian burial vault, or more precisely, a pair of chambers underground, declaring them constructed by the Christian builder "for self and children" (the usual formula); anyone trying to slip an alien corpse into this holy place would have to pay a fine to the church. The builder calls it a "heroon", a place for the venerating of some wonderful person.[16]

38   THE SECOND CHURCH: POPULAR CHRISTIANITY A.D. 200-400

Besides this heroon, Philippi at its very center held another as well (fig. 2.3). Along the great trunk-road, the Via Egnatia, which ran clear through the city from Constantinople westward, the forum was aligned; and not far from its southeast end lay a cluster of

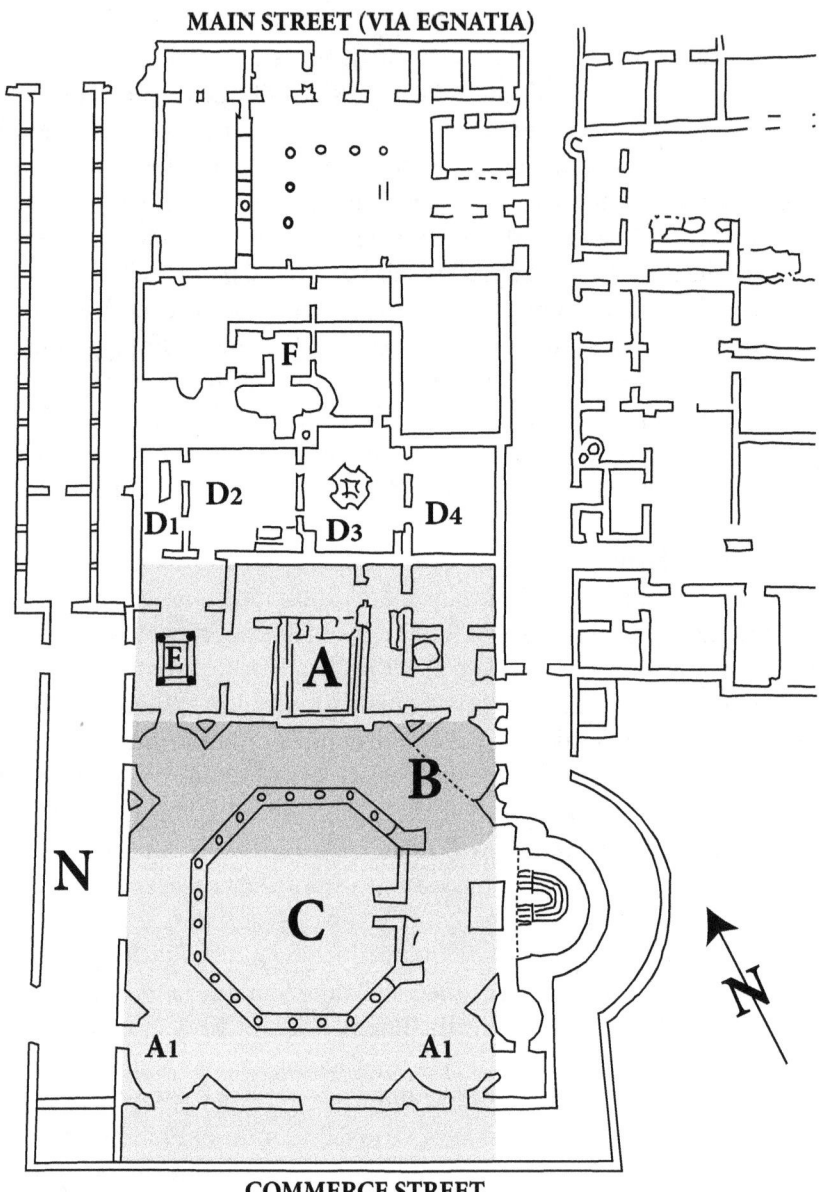

Fig. 2.3: Three phases in worship at Philippi
In light grey, lying between the city's two main avenues, the temenos with heroon (A) and front court (A1); in darker grey, the "Apostle Paul basilica" (B) of the 330s and its narthex (N). The Octagon (C) of ca. 400, with (D1) its undressing room, its catechumens' room (D2), its baptismal font (D3), its anointing room (D4), and communication to an older Roman baths (F)

buildings and rooms, and a rectangular walled enclosure, a temenos, protecting a place of worship. On one side of the temenos was the purpose of it: a square chamber about 7.5 m on a side; within it, a huge number of bronze coins as offerings, and a platform with three steps to dignify some now-lost temple-shaped memorial. In the ground underneath lay the object of the cult: a stone coffin inscribed with the name of the deceased and inside, resting on the chest of the deceased, a lovely gold pendant bearing many religious symbols.[17] The original consecrating of this shrine can only be loosely dated to Hellenistic times. From its position in the city, clearly the *hero* in the Greek sense of that word was a great figure, seen as a founder or protector.

Fig. 2.4: Mosaics of the "Paul basilica" under the Octagon

His cult continued for many centuries, not interrupted by the growing number of Christians in the city. Not long after the Peace, these latter got permission to take over the temenos and there constructed a cult hall of an almost basilical shape and of some luxury and taste; its nave was divided into two large squares covered with mosaics. Still, the ancient customs were maintained here without disturbance. Of the ground plan today, most lies hidden beneath a later octagonal structure, but enough remains to indicate an entry, and an area reserved for an altar and clergy, and in between, space for the laity measuring roughly 17 x 10 m, enough for 150 persons at the most or, more likely, 125. In its lack of a full apse, lack of an ambo, screens or barriers or built benches for the clergy—in short, in its simplicity—it recalls the Dura meeting hall. The mosaic panels, however, in their dimensions and beauty, show us a far larger and better funded.

In one is written: "Bishop Porphyrius was responsible for the decoration of the basilica, in Christ". He is known to have attended a council of 343, suggesting a date for the construction of the hall at least a decade earlier.[18]

The hall was approached from the Via Egnatia on the north by a columned passageway. It led right past the doorway to the heroon; and here beneath one's feet as one went on into the temenos was a mosaic inscription with the prayer, "Christ, help your servant Priscus with all his household". In the passage, two faiths in two streams mingled, living waters both.

Finally, on the site of this hall of the second quarter of the fourth century, after another century, a more ambitious octagonal church was put up in conjunction with a grand complex of rooms and buildings for baptismal instruction, the episcopal residence, and administration. Bishops still in the tradition of Porphyrius presided over worship which tolerated the continuation of the ancient hero-cult; for, in the heroon, the coins of offering continued through the fourth century into the fifth and the sixth. Additional arrangements for holy water in a room adjoining the heroon are best explained through traditions or relics associated with Saint Paul. Indeed, Paul is likely to have been the object of veneration and the reason for the building of the basilica back in Porphyry's day.

In the story told by these Philippian ruins, I notice two points of special interest: first, the pattern of growth in the Christian community, which ultimately required not only a new inner-city center, the octagon, but the much larger basilica A in the suburbs of about the same date. The curve of increase in membership is slight in the early decades of the Peace and throughout the fourth century, but after 400 it becomes most dramatic. A second point is equally striking: that reverence and devotion are focused most readily on a Being not quite Zeus, not quite God—the hero, his name unknown, whose perdurable cult survived the construction of the Apostle-Paul church around it.

Turning next to Salona: this was favored by its position on the coasting route up the Adriatic toward Aquileia and points north and west; and for this reason when the emperor Diocletian retired in the early fourth century (incredible act!) to live out his days in peace and quiet, he chose this site to be a little removed but not cut off from affairs. From his proximity, the population of Salona benefited in pride and size. In the period of interest to me, the city may have held 20,000 residents.[19]

Diocletian's reign had been the most changeful and dynamic in many generations; and a long one, too. Christians of Salona, however, could only remember him as a persecutor.

They had suffered in that bad year 303/4, when their bishop Domnius and another member of the clergy with several men in the army gave their lives for their faith. The most honorable resting place for these heroes was the cemetery today named Manastirine, a few minutes' walk along the main road north from the town. Here their co-religionists found a place for them among other specially known and respected non-Christian citizens of the town.[20]

The three or four hectares of the site seen in fig. 2.5 amount to a great jumble, much of it being accounted for by some 450 sarcophagi. They lie in and around the outline of a basilica which can be made out at a glance, today; but its lines don't appear clearly, and the layers of confusion are many. The confusion has been studied to unriddle it in some thousands of pages of close argument over the course of many generations, a remarkable effort!—archeology obsessed with its stones, one might say, not because of their historical role at all, in this quite obscure corner of the ancient world, but simply because they are so many and have been so little disturbed over the past fourteen hundred years. In the security of their oblivion they have survived as an almost unique object for study.

You can see to the right, which is due east, the curve of an apse of a basilica (which I use only as a point of reference—its date of construction is too late for my purposes oth-

Fig. 2.5: Air-view of Manastirine cemetery

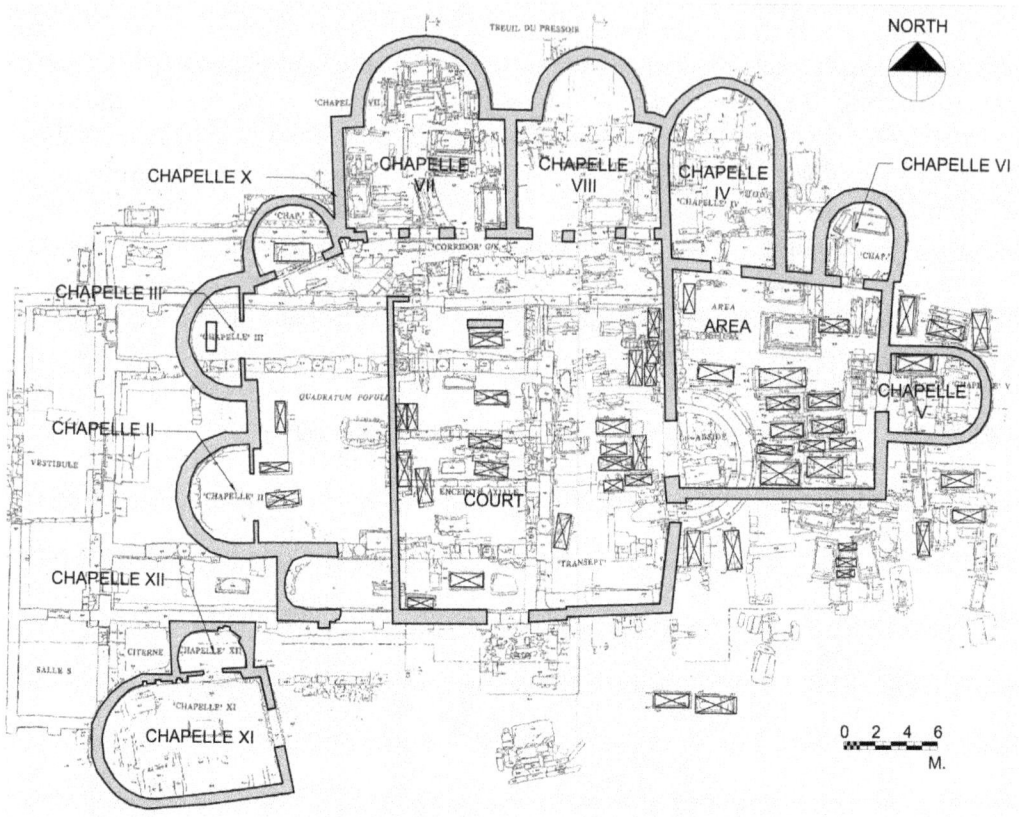

Fig. 2.6: The excavation results in Manastirine

erwise). To the left of this apse, westward down the center of the church, you can see the next prominent feature: a pair of columns still erect. They mark the edge of what was once a chancel; further still to the left, the nave and laity space. The results of study are clearer in the plan (fig. 2.6) which is given here on the chance of its being useful to show how excavation works, peeling off the layers of covering earth and successive construction. The more important lines of wall have been emphasized without concealing the complexity with which archeologists have had to deal, and which in this site required a lot of second thoughts and re-interpretation to arrive at the present view.

It is what once lay in the lower levels of these ruins that interests me; for here, inside the chancel, was the reason-for-being of the entire jumble: the community's martyrs. It was here that they had first been buried; it was from their graves here that their relics were in time taken up and moved a few feet north to more elegant lodgings; and over them was placed the altar of that church which, in the fifth century, was at last constructed, a memorial basilica. By then, many of those hundreds of sarcophagi that I mentioned had already been deposited as close by as they could get to the saints, *ad sanctos* as their privilege was expressed in Latin (Greek being attested in epitaphs here as the language of only a small minority).

The entire space was tightly controlled. That fact is clear. According to usual practice often attested throughout the region of this and the previous chapter, anyone could sell a bit of land for burials, and the buyer then could mark off what he had bought with a declaration inscribed on a marker posted at one corner or with a wall to make an enclosure. Threats of penalties against unauthorized inhumation would be posted also. The Christian community according to this practice had evidently moved quickly to secure two pieces of property at Manistirine for their own use. The smaller piece that excavators call the *area* (Latin for graveyard) can be imagined lying under the apse of the later church, in fig. 2.6. It was an already-walled "garden" where both Christians and non-Christians had long been buried; on its western edge stood, later, those two columns that I used, above, to identify parts of the site.

The larger piece adjoining it on the west side formed a court not quite square containing a little under 50 square meters, a corner of which was *ad sanctos*. Here, the raised gravestones of the most revered tombs of the bishop and four martyred soldiers probably received an ornamental covering of some sort, a wooden baldachin not surviving; and stairs led down to a crypt where these earliest heroes lay together, open to access by their worshippers. Above-ground over Bishop Domnius' tomb a marble slab—a mensa, a dining table—stood up a meter or so atop some little built structure. Nearby, Domnius' nephew Primus, rightly so-named, was the first after him to lie with the martyrs, he too a bishop; and in time thereafter, others of the rank, Gaianus and the rest, joined these two. They were the privileged, all, the martyrs and highest clergy equally revered; the date of their decease was marked on their memorials as instruction for their festal day. And to set them more splendidly apart, a light, low wall was built all around the larger piece of burial space, the court—this, in the 350s.[21]

Fig. 2.7: Martyr-memorial services (ca. 375)

We can animate this scene thanks in part to what the martyr-eulogies tell us, pronounced at similar eastern sites. Among some hundred persons shown, we can see women dancing before the holy burials in prayer and tribute to them, and men also to one side. We may suppose (but they are not indicated) someone with a small drum, someone with a kithara, someone else with a pipe of that shrill oboe note that one could hear at village feast days a half century ago in the hills of Cyprus or those to the north of Rome. Dancers do better with an accompaniment; but they may supply it as song by themselves. Crowds watch and listen. Near the principal tombs beneath the ground just in front of him and to his left would be the bishop, presiding.[22] He may have responded to the music with a conductor's wave of the hand. The mood of joy is contagious.

The hey-day of such festivals at Salona, however, is not yet. There are later beloved bishops yet to complete their lives and terms. They will be buried under their own marble mensae pierced with holes for libations. Toward the end of the fourth century and more clearly in the fifth and sixth, the apogee will come with streams of pilgrims, eager to join in but not, after all, in huge numbers. The country is not very populous and even in the cemetery-church to serve the events, when it is at last built, perhaps 250 persons might fit within the aisles and half the nave (the other half being reserved for the solea).

Disposed about the tombs of Domnius and the rest, a number of round-ended private chapels may be seen. Eventually they were twelve. Their construction began soon after the martyrs' cult here took on some popularity. They crowded in as closely as the owner of the court and *area* allowed—the owner of record being, of course, the organized church of the city. The point of the chapels was, however, not to join in the cult but rather to insure proximity *ad sanctos* for the persons buried in the sarcophagi inside on the floor. Some of these are shown, just visible. It was believed by all that touching the body of a holy person brought good things; or touching a garment or any other possession; or any fragment of the body; or anything that had touched any fragment. Touching was good but mere proximity might be enough.[23] Enough for what? By a Christian, no gift was more urgently to be sought than salvation, and no Power more naturally to be applied to than one's fellow townsman transfigured by his devotion and sacrifice: a martyr or perhaps a beloved bishop. To provide burial for one's self or one's parents, children, or spouse near such holy figures and their relics—nothing could be more ardently desired. But proximity would give force to prayers for help, too, on earthly needs. They were after all more real and pressing. Accordingly the devout built chambers to hold their own remains and their family's as close to Domnius as was allowed, counting on the advantage.

Their hope explains the position of the chapels; but it does not entirely explain what else has been discovered in them.[24] The series was built over the course of a generation and, as would be expected, where the epitaphs survive, careers and official titles may be given. Thus we know that some, and we can suppose that all, belonged to wealthy families of a high position. Some of the buried were their children; some epitaphs specify the day of death, to be remembered in the usual memorial picnics.[25] It is these funerary texts that tell us something about the reason behind the chapels: they could serve the needs of cult for family members, and as more of the deceased were placed in the earth beneath the floors, and as the burials included saints, more occasions in the year would draw in the family. We can suppose that a chapel might have visitors several times a month, always in the evening since that was the conventional time.

The proof of the practice in its broad outline lies in mensae: stone dining-tables to sit atop a burial. Wealthy people had these made out of good marble, all too easy to break and tempting to re-use later as paneling or other elegance. Today, therefore, displaced fragments are scattered all over Salonitan sites and in local museums. Nevertheless a number have turned up in their original position. Some are inscribed. One of the displaced pieces, not from a chapel but from close-by in this same Manastirine cemetery, declares in bad Latin: "Aurelius Secundus who bought the *piscina* from Aurelius Alexius, for two burials (me and my wife Renata), and God forbid us parents that we put our daughter in this *piscina*, we plainly contract no further burial on top of the girl...."[26] Secundus employs a word, "fish-pond", that must originate in the puddling of rainwater in the slightly recessed round area of a mensa when not in use; so, in time, the term for the tomb-top was applied to the tomb itself. Today, specialists when they speak about a *piscina* mean only the slab—a round one at that. Often its circle is marked out within a square piece, typically a meter across. The round rim will be raised a few centimeters and a hole will be drilled right through the slab at its center.[27] The whole is of a size to cover one third of a coffin, to receive a splash of wine from the glasses of a circle of family-members all together, while the hole in the middle allows the libation to run down into the coffin for the enjoyment of the beloved below; for, as everyone knew, the dead needed food and drink. Throughout the region of this chapter, stones of this cut are found and easily identified.

What is more commonly meant, however, by the term mensa is a square or rectangular slab with a U-shaped carved-out area, or the whole slab itself in that shape. Examples are found to the north at Sirmium, or at Iader, or to the south at Thebes, Corinth, Larissa, or elsewhere in the region covered in this chapter—and especially at Salona. However, I reach back into the region of my first chapter for an example that is particularly fine and, so to speak, expressive. It was found in one of the side-rooms of an early church at Ephesus, amid all the signs of informal meals in fragments scattered around it: broken lamps, crockery, and so forth. It has (fig. 2.8) a row of a dozen bowls around the curve, plus another five along the bottom edge—seventeen of them, offering an elaborate menu of Today's Specials.

Fig. 2.8: A mensa from Ephesus

The shape itself declares the manner of dining, with guests semi-recumbent in a semi-circle in the traditional Greek fashion, on the three couches, the *klinai*, set in a square C to form a *tri-klinion*. What they looked like was seen in fig. 2.7 in a typical form, non-Christian, or can be seen in a form very similarly but Christian, in another funerary relief which

I don't reproduce because it is damaged. It was found at Tanagra near Thebes in central Greece, around the year 400, inside a church, along with an inscription beneath it, offering instructions from the person who commissioned it. "Bring," he says,

> bring next, within the sacred precincts, to the all-ruling Trinity, on day Six, your gifts pleasing to God, Christ, in the name of your brothers, children, parents, husbands and wives, kin of former times, a dozen loaves and sweet wine like the sun's rays or the flakes of snow; for the offerings to the dead must be celebrated enthusiastically.

The instructions are elegantly expressed in verse.[28]

In many mensae (not in the example shown) there is a hole at the center, through which we must imagine the mourners pouring a little wine with a prayer to accompany it, themselves recumbent around the tomb. After communication with the dead, the living could turn to their own meal, sampling whatever stews or casseroles they had brought. Fifty years ago my friend D.G. was doing something like this as a teenager in the local cemetery with his uncles, in a Greek setting. He remembers the experience very pleasantly. It was religion of the family.

At Corinth in the suburbs, a row of hillside tombs contains two that illustrate the practice of family funerary picnics. One has a walled enclosure in front of its entrance, evidently to keep the parties more private; another has a number of sarcophagi in it, a built bench, facilities for heating food and eating, and a stone table in the center.[29] Such arrangements illustrate the requirement in inscribed and posted wills that on such-and-such a day all the kinfolk of the deceased shall gather for a feast of remembrance. Mensae might then add form and formality to the guests' prayers. A good rain would clean them out after use.

Mensae like the one from Ephesus naturally figured in the cult of the saints. How the application might be made is illustrated in Constantinople, where "a table of the martyrs" was commissioned by a pious woman's hoarding, as it were, of certain precious relics from the persecution of the 320s, for her personal benefit, in a casket with a hole in its lid; and she, Eusebia, was eventually buried with it. A mensa on her tomb above her head, likewise with a hole, allowed communication with her spirit after death as with the martyrs themselves.[30] So our ancient church historian tells us; and if the account has been embellished, nevertheless it is perfectly representative of the realities. The correspondence can be tested at Manastirine, where Domnius' tomb lay beneath a mensa equipped with a hole; likewise Bishop Gaianus'; and so also at Thessalonica.

At Thessalonica the hole lay at the center of a huge chrisma inscribed in a thick marble slab covering the crypt of Saint Demeter. In the crypt was what the excavator called an omphalos, which is indeed its shape, less than a meter high, its tip directly under the hole of the slab, sitting in a cruciform chapel among several other surrounding rooms. This had been the primitive shrine for the cult. Its treasure was enclosed in a small box and a smaller glass flask with a red deposit in it, taken to be the martyr's blood.[31] The local Christians had moved into the apsidal remains of a baths-building and transformed the space into a tiny basilica, on top of which was built, a century later, the grander church in which the slab was made a part of the floor.

All these testimonies to the focus and physical arrangements of worship explain the officiant at Manastirine (fig. 2.7) who stands at a table set directly over the saints. Chief

Fig. 2.9: Saint Demeter's crypt at Thessalonica

among them was the bishop who had given his life in 304. But there were other cemeteries along the roads from Salona, long known if not so carefully studied. At the modern village of Marusinac, a half-kilometer outside the city to the north, the ancient graveyard enjoyed a special prestige, attracting or being open to the wealthy and martyrs exclusively. Here in the fourth century, and beginning very soon after the Diocletianic persecution, several small chapels were built for Christian families but in traditional fashion over private burials and those of martyrs, alike, and in one case, the two sorts together: serving for both Saint Anastasius and a rich woman whose name is preserved, Asclepia, with her husband. Among these various chapels there was a large, walled burial "garden" in one corner of which was a chamber for the cult of a certain Valentinian. Here too at Marusinac, a number of mensae were recovered, both round and square. One of them was used as an altar-top.[32] At a third Salonitan cemetery, Kapljuc, a basilica was built in the mid-fourth century, making it one of the very earliest known

The Kapljuc evidence gives us one more instance of martyr-cult in its development from the moment of first burial, to the construction of a full-scale basilica, on a modest scale but quite elegant in its details (fig. 2.10a–b).[33] These latter can be pieced together from

Fig. 2.10a: The Kapljuc basilica   **Fig. 2.10b:** Chancel-reconstruction

the surviving architectural fragments. At the beginning, an outdoor memorial dining room was erected over the resting place of four martyrs later venerated as a group. This was a thing of the early 300s, perhaps in the wake of the persecution of 303/4. A fifth martyr was the priest Asterius who suffered at the same time. A half century later, a basilica with the usual synthronon for the clergy was built in their joint honor, with an altar above the priest in the apse (fig. 2.10a).[34] People wanted to be buried close to them all and the usual competition for that privilege resulted in one important applicant finding a place at the foot of the ambo. Above his tomb was a roughly carved mensa with four cups or bowls carved into its surface and between two of the cups, a rectangular cavity to receive libations. The excavators in the reconstruction shown here don't provide the chancel-screen with a triumphal arch. That might come later, as Anastasios Orlandos indicates from other sites. Kapljuc was well out of the mainstream of change.

It is not clear, from the Salona evidence alone, just who placed what in the cups, nor who poured wine into the hole cut into the mensa on the anniversary of the nameless honorand; but the African evidence in the next chapter will certainly suggest some answers. It is agreed that the Eucharist was celebrated on the martyrs' mensae in cemeteries both before the Peace and thereafter, on the anniversary of the death; and at these times the crowds must have been considerable, as may be seen conjecturally in fig. 2.7. In time, memorial buildings were put up over the honored graves which determined where the altar would be set. Here, the anniversaries were celebrated indoors and a mensa would serve as an altar top.[35]

That the cups and hole for libations were wholly symbolic—that nothing to eat or drink was shared with the honored dead—seems to me out of the question. The modern consensus is against it, too. In mensae, after all, there are carven representations of food; there are channels to permit run-off of liquids; and other details could be brought out, too, regarding family worship. How much of the practice of private memorial celebrations in cemeteries was imitated in those for the martyrs in churches, is perhaps beyond conjecture. It is still more difficult to say how much of traditional usages were retained in the celebration of the Eucharist over the tombs of the martyrs. This last question may be left until the next two chapters where there is more evidence to work with.

Einar Dyggve, the name most closely associated with the excavation and study of Salona's ruins, has aligned the Kapljuc material with that of the city's other cemeteries to explain further developments in martyr-cult: among other pieces of evidence, the open-work marble screens found whole or more often in fragments. Called "little windows of the Testimony", *fenestelle confessionis*, these allowed controlled access to a burial "for worship and edification through the observation of the holy remains". They also "made it possible for the worshippers to obtain pseudo relics" such as a sponge or a cloth that could be introduced into the burial and then taken out for preservation as effective in its own right.[36] Belief in the efficacy of these has had a long history.

Salona itself, the city, remains to be considered. The presence of Christians inside would be expected in the third century and two possible places of prayer, little shrines, have been identified in the amphitheater off in the northwest corner against the city wall. It was here that the presbyter Asterius was remembered to have lost his life; his figure and his name above it in a wall-painting identify one of these two sites for prayer.[37] Their dating, however, is problematic. Elsewhere at the city's edge, a large church went up in the 320s, able to accommodate crowds of up to five hundred, if the chancel did not extend any distance into the central aisle; but it probably did, and the figure should be reduced. In the general population, this would mean 1.5 to 3 per cent, quite in line with the proportions found in other cities of the eastern half of the empire.

Meanwhile, however, it is clear that martyr-cult had found expression in no less than three cemeteries out of some unknown total, making Salona a center of pilgrimage (which, for the centuries beyond my reach, is a fact well attested). If the material remains from the past are to be trusted, the balance of belief and ardor inclined toward this latter realm of worship. Asterius, Anastasius, Domnius, Justus, Maurus, and the rest—devotion to these Salonitan figures had arisen out of local experience and devotion, not out of scripture. Scripture was what was read aloud in synaxary services and commented on in the city's church by a hierarchy increasingly educated, even so far from the great cities. Their teachings and rituals must have seemed increasingly remote; their bishop when he returned in the 340s from a church council, there having met his peers from every corner of the empire east of his home, cannot have had the same vision of things as the ordinary members of his flock. It was a big world for him, but not a world for them; and as the eastern church became more and more engaged in theological questions, the everyday concerns of everyday people would hardly compete for the bishops' attention.

Perhaps. There is no source surviving to say so. Instead, there are only the stones. Yet the patterns they take on do invite some interpretation. At the very least they show ardent private action in the instituting of religious rituals at private sites outside the city, in the cemeteries—a thing then to be shared and monumentalized, in time. So far as the stones declare, the church inside the city remained unaffected by such enthusiastic initiatives. Outside there was experiment seen for example at Manastirine, where no controlling authority is visible. Quite the reverse: the chapel-builders clustered up against the martyr's site *ad lib*. At Marusinac it was the pious Asclepia who built a memorial church by herself, a fact rightly understood as a demonstration of lay spontaneity.[38] While the hierarchy were preoccupied with such abstract matters as the Trinity and the interrelations of its personae, the masses expressed their religious impulses in the cemeteries. They were focused on the simplest realities: the merit of those who dared to face the persecutions, the saving power earned by such champions, and their power in turn to answer to the needs of others in this life on earth. It is this last that is most often and most powerfully attested, if we care to reach up beyond 400 and the archeological data, to saints' biographies.[39]

But there is no need to do so. Within my chosen circuit of proof, tomb-tops that become altar-tops are testimony enough to the great popularity of martyr-cult, taking bishops as well into its embrace. The meaning of the physical traces and their ubiquity have been generally recognized. What is striking about them is their series, unbroken in Salona as elsewhere, from receptacles for food carved into the lids of the gable-shaped tomb-tops that are so common around the city as elsewhere, to the flat slabs fitted on to a coffin with a hole over the region of the head of the deceased; to the same arrangements for the saints under private protection; and so to the saints ensconced under the altars of basilicas, altars the tops of which are mensae.[40] No difference in style or shape distinguishes the non-Christian mensa from the Christian, for purposes of private cult, nor any that distinguishes the latter, if Christian, from mensae for martyr-cult. Nor, it can be added, is there any difference between these latter and altar tables which have no martyr connection. There is an unbroken flow of belief and practice across all these several manifestations of piety; all lie within the world of the masses and tradition. They assert a degree—sometimes seen as an alarming degree—of lay independence, in search of an answer to everyday prayers. Where answers were indeed available to prayer and piety, the church inside the city could be left to one's betters—who were perfectly content with the bargain.

3
North Africa

411 was the year of census, when the Christian population all along the coastal areas of Africa, from the Gulf of Tunis to the Straits of Gibraltar, counted sees. They had been for a full century divided, some deriving from one bishop and his followers, Caecilianists; the others, from another, Donatists. At stake was a doctrinal question a little like that which embroiled the Anabaptists with their neighbors, many centuries later: a question about the validity of baptism by impure hands. One side called the other heretical, and an imperial judge was sent to Carthage to weigh the merits of both. At last it was to be determined which was "right". Numbers mattered. Caecilianists and Donatists both turned up for the hearing with as full a complement of their bishops as they could possibly muster: 284, each.[1] Though some of these were rivals for the same see, many were not; and it is often supposed, and reasonably enough, that the total of sees may thus have been close to 500 or even more.

At least in the back-land parts, in Numidia especially, quite tiny towns within a half-hour's walk of each other each had their own bishop in Cyprian's day, the mid-third century. No one supposes, however, that all the various regions together in 411 could boast of so many as 500 urban centers, if "urban" is to mean anything. Such a number would be well above Italy's total—a half of which is about as much as you would expect in the north African provinces.[2] It seems more likely that by 411, in competition with each other, the two branches of the African church had put a bishop in every place they could possibly think of, villages included. The shape of Christendom in Africa was thus quite different from that of any other region; and the point is worth mentioning when we try to visualize the Christians of those parts. They shouldn't be imagined as much more densely packed nor a much larger percentage of the whole population than could be found elsewhere.

The split in north African Christendom found expression principally in the veneration of its heroes; for it was the memory of martyr-bishops in times of persecution, set against the accommodating bishops, that had given rise to the split in the first place. To shed light on this cult of martyrs, Yvette Duval made an excellent inventory of archeological findings—inscribed testimonials, chapels, and whole churches—in at least that part of the Roman provinces that is modern Algeria. All this material, and more still from other African sites both east and west, has much to reveal about rituals and how these grew out of older traditions for private mourning and memorializing. The story is useful in explaining cult practices in other parts of the empire. Hence, my emphasis in this chapter.

The early presence of Christianity in the chief centers of the African provinces is easily shown. Beyond minor figures and testimonies, there are Tertullian, Minucius Felix, and

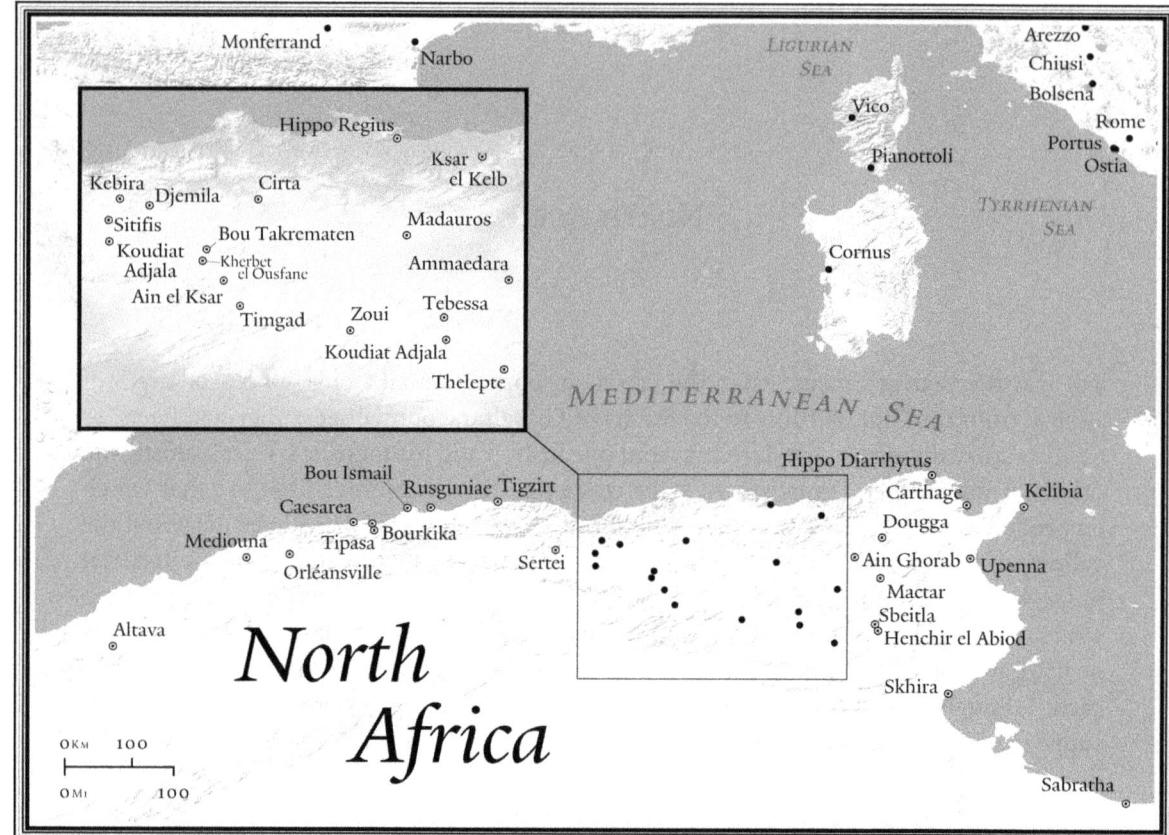

Fig. 3.1: The North African provinces
(locations appearing in the appendix)

Cyprian into the 250s. Of course, in their day, meeting places were still private houses; and archeological traces of such may perhaps be found at one site, Augustine's own Hippo Regius; but these hold no particular interest, even if they are rightly identified.[3] We learn more from the cry of hostile fellow-citizens, "An end to the cemeteries!" Still past 300, a small-town mayor addressing the Christians before him speaks of their cemeteries "where you all make your prayers". These were the places Christians gathered in, or where they were generally to be seen.[4] In sum, what little we learn of their practices and places of worship in the third century fits with what little also can be learnt of other regions.

By a fluke, in consequence of the endless bitter wrangling between the Caecilianists and the Donatists long afterwards, the events in one town, Cirta, of the early fourth century were looked into and the results of the inquiry were written down. They show us what local records were kept in the course of the persecutions of those times, and how long they were preserved, and thus, where the Christians were to be found. The records placed them in a building in the cemetery in the suburbs. Everyone knew about it. The scale of activities there suggests a congregation a good deal bigger than Dura's of a few decades earlier—say, several hundred people, some 5 per cent of a town about the same size but with a larger territory than Dura.[5] They had had a dedicated building for their use; they lost it briefly as a consequence of persecution; but they nevertheless continued to meet and keep accounts of their stores of clothes and food for the poorest among them, the most vulnerable. These were mostly elderly women.

Nothing tangible remains to bring these details to life until the declaration of religious Peace in 313. Thereafter, what was built had a better chance of surviving, at least in architectural fragments and footings. With such evidence, an attempt at a reconstruction of life may be possible; and Augustine's writings are very helpful with details about standing throughout services (nobody sat but the bishop), with moments and particular services in which the congregation knelt repeatedly or prostrated themselves on the ground.[6]

Practices seem to have been just such as you would find in other regions, at least in all major respects. There does seem to be more eastern than Roman influence at work; but there were no ambones. The construction of some churches with an apse at both ends was characteristically African, but it cannot have accommodated any particular liturgy since written sources which should have mentioned such a thing, do not; nor do they mention the consequences of having the apse, if only one, or the chief apse if one of two, at the western end instead of the eastern. The officiating priest still faced east for prayer, the congregation likewise; and the position of the altar varied according to local preferences which must remain unknown.[7]

Sometimes the altar was halfway down the central nave, as at Carthage in the basilica called Cyprian's memoria. Noël Duval picks out one feature as particularly characteristic of Africa, namely, the higher elevation of the chancel which made it easier for the clergy to see and be heard; and the bishop's *cathedra* was up several more steps above the synthronon where his fellow priests sat, in a curve beneath him on both sides. The model employed may have been the platform and elevated seat common in secular basilicas.[8] Other points of architecture are easier to find in other regions: for example, the strict separation of women from men, as also of catechumens from the rest of the congregation.[9] The chancel might lie behind a low protective marble screen, with perhaps six-foot-high curtains as well, which were closed when the officiants and their actions needed to be hidden; or occasionally the chancel took up the entire nave.[10] The clergy's gradual taking over of the laity space has been noted in its eastern contexts, above. As this happened, spectators were forced to the sides, to watch rather than be a part of worship, and to take note of the distinction between laity and clergy. Augustine indicates the unwelcome crowding this might cause, to be able to hear the bishop as he spoke.[11]

A certain type of church, however, invites separate comment: the so-called funerary or cemetery churches. Their size and number draw attention to the popularity of memorial rites for the dead, which began with family members and family gatherings but, in time, embraced the local martyrs emerging out of the persecutions. This flow of ritual, from private to public, has been often traced in Africa, as I hope my acknowledgements will make clear in the notes.

At Carthage in the great church just mentioned (fig. 5.1) there are many burials beneath the floor dating from the late fourth century; and so, too, at Sitifis, in the basilicas "A" and the very much larger "B" (fig. 3.2). These buildings were put up simultaneously, perhaps, or at any rate in close succession ("A" first, before or during the 360s and "B" in the 370s?), in a part of the suburbs being opened to new housing. In the center of "B" was an enclosed prayer platform with a dedicatory inscription.[12] "B" in particular was crammed with burials making it by itself a cemetery in use for a generation and evidently serving a great many families. Its laity space of 575 square meters excluding the apse was, by provincial standards, very unusual: larger than Augustine's cathedral in Hippo, larger even than Timgad. Even this was not enough. "A" also, or already, could be used for the same purposes; here, if an aisle was not reserved for catechumens, there would have been room for another seventy-five persons or so. A second, bigger church was only needed to meet great demand for burial-space. In both, everyone who could do so, at the end of life, crowded into the earth beneath the paved floors; the lucky ones, husband and wife, fitted tiny graves between them for their infants; and above them, to be noticed as you walked about, many of them had recorded their names in mosaic inscriptions.

What interests me here is the sign of a particular religious enthusiasm, or rather, the sign of its dimensions: three or four times as much for what could be satisfied in "B" as in "A". More can be said about this, below.

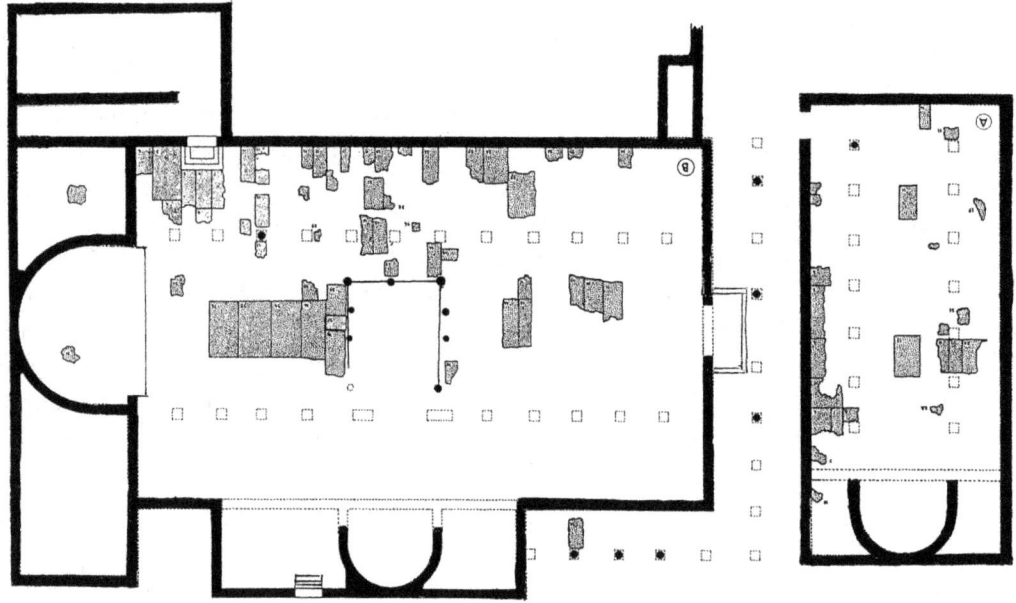

Fig. 3.2: Basilicas of Sitifis, "A" at right, "B" at left

At the time when Sitifis' churches answered to such eager throngs, a quite little church was constructed to the east, at Kelibia on the coast of Cape Bon not far from Carthage. It was destined to serve exactly the same purpose: as a roofed-over cemetery.[13] Its initial plan suited conventional religious services, with a chancel extending far into the central nave and the altar at its edge, leaving to the laity only a minority of the floor space and the sides (there were no aisles). Then, however, it was remodelled to a new use: the chancel was removed around the turn of the fifth century; burials began throughout the interior and more still in chapels built on the outside against both side walls. They had doorways into the church, essentially expanding its area for more inhumations. Their outline recalls the cluster of chapels up against the basilica at Manastirine cemetery in Salona (figs. 2.6–7) as well as the large single exedra on the east side of "B" in Sitifis. Predictably, the choice for inhumation was that place of honor, in the apse, where no one had a better position than a member of the local clergy, by name Felix; and his burial there raises the possibility that he was regarded as a saint, and that his sanctity drew in the other burials, giving the whole funerary operation the quality of *ad sanctos*.

And there is Tipasa: a city of no less than 20,000 lying along the coast, spectacularly Christian at the turn of the fifth century with a gigantic church just inside the west wall where 7 or 8 per cent of the population could have attended (so many at least if they were packed in like sardines). In addition, there was the much smaller "Peter and Paul's" just outside the east wall, the St. Salsa church also there in the midst of the cemetery (figs. 3.3a–b), and a fourth, trapezoidal, church named after the bishop Alexander in the middle of the other major cemetery in the eastern suburbs.[14]

Of these four buildings, so different, of course only ruins remain; and yet they need not be entirely silent. In the "Alexander" church, most helpful is a mosaic inscription giving a name to the founder, praising him and the glories of his work, the basilica itself, while at the same time directing the greatest honor toward the bishops who preceded him on his throne. Their relics occupied the apse, or rather its underground area; the nave was one huge mosaic floor, dotted with memorial texts; and in the aisle on the bent, western side, which was filled with burials, was a large built mensa in the familiar semi-circular form. The obvious point of the structure was to memorialize the most holy of the dead, the city's bishops. Their sanctity attracted other burials; which is why it is, by the excavators, rightly called a "funerary church."[15]

On its south side against the church was an irregularly shaped *area*, a walled enclosure such as cemeteries often had, with dozens of inhumations in it and at least one built mensa right in the center—"built," as a semicircular low platform made of rubble and cement, smoothed over and sloping away from its middle, where an indented half-circle would hold food for the diners as they lay on their cushions on the slanting sides. A match for such a thing is easily found in the regions described earlier and later as well (figs. 4.6–7).

On the other side to the north, at a slightly lower level, was another *area* (fig. 3.4) where a half-dozen memorial chambers, predating and accounting for the church, ran along the east side under a portico. All the chambers were dedicated to martyrs. Each had a dining-table in mensa form resting upon and giving names to the inhumations below-ground. One commemorated Rogatus and Vitalis, otherwise unknown; the rest are destroyed. The burial of a *martyre professus*, a hero proven by his willingness to die, faces them across a few feet of open space and also supplies the date of his sacrifice, most likely in Constantine's reign and in sectarian strife; and a wall is dated by a coin (Valens) to the third quarter of the fourth century, the same time of construction as that of the basilica itself.[16] Conveniently in a corner of the martyr-shrine was a well to serve the mensa; for wine had to be chilled and diluted. Epitaphs identify other burials as clergy.

This triune "Alexander" complex with a church in the middle (but without an altar or chancel), an *area* on both sides, and dining arrangements in all three parts was, needless to say, not one big restaurant. It was rather a place where the devout addressed themselves to Beings above themselves, and did so by their words, gestures, thoughts, and general behavior, in some traditional fashion. All these elements together amount to religion, surely, and its particular form may surely be called "cult" or "worship" (the terms have been a cause for argument, quite needlessly).[17] The facilities that once served this address tell us about behavior, which in turn may perhaps be read to reveal the participants' ideas and feelings. Along such familiar lines of reasoning, however, there is more to be said in my concluding chapter.

First, however, Tipasa's other cemetery (fig. 3.6) outside the city's east walls and the shrine there on the south side of the basilica. It was dedicated to the thirteen-year-old Salsa. She had attacked and destroyed an idol, and suffered for it. Her remains were first committed to the earth in the wake of some early fourth-century persecution. Hers was a memorial of very modest dimensions (fig. 3a–b), lacking a proper complement of right angles and straight lines; only a lintel-inscription supplied her name. The date of construction may have been around 320. In the rectangular room on the south (right-hand) side, across the corridor from an apsidal room, was a large mensa (M) originally without walls around it, serving whoever came to her burial in the apsidal room on the north (left). A few decades later, this slanted eating structure was surrounded by a wall, dignifying the rites that there took place; and when before long the saint's fame spread, and she received the tribute of a church a few hundred yards away, still her original resting place was remembered and burial in its vicinity sought out.[18] That story, however, lies beyond the limits of my study.

Tipasa had another martyr-memorial dedicated to a group of three, Sperantus and others, in one of its cemeteries. At some point in the fourth century they had fallen victim "to the blind wickedness of this world" (it is natural to think of Caecilianist-Donatist violence, so well attested); they were afterwards honored by four "brothers". So reads the tablet set up where they were buried. The four may have been co-religionists or real blood brothers.

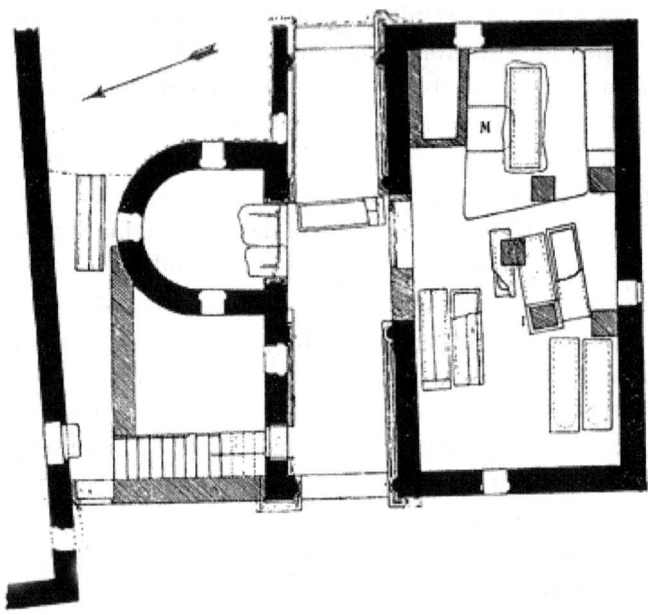

Fig. 3.3a: Plan of St. Salsa's chapel

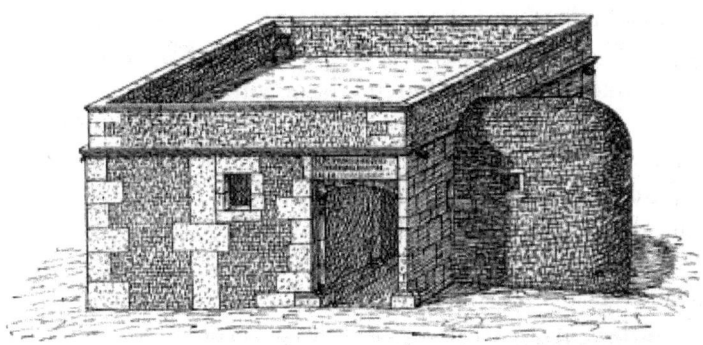

Fig. 3.3b: Reconstruction of St. Salsa's chapel

In favor of the latter interpretation, Paul-Albert Février compares another memorial tablet found near Castellum Tingitanum (modern Orléansville) some twenty-five miles west of Tipasa, dated to 329 and dedicated to four young martyrs, the dedicants being their own father and mother. Similarly, not far from Sitifis, a local priest "and all his family" joined together in offering a built mensa inside a chapel, this one to Saints Nabor and Felix. Another priest in a second small town in 361 similarly combined the building of his own resting place with a martyr-shrine; and there are many more shrines that could be instanced with the same kinds of originating impulses, essentially private, spread across the African provinces.[19]

They are touching testimonies, reminders of the emotions that might be wrapped around the rituals for the dead. Their party atmosphere should be acknowledged, too; for, in what must be the earliest inscription to tell us about African martyr-cult, the devout are told, "[Here is] the mensa of Januarius the martyr. Drink up, live long!"[20]

We are struck by how simple were, or might be, the beginnings in martyr-cult. We have the various examples just instanced; also the little martyrium for St. Salsa, above, or the action taken by Eusebia at Constantinople (ch. 1) or by other pious persons like her attested through their chapel-building at Trieste, Manastirine or Kapljuc (ch. 2). The dedicants acted in a manner as close to unplanned as possible along entirely traditional lines. Tradition, being so long familiar and approved, gave them confidence. Church authority didn't have to be involved in the process; nor is its hand always apparent at all, any more than in the veneration of relics carried about on one's person—veneration which some clergy approved of for themselves but others would have prevented.[21] Similarly, the authorities did sometimes step in at an early point in the creation of a regular church for martyrs, thus taking over what had had a more spontaneous commencement.

Our picture of rituals surrounding the saints in Africa must be largely drawn from the archeological data. Any written story like Eusebia's in the east is rare indeed; but one important piece of such evidence is often brought in to help. At its center is Augustine's mother, Monica. She had learned her Christianity in a town twenty-five miles inland from Hippo, his eventual see, where she was used to going about the martyr-shrines with a jug of wine and a basket of cheesecakes for herself, and something extra to share with others. In 385 she found herself in Milan. She attended at the saints' shrine, most likely of Saints Nabor and Felix, hugely popular; but the bishop Ambrose had recently placed a ban on any jugs and baskets in churches, and she was corrected.[22] The incident tells us that in North Africa at this time, and as far back as the 330s when Monica was growing up, real food and drink were brought into the martyr churches in quantities beyond what might be needed for a snack; private as well as martyrs' mensae might be found inside churches; and we have, thus, the explanation in writing, as common sense would suggest anyway, that a dinner-table, a mensa, would have a real meal on it; further, that the wells so frequently dug in proximity to mensae in chapels (not in churches) were for the service of the wine; likewise the grooves often cut into the table-tops for the flow of water to chill it. What Monica's story reveals is confirmed by what her son the bishop saw as the practice many years later.[23] The question of behavior raised a few pages earlier is thus partly answered. Whatever else they did, worshippers in a martyr church or chapel ate and drank as Christians had been doing at graves and shrines since the second century. Eating and drinking was worship.

A strange idea, or at least unwelcome!—unwelcome because of its pagan origin. Yet, considering the religious manners of the Christian population as one whole, Augustine advised,

> Let it [that population] bear in mind that its future members are concealed within its very enemies, and let it not be thought that even among those very persons there can be no harvest. Let it put up with those who are hostile until they declare themselves Christian; for God's state includes even some of them in its company during its secular wanderings.... Surely these two states are tangled together and thoroughly commingled one with the other in this world below, until the day of judgement.[24]

It was this very commingling, however, that bothered Ambrose about the North African practice (which has been seen also in eastern churches like Ephesus', fig. 2.8). It all too clearly recalled non-Christian rites. They are attested, as we have seen, in the mature or later Roman Empire wherever Italian families had settled;[25] and a match to them can be found in the indigenous rites of other peoples, too, as appeared in the first chapter, above. As to their origins, they recede into the mists of the past under that name naturally familiar to Ambrose, the *parentalia*, but under other terms also and with particular dates and rules for the non-Christian pious to observe.[26] To address one's self to the dead was then and is still today a common practice—at least common enough so that we ourselves have no trouble understanding, across a great gap of time, space, and way of life, the following dedication set up at Satafis,

> To the memory of Aelia Secundula:
> We all have already spent much, as is right, on the burial, but we have decided furthermore to put up a stone dining chamber where Mother Secundula rests, wherein we may recall the many wonderful things she did, the while the loaves, the cups, the cushions are set out, so as to assuage the sharp hurt that eats at our hearts. While the hour grows late, gladly will we revisit our tales about our virtuous mother, and our praises of her, while the old lady sleeps, she who nourished us and lies forever here in sober peace. She lived 72 years. Dated by the province's year 260 [A.D. 299]. Statulenia Iulia set up [the memorial].[27]

The dedicants are Christians, although in the old style or tone. This, the ecclesiastical authorities evidently could accept. Augustine, for one, tells us that Christians celebrating the anniversaries of the deceased at their graves, at the traditional points in the year post-mortem, might even ask for the Eucharist. That was their choice.[28] And such meals as Secundula's children enjoyed in her company might be tolerable in a room or chapel that would be, after all, privately used and owned. Their setting would resemble that seen below, in fig. 3.5. But Augustine didn't want to see them enjoyed also at shrines and churches where martyrs were buried, or where they were at least remembered with the Eucharist, and this, not only on saints' anniversaries but daily.

Then too, from his description of the model or habit of *parentalia*, evidently the participants believed the festivities were a solace to the martyrs just as they were to the ordinary dead. The dead were after all only asleep; they could in their sleep still sense what was offered to them. For this reason anyone not a believer must naturally suppose, looking on, that the object was to propitiate them with wine and things to eat which would make them happy. In return, their favor might be hoped for.[29] But the idea that they themselves might have favor to give, rather than the privilege of asking on another's behalf, made them too godlike for the bishops' comfort. That was the trouble with the unbroken flow across the period of my study, from third century non-Christian (and earlier) religious practices, to Christian and fourth century (and later).

To demonstrate this derivation, as long ago as the 1940s, Henri-Irénée Marrou assembled the most informative passages. He made use of evidence from the African provinces, adding such items of archeology as were most helpful, too: for example, in the basilica at Timgad, a sarcophagus with a wine-strainer in a carved-out cup on the lid, communicating by a tube down to the box for the corpse, just above the mouth of the deceased. Libation tubes elsewhere in African graveyards are a not uncommon feature; and the arrangement, only a little more explicit than the hole for wine in the mensa at Kapljuc, is matched by the libation-tubes in the tombs of Huarté, above, or in a burial under the floor of St. Peter's.[30] From another African cemetery we have the quite elaborately shaped, heavy stone table, a mensa with a raised rim to invite and hold the offerings of wine, the whole dedicated by a certain Felix to himself and his mother Rogata "in honor of the blessed martyrs"; so anyone seeking the favor of the saints must share his drink-offering with the shades of "Lucky" and Rogata. As to the food, we have the various items in relief on slabs made to fit over stone coffins, depicting fish or fruit or loaves.[31] For dining, there are for example the sarcophagi in the St. Salsa cemetery at Tipasa, against some of which, on their long side, a slanted dining couch has been built, the usual mensa in the expanded sense of the word, with a low space at the center around which would lie the usual number of guests. Non-Christian burials with cooking and eating vessels found in fragments around them show the models and earlier generations that lay behind the later Christian practices.[32]

These private rituals we can see at Tipasa in one of the funerary churches mentioned early in this chapter, along with others at Sitifis and Kelibia. It is convenient now to return to them. They were, it will be recalled, simply cemeteries under a roof. Now, we can hardly suppose that what was permitted by the clergy in the open ones, and well understood to be very important to families, would be forbidden in structures specially designed for them and for their loved ones after death—especially considering the deep roots of memorial practices and their acceptance by earlier spokesmen for the church like Tertullian.[33] What they meant to people generally may be inferred from the discovery of some fifty mensae in the cemeteries of Tipasa alone, representing only the richer members among the faithful of that city.

The space in one of the churches, the so-called "Alexander" chapel at Tipasa, may be imagined as a great picnic ground, with some portion of the families present in little circles, close-packed but no more closely than they would be in a suburban necropolis. The scene would be just such as is shown in fig. 4.10, below. Since it was open to celebrants of the anniversary of a death, or of the third, the ninth, or the thirtieth day after decease, if the clergy were to attend and administer the Eucharist, we may imagine a portable altar somewhere in the picture; or we may leave it out. There is no evidence on this possibility. As to the picture of these anniversaries, it may be more easily evoked in the adjoining enclosure (figs. 3.4–5) where the richer families had their private mausolea worshipfully close to the saint, but still their own. A half-dozen built mensae can be seen, here, some of them in a portico. They recall structures and arrangements already seen at Salona.

Martyr-cult evidently developed from private commemorative beliefs and rites. In smaller chapels built out of such traditions, this has been shown in the various arrangements for memorial meals; but the derivation also explains what is found in conventional basilicas to which martyr remains had been transferred. Monica's story of the 380s in Milan, and Augustine's response, are once more useful. He had agreed completely with the strictures directed against food and drink in churches, issued by his admired model of a bishop, Ambrose; and when he returned to Africa, he enlisted the bishop of Carthage, Aurelius, in a campaign to change things in that province, too. The practices established there in honor of the saints they both found detestable: noisy, self-indulging. People ate too much, they drank

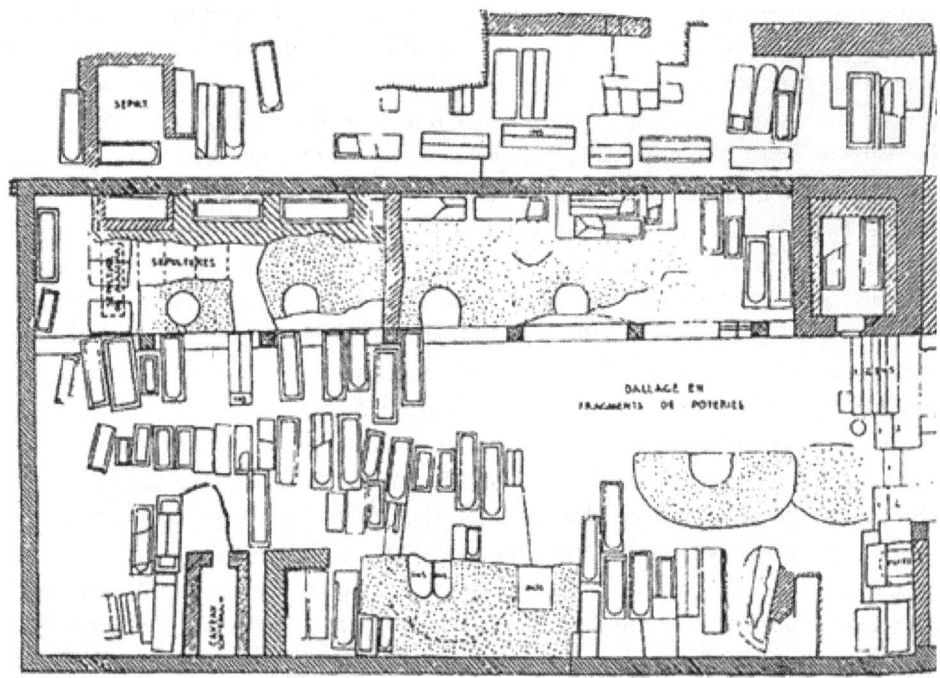

Fig. 3.4: The *area* adjoining the "Alexander chapel", Tipasa

Fig. 3.5: The cult of the family's dead at Tipasa

too much; and they had too good a time, stayed up late or, indeed, all night: "Drink up, long life!" as a tomb inscription exclaims. People enjoyed music in their celebrations of the dead, and even danced. Dancing was especially disgusting; it called for instruments associated with vulgar entertainments. Augustine witnessed it in Carthage, where it started among a group of worshippers outdoors, no doubt in the surrounding cemetery, before they moved into the basilica where Cyprian's burial was the centerpiece.[34] Aurelius had, some years earlier, expressed his misgivings about this sort of thing. Now Augustine, rousing those thunders of outrage which ancient orators had ever at hand, urged him to follow up with some action. Nothing but a provincial council would do. Aurelius heard him, and a council in 397 condemned the gross expenditure on meals eaten in the martyrs' honor. A second council a few years later condemned dancing in the streets and plazas and deplored the pressure from non-Christians in many cities to join religious parties, on martyrs' days.[35]

These old ways died hard. Bishops couldn't simply kill them by ukase. Recognizing realities, the earlier council had denounced what it didn't like "only so far as it can be forbidden"—which indeed proved a problem. In the same tone of caution, not to say defeat, the bishop of Hippo described how, in the face of his reproaches, "the rowdies declared they would never abide a ban on that ancient custom which they call their 'joyful'". He had to concede that, in their minds, it amounted to religion; this same recognition he extended to the cult of the ordinary dead.[36] Its devotees saw it as a spiritual thing, a rite of worship; and certainly they meant no disrespect to the saints, indeed the reverse: they sought a happy communion with the admired and beloved witnesses to their faith, a communion sought in a spirit of homage. This, we must suppose because it was what tradition had taught over the course of as many generations as anyone could remember. But for the bishop, the perpetrators remained "the rowdies", "the carnal ignorant masses", "clinging to their practices with an obstinacy proportionate to their ignorance." Thus a matter of style and shocking bad manners, also called "joy" as worship, set the few against the many.[37]

In a defensive passage, the bishop

> explained by what necessity this bad custom seemed to have arisen in the church. For, when peace came after so many and such violent persecutions, crowds of pagans wishing to become Christians were prevented from doing this because of their habit of celebrating the feast days of their idols with banquets and carousing; and, since it was not easy for them to abstain from these ancient but dangerous pleasures, our ancestors thought it would be good to make concession for the time being to their weakness and permit them, instead of the feasts they had renounced, to celebrate other feasts in honor of the holy martyrs, not with the same sacrilege but with the same elaborateness.[38]

Rules of behavior in society, familiar and enforced among the upper classes, had been thus challenged.

The challenge could be borne, it could be managed. But it was an altogether different and more serious thing actually to nominate a new martyr. To do so was the prerogative of authority, not of enthusiasm; and its usurpation was most feared by the Caecilianists such as Augustine or Aurelius. Donatists, glorying in their heroes, all too readily enrolled the new. In response, as early as the 340s, in a council that excluded Donatists, the Caecilianists agreed to deny the title martyr to any candidates whose deaths were suspect (suspect surely in the eyes of the Caecilianists). In 401 the question came up for discussion again, with the determination that

> altars erected randomly in the countryside or along roads, as if they were martyr-shrines, if they don't have the bodies or remains of martyrs in them, shall be destroyed by the local bishops; though, if popular disturbances make this impossible, at least the populace shall be warned not to hang about such places, so that sensible people won't be taken in by any superstition and so that shrines of martyrs, martyria, shall be approved in due fashion.... Altars thus set up by reason of visions and empty revelations, by who knows what individuals, everywhere, must be entirely rejected.[39]

A generation later, the legislation had to be repeated word for word, suggesting that not much had changed. As Yvette Duval says, carrying the story far into the fifth century and so beyond my focus, "the tombs remained centers of fervent cult for the faithful."

And the appeal of this alternative to ordinary church services appears in a limited but still revealing part of Augustine's activities. After being so disapproving of martyr-cult for so many years, in the later 390s he accepted an invitation from Aurelius of Carthage to visit that city as a guest speaker. It would mean a fortnight's travel. He accepted, indeed from then on he often went to Carthage to preach. He did so most often in one or another shrine dedicated to St. Cyprian (one of them named "the Dining Rooms", for reasons easy to guess). Sometimes he preached day after day. But he preached also in the church of Saints Perpetua and Felicitas, and of Faustus, and of Leontius, and of the so-called "Martyrs of Scylli". At Hippo he preached at St. Eulalia's, and Theognis', and Fructuosus'.[40] Many of his sermons celebrate saints' anniversary days whether or not in churches named after them. For these exhibitions of his eloquence he naturally sought out the largest possible audience, that is, in the cemeteries.

Which leads into the question, Where should one expect to see the Christians? At ordinary services inside the city? Or instead, at commemorative services with or without picnics in the suburbs?

Surveying Carthage's churches within the period of my study, Liliane Ennabli found the stones of only one very modest structure inside the city walls: a narrow hall without apse able to accommodate 300 people at the most. This was to serve a population of 200,000![41] By contrast, outside were the St. Cyprian cemetery-basilica (fig. 5.1) and close to it, many other large churches, of which the first by itself could hold close to a thousand and all these structures together, a total of 10,000 to 15,000.[42] Yet still, the total, put in perspective, is not large: 5 to 7 per cent at the turn of the fifth century.

A review of the African churches in the appendix shows three quarters or more to have been built outside their cities. Some sites may to this day conceal a big intra-urban cathedral which, for whatever reason, has never been uncovered; but significant misrepresentation of the realities of ecclesiastical construction in this way seems to me unlikely. If there is in fact some misrepresentation of religious preferences, it may not be so much in the unexcavated sites, as in the literary evidence. The latter, from the death of Cyprian in the 250s until the Vandal invasion in 430, is Augustine's. He is virtually the whole story; and it is he who exclaimed "all Africa is full of bodies." Frederik van der Meer put it another way, equally graphic: "mensae shot up everywhere out of the ground like mushrooms."[43]

To the mind's eye, African Christendom must thus have been very much a thing of memorial worship, and therefore most active and vital among the dead. Both communion with the dead by their families, and communion with the martyrs by congregations at large, appealed to great numbers of people, to judge from the size of churches; so it may fairly be called a mass phenomenon. Certainly Augustine saw it that way, and with misgivings. What the masses initiated inevitably had so much in it that was of the unregulated past, so much that answered to needs and a way of life quite different from Augustine's or Aurelius'. The latter from their high thrones might insist that the church was theirs; yet the realities in stone seem to tell us something else.

Which is not to deny to the upper class its place in the cemeteries as well as inside the urban churches. Above, I instanced a number of relatively modest buildings to mark where a martyr's body lay, and where saints might be recalled to a banquet in homage and remembrance. Only persons of some wealth could pay for these. They often doubled as mausolea for the future burial of the builder and his family. He or she would desire that proximity; for, at least in traditional terms, it could not be imagined that such holy personages would not avail to save. And save from what? The words that are so common, by the thousands of examples in Latin Christianity (and their equivalent in Greek), *votum solvit*, "paid the vow", tell us nothing of what was in the dedicant's mind, to impel the promise in the first place.

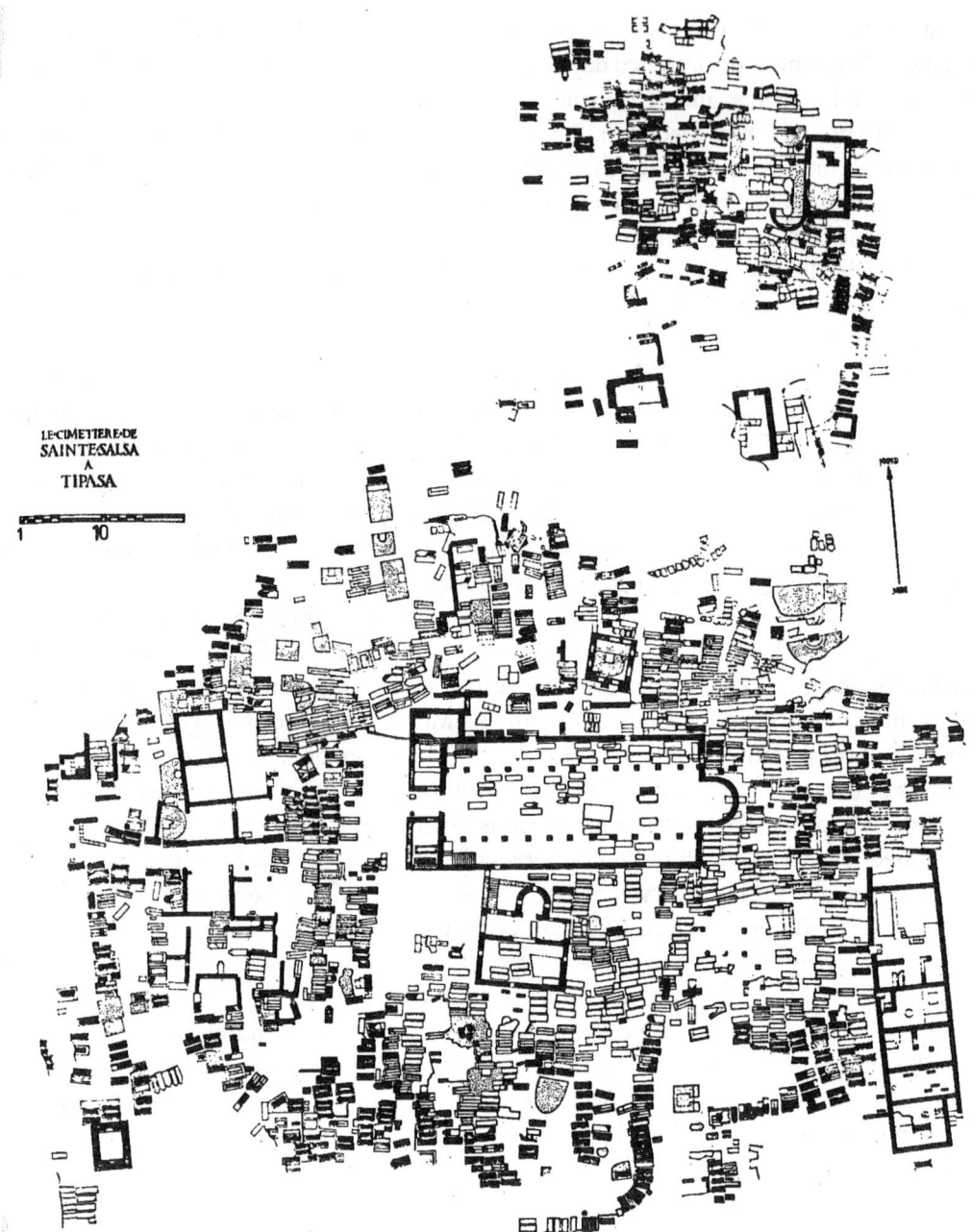

Fig. 3.6: St. Salsa cemetery, basilica, and chapel

Salvation of the soul is the answer that modern interpretation will most often suggest. And correctly? No doubt martyrs, being at the very instant of death wafted above to heaven (though also resting here below!), could there speak up for you.

The ardor for nearness can be judged from the frantic crowding around little St. Salsa. Here (fig. 3.6), a glance will pick out among the inhumations four or five of those tell-tale horse-shoe shapes that represent mensae; and peering more carefully and including the square-cornered ones will raise the count to a dozen, with a particularly large, luxurious example in a one-room building of its own, handy to a door on the basilica's left side. Above the door was inscribed the Christian password, "Ichthus".[44] All the rest were the tombs of plain folk.

Church authorities built the basilica to the martyr, it is not known with what funding. They therefore naturally controlled and parcelled out the area for burials, including some fifty under the floor of the nave and aisles and hundreds more outside. These have almost all lost the covering by which they were once identified; but there is no reason to think that the general rule, clergy first, the lucky rich second, did not obtain here as elsewhere.[45]

Enthusiasm felt first as an individual faith, even as a private or family thing, rapidly spread upwards in lay society. The clerical reaction was not so welcoming. "Their tardy reaction was a sign of their uncertainties about the doctrinal justification for a phenomenon the original impetus for which no doubt lay among the people lacking instruction". Yet the clergy came around. They admitted huge numbers of saints to their calendar of annual celebrations; we know their numbers in Carthage.[46] Near the end of his life and of his great work on the *City of God* (book 22.8), there was no more ardent believer in the martyrs and their miracles, no more effective promulgator, than the bishop of Hippo. He regularly informed his congregation about them: how a very poor man had prayed at the shrine of the locally celebrated Twenty Martyrs, and been made rich in reply; how prayer at the relics of Saint Stephen, in a dozen instances very dramatically detailed, brought instant healing to the dying, the blind, the palsied; how a martyr had even visited a woman in her sickbed, no doubt in a vision, and then and there healed her; and how his own records of some seventy miracles at the same Stephen shrine were out-matched by those in the nearby town of Calama, where other relics of the same martyr were on display, and more still at Uzala. Carthage had its share of such relics and there too the records of the martyr's beneficent powers were kept, and retailed in an anonymous *Of Saint Stephen's Miracles*: how he granted relief from burns, broken bones, paralysis, loss of speech or sight, any ailment at all; relieved awful anxiety about an absent spouse or a man buried under a house-collapse. "I beg, I implore," the suppliants called out at his shrine, as they lay prone before him.[47]

In his sermons Augustine often and especially paid tribute to the martyr Crispina.[48] Though not a virgin, still, she deserved to be mentioned in the company of the very first names in sanctity: with Stephen, Agnes, Gervasius and Protasius. She had been a great lady "of whom, brethren, surely there is no one in Africa who is ignorant" (it was the practice of bishops in all of the empire's pulpits to address the male part of their audience principally or only, even when speaking of female role models). The day on which she was executed for her faith, the 12th of December, was to be faithfully celebrated at Hippo. No doubt it was celebrated in many churches elsewhere, too, most obviously at her home, Tebessa; for she was Tebessa's own, if not born there, then at least dying there—a celebrity in that remote little center 150 miles from Carthage, population 5,000.[49] Remote—yes, but all the world knew of Crispina. From across the seas as well as from other parts of the North African provinces, many came streaming in as pilgrims to her shrine. No more spectacular point of martyr-cult is known in the African provinces, even to this day impressive in its remains and a tourist attraction.

Despite its lying at the center of a cemetery, and alone among African churches so situated, this was Tebessa's cathedral church, and the altar in the chancel and the patterns of panels in the mosaic floor were suited to regular services, baptism, and the Eucharist. The entire nave was reserved for the clergy and their ceremonies, leaving only the aisles for perhaps three hundred of the laity. Regular services, however, were not the point of the building effort here; for, surrounding this church on three sides was a walled enclosure, a trapezoid in shape, on a truly vast scale (roughly 115 x 75 m) that announced the importance of the site over-all and far beyond any day-to-day liturgy. Further, on the fourth side of the church, seen at the bottom of the view in fig. 3.7, was a porticoed open square with a baptismal fountain in the middle. It was in turn entered from another open space on the west nearly half the size of a soccer field marked off in four squares of low walls with a portico defining their western side. Those squares—where another town might have turned its aqueduct into the public baths—were so many cool, neat ponds that "surpassed all the ornamental basins and fish-ponds of the grandest, most luxurious country-houses" (fig. 3.8).[50] Adjoining them, utilitarian but decently concealed behind a blank wall, were great stables for travelers with a score of stalls. The scale of everything was in keeping with the renown of Crispina.

Her shrine was entered from a corner of the church, just at hand by the doorway and then by a little turn into a very ample tri-apsidal annex, seen in fig. 3.7 in the shadows to the right (the south). Beneath its floor in the southern apse had once been Crispina's martyr-

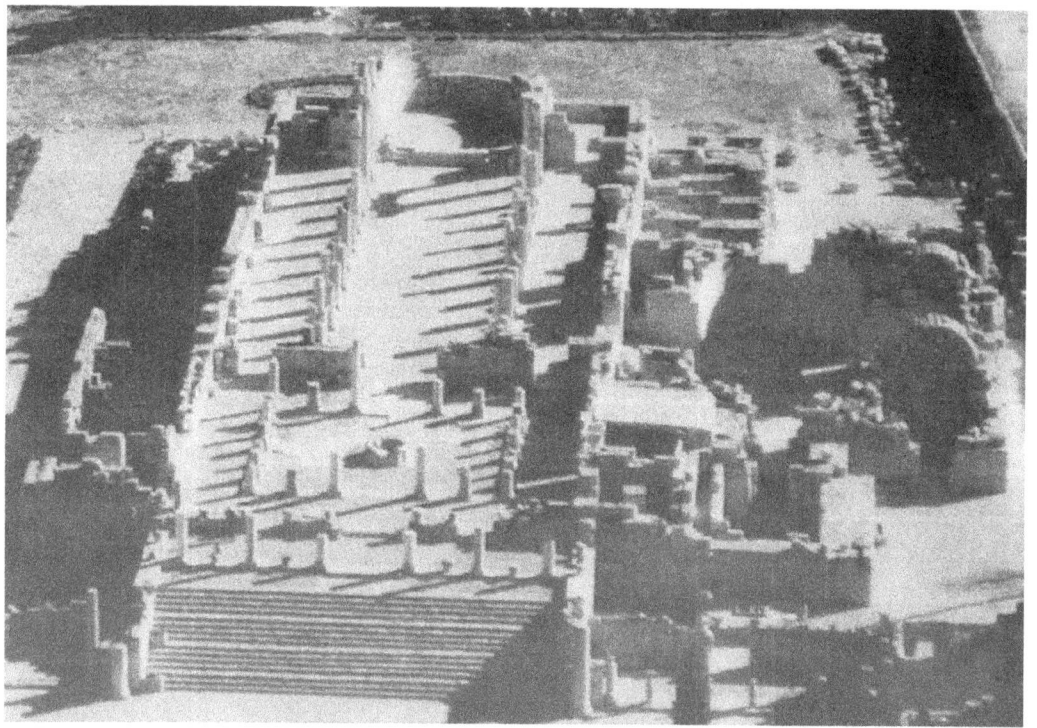

Fig. 3.7: The cathedral at Theveste (Tebessa)

Fig. 3.8: The entry-court and grand stairway, Tebessa

tomb and memorial. Here, after her death in 304/5, had been her mensa. It must have been so; for graveside picnics are attested in this city's cemeteries as in every other site, to a date centuries beyond my scope.[51] Then, as her fame spread, something better had to be thought of. The church was built and along with it, the triconch, together conceived of and begun as a single complex in the 380s or 390s, on which the masons labored still perhaps in the 420s, till the vast walled enclosure on the north also was completed. It would serve as a sort of caravanserai.

In its dates, coming late in the fourth century and declaring its ambitions in the fifth, the Tebessan shrine fairly represents the full flowering of martyr-cult in the African provinces; and in the scale and theatricality of the complex—from its water-squares to its stables, and from the grandiloquence of its arched entryways and broad staircase to the cool dim-lit confines of the martyr's sanctuary itself—it represents also the meaning of that cult.

There is only a note to be added about a catacomb, a burial-gallery reached by a long flight of steps quite deeply descending underneath the western, "water-square" area. The walls contain only a few burials (*loculi*, to use the term familiar in the setting of Rome); but at the end is a triangular chamber some six meters on a side, containing *arcosolia* (I use another Roman term) carved out of the walls as vaulted niches to receive sarcophagi. These are identified by epitaphs.[52] It is a puzzle to me why in a cemetery anyone would dig down three meters to prepare an inhumation, unless out of the necessity of concealing some ritual in a time of religious tensions or persecutions. The circumstances would then suggest a date before the Peace and a comparison with the Roman catacombs.

4
Italy and the Northwest

1. Rome underground

The catacombs of ancient Rome almost define earliest Christianity in the western empire, and quite understandably so. They give visible form to the accounts of Paul and Peter, reverently remembered in the capital, whose primitive shrines have been in modern times uncovered and so often described. But the faithful who once attended them in the distant past, these too, are visible if we turn our mind's eye on what has been found underground. There, objects and built features alike have much to tell us about the Christians of long ago.

What is most easily seen is the plain fact that poverty ruled over death as well as life. It was money or the lack of it that determined the mode of one's burial. For the less fortunate, there might be no burial at all. At the worst, pauper bodies were picked up off the streets by municipal slaves and tossed into huge rubbish pits called *puticuli* beyond the wall to the northeast, pits still disgustingly malodorous when they were dug into in the nineteenth century. Those luckier mortals at their death, who were of course the vast majority, would have some family to take care of their last rites and a resting place; but whatever the chosen form of inhumation, whether the narrowest grave or a marble sarcophagus, it reflected the realities.[1]

In the period of my study, true, there were built mausolea along the roads leading out of the city for those few who could afford them, and they will need some mention later on; but underground burial was most likely to be in a catacomb. Here, like bunks in an overnight train or in some freighter's foc'sle, spaces barely adequate to the human form were carved into the soft rock on each side, up to six feet or so, horizontally, for each; and thereafter, to expose more usable wall area at a convenient height for excavation, the floor might be lowered and another couple of rows added, making eight or ten burials closely arranged on top of each other; and then, beneath that level of galleries, another might be dug, and a third, a fourth, underneath that first, so as to make maximum use of the site—at a most awful cost, surely, for the wretched family that must now be introduced to the new home of their materfamilias, deceased, or of their child, deceased, being led down and down into the bowels of the earth by the digger with his little oil lamp, to that hole in the wall that he had assigned to the loved one in the infinite, everlasting darkness.[2]

> Step by step
> Carefully in the dark, tracing my way,
> Backwards the way I came this way in the dark,

Everywhere as I go fills me with terror,
the very silence around me fills me with terror.

—these, the lines from Vergil that Jerome thought of when he recalled his own samplings of a descent into the catacombs, a little after the mid-fourth century.[3] It would be easy to present the diggers' handiwork in a more attractive light but the realities might then be lost (fig. 4.1).

Whether Rome's early Christians were in fact generally poor can best be shown through their choice of language. The catacombs themselves offer an entry into the subject. One among them was evidently spoken of in Greek, *kata kymbas*, "at the Hollows"; hence the term that came into eventual use. It was mere chance that it spread from the one location to many;[4] it was not mere chance, however, that it spread at all. Rome was in fact almost bilingual; but it was so, differentially. Patterns of everyday use, Greek or Latin, corresponded with economic position, at least to a large degree. Greek meant poor.

To explain: a great many of Rome's inhabitants were first-, second-, third-, or fourth-generation transplants from the eastern provinces where Greek was their only tongue or had served them as

Fig. 4.1: Catacomb gallery, six *loculi* on each side

the lingua franca. Certainly some had come to Rome freely; a majority, however, as slaves, willy-nilly. Though they could then hope, with luck, to be freed from their condition after some decades of service, nevertheless, in the third century, the population in servitude certainly numbered 150,000 or more.[5] Together with freedmen they always constituted a very significant minority in a city of, let us say, a half-million (this latter figure being only my best guess, demographically or *grosso modo* as a modern Roman would say).[6]

If we found Rome's Christians largely Greek-speaking, in the early centuries, this would place them in the midst of the impoverished immigrant population. Their preference in speech is in fact clear from their conducting their religious services in Greek and in that language composing their internal administrative manuals well past the mid-fourth century.[7] Their leaders, meaning bishops and then by gradual change of title, popes, bore overwhelmingly Greek names: Eleutherus, Zephyrinus, Callistus, Xystus, Stephanus, Dionysius,

Eutychianus, and so forth through most of the third century, with only a rare scattering of Latin Roman ones, until we get to a Gaius, a Marcellus, a Marcellinus first to be titled *papas*, and so forth in the 280s and later. Throughout these many generations, even for the formal public act of putting up an epitaph amid Latin-speakers, Christians often used Greek;[8] and it may be worth mentioning, too, that a good bit of Greek turns up among the Christians in other Italian cities north and south of the capital.[9] Only slowly could this depressed population rise in the world, into the strata where Latin prevailed.

We would expect them, then, to make do with cheap burials for a long time; and such is the case, explaining the catacombs.

Centuries ago when the study of these sites was in its infancy, and thereafter for many generations, it was supposed that Christians burrowed into the ground to escape their oppressors and worship in safety. The catacombs were their church. In the end, however,

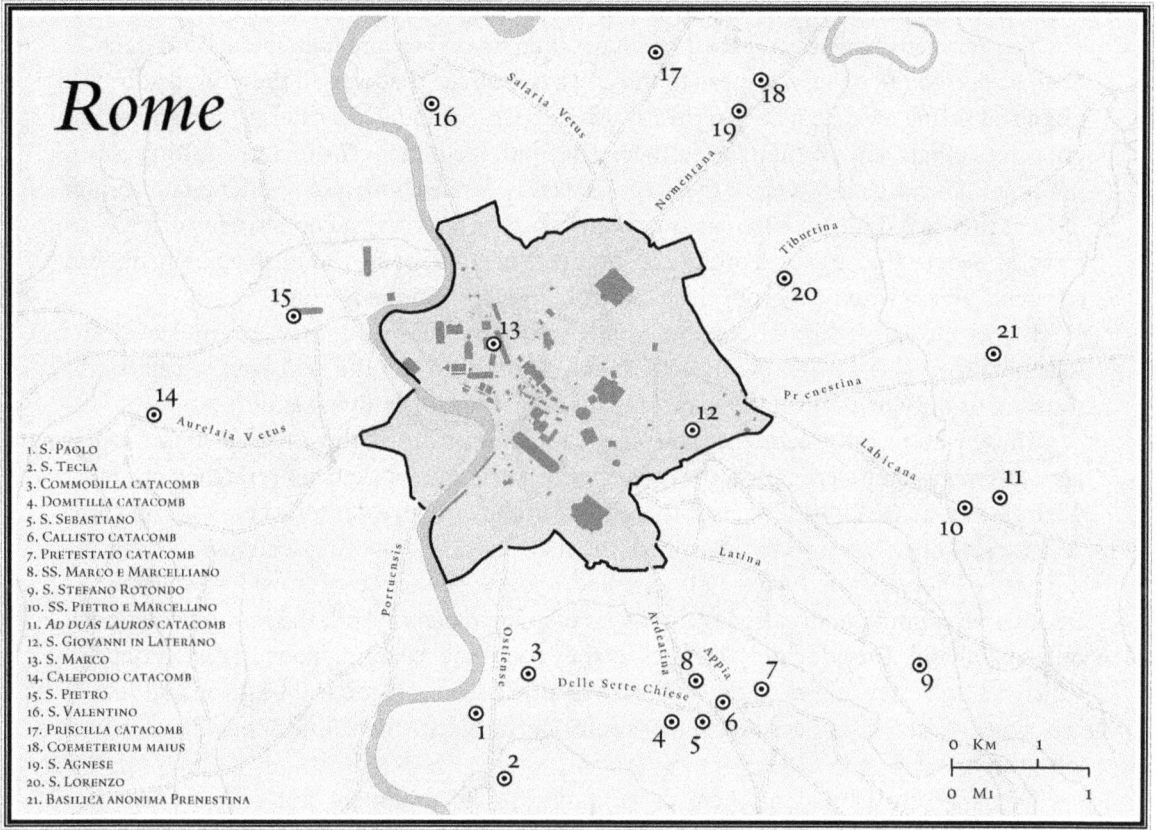

Fig. 4.2: Selected church sites pre-400
1. S. Paolo; 2. S. Tecla; 3. Commodilla catacomb; 4. Domitilla catacomb; 5. S. Sebastiano; 6. Callisto catacomb; 7. Pretestato catacomb; 8. SS. Marco e Marcelliano; 9. S. Stefano Rotondo; 10. SS. Pietro e Marcellino; 11. *Ad duas lauros* catacomb; 12. S. Giovanni in Laterano; 13. S. Marco; 14. Callisto catacomb; 15. S. Pietro; 16. S. Valentino; 17. Priscilla catacomb; 18. Coemeterium maius; 19. S. Agnese; 20. S. Lorenzo; 21. Basilica anonima Prenestina

this explanation for the choice yielded to another that made better sense of the evidence: what in fact controlled the choice were cost considerations.

Demography explains why. We have only to imagine that gigantic, heterogeneous, teeming, jam-packed confusion of humanity on the Tiber, the size of Carthage and Alexandria both together, "a population sink" as it has been described.[10] The worst of it was infant mortality; true, but over-all, the death rate is best estimated at no less than 45 per thousand.[11] That would mean 22,500 burials year after year, enough to explain, without need of any more arithmetic, how costly land was bound to become by the second century, and still more so as time went on, in the preferred areas for burial: that is, right along the edges of any one of the highways leading out of the city, and as close to the walls as possible; for burial practices, no different among Christians than non-Christians, were not just a matter of putting a corpse into the ground. Rather, they required many subsequent visits in the first thirty or forty days after decease, and annually thereafter. Even for such important purposes of piety, families would rather not travel too many miles.

The alternative answer for the poor must then be two square meters dug into the side of an underground gallery, as near to the city as possible. That was all they could afford. It was a real saving over even the narrowest grave above-ground. Nevertheless, some were less poor than others, and so they sorted themselves out, the better-off somehow getting places not so far down a gallery, nearer the access-stairway. Some chose also to offer an indication of what they had done for a living, as a green-grocer (a woman), a cooper, a farmer, and so forth, known by the inscribed outline of some tool of work, or a word in an epitaph, or even a fresco. "This is who I am," they declared with dignity from the Beyond.

It was the same throughout the empire. Only the Haves lumped all the Have-nots together. The Have-nots knew they were not all alike. So say the signs in the catacombs showing us the Christians in their various rungs up the ladder, living and dying.[12]

Those who actually made the catacombs should be included: those tireless ants, the diggers, *fossores* as they were called, they too appear in frescoes or sketches scratched on stone. Theirs was a tremendous task, as it turned out in the end: two centuries of work on some seventy sets of galleries so far identified, the maze of one alone (but a large one) measuring twelve kilometers if it were all in one line, and the extraction of stone necessary for all together amounting to hundreds of millions of cubic meters.[13] Still, the *fossores* responded only to demand. They dug only as much as they could sell, charging their customers a price which we find often engraved on *loculus*-covers. The seller's name will be given and that of the owner of the *loculus*, and how many bodies can be placed there, one or occasionally two, even three.

Diggers were Christians themselves, it mustn't be forgotten; not only so, but they counted as members of the clergy, though only at its lowest level. In time, and at the latest by mid-fourth century, in ordinary Roman fashion they had organized themselves into a trade association bearing a Greek-transliterated name, *copiatae*.[14] It meant "toilers", unskilled and very poor; for who else but the necessitous would care to spend their days in semi-darkness and 95 per cent humidity? To make it pay, they kept the galleries to a minimum width that barely allowed them to swing their little pickaxes; they arranged inhumations in closely serried ranks; and sometimes they deposited the fill from one stretch of work into another stretch already fully sold out. Too bad for the families of the deceased, one might think.

From the turn of the third century on, when the Roman church as an organization took a hand in the purchase and administration of cemeteries and, thereby, of access from them into subterranean galleries and chambers, these latter means of inhumation became increasingly popular.[15] The possibilities were further explored as land continued to rise in price. In time, the rich took them up. They could of course afford something conveniently near to the city and near to the staircases that led down into the ground, at a price, both for themselves and their dependents. In consequence, we begin to find those commodious, often elegantly decorated, sometimes quite glorious buried rooms, *cubicula* (as they're called) opening off the galleries—often featured in picture books or guided tours brightly illuminated by colored lights. They served private families, not individuals. The style of them is suggested by one in the so-called Grand Cemetery (fig. 4.3); but there are many hundreds that properly deserve the name, of all sizes, with many or few *loculi* in their walls or sometimes carved-out cavities with an arched top, *arcosolia*, on the floor of which a further cavity received the burial and suggested, with its flat top, a dining table, a *mensa*.[16]

By mid-fourth century the more prestigious catacombs had established their ranking and were eagerly bid for. Clergy sought them out for their own burials and, as the fourth century went on, big government officials and other members of the real aristocracy joined

Fig. 4.3: A *cubiculum* with an *arcosolium* to the rear

them. A star among sites for ornament and display was the S. Callisto, containing many scores of fine *cubicula*. They are representative, of course, of only a very small percentage of the whole catacomb phenomenon, which continued to pile up the dead in stacks of eight or ten or more *loculi*, and in deeper-dug levels, down to the third, fourth, fifth.[17]

Between these latter burials representing the have-nots, and the haves, nothing in my reading addresses the question: Just what was their ratio one to the other? For obvious reasons, not least the fact that the poorer remain in large part unexcavated, quantification is very difficult. Still, Jean Guyon did work out the figures for tomb frescoes in the *cubicula* of the half-dozen showiest, best known catacombs (the earliest of these being the Callisto and Domitilla). Percentages range from 7 to 21 per cent; so there is a beginning in quantification. Clearly, some catacombs attracted or served a more fashionable clientele than others. Indeed the over-all rise of Christianity in socioeconomic terms can be clearly seen in the increasing size of this clientele from the later years of Constantine's reign, the 330s, attested archeologically in the commissioning of more *cubicula*, and more big ones, more wall paintings, and so forth. The evidence is usually datable only in terms of a generation. Nevertheless, in any decade of the fourth century, it is safe to estimate *cubicula* at less than 5 per cent, compared to the number of *loculi*.[18]

In these relatively prosperous times, some Christian visitors to family graves would be attended by their slaves. Their burial ceremonies would be more ceremonious, set off by more elaborate structures and decoration. Not for them a mere *loculus*. Among the amenities they could afford would be mourners' benches and a chair for the deceased, both (like the room itself and the *arcosolium*) hewn from the living rock by some clever pick-man (fig. 4.3). Above the arch of the niche might be a painting, with others on the two sides framing the niche, or on the walls to either side of the room; perhaps also a stone table in the form of a round or a square or polygonal column waist-high against a wall, a sort of abbreviated pilaster, with a ceramic plate sitting on top, or the invitation for such a thing, for an offering of food. Chairs, tables, and plates, even if not common furnishings, are enough to indicate how tomb-side rites were envisioned by the families commissioning them; and wall-paintings by the dozens (but not the scores) complete the vision. They depict semi-circles of happy diners, sometimes boisterously gesturing and calling for more wine (as inscriptions above their heads make plain), where the men sprawl at their ease on individual cushions or on a big couch and where the women most often sit on chairs modestly positioned at either extremity of the group (fig. 4.4–5).[19] Two of the most often reproduced give an idea of the scene where, in one, the shouted instructions of the diners are written in above their heads (to the slave-girl, "Irene, hand me hot water" and "Agape, mix me some").

Of the two depictions shown here, the first, in the so-called Vibia tomb of the Callisto catacombs, has an odd history. Its nature as a religious meal was described, back in the 1750s, by its discoverer; but he nevertheless took this tomb to be Christian because of all the others around it. The authorities that licensed excavation at the time knew better. They knew that the actions and inscriptions of the painting showed a moment in Sabazius cult. The underground area was accordingly blocked off and any account of it erased from the records. So, nearly a century passed before its re-discovery and the new and further discovery, adjacent, of a Mithraic burial. In time, the idea that these two horrifying neighbors must have been walled off by the faithful and their innocence in this way protected, had to be abandoned. Mixing had to be accepted as a fact of life, in those imperfect early centuries.[20]

In the decades post-Constantine we must certainly imagine a lot of recent, well-off converts buying a *cubiculum* for their loved ones rather than a place above-ground.[21] They favored the elaboration described a little earlier. From its various elements we can understand the routines of a funerary meal. However, underground facilities for meals such as a mensa were not actually used very much. Their value was symbolic. It was supposed otherwise, at first: either that church suppers of the early Christian *agape*-type were celebrated there below, or grave-side meals in the old Roman, meaning non-Christian, tradition. A

Fig. 4.4: A *refrigerium* (the Vibia tomb)

Fig. 4.5: A *refrigerium* (SS. Marcellino e Pietro catacomb)

better view of the realities of that subterranean environment, where no one would willingly linger for very long, saw evocation rather than reality in the elaborated features of *cubicula*, intended as a sort of reassurance to the deceased down there that the proper celebrations had not been forgotten. Families might indeed visit, leaving gifts of sweet-smelling spices or oils or tasty dishes; but then they returned to the sun for their picnics.[22]

This was the ancient reality; and for it to gain acceptance among the learned required only thirty years of discussion.

2. Rome above-ground

Into the sun, then! An end to darkness! Let it be accepted that man must die, yet in death he need not be remembered only or ever in the dank confines of the catacombs. Above-ground would do just as well, where the departed ones could be notionally present in the company, they in their family's loving thoughts and the family, in theirs as well—a mutual thing; for, among Rome's Christians as among people of the traditional faith, there was no doubt that the dead were sentient beings and could be reached by the living, for happiness' sake. The prevalence of this view among the general population of the lands lying to the east and south of Rome appeared in earlier chapters. It may be noted, too, to the west, in the discussions of the council of Elvira.[23] In Rome in the texts inscribed on *loculi* and elsewhere, the dead were invited, as we would say colloquially, "to chill out" (*refrigerare*) and to enjoy the experience. A *refrigerium* was a party attended as an act of communion. If bishops like Ambrose could hardly abide the idea or the practice (ch. 3 at n. 22), they were nonetheless unable to talk it out of existence. It was in fact—and a most significant fact—the favorite subject to be shown on *cubicula* walls, giving us dozens of easily identified banquets, however crudely painted. No Bible scenes are so common, no figures of prayer or allegory.

For Ambrose and his like, the problem lay in the identity of Christian with non-Christian religious usage. Their view of such common practices was entirely natural. So, too, was that of the 95 per cent who thought otherwise, at least at first. They had joined the church from a traditional background, or their parents had done so. They had thus been raised in beliefs that lay beyond the boundaries of any church and were close to the heart. They believed the dead needed a helping hand, as we must suppose from the common leaving of coins in their sarcophagi, or a variety of little gifts, it might be only in fragments, or again, for children, toys and diversions stuck into the plaster that closed a *loculus*. The unseen interim-world had its needs, so everyone believed; it had a reality and life known also in the form of its guardian spirits, the Manes, who *were* the deceased, and to whom epitaphs were routinely addressed. The formula was, in abbreviation, "to the gods and Manes," *D*(*is*) *M*(*anibus*) on hundreds of Christian tombstones.[24] In so many way, Christians and non-Christians were thus at one.

But Ambrose's problem became, in modern studies, a problem also for those who brought to the ancient world their own conception of Christianity. Christianity must surely be not only itself, at its core, but a repudiation of every alternative as well. Such was the model to be imposed on the past.

In the first place, it was assumed that Christians kept themselves apart for religion's sake; so no family of the faithful would willingly share in the cemetery of non-Christians.

Did not Cyprian express shock that a Christian would bury someone in the property of a burial-insurance club? The setting was Carthage of the mid-third century; he pointed to a particular excess. No other text to the same or a more general effect can be cited.[25] Rather, Christians in his region of the empire as in every other as well, in the third century, made free use of the community's cemeteries side by side with their non-Christian neighbors. Later, post-Constantine, they could more easily afford to buy some room of their own for their dead, and they took advantage of this and can be seen gradually segregating themselves. In Rome, their own burial areas began to appear in the early third century; but self-sufficiency across the board was not attained for a long time, a matter of many generations.[26]

In the second place, as to the attendant funerary ritual, this too presented a challenge to the model. Christians clung to the old tradition, which had even to be incorporated into new saints' days. It was described in other chapters, involving a set of three days of remembrance post-inhumation, and then a fourth day on the seventh or ninth day, and then a fifth day on the thirtieth or fortieth, and then annually thereafter on the birthday of the deceased, on January 1, on a universal week in February ending on the 22nd, and on a later day or days (March, May, June) celebrated with flowers and a more elaborate liturgy—which is not to say that every family observed every one of these occasions.[27] We have no information about ordinary practice. At each occasion, however, there would be a picnic in the old style, a *refrigerium*.

To see it in the mind's eye is easy enough, though not to be done from written description. Instead, it is the physical remains that explain things. They include, as has been shown, a place set aside for the deceased as if he or she were present, and a share of whatever there was to eat and drink, and tributes in the form of a toast or a little libation poured into the coffin if that was at the center of the celebration, either set upon the ground or accessible beneath through a hole in the grave-top. For food, there might be need of a charcoal brazier; for wine, to chill it and dilute it, a well if possible or at least a receptacle for water that was brought to the occasion. In the very grandest of the catacombs' *cubicula* we have seen all these necessary items of equipment actually present or suggested; but naturally they were not easily accommodated below-ground; so it is in cemeteries in the fresh air that the meals were ordinarily enjoyed, to a late hour, with good cheer and drink, song and dance, at least if we may judge from martyr-day celebrations.[28]

Perhaps (in parentheses) we may judge also from a scrap of poetry, where Ovid in the early first century describes how the common people in the best old Roman tradition met in the suburbs to offer their devotion to the goddess Turn-of-the-Year. There on the banks of Tiber (who was another god, himself) they stayed up all night in her honor, enjoying "many wine-glasses" that inspired the women present to form their lines and dance about in the moonlight, their loosed hair flying about their heads.[29] And as to a musical accompaniment, which must also be imagined, we have the words of a pope condemning those "foul songs" which he heard at the February celebrations of his people. The ban takes me past the boundaries of my chosen period, but in service to my assumption: that Christian usages drew upon non-Christian in many ways and settings, and for a long time, too.

But to return to *refrigeria* above-ground: it must be said that our picture of them has to be pieced together from little glimpses and particles of evidence, because of the almost total destruction of the city's cemeteries over the course of some fifteen hundred years.[30]

Fig. 4.6: Isola Sacra *mausolea*

What were they once like? The ground, we know, was mostly chopped up into those *areae* which have been encountered in earlier chapters (Greece and Africa), abutting on a main road out of the city and walled to afford some privacy or at least to stake a claim against intrusive burials; but for any better picture we have to look to the delta island at the mouth of the Tiber, Isola Sacra, a long day's walk from the capital but only a little distance outside the port-city of Ostia. Here, along the main road, are the predictable built tombs, their doorways surmounted by an inscribed plaque (some, torn away, fig. 4.6) to identify the occupant or family and, in a good state of preservation, the built mensae for the dining family outside (fig. 4.7). In front of them also was space for a brazier and the fresh air to carry off the smoke (significantly, even in Rome's best-equipped underground *cubicula*, there are no signs of a fire). Exactly the same shape of their dining-couches is to be seen in an even better state of preservation in Herculaneum or Pompeii. Where there is no doorway to consider, the slanted surfaces will be built in the usual square-C form. Funerary picnics with or without mensae were general features of life, evidently; for among the hundreds of stone coffins at Isola Sacra serving even ordinary people of no great wealth, most have a hole for libations.[31]

We can accept all this evidence from Isola Sacra for Rome of the third and fourth centuries. There is no reason to doubt it. There is even a little (but very little) direct confirmation. In the Roman suburbs, to repeat, the existence of *areae* is clear, though not very fully revealed by excavation. The existence of mausolea is clear, too, two rows of which are known archeologically. They were once strung along the thoroughfares outside the city's walls; but they were later buried. The fill above them was needed to make the terraces on which were then built, respectively, the basilicas of St. Peter's and S. Sebastiano.³² At the former site, among the score of mausolea, some had burials under their floor with libation-tubes reaching down to the head of the deceased, a testimony to *refrigeria*; so also the bones of demestic animals scattered about the shrine to the saint, the *aedicula*; and at the latter site, under San Sebastiano, tomb-owners provided for funerary meals with a well in an open space in front of a dining porch, a *triclinium*. It had benches along two sides sufficient for 25–30 worshippers. Where they sat in their all-night *vigilia*, they left hundreds of graffiti in honor of Saints Peter and Paul from about A.D. 260 on. Their commemorative liturgy may have been directed not at the saints' relics but rather (as so often elsewhere) at venerated objects that had had contact with the relics elsewhere.³³ The remains thus testify to the practices here that we would expect to find, given our literary sources for non-Christian times and settings.

From Rome or Ostia to the family plot or tomb on the anniversary of some death, the paterfamilias would, I suppose, lead a donkey hired for the day to carry a small amphora of wine slung on each side; a couple of baskets of bread and cheese and covered casseroles of stew; a jug of milk for Adeodatus, aged three; kindling and charcoal; some sacks filled with straw for a couch; and on top of it all, steadied on his perch by a parental hand, Adeodatus

Fig. 4.7: Isola Sacra *mausoleum* and built mensa

himself. Any donkey would rise to the task, if only for two or three miles. Arrived at the cemetery, the family would find others; if it were a universal anniversary of the dead, for example, on February 22, there would be many, many more; and as the evening wore on and the children dropped off to sleep, the adults might visit with each other across groups, in a sociable style that the bishops in Africa at one point publicly deplored. It brought Christians into the company of non-Christians. The bishops' complaint is a reminder that such celebrations were in their view more than meals. They were religion; therefore it is safe to say they were everywhere marked or accompanied by fitting words and mood. But just what their liturgy may have been, we can't say.

The effort to imagine *refrigeria* thus has only a limited reward; and it has to be remembered, too, that the archeological evidence is most informative about the luckier 5 per cent of the population. Their better arrangements present us with what Paul-Albert Février called "a conflict of class". We have the rich with frescoes and space; the poor, without.[34] He was speaking only of underground Rome. Well, as his *cubicula* are to *loculi* in the catacombs, so mausolea were to ordinary inhumation in cemeteries above-ground. For the poor, a resting place for the dead could only be managed in some clumsy, tile-lined hole, perhaps even on top of an earlier inhumation, and with little space for later celebratory rites, since, to repeat, by the conventional logic, the very reason for the catacombs was the lack of room on the surface, except at a high price. The logic seems to me perfectly persuasive.[35]

To relieve a situation so painful to so many must surely have been a concern of the church authorities—a concern especially in Rome because of its gigantic number of residents, annual deaths, and pressure on the suburbs. Then, a miracle! Of a sudden, by the events of 312, they beheld on the throne a man of their own faith, in command of all that he cared to seize from the great estates that had supported his rival. And he proved open-handed beyond belief.

At his command, with remarkable speed, grand places of worship were constructed. For ourselves, seeing Rome's Christians at worship above-ground now becomes possible for the first time, and more than possible, in the space of only a generation. The change is dramatic, overwhelming. A long list of new basilicas (for that was the shape of them all) begins with the Savior's (now S. Giovanni). It was provided with two almost life-sized silver statues of Jesus displayed on the triumphal arch above the chancel. Next to be finished was either St. Peter's or the Church of the Apostles (now San Sebastiano). Then followed SS. Marcellino e Pietro (Peter the Exorcist, not the Apostle), and S. Agnese, and S. Lorenzo, and the "Marciana" named after the pope Marcus, and what the excavators could only call the "Anonymous on the via Prenestina". Perhaps the sequence of them in construction was as it is given here. The first of them, S. Giovanni, dated from that moment not many months after his victory when the emperor met with the pope Miltiades; then, subsequently, with Silvester (314–335), at whose urging S. Paolo was built;[36] and the last two basilicas rose under the next emperor. So the full satisfaction of piety took shape in stone.

Constantine was certainly an impatient, opinionated autocrat; but on the question, how should a great patron, the greatest imaginable, show his favor toward his co-religionists, I cannot imagine him arriving at an answer without seeking the counsel of their acknowledged head, the pope. Indeed, it must be a three-way conversation. "I've always had the notion," said Richard Krautheimer,

I've always supposed that affairs in those days were transacted like this: the architect has an audience with the emperor who tells him, "I want to build a basilica for the Christians of Rome." "Basilica" would mean generally an assembly hall. But exactly what sort of hall? So the architect goes to the bishop. "The emperor has directed me to build a basilica for the Christian community. What ideas do you Yourself have?" Surely that's how it was.[37]

And for more detail, there is an emperor in 387 addressing the mayor, "As it is Our wish, in view of the reverence long devoted to the basilica of the holy Apostle Paul, to embellish it in a manner befitting the piety of faith and to expand it in accord with the crowds assembling, … Your zealous energy has been welcome to us," to look into "the site and location" carefully in consultation "with the venerable priest [the pope] and all his associates", and then to

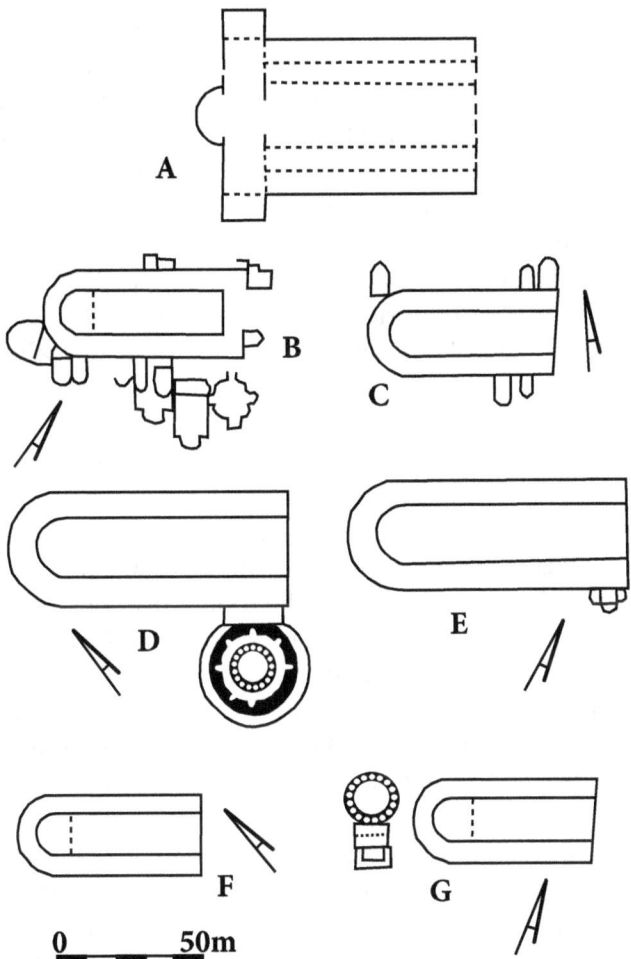

Fig. 4.8: St. Peter's plus "the Six" (all to the same scale)
A: St. Peter's; B: S. Sebastiano; C: SS. Pietro e Marcellino; D: S. Agnese; E: S. Lorenzo; F: "Marciana" on via Ardeatina; G: "Anonima" on the via Prenestina

report "to the Senate and the Christian population, "so long as Your Sublimity shall decide with the architects on the plan of the basilica to be constructed."[38]

By such consultations no doubt the first basilica was commissioned, on crown property within the city's walls. It would serve the pope and city congregants for routine services. All seven of the others, however, were in the suburbs, all arose over catacombs, all had a close connection with martyrs, and, after St. Peter's, all were shaped like a race track: not exactly like the centuries-old Circus Maximus in Rome's midst, but like the new Circus outside the city. This had just been finished as a part of his palace complex by Maxentius, Constantine's enemy and predecessor. It was next door to the site of the Apostles' basilica, S. Sebastiano; and, strangely enough, S. Sebastiano had its entrance-end slightly on a slant just like the starting line that evened out the distance chariots must traverse around their course in Maxentius' structure. Three others of the Six churches show the same slanted end. Who or what dictated the oddity, no one knows.

The Six (fig. 4.8) shared two other features: there was no built provision in them for religious services, no baptistery, sacristy, chancel, ambo, altar, nothing; and, in the second place, their floors were rapidly filled up with burials until absolutely every square inch was accounted for. They were simply carpeted with gravestones. In S. Sebastiano more than 150 can be counted; in the "Marciana", when such stones were revealed and taken up from their sarcophagi in the course of excavation, the eastern corner of the basilica looked as it is shown in fig. 4.9. We behold the most remarkable congestion; we can easily imagine the one to two thousand burials fitted into the whole floor area of the building if it were uncovered. Over the course of two or three centuries, one body might be piled on top of another, to a depth of four! On a less rational level, we can feel also, within our selves, the passion for proximity to holiness that explains the phenomenon before our eyes.[39] It explains the close clustering to be seen outside a North African church (fig. 3.6) and the chapels or mausolea facing in toward the focus of worship in Manastirine (fig. 2.6–8); or, in Rome, around SS. Marcellino e Pietro and, especially, S. Sebastiano.

Inside the inner curve, at the center (fig. 4.9), was the place of greatest honor. Here are those slightly larger sarcophagi that indicate persons of importance—as, for example, Ambrose who secured a burial for himself in the church that took his name, and for his brother in another, each of them next to the martyrs at Milan. We have seen the bishop of Nyssa arrange as much for his parents. Twenty miles south of Rome in the little city of Velitrae, a woman of rank illustrated the same general truth, that importance meant privilege. She "who for so many good deeds gained a burial in the precincts of the saints … received what many desire but few get."[40] Control was naturally in the hands of the authorities. At Rome, it extended to the right of approaching a martyr's tomb for worship, so Jerome tells us. There had always been patrons and donors who had to be rewarded, including as we would expect an occasional senator, or high officials, or the merely rich; but in the decades post-Constantine, increasingly it was the clergy themselves who qualified at least for burial *ad sanctos*, as it was termed, while being also increasingly numbered among the saints.[41]

To return to the Ardeatina church: here, by exception among the Six, a line of stones is visible that marks a sort of chancel area within which there may have been an altar placed for the celebration of the Eucharist. Or perhaps not. The conjecture is supported only by S. Sebastiano.[42] It is of course natural to wonder exactly what went on in the Six. Even

Fig. 4.9: A corner of the "Anonima della via Ardeatina"

before the last two had been identified and studied, sixty years ago, a conclusion could be drawn from the abundant remains of cooking vessels in and about the sites; and in time, a mensa was found in one as well. The basilicas, then, must have been roofed-over cemeteries accommodating the usual funerary meals, *refrigeria*—in short, "gigantic dining rooms," as one scholar put it. Each also served whatever saint was there held in memory, for whom a portable altar might be put in place on his feast day. That might account for the chancel-barrier in the Ardeatina church, just referred to. In S. Sebastiano, well down the nave to the north side, was an entrance and staircase to a crypt, where lay the saints' burials determining the choice of the site in the first place; but the unsanctified dead, too, were served by rites of remembrance, lying below in their thousands. Hence, in attendance, thousands of families. The gallery running around the outside may have served them for the mourners' procession, the *circumambulatio*, traditional in a Roman funeral. Ordinary people were buried here, not out of some egalitarian impulse but because there could not have been the necessary thousands of rich to assert their priority.[43]

In active use, then, any one of the Six will have presented the scene shown in fig. 4.10—though it most closely fits S. Sebastiano. There we can see, evoked as all the evidence requires, a round hundred in family groups with others beyond our view, celebrating communion with their dead and perhaps simultaneously with the martyr. The dead lie under the stones that are the floor, known through their inscribed epitaphs; they are the reason, the foundations for the building. In the shallow niches along the walls, not statues or other ornamental feature but more burials have been placed, many hundreds of *loculi* stacked up as one can see them still in the catacombs beneath the church. Braziers would give light after dark, allowing ritual remembrance to carry on into the night.

Fig. 4.10: A feast day in S. Sebastiano

I leave unspecified the nature of the feast imagined here, whether the Cara Cognatio or some similar, universal day of remembrance for the deceased of one's family, or a private celebration. If the latter was the occasion, then we have an indication of what it would look like on the very grandest scale. We are told of a great senator Pammachius in 397 adopting and adapting a common practice among the municipal elite throughout the western provinces. He offered a great banquet to his fellow citizens en masse—but with a Christian twist, to make it a gift of Christian charity, and not in the forum but in St. Peter's. The host was himself present to preside; the happy occasion was the death of his wife; and the invitation was extended to all, who were most obviously the poor. Crowds of them were disposed on the floor in their dining circles crammed close together as the senator directed them, and they even spilled out onto the steps. Those who brought their own baskets could take away anything left over.[44] Whether this was the only such public banquet ever known in a church, there is no saying; but that seems unlikely. A rare event or merely on a rare scale, our reporter Paulinus salutes it with ecstatic praise.

Or, instead, the feast might mark the anniversary of a martyrdom. In the Six, both sorts of occasion were celebrated, though according to what calendar, with what frequency, and with what liturgy can't be known. For the saints' day the celebration of the Eucharist is assumed and, indeed, the siting of the altar over memorial burials does support such an idea. This was common—probably the rule in the west where Augustine took it for granted.[45] The tangible evidence indicates libations to the martyr below-ground through tubes communicating with the head of the corpse in its sarcophagus, or with his or her relics; and the implication is obvious that it was the focus of a *refrigerium*, a communion through feasting. The saint had a mensa, so-known to the devout in Rome as we have seen it in another Latin-speaking land, North Africa. No mensa was more revered than that covering the sarcophagus of Paul, with its libation-hole, in the basilica that Constantine built in the suburbs.[46] In St. Peter's itself at the turn of the fifth century, it has been suggested that the mensa served as the center of *refrigeria*, meaning big meals and wine; and at the sites of the Six a good quantity of broken cooking- and eating-vessels turned up in the course of excavation.[47]

Martyr-cult liturgy, as one may call it, was *par excellence* a funerary meal attended by reverent good wishes and, it might be, by a prayer as well. Prayer was of course the most private of religious acts, hence the silence that surrounds it still. To my knowledge nothing survives of its inner nature except in non-Christian sources, and even there, anything of the sort is very rare.[48] The outer appearance of it is well enough known in art and literature. We can see the Christians like non-Christians kneeling, or with arms outstretched, standing; but we see only the outer man. Within, as we can only guess, the believer called up before his mind the image or the affect, or both, representing the Power he addressed, and then expressed his wish, perhaps wrapped in praise of the deity and self-abasement. Even with the help of this conjecture we have not reached the center of the act. Among non-Christians and Christians, the wrapping may be attested, true; not so often, the reason for the act in the first place.

Its occasion was a wish, often but not always matched with a promise, *do ut des*. If the Being addressed should grant the wish, then the suppliant might return thanks. Mutuality is not uncommonly revealed to the world in temple-inscriptions, if they are Greek; but it is a rare thing in the more laconic Latin. Ordinarily it found expression only in a brief formula or a variant, *votum solvit*, "So-and-So fulfilled his vow".[49] The latter convention prevails in Christian epigraphy of Rome as in non-Christian, though the body of Christian material is all pre-Constantinian and certainly not very satisfactory: graffiti, whether in the Pretestato catacomb or, best known, on the benches of the grave-side dining-portico under S. Sebastiano. They date to the half century leading up to the Peace. After 313, petitioners in their scribbled messages beg, or they repay a promise, or they offer an inducement, perhaps specifying that God has answered them; and they declare and seem to boast that they have dined with the saints, by which they indicate they have established a claim on the saints addressed.[50] They ask the saints to "bear in mind" So-and-So, for reasons most often not expressed—or sometimes, to insure a safe voyage or good luck to their favorite in the races (the track being next door).[51] In later and more formal inscriptions on stone, the wish is often for the salvation of the soul; but these third- and early fourth-century graffiti under San Sebastiano speak in more traditional terms and, from their bad grammar, seem to include many a visitor from those same poor folk that later accepted Pammachius' invitation.

To recognize the virtue and power in a martyr didn't require any official act. Unauthorized cult is occasionally demonstrable in other parts of the empire, as earlier chapters have shown, but also in Rome, where a catacomb-space taken up by a family for its own dead incorporated martyr-burials; and, when they were recognized, the complex underwent expansion through the knocking down of a wall to another chamber so as to form a quite grand setting in the martyrs' honor. They were Marcellinus and Peter the exorcist, or Urbanus the bishop, or the martyr Quirinus.[52] Piety born in a private setting could thus reach out and become established by word of mouth among the community, and so be generally accepted and assume grand dimensions. A proof of the potential for growth from the ground up, and the dynamic nature of the phenomenon, lies in the forty-six saints' days in the Roman church's calendar by the end of Constantine's reign, an astonishing and revealing number which rose rapidly thereafter to 150 a century later.[53]

By that date, the Six basilicas were all in operation. All, and St. Peter's, were martyr churches.[54] It is a remarkable demonstration of the martyr-cult dynamic, that over the course of little more than a generation of Peace, the church chose to devote *one* eighth of its new-found freedom and funding to its bishop and his in-city needs for daily or weekly services, but *seven* eighths to the martyrs, in the form of several sizeable, costly buildings, and several more, really huge ones of the highest ambition, of which in turn, Six were funerary churches.

Not long after the last of the Six was finished, a dispute broke the Roman community in two and, in the struggle over who was to be a new bishop, the party of Damasus set upon its rival with force, and left some 150 bodies strewn about the floor of the church (A.D. 366). This was apparently S. Sebastiano; the event recalls the slaughter in the other capital mentioned in the second chapter, above.[55] Shortly afterward the victor now as pope—it is supposed to ease or cover up the wounds that the dispute had inflicted—began a campaign of advertisement of martyr-cult in the course of which he sought out the names of scores of forgotten heroes, identifying them most often in the catacombs, and glorifying them in short poems most beautifully inscribed on marble plaques *in situ*. The renown of his long reign (366–384) was communicated to the saints' lives and deeds and, therefore, to their powers. It led to the imitation of his efforts in other sees of Italy and beyond. That story may be picked up, below, in section 3.

My account of Rome's Christians at worship has so far centered in the rites and devotion offered to the dead, both those merely mortal and the immortal saints. The scene has lain entirely beyond the city walls. Perhaps my choice of focus should be explained. First, then, arithmetically, it is dictated by the ratio of one to seven noticed just above. This by itself might seem justification enough. Historically, however, the in-city facilities in the period of my study do need to be mentioned, beginning with "house-churches" similar to the one at Dura in Mesopotamia.

The search for any such thing archeologically detectible in Rome has been quite in vain, despite being very diligent. Whenever some set of walls has been proposed as a possibility, it has been argued out of existence. Of course the fact may not matter very much; for, really, unless some built features inside were to indicate details of liturgy, it is hard to see the benefit in knowing that Christians had met in this or that room or rooms underneath this or that later-built basilica.[56] No one doubts, of course, on the basis of first-century literary evidence, that such houses or rooms did exist and that some of them continued in use at least until the Peace.

By then, it is supposed, some adapted rooms or houses may have become more ample, and so qualified as precinct or parish churches. True, in explaining where early Christians conducted their services, even these have been called in question. The usual term for them, *tituli*, came into use only in the fourth century, to designate buildings that had a name and a sign on them, and it is no more than conjecture to treat these titled ones as earlier churches re-named. The dividing of the city into seven church precincts for administrative purpose in the mid-third century is, however, rightly taken to mean that each of them must have had its own place of meeting, no doubt unadvertised.[57] Perhaps some house-churches existed as well. Accommodations for worship pre-313 appear to have been very limited both in the number of places and in their dimensions.

If the *tituli* were as big as subsequent churches whose plan is known—excluding the Lateran, St. Peter's, S. Paolo and the Six—then together they could hardly have held 4,500 worshippers on a Sabbath; and this, even if attendance were such as every priest dreamed of. The calculation is based on a length of church around 30 meters, whether of the single-nave plan or, like the majority, with side-aisles. This length would be an average and typical for both *tituli* and the untitled churches, suburban or in-city, post-313. Of course there was considerable variation. The 4,500 at worship at one time wouldn't amount to 1 per cent of the city's residents. If it should be increased by some number of unknown and unattested house-churches, and again, by imagining certain worshippers attending at one time, others at another, the total would still hardly top that 1 per cent.

After 313 the whole community could come out into the open; but its in-city needs or at least its building efforts for a generation and more remained (except for the Lateran basilica) only "large but modest halls." The description is Richard Krautheimer's, as good a judge of ecclesiastical construction as anyone could ask for. A number of papal-built *tituli* were added, both in-city and suburban, most of them in the last twenty years of the fourth century. Along with the untitled, the increase to Rome was around twenty new churches;

these, too, Krautheimer described as "amazingly small" in their total capacity.[58] They may have accommodated 250 persons each, able to take in a total of some 5,000 worshippers.

All these churches just reviewed, added to the Lateran and the eight other large basilicas, approach the figure "more than forty" which a bishop ascribes to Rome toward the year 380.[59] The added nine may have had had room for a further 17,000, though a reality of 10,000 or 12,000 is more likely. The 17,000 and the 5,000 of the more modest churches would constitute a total capacity of 22,000, arrived at through maxima. It fits not too badly with the space-requirements in the catacombs, say, for a thousand inhumations a year, or two kilometers' worth of galleries per annum.

This total, however, certainly doesn't fit with modern estimates of the Christian proportion in the city over the two centuries of my study. Those estimates are not hard to find. They range from 2 to 10 per cent in the year 250 based on a false premise, as it seems to me,[60] and rise, unsubstantiated, to a range of 50 or 75 per cent for the second half of the fourth century.[61] In contrast, the archeological evidence points to an organized community about a tenth of the size generally assumed at that latter date: say, 5 per cent or less. What's to be done with the discrepancy? Discussion surely needs to include similar evidence from everywhere else in the empire, and for that reason may be deferred to the next chapter.

Fig. 4.11 St. Peter's façade (the Pola casket)

If modern estimates had the truth in them, facilities for worship would have been obviously and painfully inadequate; but church design for day-to-day or weekly worship, the synaxary, indicates no worries about space in those floor-plans, post-313, which are available for study: that is, much of the nave of a church will be reserved to the clergy by the chancel and by a long solea, one even reaching from chancel to door. In both St. Peter's and S. Giovanni this is noticeable.[62] The altar may be set far down the nave, encumbering it the more;[63] so also the pulpit, a moveable wooden one explaining why an ambo doesn't appear in the city's churches.[64]

Besides altars, pulpits, chancels, and soleas, which determined where and how people stood or moved about, a last feature of fourth-century churches should be mentioned: their orientation. It should rather be called occidentation. Rome's churches faced west. In consequence, we have a vivid account of worshippers turning around on St. Peter's steps and bowing deeply to the rising sun before they entered for the morning services—a custom obviously non-Christian and deplored by the pope.[65] The direction in which the churches faced required women to be sequestered in the northern aisle, men in the southern; for, to an observer, the left of the altar was its right side, the more honored, where Jesus sat with God. In depictions of pilgrim crowds at the altar end of St. Peter's, S. Croce, and S. Lorenzo (fig. 4.11), in all three on the front and side panels of an ivory reliquary of 425, we see the men grouped to the left, which was the south; the women faced them across the nave.[66] In prayer, however, men and women alike faced to the east. Rome's example exerted a great influence on other sees and regions to the north and west.

3. Beyond Rome

Among the realities of Christian worship as they have been seen in the empire's capital, the most striking seems to me their dynamic nature, on view in the cult of the dead. This accommodated both the family's honoring and communing with its own, mere mortals that they were, and the individual and general honoring and communing with the saints, immortal. It dictated the principal use made of Constantine's and his successor's unstinting generosity—"principal" in the proportion of seven to one. This was the ratio of expenditure on construction; such was the attendance expected at St. Peter's and the Six, as against the Lateran basilica of Jesus Savior, with its silver statues.

To see these realities any more clearly, however, is not easy. In the administrative and liturgical manuals of the third and fourth centuries, generally taken as operative within the Roman church, and in the surviving correspondence and other records of the see, I find no hint of what actually went on in the seven great basilicas that served this communitarian preference; and the sources of information eventually dry up. By the eighth century all seven had been adapted to some new use or were disused entirely and in ruins.[67] They had emerged from the ardor of what was only a moment, *sub specie aeternitatis*; and yet it was of great consequence.

To see this ardor on display and in action elsewhere, Milan, Nola, and Geneva may serve best, beginning with Milan. Here Aurelius Ambrosius, with crucial support from Damasus, was chosen to be bishop in 374. He was the son of a great official, educated at Rome in elite fashion in both languages. At the time of his election he had his foot on a high rung among

Fig. 4.12: Italy and beyond
(locations appearing in the appendix)

imperial offices, as a provincial governor. His first ten years in the see coincided with the last ten of Damasus, and reflected Damasus' highly publicized discovery of and enthusiasm for saints' relics noticed on an earlier page.

Milan, not Rome, had served emperors of the west as their capital for nearly a century. Its population in consequence was very large and has been estimated in Ambrose's day at well over 100,000.[68] Here, early in his episcopacy, he was directed in a dream to the burial place of the local martyrs Gervasius and Protasius—unless he was "acting in response to popular demand, perhaps well managed and orchestrated"—and had the relics dug up and brought in triumph to a proper church. They began performing miracles of healing before his eyes on the instant.[69] Their fame and worship spread rapidly to Africa and other regions.

Among the cemeteries where families celebrated their *refrigeria*, and where a memorial in honor of Saints Nabor and Felix already stood, the bishop promptly began (A.D. 379) construction of the grand basilica given his own name. Here Gervasius and Protasius found their new home.[70] The basilica Ambrosiana did not put an end to the bishop's building: at the end of his episcopacy Milan's cemetery churches could accommodate several thousands, while the churches in-city had room only for a half as many.[71] Christians in the total population may have accounted for some 3 per cent, if we may judge from the capacity of all the churches of Milan counted together.

Ambrose preached against those who took part in martyr-cult in the traditional way of *refrigeria*, "who bring wine cups to the martyrs' sepulchres, where those people drink till dusk in the belief they won't be heeded otherwise".[72] His understanding of their faith was of course correct. In nearby Verona some years earlier in a similar sermon the local bishop had spoken out against "people who circulate among the graves, offer banquets to the stinking bodies of the dead and, out of their taste for self-indulgence and drinking in disreputable haunts, make martyrs out of them on the spot, by their wine-jugs and cups."[73] From both bishops, harsh words indeed!—and not easily fitted into the picture of martyr-cult and its reception so far presented. Their explanation lies in the persons making the discovery of relics, who should be clerics, not common folk, and certainly not within the frame of detestable beliefs and an outdated and scandalous liturgy. No lessening of enthusiasm for the cult in itself was intended. Rather, when the bishop of Rouen, Victricius, returned home after a well-received visit to Italy in the 380s, he was followed by a rich assortment of relics sent to him by Ambrose among others. The gift included parts of the Saints John, Andrew, Thomas, Luke, Eufemia who has appeared in my first chapter, she of great fame, and inevitably also, Gervasius and Protasius. At their welcome and praise at Rouen, "prone upon the ground, watering it with our tears, let us call out," Victricius urges his congregation, in a great display of high-flown oratory; "with staying up all night, with fasting" let the new arrivals be greeted! "And do thou, O holy and untouched virgins, play upon your instruments, play upon your instruments, and mount the paths to heaven with your dances, striking the ground with your steps."[74] Yet at this point Ambrose might have disagreed. He reproached his own people for their habit of dancing in the course of prayer.[75]

The absolutely right way to handle the matter of martyr-cult was shown by a bishop to the south, Paulinus of Nola. He was like Ambrose, an aristocrat and a governor before retiring to the town ten miles up the coast from Pompeii, where he was elected bishop: an excellent choice for the Nolans, given his wealth and connections with all the best, the most wealthy and prominent people. He didn't disappoint his fellow citizens.

Their local hero was the martyr Felix. His memorial in a cemetery less than a mile out of town had been honored with a clear space around it a few meters removed from a line of ten earlier mausolea (B in fig. 4.13). He was joined by two other burials of privilege, presumably two bishops—this, by at least the early third century. An apsidal memoria plus three mausolea were then added, the three mausolea enviably near to Felix and thus, to extra blessings.

These latter little buildings in a ragged row almost closed off a sort of plaza where we may imagine regular memorial picnics. Its features recall the space around the apostles under St. Peter's and around the burials at Manastirine. Here at Nola, communion could be conveniently enjoyed both with Felix and the venerated bishops next to him, and with the deceased of the families also who had built the mausolea, his close neighbors. Replacing the string of three little mausolea, however, an apsidal hall was built (C in fig. 4.13) to cover and further dignify Felix's remains, from which the two bishops' were removed a little distance to an also-honored site. This hall of late Constantinian times was made much larger on its northern side, a generation later, to form the so-called *basilica vetus*, the "Old".

Such was the long story and the scene to which Paulinus arrived, open-handed, toward the close of the fourth century. This was the setting to which he gave a New basilica far grander than the Old as a fitting center for still more widely advertised and valued celebrations. While the Old had been intended for a few hundreds of residents in a town of 5,000 to 7,000, with some admixture of visitors to the saint, the New more than doubled the space available. It promptly received a deputation of approbation. Another bishop came with representatives from Augustine and the nearest thing the Roman empire could show to a bil-

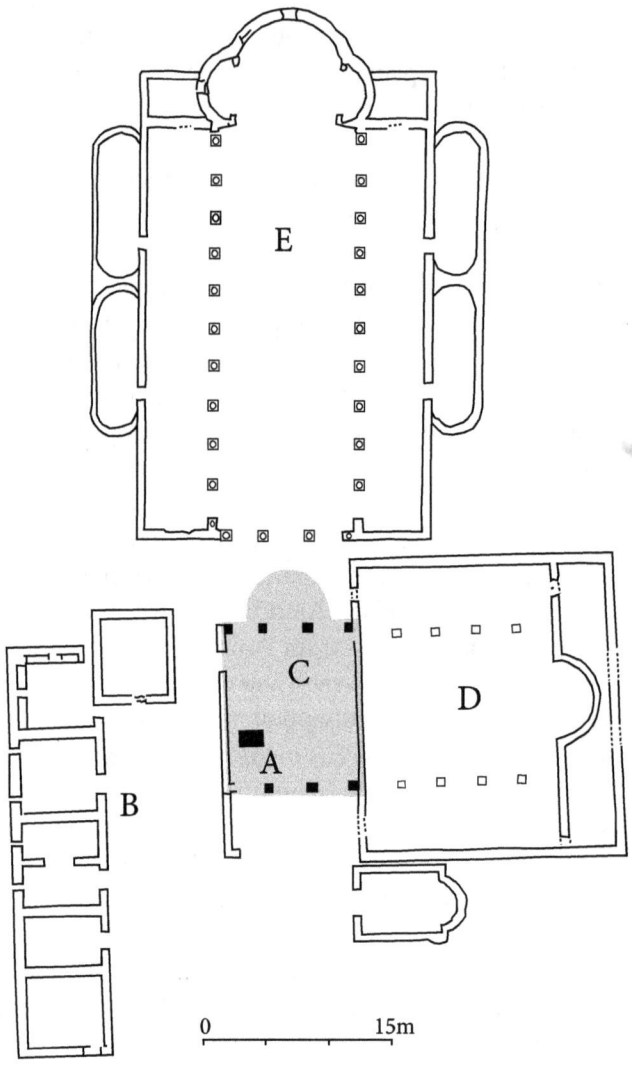

Fig. 4.13: Felix' cult center in Nola
Felix' burial (A) originally in an open space a little removed from a line of mausolea (B); honored in the 330s or later with a small apsidal church (C, in grey) built around it; this incorporated into a basilica, "the old one" (D) in the last third of the 4th c.; and "the new one" (E) built at the turn of the 5th c.

lionaire, the lady Melania; Ambrose sent precious relics. The interior walls could boast of frescoes showing Nazarius of Milan and John the Baptist, Thomas, Luke, and Euphemia.[76]

The steady development to be traced here through the surviving stones and layers is interesting in part because it is easily matched by others very similar in the cemeteries touched on by my earlier chapters. A little idea, a little focus of awe and piety centered in a Christian exemplar, established itself. It couldn't be crushed, it couldn't be rushed, its fame spread slowly by word of mouth. Here upon the saint's head, or on those relics that lay in the upper end of his tomb beneath the floor of the Old basilica, worshippers could pour sweet-smelling liquids through a tube that opened at floor-level, in the belief, as Paulinus explains, that Felix rejoiced in such tributes (though the bishop didn't).

And, for another example of the birth of cult in private initiative before its more official development: Paulinus was invited by his friend to the north, Sulpicius Severus, to compose a verse-dedication for the remains of Sulpicius' favorite priest, Clarus, buried in 397 under the altar in Sulpicius' own chapel; and the response was not one but a choice of three poems, all, suitable for a saint who was to enjoy much popularity in France down to the present day.[77]

By around 400 the "New Basilica" as Paulinus calls it was fairly underway in Nola. You could walk around in it and see, hung up on the walls, the donor's beard-clippings from his youth (how long preserved for this display?), together with the frescoes just mentioned and inscribed texts that told of Felix' miracles. The saint's powers were confirmed by testimonials from persons whose disabilities and ailments he had cured. Beneath the altar the relics of the apostles were now placed for veneration; and all around, the earth was promptly filled up with burials of those who sought an advantage in their prayers.

Here the exorcist brought the mentally ill for healing; on the day of Felix' martyrdom, every year, people brought animals to be slaughtered on the spot and roasted, a piece of which would be given to the saint (how delivered? given instead to the poor?) and the remainder enjoyed by the pious and their guests with perhaps some left over to take home or distribute as charity. On the night before, everyone had stayed up, singing and drinking in the shrine. All such gestures and rites of worship were thoroughly traditional yet all somehow acceptable. Seen from a great height above them, wrong though they were, yet, said their bishop, "behold how many collect from every country district and how they stroll about, their untaught minds caught in error, but out of piety.... such merriment at their party tables we must forgive among such little folk, since mistaken beliefs do steal into their unformed minds and, not understanding the extent of their sin, their simple-mindedness errs out of devotion, believing as they do, wrongly, that saints are delighted to have their tombs bathed with odoriferous wine." To such celebrations, attendance drew strangers from a hundred miles away, two hundred.[78]

Geneva was another town that received relics of Gervasius and Protasius. In a little suburban settlement just across the Rhone, they were honored by a basilica in the fifth century. It was built exactly on top of the principal room or building within a complex for pagan cult going back many centuries. Who the subject or object had been is unknown: a local hero, perhaps a god. A second hero of apparently private invention toward the end of the fourth century had his shrine a little distance above the lake, in another complex of small buildings. A Christian martyr, this.[79] And honor was paid to still a third hero whose mighty bones and presence within the city boundaries testify to a savior-figure of some sort. His story has been lost; but his people remembered him so well that the site was respected and later selected for the burial of two venerated citizens of Christian times. Recent excavation beneath the apse of Geneva's St. Peter cathedral has revealed in its successive layers these centuries of changing worship.[80]

Geneva's bishop Isaac appears in records of church councils, the first to do so from the town. He had the funds for very extensive construction serving the residential needs of himself and his clergy, and his services to his people. For the latter, over the closing years of the fourth century, he could enlarge the old basilica and construct a new one. In both, the laity space was divided in half by a stone barrier by which the congregation was somehow segregated into the more privileged, and the less. The chopping up of space recalls what was noticed elsewhere toward the same date (fig. 1.10, above)—though it is a little surprising to see the fashion registering in a place like Geneva, so far away from the centers of influence.

A stone pulpit distinguished this new building, at the end of a solea. These two features also were very up-to-date. They had the effect of reducing the laity space, already intruded on by ample chancels in both of Isaac's basilicas, so that even the larger of these two could contain no more than two hundred persons at worship—if so many. The total would amount to 5 per cent or less within the five or six thousands of the city and its suburbs.

The statistic invites a comparative glance at other excavated sites in the northwest quadrant of the empire, meaning Spain, France, England, and the Alpine and middle and upper Danube countries or provinces. Within this great area, the Christians seen at worship need no special description; my findings indicate no more than the lightest scattering of convert-communities, none of them with significant mass.[81]

In Italy, on the other hand, one would expect things to be different. It was urbanized to a unique degree, the estimate of course being relative to other regions and requiring a definition of what a "city" may be; but perhaps 400 centers of 1,000–5,000 inhabitants can be counted. In fewer than thirty of these 400 is some place of Christian worship attested archeologically within the urban circuit; and the number of cities that could each claim its own bishop is perhaps not very much greater. Milan, Aquileia, Ravenna, and Concordia in the north, and Rome, are chief.[82] To explain the lack of any Christian mark on the map of the remaining centers—more than 300 of them—we could blame the deficiencies in our data, archeological or written; but it might make better sense to suppose that, in these many centers, very little Christianizing had in fact taken place. Weighing the two possibilities, we should consider how closely the past and our knowledge of it correspond. The site of Rome itself provides some reassurance; for here, today, we can identify thirty-nine churches, while a bishop may be recalled from an earlier page, speaking of some "forty and more churches" in the capital toward the year 380. His total and ours today are pretty close.[83]

The fit suggests that the modern tools of discovery work pretty well, and the archeological evidence or lack of it throughout the peninsula, as also to the north and west, ought to be taken seriously. However, the possibilities are better tested comparatively in the next chapter.

5
Conclusions

Christendom, the City of God, was very different in the year 400 from what it had been in 200. Among the changes it underwent, nothing was more important than the sheer increase in its numbers. The amount of new construction is the proof of this. The City grew at a great rate post-312 not through a natural increase in population but through conversion. Growth necessitated, and was conditioned by, adaptation to the needs of all those new-comers. Before, both numbers and needs had been quite small-scale and the City, relatively homogeneous.

Adaptation can be seen in many points of practice and belief. It is natural to ask where they all came from—to what extent they were all internally generated and, so to speak, organic within Christianity, or were instead brought into the City by the converts. At the time, as the bishops reminded those newly won over, every trace of ancestral religion should have been left at the door. Converts, however, were reluctant to renounce their traditions, lock, stock, and barrel. Various details in the religious scene on which my earlier chapters have dwelt show bishops and the masses pulling in opposite directions. They had different ideas about the language of gesture and voice that one should use toward the divine, its style or propriety; different ideas about the reality of relations with the dear departed; and their own sense of what were the best answers for ordinary people faced with the needs of this secular life, not those of the life to come.

From time to time the question even arose and was articulated by the bishops, whether some in their congregation were Christians at all. Yes, these people came to church, sometimes, and were ready enough to call themselves Christian; but they didn't always act like Christians. They didn't disagree with their bishop's teachings, but those teachings were not the whole of their religion. For the historian, their condition and their numbers within the City—or perhaps not within it, and how that might be determined—are all matters of interest.

1. The model church

Our understanding of worship itself is, however, a problem for us still, an encumbrance to our reading of the past. We in the West today, as a sort of reflex, naturally suppose that in our human address to superhuman Powers—whether Jupiter or Penates, Yahweh or the Trinity—there may be some quality or moment that is really of the inner man, "spiritual"; and this is "real" religion as opposed to "cult" or "ritual". The definition is sometimes insisted on; it springs from living experience, not just the study of the past.[1] It discounts physical acts, gestures, movement, especially if communal. It favors the activity of the mind alone. The former expressions are *mere* forms, routines, rites, practices, customs; or if they are more than that, they lack any deep mystery; they are superstition in the sense of having no thought to them—automatic, irrational, undisciplined.

"Mere" routines: we know very well what they're worth. I quote a serious scholar, specialist in the subject of religion in Antiquity, to remind us of ideas so common, they amount to a modern consensus:

> It is perhaps misleading even to say that there was such a religion as "paganism" at the beginning of our period [of the Roman Empire], which could be offered to a potential convert from another religious tradition. It might be less confusing to say that the pagans, before their competition with Christianity, had no religion at all in the sense in which that word is normally used today. They had no tradition of discourse about ritual or religious matters..., no organized system of beliefs to which they were asked to commit themselves, no authority structure.... [Paganism] did not contain or control morality, philosophy, eschatology, and so on.[2]

The writer is perhaps not even conscious of taking a Judeo-Christian model as "religion", and looking for it in ancient times, and not finding it among those who were neither Jews nor Christians. He knows, he doesn't have to be told, that the only religion worthy of the name is the Judeo-Christian. It has what he says is everything needed to make a religion: a hierarchy, an enforced credo, a theology, a single and obligatory liturgy, a pressing sense of the hereafter, and moral imperatives. True, certainly true, such structural features are not to be found in ancient polytheism. *Q.e.d.*

As to polytheism, none of its gods could be received. Let this great difference be acknowledged; but the model that is proposed as "real" religion and Christian is a relatively modern one. The ancient was not so distinct. In illustration, a representative outburst was quoted in the last chapter, from Ambrose, directed at the roisterers around martyrs' sepulchres "where those people drink till dusk *in the belief they won't be heeded otherwise*." He readily concedes, there is reason behind their behavior. It is religion. That is exactly the problem. His pagan opponent in Rome, the senator Symmachus, speaks of a Christian's devotion to *religiones* in the plural, where the word means all the pious acts to which a Christian might be attached, including (or principally) things done and visible. These were nevertheless taken to be expressive of true devotion. They were "religion" in the singular, as we would say in our own understanding of the word.[3]

Neither the ancient bishop nor the senator saw routines as meaningless. Rather, routines addressed a universe that we today happen not to believe in. Let our own focus be on morality, theology, eschatology and eternal punishment. Early Christians, however, included not only all this but a great deal more besides.

Back then, everyone knew that whatever could go wrong in the world, from floods to rebellions, was the work and sign of some of those certain Beings that are bad, legions of which are ubiquitous and actually immanent in our very selves, and are well known to be so from their being driven out of catechumens by baptism and out of the possessed by exorcism before the very eyes of the most reliable witnesses; while at the same time other Beings, which are good, manifest themselves in the driving out, and in other beneficent acts, or inflict merited punishments on wrong-doers. All this body of common knowledge was illustrated in my earlier chapters, if only in scattered mentions as they might help to explain the archeological record.[4] They are, I hope, enough to show what ideas prevailed in Ambrose's day and shaped prayer or supplicant gestures.

Among the good were Beings who had been like ourselves, once. They were the departed who indeed slept but yet remained still sentient—a fact of life or death acknowledged by Christians and non-Christians alike. We have the vision of a desolated husband at his chaste wife's tomb, promising her, "I will pour down upon your bones that wine which, living, you would never touch".[5] The text may stand for a score, or rather, many hundreds of others of a similar character, inscribed in the certainty that the dead do hear and in their sleepy way do find a special solace in living memories ritually expressed. The dead need this for their very being. Even unwritten evidence speaks to the belief. I instance at random the decision to build a mensa adjoining the tomb of S. Callisto/Callixtus in the Calepodio catacomb, since the saints just like ordinary mortals were comforted by being remembered; or again, all those other hundreds of mensae adjoining or more often directly above some private tomb; and for both, there were toasts and libation tubes. Cemetery rituals had a point: to provide for others what one would wish others, after one's death, to provide unto one's self. The point was explained and supported by certain beliefs about the Beyond.

In accordance with these beliefs we have not only visions but vows, too, like that of the bereaved husband, just quoted. Such vows were very common. In proof of the ideas behind them, the yield from prayers was mentioned in the previous chapter (at nn. 49ff.). Inscribed promises are addressed to Beings once on this earth, just as to the Immortals, in the form, "So-and-So paid off his [or her] vow", *votum solvit* (or the equivalent in Greek, *kat'euches*). They may also be offered to the saints in terms like those chosen by the grieving husband, above. To the saints, in addition, thanks were due if the vow was answered. Answers themselves supported belief in the connection between asking and getting. Thus and therefore, said Tertullian, "faith in Divinity is produced through certain signs, miracles, prophecies".[6]

This graveside evidence suggests how much "religion" has been left out of the modern model; for, though the people who engaged in the practices just described were certainly Christians, what they did and thought represented "no tradition of discourse about ritual or religious matters", "no organized system of beliefs to which they were asked to commit themselves, no authority structure"; nor were their practices to be found in the Bible, whether the Old Testament and Judaism or the New, save for a single mention in Revelation (ch. 1).

The modern model is not, of course, an empty fiction. A great number of the most familiar texts show us real preachers speaking to real congregants in attendance at real churches. What we read about them, we have no reason to doubt; indeed, it fits easily into the experience of the present day; and in the scenes presented to us we can identify the very elements insisted on as definitive of religion: "morality, philosophy, eschatology, and so on"—to say nothing of biblical authority.

We have, for example, Augustine seated on his episcopal throne. Attentive at his side would be his short-hand writer, thanks to whom we have our texts today. In the audience the female part would be strictly kept apart from the male. Augustine was insistent on this. Only the men would be addressed by him, as "my brothers", "brothers", "dearest brothers"—for example, at the little town of Thignica a couple of days' journey to the south of Hippo, in one of the opening years of the fifth century. Here, he was little known; perhaps had never paid a visit before. He chose to preach on God's severity. As a way of winning over the audience, he adopted, as often, an almost conversational style: "To begin with," he says, "just look at everyday life, where you can discern the right path.... And what is it that I'm saying? You punish your slave"—as God punishes you, so you punish the insolence of a slave by inflicting the proper pains. A parallel is drawn to the *vita cottidiana*, which is my point of interest in the passage; for it betrays the speaker's assumption that everyone present would be a slave-owner. The socioeconomic stratum he sees before him could hardly include more than one man out of twenty in the city's whole population, where such an indulgence as a single slave's purchase would amount to far more than the year's earnings of a day-laborer. Augustine's audience of owners was, then, just that 5 per cent to whom I have referred in earlier chapters. What can be found in his sermon can be found equally in the whole homiletic corpus of the fourth century, from every region and province.[7]

Thus, to the extent that the modern model of religion derives from and reveals to us the Christianity of these great teachers and their classrooms everywhere, it must appear to be the possession of only a very few. It can hardly represent the whole City of God. As much may be said about the photogenic columns or elaborate decoration of a classical temple or a cathedral looking up at us from some coffee-table picture-book. They certainly do not represent the whole of religion in any ancient community. Rather, every brick or stone regardless of its size or shape, as every citizen, must be considered; for all are equally a part of the reality. History is a democrat. It is or it should be respectful of all human beings alike, not only those that dominate in the report through their position and their art.

2. NUMBERS AND CLASS

A flood of conversion defined the turn taken by the City's history in the period of my study. It registered in a great many ways, differently on different aspects of religion and in different parts of the Christian population. Jeradé's church (fig. 1.4) illustrates a change experienced among the ecclesiastical authorities. These latter had their ideas about good manners suited to, and acceptable among, a higher and higher class as the City prospered decade after decade. They knew better than their forebears how one should properly show respect to the Almighty, and acted out their knowledge according to the usages of their own rank in society. Those were the manners of address that would be equally appropriate in an entirely secular approach to a governor or still more to the emperor, in his *secretarium*, his audience chamber, up on a platform, beyond a barricade of attendants, behind a great curtain, in a place defended by a latticed screen, a *cancellus*, surmounted by a special arch. Illustration was offered from the Syrian church. The architectural features for worship were contrasted with those of Dura. They laid out the rules of it in visible form, they laid out the mosaic panels on the churches' floor by which everyone's path should be instructed, either to step elsewhere, or to step forward. It is very largely through the study of the stones that we understand the changing liturgy in the period that interests me: the stones, the tesserae of mosaics, the nicely carved thin marble slabs that still survive, generally out of place and broken in bits, once serving to define the sanctuary and set apart the aisle for catechumens. I must not forget the stones that made up the whole grand basilica in Tebessa (fig. 3.8), those grander in Rome by Constantine's gift (fig. 4.8), or those walls and columns at Carthage in an air-view (fig. 5.1) where sheer enormous size was a declaration of homage in itself and, at the same time, a sign of the grandeur of God. Here in Carthage at Cyprian's shrine hundreds of worshippers often gathered to receive Augustine's instruction.[8]

The same classes that decreed such ambitious construction can be seen monopolizing the places of highest honor within its walls not only in their lifetimes but even afterwards in their burial beneath its floors. In the catacombs of Rome they have been seen clustering together in the better parts; here were their own more ample frescoed chambers and broader corridors.[9] They bought up and kept among themselves the most prestigious cemeteries, entire, like Marusinac or, within cemeteries, the square footage most likely to get them into Heaven, thanks to the intercession of the saints. They advanced from lower clerical ranks to higher, from a smaller church to a more renowned, and so in the end to win a final resting place *ad sanctos*. In death they even claimed an equality with the martyrs thanks to being

Fig. 5.1: "Cyprian's memoria" at Carthage

voted martyr-status, it is not clear just how or why; but certainly bishops became saints pretty frequently, post-313, without need to give their lives for their faith, and in good time were credited with their share of miracles, too. In the diptychs—lists read aloud at services for an especial blessing—the names of bishops took up the larger part, while lay benefactors were immortalized in the mosaic panels on the floors as, no doubt, in other inscriptions on the walls, now lost, declaring that so-and-so had contributed so-and-so many dollars to construction costs for so many square feet. The reminders were made by the donors along with the gift. Many were clergy, since, increasingly, clergy were rich. It might then appear, because it was so nearly the fact, that the rich had paid for and thus had bought the church, and it was theirs. In token of the fact, episcopal elections which had once been the right and business of the congregations at large passed into the hands of the local elite, the *honoratiores*. It was a gradual thing but an indication of emerging realities; and, along with this change, the honoring of titles among the lay elite, in mentions or records of them, and the growing attention to the various grades of honor among the clergy—close to an obsession with rank—gave a new character to the church from the mid-fourth century on.[10]

To point this out amounts to saying that the shape of society was reflected in its religion. Surely nothing else would be expected, in this particular aspect of life as in any other. The traditional cults, to the extent they were communitarian in any sense, were no differently composed; that is, in Rome, Vestals and Arval priests still in the fourth century working their way through their super-sumptuous festal feasts, and in eastern provinces the boys' choirs and the generous persons urged to take on the presidency of some religious event with its incumbent costs, all, could only be drawn from the urban elite.[11] Such was reality, socioeconomic reality. The elite could of course have said no. Instead, they came forward gladly to play their roles, to assert their rank and earn an even higher one, whatever its cost. Within an established Christianity, in due course, that was how the world still worked. As a certain great nobleman (Praetextatus, non-Christian) more than once declared to Saint Damasus, "Make me bishop of Rome and I'll be Christian overnight."[12] The two were friends and enjoyed the joke.

Praetextatus may be compared with others of the elite whose sincerity of belief we can hardly be sure of. The bishop Synesius and the poet Claudian are two instances.[13] They support the suggestion that Praetextatus would have made, not a sincerely pious, but a respectable pope. That is, under his hand the Roman see would have had an officiant bound to do his job in good style, vigorous and effective and ambitious for his charge; able by his eloquence to enhance its image and its mission alike; in sum, a faithful servant. Like a college president today, he could insure a good inflow of support. He knew, he had always known, he daily met and talked with, that set of people who were best able to give such support; and the churches of Rome, or of Tebessa or Carthage, were in their gift.

The upper classes who chose to support the church could have directed their energies at leveling or evangelical goals. There is little sign of any taste for this. In the spirit of Mt 6.6, to pray only in one's own room with the door closed, no showy places need have been constructed, either. There was no need for any grand entrance of the clergy, devised and reverently acted out, or for a triumphal arch above the clergy's heads as they mounted from the nave onto the chancel, symbolically set above everyone else; no need to sequester the laity by physical arrangements at worship and by reminders to women and catechumens of their differing degrees of acceptability. But all these features had something sacred about them. In communication with the divine, there must be no slight, no disrespect, no unintended message conveyed. Forms *were* content.

Propriety was of course to be determined by those who led the church and by those laity who gave it eminence and strength. The two were nearly one, within a generation or so after 313: that is, a majority of gifts for church construction were by that time coming from the clergy themselves. The class from which they were recruited must be assumed to have supported their lead generally. It was their church, its forms and gestures were theirs. It spoke to the lay part of them through the terms of personal address scattered across the whole corpus of sermons. "We", and more often "you" who are addressed, whose style of life is the norm, are moneyed folk. "We" and "you" are used to luxury and expense—have never wanted for a servant, have never had to cook a meal, let alone do without one. The homiletic tone, while often philanthropic, was decidedly not inclusive.[14]

We are drawn into this world through its sermons and letters, church manuals, tracts, memoirs and biographies; we know the writers and many of the laity, too, with their career high-points spelt out in inscriptions. We would say we are familiar with them all, very much as we might say we know Cicero and his friend Atticus from an earlier time. But did these eminent, affluent, eloquent people constitute the City of God any more than Cicero and Atticus constituted—really *were*—the whole of Rome? I raise again the question asked at the close of the previous section. Can the whole be fairly known through such as these? Or are we seeing only as much as we take the trouble to see? This is but the first of two impossible questions—impossible or at the least, very uncomfortable to answer.

A second question broadens inquiry to the entire body of Christians, combining the few with the forgotten many and asking if even the grand total should be called the Christendom of the period. Here too there are uncomfortable possibilities; for, out of some 255 churches in some 155 towns and cities, wherever the remains survive for the record, the expected attendance ranged between a mere 1 per cent and 8 per cent of the general population. Such are the figures we have seen at Alexandria, Constantinople, Rome, Antioch, many little Syrian centers, Salona, Philippi, Oxyrhynchus, Carthage, Cirta, Tipasa, Nola.... They can be checked in the three greatest of these centers, where we have reliable lists of the fourth-century churches. By no estimate of their total seating or standing capacity could they have accommodated great crowds, compared with the whole urban population. Only by exception, in the major centers, is a church built to accommodate more than 500 persons; a more usual figure for cities that had perhaps 20,000 in population was 350 or 400 per church; and no great efforts were made to multiply the number of churches. Except at certain pilgrim centers (and the exception is instructive), special measures were apparently not needed. Need could be measured by those contemporaries who were best suited to do so, namely, the local bishops. They were guided in their planning by their experience of normal attendance, not by their lack of construction funds; and, as the fourth century draws to its end, and so into the fifth, we can see them sometimes *cutting back* the laity space in favor of the clergy, to make room for a more ample chancel, a solea or an ambo.

All these urban data are worth thinking about because, as has been more than once recalled, in estimating the place of Christianity in the whole empire, the weight of representation must fall on the cities, not the countryside. Everyone is agreed that the new faith only very slowly reached out into the farming population. There, Christians would have been far fewer, thus to pull down the over-all percentage.

Yet Christian texts encourage the impression, and sometimes insist on the fact, of a near-perfect triumph of belief over darkness throughout the ancient world well before the end of the fourth century. Claims of the new religion's great success are common in more or less contemporary church historians or casual commentators of the second and third centuries. We have Tertullian in 211 claiming a half of the empire's population for the church. Later, there are more statistics: at Antioch in the 380s, not far from half of John Chrysostom's fellow-citizens were also his fellow Christians, as he told his listeners; and empire-wide, they were close to a totality in 423, as the emperor Theodosius saw it.[15]

If such statements are doubted in modern accounts, still, the historian has almost nothing to work with: only a number extrapolated from the roster of dependents supported by the Roman church in the mid-third century, and a second figure offered for Antioch in the latter fourth century. This latter was just referred to. I have indicated my doubts about both of these items.[16] Otherwise, so far as I can see, the written sources deal only in words, not numbers: in some given time or place, Christians will be described as "crowds", "numerous", and so forth.

But such terms are really of no help at all. Anyone interested in how the church grew, the rate of increase, its effect and its historical consequences, must have specific numbers to be compared with each other across time. For such a purpose, words without numerical meaning have no meaning at all.

If what's needed can't be found, let it be invented! We find in our texts all those Christians who turn up anecdotally or historically in hundreds of towns and cities (out of some thousands) during the period of my study; and there are lists of bishops, too, in attendance at councils. From the accumulation of such mentions Adolf von Harnack in successive editions of a work published more than a century ago could venture an estimate of Christians in the empire at the turn of the fourth century in percentile terms: 7–10 per cent. The figure was developed out of a great deal of very careful gathering of materials from the written sources, a true specialist's best guess. Still, it wasn't supported by any argument.[17]

Some sort of very loose control was or is possible. Using such "facts" as ancient historians must ever be content with, it could indeed be demonstrated that an estimate of 1 per cent would be too small while more than 40 per cent would be too large, empire-wide. Those terms I think would be agreed. But fixing a more precise figure between the two extremes remained a perfectly arbitrary exercise. Never mind, Harnack did his best, and others (myself included, a quarter-century ago) joined in the guessing game. His estimate for the Christian part of the empire's population, in some critics' view, needed to be raised to 12 per cent; by others, reduced to 4–5 per cent.[18] Jean-Marie Salamito, however, dismissed these proposals (instancing my own, it so happens) as "impossible to verify".[19] I accept the verdict as a fair one, perfectly fair.

Next, whatever the specialists' preference, their choice could be used as a benchmark from which to deduce a rate of increase up to its point in time, A.D. 300, from the initial 120 believers of our text, Acts 1.15, in the A.D. 30s; and the same rate could be projected beyond A.D. 300 so as to support a figure for the Christian share in the population a century later: 60 per cent. The effort invited statistical modelling with tables, graphs, projections and parametric probabilities. From these in turn flowed various significant conclusions: for instance, that the rate of growth was so marked, the resulting numbers had made it expedient for Constantine to be converted; so marked, that it required this or that explanation of the age-groups recruited, their gender, their economic status, the diversity of sects; and further, that only the persecutions and civil wars sufficed to explain that rate, at least in the third century.[20]

My reason for going into all these airy calculations will be clear, I hope. It is important to see how an undefended surmise based on written sources alone can turn into a given, a number in A.D. 300, something on which then to hang quite elaborate reconstructions, without in the least enhancing their fundamental credibility. They remain as insubstantial as the surmise itself. If the latter is wrong, then whatever is deduced from it is valueless. And the figures which are in fact most in play in the most modern discussions, drawn only from written sources, are in obvious conflict with what the archeology tells us.

What the statistical models expressed in graphs and tables, W. H. C. Frend showed in another form: a map representing impressions quite conventional in the 1980s as they would be today (fig. 5.2). It showed conversion at the favorite point of measurement, A.D. 300, to have attained to a "strong minority"—which can hardly mean less than a quarter of the total population—along the coasts and the areas behind them as well, throughout the eastern Mediterranean and parts of North Africa, while, in the western parts of what is Turkey, today, Frend imagined Christians to be an absolute majority.[21]

A majority—can that be true? In the year 300? Exactly in these provinces, four deacons and their animating bishop in the 540s and 550s were given money to offer to converts, and could distribute rewards in lump sums larger than most recipients had ever seen in

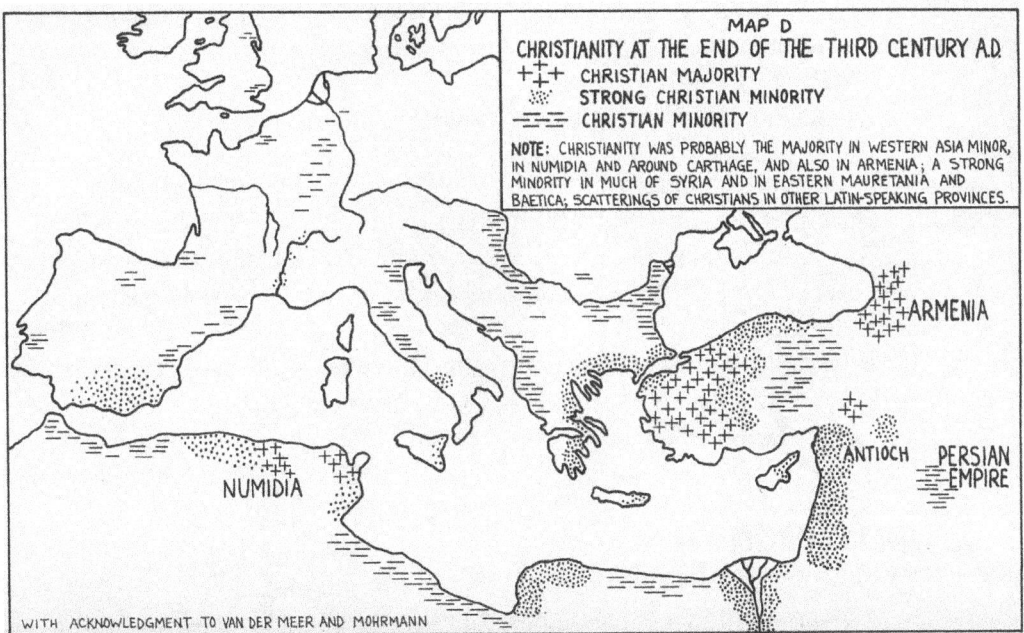

Fig. 5.2: Frend's idea of the place of Christianity

their lives; with the result that 80,000 professed themselves new Christians. As strangers in a village, without scandal, the missionaries could have addressed and paid only adult males (heads of households and guardians of widows), by whose conversion, and therefore of their families, the total of converts must have included some far larger figure—in sum and in short, "a strong minority" in Frend's terminology, and perhaps even a majority. So great a number of non-Christians two and a half centuries after Constantine, though quite at odds with the common view of the empire's conversion, fits not badly with another specific glimpse given us by a good source, this one in a western context. From a port in the most urbanized, most anciently Christian province of Provence, a big crowd got on board a ship one day with our reporter, a Christian, bound for Italy. Among them all, described as country people, *pagani*, not one other Christian could be counted; so, in what appears to be a random sample of the 580s, the reporter was outnumbered twenty-five or fifty to one.[22] The implication in the two pieces of information can be supported with a great deal of other evidence, less vivid and specific though it may be. It raises a problem easily understood. Our idea of Christianity's place in the empire must be reduced not only in the cities, judged by the size of their meeting-places, but still more in the rural parts.

These written accounts in their contradiction of our usual way of seeing the early Christians return me to the two "impossible" questions I raised some pages earlier: Really, what was or constituted the City of God, and what were its proportions within the whole of the empire's population? Answers from the traditional sources don't seem to fit; nor can they be verified, as Jean-Marie Salamito would remind us. There remain, however, the answers afforded by the stones. From their testimony, at least in urban and suburban settings at scores of sites, numerically based estimates have been derived at many points in earlier chapters.

And if it is fair for Salamito to ask for facts, it seems to me equally fair to ask for contrary evidence as good as the archeological, before dismissing what the stones have to tell us.

3. Two churches

To address the apparent contradiction between the common idea of the City's size and its tangible imprint on the ancient world, I return to the title of a section, above (ch. 1 §3): "Suburbs". A lot of religion went on outside the walls. The picture familiar to us is of course drawn from the written record. It most often places third-century Christians in the cemeteries and there they are still to be found at their services well into the mid-fourth century. The fact is little noticed in modern accounts, therefore surprising. Later, of course, in eulogies delivered by bishops like Basil or Victricius in sermon form or in poems by such as Damasus or Paulinus, the cemeteries are seen as the setting for the celebration of martyrs' anniversaries, and these are acknowledged to be of great importance in worship at the time.

For martyr-cult the literary evidence is thus undeniably useful. Reliance on this alone, however, may lead to very strange conclusions (I leave them to a generation now past).[23] In contrast, the evidence from excavation is more inclusive and therefore less likely to mislead. Every province contributes to it, every rank of society is represented. It even allows a statistical approach: among all the places listed in the appendix, only one in ten can be shown to have had an in-city church, whereas in half of the sites the suburbs contained a funerary basilica or martyr-memorial. Regular mass could be celebrated in these without their losing their particular quality and purpose, in proximity and service to the dead, meaning not only the saints but the merely mortal as well. They might be (as they have been called) "roofed-over burial grounds" or "cemetery churches".

Particularly striking is the understanding of these Christian realities shown in the building program of the first Christian emperor. Whether he was so advised by some ecclesiastic like Ossius, as I would suppose, or whether he trusted to his own observations, he bestowed his favor on the memorializing of saints, Peter and Paul and Marcellinus in Rome and in Ostia, too. This was his decision in his first capital, to immense effect, since his favor was immense. But in an even more spectacular way he monumentalized communion with the dead in those six huge basilicas described above (fig. 4.9), each with a capacity equalling or close to that of St. Peter's itself. The fact invites reflection.

It invites reflection not only because of its scale but because of the silence that in time erased it, first on the ground and then from memory. Evidently it didn't fit within the religious preferences of the ecclesiastical authorities. Arrangements in a couple of these six structures were eventually adapted to a different, more enduring liturgy; in the others, worship declined, roofs collapsed from neglect, the stones of the walls became fair game for the casual depredations of builders needing a block, or a hundred blocks, or a carved lintel which could be easily pulled free and taken away in a cart. The entirety of the ancient capital as is well known became a gigantic quarry, wherever there were no occupants to protest and protect. Suburban structures were not exempt from pillage. By some point in the early Middle Ages, there were no longer any guardians in Constantine's great covered cemeteries. In the past these had served a far larger population than ever attended St. Peter's, to say nothing of all the smaller structures within the city wall. Once, they had served the requirements of obviously more favored rites; but favor faded, the rites themselves were in time given up. The fact points to a difference in worship between those who were at first served by these basilicas, and others who controlled their use: two kinds of Christianity.

In earlier times, even before the period of my study, rituals of private, familial remembrance of the dead were adopted for communion with martyrs as well. The two shared the same space. The gradual easy incorporation of the newer tradition into the older, that is, the development of martyr-cult out of family rites, has been often described (by Marrou, Février, Noël Duval, Jastrzebowska...), and on such scholars as these my own pages of description at various points depend. Beginning in Palestine, as was pointed out in the first chapter, above; then turning up by the second century in the province of Asia; next, in Africa in Carthage and to the south; so, across the generations, the Christians' celebration of their more glorious dead took hold everywhere. The proof is before us in stone. The growing number of churches which focused on the victims of persecution is very striking.

Most familiar are of course the Constantinian ones or, in Jerusalem, the examples of Constantinian inspiration but somewhat later. By the 350s, post-Constantinian martyr churches appear elsewhere in the east; pilgrim centers grow bigger and more numerous. Perhaps in the 370s Chalcedon's Euphemia-shrine was built. Its remarkable dimensions and rotunda are known to us in only written sources, summarized in the appendix. In the west, pope Damasus by the same decade had focused publicity on the discovery and enshrining of relics. These, every bishop wanted—or his people did. In the African provinces, Tebessa's cult-center almost matched Euphemia's (fig. 3.7). Martyr churches constructed over the victims of the Caecilianists were naturally re-dedicated post-411 by the victorious sect and sometimes no doubt lost their name, so as not to be identifiable as martyr churches at all; yet they may underlie buildings of a great size in continued use. Many others arose to recall the persecutions under Diocletian. Clearly there was a growing enthusiasm throughout the empire, ready to find expression in new construction; and the pace picks up dramatically after the period of my study.[24]

The scale of martyr-cult is clear both in the ample remains of memorial churches and in their number. This was where the action was. This was where the priest or bishop met with his congregation in the largest numbers—so the physical remains indicate in the west and the written descriptions show in eastern cities. The cult answered to a natural need; for address to divine power was never an idle exercise. It was meant to draw strength and assistance to the worshipper. You prayed *for* something, you were a suppliant: "begging", "requesting", "promising".[25] In reply, the martyrs represented that superhuman power which was accessible to the mass of people in a way the Triune God was not. The latter, the great judge, the divinity whose invoked descent in the eucharistic sacrament should be felt (so officiants declared) as "hair-raising"—this Power was not easily appealed to for life's ordinary difficulties that seemed so big to ordinary people; and extraordinary people, the eminent and wealthy, had difficulties of their own that even their wealth and eminence could hardly solve.

Augustine and other bishops tried to persuade their congregations to turn rather to the Triune God.[26] Their efforts were in vain. The saints, the focus always of pride and veneration, took over as the active agents of divinity on a level that could be approached by Everyman. The miracles they worked were increasingly sought, increasingly attested: sought from the blood-soaked garments of Cyprian in the mid-third century, attested in our sources from the first quarter of the fourth century on.[27] By then they were, for most believers, the center of belief. Hagiography in due course reflected the fact; graffiti, too, in the Roman catacombs and elsewhere, giving us the thoughts of pilgrims. New accessions to the sanctified rank were found in forgotten tombs, through visions, or in the person of a favorite bishop, a favorite priest or a celebrated ascetic—all, saints-in-the-making as they may be called—once they had passed into the Beyond. So urgent was the demand, their bodily remains in little bits or objects that had touched them might be made accessible to distant throngs. The practice is attested as early as Constantine's reign, that pioneer of piety bringing tokens of Saint Euphemia almost to his palace door. The bishop of Nola much later counted her among the holy ones whose dried traces, mere dust, he could receive and treasure in the basilica that he had built. She it was who presided over the Council of Chalcedon in 451.

In the generations leading up to Paulinus, to Chrysostom and Theodosius, church leaders spoke out against what they saw as the excesses of such piety, meaning, piety unregulated by the clergy. The widow Lucilla provoked harsh mockery from her bishop—this in the early 300s in Carthage, where she carried about a tiny precious box. It contained the relics of a martyr—"which one it was, who knows, and who knows if it's any martyr at all?" Just in this way, a much-engaged Christian visitor in Syria two generations later ridiculed "those who carry about some little container everywhere, wrapped in precious cloth with a bit of who knows what dust inside, kissing and worshipping it".[28]

Lucilla was a power in her church and for that reason, perhaps, not friendly regarded by the clergy. Her story concerns me only as a reminder of two other women who had money and used it in the service of martyr-cults of their own invention: Eusebia and Asclepia (ch. 2 at nn. 30 and 32). Their example may be aligned with the quite different hero-cults in Geneva and Philippi carried on into the local church from far earlier times. The impulse of worship can be seen bubbling up from these layman circles with a force the bishops couldn't withstand. The term "citizens and fellows of the faith" should be remembered, too, to indicate the originating force of martyr-cult in a city of the east (ch. 1 at n. 82); and many instances have been recalled, too, of low-level, low-key devotion to a martyr that eventually took form in some tiny shrine, and then a church, and then a pilgrim center (chs. 1, Huarté; other instances in chs. 2, 3, and 4).

More central to martyr-cult were anniversary observances, evidently involving great crowds of participants and occasionally exclaimed upon in a way that allows us to see them: for example, in a memorial church in Pontus, a very large one but not big enough to hold the crowd, or in the race-track outside their town, or near an open space allowing the parading about of a martyr's relics. The customs on display were taken over for the saints from the traditional family rites: staying up late, often all night, and eating, drinking, and dancing in a celebratory fashion, exactly as non-Christians had always done in honor of their own dead and as they continued to do in the same cemeteries, or next door (fig. 2.7). Such behavior was a common target of the clergy's reprobation from the mid-third century on. They were obliged, however, to speak with restraint; for, as Jerome and Augustine among others explain, the offenders were very many and their numbers made them important.[29] One more point of tension was, however, thus revealed, between two forms of Christianity. In rough terms, one was the choice of the Establishment, principally the clergy, in-city; the other, for everybody else, including some part of the farming population, beyond the city walls.

Between the established church, as it may be called, and the Christianity of the many, tension appears in further matters of worship a little after the persecutions had ended. Full public discussion of ecclesiastical affairs then became possible, and a council outlawed the lighting of candles at the tombs of the saints; yet this was a ban certainly not observed.[30] In mid-century, another council meeting at Laodicea (§28) forbade the holding of banquets in churches and the singing of psalms not properly authorized (§15). There is no saying how this could be reconciled with the attested practice and facilities of Antioch, Nola, or Carthage. Individual bishops forbade the adoption or advertising of martyrs unlicensed; new ones went on appearing. The authorities also showed their hostility to traditional forms of worship: you shouldn't dance, as only the heathen did; or you should do so, but only shuffling your feet a little; you shouldn't make it a party, or sing too loud, or throw happy glances about, and you certainly shouldn't have enough wine to affect your behavior. On certain days of the year, for good believers, *laetitia* might be quite proper; but it should be joy without merry-making. Observance of the high points in the year, at winter's turn, or again in the first full days of spring, should never get noisy. If it was a dinner put on for religion, then—no interrupting, no arguing or rude words, no reaching around the table, and always, modest portions. Leave a bit on the plate. A Christian also would be well advised to avoid memorial picnics for the dead—this, a real problem, given the universal importance of the rites and their deep roots in people's feelings and traditions.[31] The proper manners were thus taught to you by your betters, whose manners at their own dinners were so different and whose clothes made you ashamed of your own.

How your betters conducted their own selves in church is sometimes described. Their bishop protests, they sniggered and whispered.[32] Such behavior wasn't usual, however; and the usual, inviting no comment, is largely hidden. Some indications were gathered in an earlier chapter. Whether the setting may be the ordinary services, in-city, or in larger crowds in cemetery buildings like Antioch's or Tebessa's (figs. 1.13 or 3.7) is also generally unclear. Whatever can be further added from the remarks and implications in sermons has more to do with secular behavior, class, and values, than with religion. In short, seeing the early Christians at worship as the bishops saw them is possible only in unsatisfactory glimpses.

As to the religious practices preferred and natural among the great majority, the "95 per cent", here too the previous chapters show how difficult description must remain. It is not clear, but it is certainly not probable, that the very same members of the upper class who attended in-city regular and regulated services were not also to be found in the cemeteries. There, they had their own dear departed, their own Rosalia and Parentalia exactly like everyone else, though in better accommodations. Pilgrim scenes in Jerusalem and elsewhere provide good evidence regarding martyr-cult as well.[33] A passion for this among the higher classes is sometimes encountered in written sources from the very beginning; and my earlier chapters have offered examples of third- and fourth-century memorializing of martyrs through some private act at great enough expense to show up in stone—therefore the act of a rich person. Clustering of mausolea around saints' shrines at Manastirine in Greece or Kelibia in Africa may serve as proof. The elite of course wanted the benefit of burial *ad sanctos* like everyone else—indeed, demanded this of particular right both for their own selves and their family members. Saints' relics were taken up, too, as report of their efficacy became known. John Chrysostom celebrated the wonderful fact, Basil sent relics to a fellow bishop, Ambrose advertised how they had restored sight to the blind before his very eyes. The saints, it was acknowledged, could even reach out from their graves to punish or reward. They were alive.[34] Of this truth, in the century beyond my chosen time-line, stories upon stories supplied a flood of testimony, endorsed as much by the clergy as by the mass of the faithful; and so the two Christianities drew together—a little.

Clerical approval was, however, withheld from rites and customs that too clearly showed their origin among the common people. The two Christianities remained two. Thus, out of tune with the jubilation and apostrophes of Victricius at the receipt of relics (above, ch. 4), Zeno bishop of Verona can be heard grumbling about the wine, the dancing, the unbridled party mood of the celebrants at a saint's-day vigil. It was all much too pagan. Basil, Augustine, and others chimed in. What was popular could be accepted, yes, but only in part, only to the accompaniment of sour notes and with some necessary re-interpretation.

For example, Augustine. Speaking in his home church about one of Saint Cyprian's shrines to which he was often invited and where he appeared in fact a good ten times as a visiting preacher, he reminded his listeners,

> As you well know, those of you who know Carthage, there's a mensa of Cyprian constructed just there [where the saint met his death], a mensa to God, even though it's called the mensa of Cyprian, not because Cyprian ever ate there but because he was sacrificed there and because by that sacrifice he prepared this mensa—not so that he might give or receive food there but that upon that table sacrifice might be offered to God, to whom he himself had been offered. But the reason why this table of sacrifice, which is God's, is still called the mensa of Cyprian, is this: he was encircled there by persecutors, now, where it is venerated by his friends in prayer.[35]

Faced with the same problem in Nola, Paulinus was determined to see *pietas* in *refrigeria*, and to forgive the regrettable errors of those who were after all mere children (ch. 4 at n. 76). Augustine can be seen adopting the same tone while sanctifying the practice of offerings through metaphorical treatment. The intimate connection between the altar on the floor of the memorial basilica, and the crypt directly underneath, which he refers to, was usual, whether at St. Peter's or at Trieste (fig. 2.2). This he could accept; the mensa he could claim for the Eucharist; and the story of its origin in the cult of the dead he could simply re-write.

Still, recent or potential believers obviously found it difficult to conform to re-direction from the hierarchy, where so much that felt right, so much that was familiar and accepted by everyone you knew, was to be discarded. In consequence, they simply ignored what they were told, or some did, anyway, and to some degree. The most irritating are described by their bishops in a way that makes at least one thing clear: they were of the masses. Their behavior identifies them still more.[36] They were not heretics or sinners (who are spoken of in quite different terms) but "Christians in name alone," "neither Christian nor pagan," or "the half-converted," as they have been called more recently.[37] They were also simply "the more ignorant," *simpliciores*, in the assumption that their hearts were in the right place, as it might be said, and they should be forgiven, even though their customs were bizarre or even scandalous. Such was Paulinus' characterizing of them. Language that distanced the speaker from "the lowly city masses or rustics", as opposed to "the educated", or the devout from "the populace that thinks only of its belly", was common among the elite, both Christians and non-Christian.[38]

It can't have been very pleasant to overhear such talk, for those who belonged to the middling or lower classes; nor was it always in just this way that they saw themselves. Consider a certain remote community in an eastern province whose members were asked by a traveler whether they were really Christians at all, since to his mind they had it all wrong; they had not the least knowledge of even basic truths and teachings; but they answered very indignantly, they certainly *were* Christians. Or again, in a western province, consider the man who protested, "Indeed I do visit idols, I consult inspired men and soothsayers, but still I haven't forsaken the church of God—I'm a Catholic."[39] In the course of the changes post-Constantine on which everyone puts so much emphasis, rightly, I imagine that a great many people, especially in the rural areas and the smallest towns like Nola, spent their lives in an incomplete transition, having recourse to martyr-cult and cemetery celebrations, local shrines, traditional prayers and holy days, all in their own faith-full confusion. Indeed the description of the crowds at St. Felix which was quoted earlier almost fits such types.

Still further: if among the elite there were some who never bothered to come to church, in-city, or almost never, and whose neglect their bishops often deplored in their sermons, the same proportion of the neglectful may fairly be imagined among the 95 per cent. Yet they considered themselves Christians.

What then was a "Christian"? A definition in explicit, normative terms is in fact surprisingly hard to pin down. The proceedings and canons of councils don't spell it out, nor is it obvious anywhere else that we might expect to find it. It is difficult to think about in the abstract even today. Arthur Darby Nock in one and the same year published his opinion that you were not a believer except by adherence "body and soul" as it might be "prescribed by authority"—or, *per contra*, that a believer might result on the instant, beholding a miracle, with no need of any teaching at all! As a guide through these problems, no one is more likely than Nock to be quoted still today.[40] What if you declared your faith just by turning up at services? Your pastor would count you among his flock but the mocker would declare, "so, then, it's the walls that make a Christian."[41] Or the flock might turn up, but only once or twice a year, and they might be drunk, to the bishop's dismay.[42] If the definition required the active repudiating of anything or anyone non-Christian, that might well be too much—witness the use on Christian epitaphs of "DM" to stand for the ancestral prayer "to the gods and the favoring spirits".[43] If some mastery of scripture and teachings was necessary, then there could be no room for the *simpliciores*, and the role of class became too nearly determining.

"Christians" in historical terminology, not theological, we can only know as we see them in some act of worship. This might be in the synaxary churches for regular services as, for example, in S. Giovanni. But in Rome, the other seven large, or extremely large, basilicas will also be recalled, all in cemeteries. Here, unlike set services conducted by a priest, communion with a family's own dead could be sought in private celebrations or similarly with a martyr on some particular impulse, or instead, on a general anniversary like the Rosalia or on the saint's own day. At Tanagra this was the case (above, ch. 2), and in Carthage (fig. 5.1, with its many burials beneath the floor), or S. Sebastiano (fig. 4.10). No priest need preside (though on a martyr's anniversary, likely he would be present); the worshippers of one moment need not be the same as on some other. Thus the size of facilities need not have limited the number of worshippers who could be served over the course of a given week or year.

All of which suggests that what is needed for a good sense of the size and nature of the City of God is a model utterly different from the one presented and discussed in the first section of this chapter. What is needed in its place is the notion of a spectrum of religious affiliation ranging from the model itself and Jeradé (fig. 1.10), approved by the hierarchy and the elite, to an opposite extreme approaching total deviance or indifference—the latter amounting to something quite separate. The archeology seems to require this; common experience doesn't resist it. At the more familiar end can be seen the Establishment: ecclesiastical leadership, councils and theology, scriptural citations; at services, the synaxary, bishop, clergy, the two sexes separated; indigent enrolled women and catechumens, each group by itself; solea, incense, chanting (but not singing), and the chancel arch called the "Triumph"; in attendance, a laity almost wholly recruited from the local aristocracy—all this, one Christianity. In the other were the 95 per cent, worshipping in their own way. Except in the cult of the saints and a most bare-bones belief in Hellfire and Judgement which expressed itself in the press for burial *ad sanctos*, the two seem to have had little in common. Each had its own ways. Even on their common ground they stood somewhat apart, the clerical authority ranged against the faith of the many as it was expressed in traditional practices. These latter are not often revealed in the written record; or if mentioned, they are corrected. The archeological record, however, brings out a more ample, complicated reality than is usually allowed—more complicated because more human, and less perfect.

4. Numbers, again

"Perfect", however, is a word that hardly belongs in the assessment. It is normative; it is theological. What rather counts in historical terms is the weight of a development or institution in the shaping of people's lives. Now, of the two churches, it is obvious which is the more important, measured at least by the numbers provided for in built structures. At Rome, the space available for worship in-city, compared with the space available in cemeteries, was as one to ten or one to fifteen even without consideration of the casual off-and-on attendance I suggested above.[44] The same uneven ratio, more or less, can be found and I think easily defended across the empire. Perhaps in cities less minutely studied than Rome we should allow for the possibility of construction that has left no discoverable trace. To that degree, archeology will fail us, true; but there is no likelihood of any gross failure. A variety of sites serve as a control, where in fact digging has been quite extensive without yielding a very different picture from those sites less well reported, either in the number of places of worship, or in their size, or in their location. The surviving evidence is quite consistent in its indications, allowing us to meet the challenge of the doubter: "vérifier", said Jean-Marie Salamito, "prove it".

The congregants at in-city churches I have called "the 5 per cent", referring to their socioeconomic status. In Rome's catacombs, quantifiable indications of wealth and poverty can be teased out (at n. 18 in the preceding chapter) but not in any way that can be tied to one or another church. They only show how the city's Christians differed in what they could spend on burial arrangements. To go beyond this and show that the in-city churches served their own clergy and the wealthy, who were the few, we depend only on written evidence of such things as slave-ownership. But numbers are certainly not the whole story for the historian any more than they are for the theologian. The historian recognizes that the 5 per cent had the louder voice in the City of God just as they did in civil society, always—only, it is one thing to speak, and another to be obeyed. What can be learned from the cemeteries shows a large worshipful population "doing their own thing," as we would put it nowadays.

The capital conveniently supplies another statistic. It shows us not only the ratio between in-city construction and construction in cemeteries, that is, the suburban. Measuring the physical space available to the laity both within and without the walls, we can also determine the Christian total within Rome's general population. This amounted to <35,000 persons or <7 per cent at the turn of the fifth century. Once again, the evidence from Rome is not at odds with the evidence from cities anywhere else in the empire. I need not bring in, here, what can be easily checked in the appendix.

Exception should be made to the west and north of Italy: Spain, Gaul and so forth. Here, the urban samplings are too few and incomplete to be of much use to us; the degree of urbanization was quite different. The success or lack of success of conversion in rural areas was, however, suggested by the casual testimony of a traveller bound for Italy from Provence: the countryfolk around him, to a man, were heathens. This was in the mid-sixth century. A quite similar report was also recalled on the same page, above, where the region was eastern. It too told about the rural population, very incompletely converted. Since this population amounted to some four-fifths of the total across the empire, we must estimate the Christian portion of that whole at far less than the strictly urban: therefore not 7 per cent but more like 3 per cent.

A religious belief originating in the way Christianity is known to have done in urban settings, spreading from the established to new ones, and drawing in some membership from the local elite, until by a miracle the very emperor became a convert, himself—such a belief might very well attain the percentages just suggested for the turn of the fifth century. It is a real success story, proven beyond any doubt. At the end it commands the heights of law and political influence, it commands great money resources, displacing immemorial institutions at the heart of public life and silencing (or almost silencing) alternative beliefs and practices. All this sufficed also to produce a widespread acceptance beyond formal membership—by which I mean to include in Christianity's embrace a large number of semi-Christians, as they have been called. They are needed to explain certain crowd scenes in such major centers as Alexandria or Constantinople in the course of the second half of the fourth century and, of course, more clearly, later. To this extent we may say they are attested. Thus a share in the *urban* population approaching one-fifth seems to me quite conceivable—in the terms used by W. H. C. Frend, "a significant minority". The *rural* world and therefore the empire as a whole unit of census remained quite a different story.

Nevertheless, a City of God in the year 400 claiming only a 3 per cent share of the total population contradicts, head on, the picture to be found in any modern account I can think of. For the historian it is a problem, a *skandalon*.

One response would be to deny the validity of the picture I discover at Rome, Constantinople, Alexandria, Carthage, Tipasa, Salona, and other sites less fully known; indeed, to deny the whole appendix on which my findings are based; and in addition, to deny or somehow explain away the limitations on conversion in the country parts. I leave it to others to make this case.

Alternatively, I may suggest that the model of religious life is wrong, in which we try to fit what we find principally in the written evidence. It is on this evidence that modern accounts rely. It naturally reflects what a particular sort of person chose to talk about: a person of a particular class, most particularly interested in religion, resident in a city or naturally sympathetic to the values and culture that prevailed among the urban elite, and of course with the ideas of the time regarding analysis and reporting, through whose eyes we try to see the ancient world.

But imagine analysis à la Jean-Marie Salamito, in terms of which nothing about success and demography would be accepted that could not be verified. Suppose that attested conversion beyond the cities in fact proceeded very slowly, far more slowly and incompletely than is generally conjectured. Such slow progress would explain patches of success here and there, but matching areas of total disregard for the message where nobody had bothered to disseminate it with any seriousness. It would explain, in the succeeding millennium up to the very edge of modern times, unreformed beliefs and rites such as I have seen, myself, remaining in many parts of what was once the Roman empire, a witness to the very reluctant abandoning of the old ways.[45]

So much for totals, the rural world included. Within my suggested model, the communitarian expression of belief that was played out in cities— the formal, organized, scripturally supported, public, well-seen and well funded parts of religion—could be left in the hands of the 5 per cent. For other worshippers, address to a superhuman Being for strength and favor in return for prayers and vows might be imagined as only an occasional thing, untaught or at least not consciously learned. Yet they were not irreligious. There was, after all, never a catechuminate in Isis-worship or the worship of Athena; yet each in her time had her millions of the faithful. They came to her when they needed to. Religion can only have been spontaneous; in people's homes it was perhaps little thought on though comforting; and that comfort, by many, was only rarely sought in any serious way.

We might for comparison try to calculate the available square footage for worship at Isis' or Athena's shrines measured against the likely population round about; as, equally, the square footage for the laity in the churches of tenth century Bordeaux and its surrounding territory (I offer the site at random, knowing nothing of medieval religious history). That footage—was it very considerable? Does it imply the attendance of more than 10 or 15 per cent of the population? What really was the place of worship in people's daily lives? The question is as obvious as can be. Anyone who wants to understand some event or development in the past considers the permeation of society by this or that belief, including the religious, of course—Protestantism and the capitalist spirit, the Great Awakening and the abolition of slavery, fanaticism and religious wars.[46] It is certainly useful to consider such factors to the extent they can, in some sense, be quantified; and if they can't be, then let that be clear.

The model, the spectrum here imagined, as it fits the ancient cults, seems equally suited to the cult of Salsa or Euphemia. The saints' petitioners felt no need to trouble a priest. By one definition it would be fair to call them Christians; by another definition, semi-Christian or heathen, depending on the temper of the observer. Their numbers are beyond our counting, not least because no observer likely to leave an account in writing at the time was much interested in them.

Further: if the proportions of the two Christianities may not be anywhere near those precise figures I have used for purposes of explanation, 5 per cent and 95 per cent, it is still more difficult to measure the pace and manner of their eventual rapprochement, by which the Established became more effectively dominant over all. This process nevertheless went on. Wealth, social standing, and above all, organization and discipline insured that something more or less like the modern model (above, at the beginning of this chapter) would eventually prevail. It would prevail and thus quietly bring to an end the worshipful life of Rome's Six basilicas and similar traditions, or independence, elsewhere, long after the period with which my study is concerned. Thus the division within the City of God would gradually became less divisive.

As to the proportion of Christians (however defined) to non-Christians in the several centuries post-400, this must remain obscure. The anecdotal evidence invites guesswork of which there is more than enough in print; the archeological suggests a very slow advance of belief.[47] But the problems lie beyond my chosen boundaries.

Abbreviations

CT	*Codex Theodosianus*
CIL	*Corpus inscriptionum latinarum*
CSEL	*Corpus scriptorum ecclesiasticorum Latinorum*
DACL	*Dictionnaire d'archéologie chrétienne et de liturgie*
HE	*Historia ecclesiastica*
ICUR	*Inscriptiones Christianae urbis Romae septimo saeculo antiquiores*, eds. B. de Rossi and A. Silvagni (Rome 1922–)
PG	*Patrologiae cursus completus*, series Graeca, ed. J. P. Migne
PL	*Patrologiae cursus completus*, series Latina, ed. J. P. Migne
RAC	*Reallexikon für Antike und Christentum*
RE	*Realencyclopädie der classischen Altertumswissenschaft*

Appendix
Churches Built before 400

Note: for the estimates of laity space, which are all obviously approximate, see the discussion around figs. 1.6 and 1.8 in the first chapter.

The Eastern empire

Site unspecified: Porphyry in the 270s reports Christians to be "erecting great buildings" just like non-Christian temples (*Adv. Christianos frg.76* quoted by Macarius Magnes 4.21, in White 1990, 104f., 110, 117, 129); Euseb., *HE* 8.2.1, Diocletian's First Decree of 303 aimed to destroy "houses of prayer", *proseukterion tous oikous*; 8.2.4, *tas ekklesias*; 8.17.9, 9.9a.11, persecution ends in A.D. 313 and the emperor bids Christians to rebuild "the houses, *oikoi ekklesion*, in which they had assembled" pre-311; and in 383 Christians are still assembling in private houses modified for worship, which they are forbidden to do if judged heretical (*CT* 16.5.11, issued from Constantinople, *nec ad imaginem ecclesiarum parietes privatos ostendant*)

Aleppo (Chaleb): a "Great Church" by the end of the 4th c. (Kleinbauer 1973, 103)

Alexandria:
(1) the metropolitan church, "the big one", built in the period 313–28 (Athan., *Apol. Ad Constantium* 15, *PG* 25.613Af.)
(2) Epiphanius, *Adv. haer.* 69.2 (*PG* 42.204B), lists nine churches in the city and its suburbs in the 'teens of the 4th c., to be expanded in terms of the number of priests to a total of 23, see Martin (1996) 180
(3) a church built by gift of a lay-person, the rich Theodora, at Athanasius' urging (Galvao-Sobrinho 2009, ch. 7 n. 1093, the *Synaxarium Alexandrinum* 2.71)

Amaseia (Pontus, north-central Turkey): in 320s, churches (plural) are razed or closed (Eusebius, *HE* 10.8; *Vita Const.* 2.2; Basil, *Ep.* 226.2, *PG* 32.843B)

Ancyra: in the city and its territory, Novatian churches in mid-4th c. (Soz., *HE* 8.1, *PG* 67.1512C)

Antinoopolis (Saih Abada in Egypt, ca. 150 km south of the Fayum):

(1) a basilica from the last quarter of the 4th c., in a cemetery (Grossman 1989, 2.1872)
(2) a church of the 4th c. inside the city (Grossman 1989, 2.1872)

Antioch (Syria):
(1) a church destroyed by Diocletian and then rebuilt by the bishop of 314–320, called "the old church" where Chrysostom sometimes preached (Paverd 1970, 8f., 12f., 17)
(2) a number of suburban churches of the 4th c. referred to in literary sources, no doubt in the cemeteries (esp. Soz., *HE* 7.3, *PG* 67.1421B, mentioning "one of the suburban *ekklesiai*"; Theodoret, *HE* 1.2, several in 320; Petit 1955, 315, 317; several for the Meletians by the 360s, Soc., *HE* 3.2 in Downey 1963, 176, 182; also Soz., *HE* 5.13, *all'idia ekklesiazon ... sphas tes ekklesias apeschisan*)
(3) a cemetery church of no great size built outside the Daphne-gate where Chrysostom delivered his *Homil. in martyres*, seen as an old one even by the early 4th c. (Paverd 1970, 9f. and *PG* 50.664)
(4) a second cemetery church in the suburbs in existence by the mid-4th c. (Paverd 1970, 9)
(5) sources declare Constantine in 327 began the construction of "the foremost church" of Antioch, west-facing, "the Great Church", "the Golden", sometimes called "the Octagon" and described in sources as "circular" in appearance, somewhere on the same small island where the 1st c. B.C. hippodrome was built next to the palace. It was dedicated in 341 but does not survive; described by Euseb., *Vita Const.* 3.50, and *De laude Const.* 9.15, an *anaktoron* which would be a natural translation of "basilica", but cf. Paverd 1970, 3f., 6f.; Downey 1963, 144; meant like the hippodrome for the emperor, as at Constantinople and Thessalonica, 118; Kleinbauer 1973, 111ff.; Brandenburg 1995a, 52ff.; Brandenburg 1998, 20; perhaps referred to for the 360s by Soz., *HE* 4.13 (*PG* 67.1144B), "THE church of the Antiochenes," *ekklesia*
(6) "the new church" to which Chrysostom refers, sometimes taken to be "the Octagon" and otherwise unknown (Paverd 1970, 13f.)
(7) two churches built from previous structures (Malal. p. 319 Bonn and Evagr., *HE* 1.16, in Deichmann 1939, 115)
(8) just across the Orontes at the modern Kaoussié, a cruciform martyr-cult *ekklesia* built in the 370s or 381, dedicated to St. Babylas, the central square measuring 16 x 16 m and the side arms measuring 25 x 11 m (Lassus 1938, 5ff., 38, 299f. plan, and passim; Lassus 1940, 1.340f., 343, and fig. 4; Lassus 1947, 123f., plan in fig. 51)

Antioch (Pisidia in SW Turkey): a basilica built in the last quarter of the 4th c., gift of a bishop-to-be, the total length being about 62 m, narthex included, but the laity space measuring only ca. 26 x 20 m to serve <500 (Kitzinger 1974, 386 fig. 59, 392f.)

Anz (Syria): oriented rural church of ca. 11.6 x 5.5 m dating to the 1st half of the 4th c., with room for <50 (Nussbaum 1965, 1.34)

Apamea: a church built out of a ruined Zeus temple (Theodoret, *HE* 5.21.7, in Deichmann 1939, 115)

Aphrodisias in Cilicia: a basilica with side aisles built in about the 360s, St. Pantaleon's, beautifully covered in its entire floor with mosaics of ca. 400, with a laity space of ca. 13 x 11 m, thus accommodating <125 (Budde 1987, 34 and fold-out plan). The mosaic was the gift of several persons—one, a deacon—for miraculous healing; and there are several burials within the church (25–28, 33) indicating that it lay in a cemetery (but unexcavated)

Babisqa: late 4th c. church (Lassus 1947, 188, 263; Sodini et al. 1989, 349)

Baris (Isparta just south of Seleuceia in Pisidia): a 4th c. church built by the bishop (Rott 1908, 9, 50)

Batuta (Syria): a church of mid-4th c. (Sodini et al. 1989, 348)

Ba'udeh (Ba'uda, Syria): small church datable to 392 (Butler 1929, 39; Sodini et al. 1989, 349)

Berytus (Beirut): literary sources show a church of unknown date burnt in the 360s and soon rebuilt (L. J. Hall 2004, 172f.)

Bosra (Syria): a civilian basilica turned into a church, undated (Butler 1929, 14 and ill. 5)

Brad (Syria): a late 4th c. basilica built by the architect Julianus, with mosaic inscriptions naming a priest-donor; with laity space of ca. 30 x 13 m, thus serving <350 (Butler 1929, 18f., 34f.; Lassus 1947, 31, 74, 169 fig. 77 plan, pl. xxix, 1–3; 231, 257, the text of the Julianus inscription, 259; Nussbaum 1965, 1.54; J. Lassus in N. Duval et al. 1972, 219, 221 fig. 4, D, plan; Gamber 1976, 2.19 Abb. 32, plan and reconstruction)

Burdi-Hedar (Burdj Hedar, Syria): "West church", a small one of the mid-4th c. (Butler 1929, 32; Nussbaum 1965, 1.58)

Caesarea (Cappadocia): shrine, a "vast edifice" to St. Mamas dating from ?345 (Maraval 1985, 371)

Capernaum (Palestine): indications that a house is that of Peter where Jesus visited, and where subsequently worship was conducted, making it a house-church; so, Corbo (1993) 71ff.; but the proportions of the space and other considerations make me doubt the identification

Chalcedon: St. Euphemia's shrine was built before (perhaps many years before) 387, where supplicants came with their prayers and requests and where famous miracles were performed. It was a complex of three buildings: an open court surrounded by porticoes, leading to a closed hall of similar proportions, opening on a rotunda containing the silver casket in which lay the martyr's remains, accessible to infusions by a hole in the top through which the saint's blood was regularly recovered by the local bishop with a sponge. Since the middle structure could hold the thousand or so clergy attending the Council in 451, it must have been as large as any church in the East (Evagrius, *HE* 2.3, *PG* 86.2193Af.; MacMullen 2006, 4, 79, 84; *Dictionnaire d'histoire et de géographique ecclésiastiques* 15, 1963, 1409; *Lexikon für Theologie und Kirche* 3, 1995, 991)

Çukurca (near Afyon in Turkey), an inscription perhaps of the 3rd c. announces the stone as part of "the house of God", a now-lost church (Levick et al. 1993, 82)

Cyzicus: a church in mid-4th c. (Soc., *HE* 3.11, *PG* 67.409B)

Damascus:
  (1) Ambrose says that two churches existed in the 360s, then were burnt, and only one rebuilt (L. J. Hall 2004, 185)
  (2) the Jupiter temple reconfigured for a church named after St. John, in late 4th c. (Ulbert 1989, 434)

Diocaesareia (Cilicia):
  (1) a cemetery church of the second half of the 4th c. memorializing a martyr; a partial plan suggests side aisles and dimensions ca. 23 x 23 m (Keil and Wilhelm 1931, 60)
  (2) St. Stephen's, ca. 30 x 20 m, second half of 4th c. (Keil and Wilhelm 1931, 61f.)

Dura (Doura Europos): a house-church by the 240s (Kraeling 1967, 3ff.; 10ff., 38, and passim; Krautheimer 1983, 16 and fig. 17)

Ephesus: the name and site of any 4th c. church unknown; the St. Mary cathedral alleged to date to the 4th c. (Sodini 1989, 421) but the suggestion cannot be right (Karwiese 1989, 27)

Euchaïta (Avkat, roughly 300 km NE of Ankara): a grand martyr-memorial described in the 380s (Delehaye 1923, 130f.; Bernard 1968, 302, 305)

Fafirtin (Fafertin, Syria): "a comparatively large" rural church datable to 372, "the earliest dated ... basilical" church in the province, built under (that is, by) its bishop, measuring on the inside 23.2 x 14.6 m, thus providing a laity space for <300 (Butler et al. 1930, 327f., ill. 370; Lassus 1947, 63 fig. 32, 177, 253; Lassus and Tchalenko 1951, 79); but here, "the whole of the central nave in front of the bema seems to have been closed to the people" (Taft 1968, 342)

Gaza: the bishop in the third quarter of the 4th c. builds a church (Galvao-Sobrinho 2009, ch. 7 n. 1094, *Acta Sanctorum* Feb. 26, *Vita Porph.* p. 648)

Gerasa (Jerash, Syria): an oriented cathedral with side aisles of the 370s? or third quarter of the 4th c. measuring 40 x 21 m on the interior, into which the chancel advances 10 m, leaving ca. 26 x 20 m for the laity, thus for <500 persons; but there are other features probably diminishing the laity space further (Crowfoot 1940, 1.324; Crowfoot 1941, 58, 60 fig. 12; and to be noted is the absence of any church in the city certainly earlier than 464, in B. Ward-Perkins 1998, 371–410 passim)

Huarte (Syria, ca. 15 km north of Apamea): a basilica of the 390s, measuring ca. 17 x 10 m, with side aisles, conjectural beneath the later basilica (Canivet 1980, 88 fig. 1 and 91)

Isruq (Syria): a mid-fourth c. church (with nothing further known nor location shown on maps in Tchalenko 1953–58, 1.336)

Jeradé (Syria): on a single page a church attributed to both the 4th c. and 5th c. (Lassus 1947, 31; Sodini et al. 1989, 356f. and fig 88, from Tchalenko)

Jerusalem:
(1) Constantine's church of the Holy Sepulchre, the Anastasis or Martyrion, west-facing, built on the site of the Aphrodite temple, with two pairs of side aisles, ca. 50 x 33.5 m measured from the top of the apse, but within the nave, ca. 37 x 33.5 m serving <800 (Euseb., *VC* 3.3.26f.; F.-M. Abel in *DACL* 7.2313–17 s.v. "Gérusalème", noting close similarities with the Nativity church plan and, fig. 6178, showing the extended chancel and solea; Deichmann 1939, 107; Orlandos 1952–57, 33, reconstruction; Coüasnon 1974, 14ff., 36–44 passim; Corbo 1981 passim, with the Constantinian plan, vol. 2 pl. 3; Krautheimer 1983, 23; Maraval 1985, 67; Deichmann 1993, Abb. 16; Brenk 1995, 98 and Abb. 16; Brandenburg 1998, 18f., Abb. 3; M. E. Johnson 2000, 490). To its west, beyond a court, was a rotunda with an external diameter of ca. 32 m and a concentric inner circle ca. 21 m across with altar area at the center. In this latter, the laity space might accommodate a few hundreds; the ambulatory around it was reserved for processing (Kleinbauer 1987, 284; Brandenburg 1995a, 54). From *Peregrinatio Silviae* [*Egeriae*] 24.8 and 25.3 (*CSEL* 39.73ff.) we see the *ecclesia maior* within a few yards of the cave-shrine so incense in the latter is enjoyed in the former
(2) another Constantinian memorial church, the Eleona, with the laity space measuring ca. 15 x 18 m (Deichmann 1939, 115; Hoddinott 1963, 35; Tsafrir 1993, 2; Wilkinson 1993, 25)
(3) other Constantinian memorial churches, of the Nativity at Bethlehem with two sides aisles and no clear laity-space dimensions, 32 x 32 m or smaller, and thus, room for <500 person; with attached octagon, razed in the 6th c. (Maraval 1985, 272f.); also at Mamre (Nussbaum 1965, 1.69; Deichmann 1939, 33; Deichmann 1993, fig. 6; Tsafrir 1993, 7f.; Wilkinson 1993, 25; Brenk 1995, 92 and Abb. 13)

Kalota (Syria): a church in which the nave is 16.85 x 6.15 m, and the ambo is only 3.10 m from the doorway, so that the worshippers can have clustered only in the side aisles each, 2.6 m wide—the laity space accommodating fifty or sixty? (Butler 1908–30, 316 and plan, ill. 349 on p. 324)

el-Kefr (Syria): a church of 392, a gift by a great imperial official, *dux et comes* (Littmann et al. 1921, 3.309 no. 670, the dedicatory inscription; Lassus 1947, 251)

Kharab Shems ("Chems", Syria): a rural 4th c. church (Butler 1929, 31f.; Butler 1908–30, 323f., ill. 363; Butler et al., 1930, 72; Lassus 1940, 1.350; Lassus 1947, xxi and pl. x; Nussbaum 1965, 54f., 4th or 5th c.); or 5th c.? (Lassus 1967, 40)

Laodicea Combusta (Kekaumene, Lycaonia): an *ekklesia* built by a bishop in Constantine's reign (White 1990, 136; 1997, 171–78)

Lebaba (Deir Ali ca. 3 miles south of Damascus): an inscription of 318/9 records the construction of an assembly place of the village Marcianists, *synagoge komes Lebabon*, by the presbyter (LeBas-Waddington's *Inscriptions grecques et latines de la Syrie* no. 2558, in Harnack 1908, 1.124; White 1997, 140)

Nazianzus (modern Nenizi in Cappadocia): a church standing by the 370s (Mitchell 1993, 68)

Neocaesareia: Dirsi Farag on the Euphrates, a three-aisled basilica built in the 340s (Ulbert 1989, 443)

Negev area: small churches dated to the second half of the 4th c. at Kurnub, Eboda, and Subeita (Shereshevski 1991, 30 and 43 and 76—the reference, thanks to J. Fitzgerald); on-site dating of the 1970s seems not to have been checked subsequently

Nicomedia: a large prominent church near city center in early 4th c. (Lactantius, *De mort. persecut.* 12.3f., *PL* 7.213B)

Oxyrhynchus (Egypt): in POxy 2673 of a. 304, mention of an *ekklesia* in a nearby village, and POxy 903 mentioning another early 4th c. church building (White 1997, 166), where the town's population may be set at no less than 30,000 (Tacoma 2006, 42f.)

Panopolis (Egypt): an *ekklesia* mentioned on a certain street, end of 3rd c. (White 1990, 122)

Pergamum: a church built out of a temple, ca. 400, with two narrow side aisles and laity space of ca. 10 x 10 m, thus serving <90 (Deubner 1977–78, 228 plan, 249)

Perge (Cilicia): a 4th c. church (Herzfeld 1930, 123; Orlandos 1952–57, 49)

Qirk Bizzeh (Qirkbize or Qirqbize, Syria): oriented rural church in a private house with no side aisles and entry on the south side, 1st half of the 4th c., for <40 persons (Lassus and Tchalenko 1951, 97, 99, fig. 2-3; Tchalenko 1953-58, 1.319, 325, of the 320s; 2. pl. cv; Nussbaum 1965, 1.34; N. Duval 1978, 533; White 1990, 129)

Qubbet es-Shih (Syria): a small rural church, ca. 15 x 5 m, built by a bishop and his priest, datable to the 4th c. (Piccirillo 1981, 115-18)

Resafa (Sergioupolis): a memorial chapel to St. Sergius outside the fortified town from shortly after his martyrdom in the early 4th c., known from literary evidence (Ulbert 1989, 445)

Roueiha (Syria): 4th c. church (Lassus 1947, 31)

Sardis: mid-4th c. church of only 7 x 6 m inside a temple enclosure (Nussbaum 1965, 1.126)

Seleuceia (Syria): of the 3rd quarter of the 4th c., a basilica with side aisles sitting on top of certain relics of Saint Thecla (Maraval 1985, 357)

Selge: in Pisidia in southern (modern) Turkey, around 400, a basilical church was built out of a disused odeon, its dimensions ca. 32 x 24 m but its laity space ca. 18 x 24 m, with two side aisles, for < 350 persons (Vaes 1984-86, 364, 388)

Serjilla: a 4th c. church measuring c. 16.6 x 11.8 m, serving <175 persons (Lassus 1947, 29ff. and fig. 12)

Shechem (Syria/Israel): an early, perhaps the earliest, cruciform 4th c. memorial built over Jacob's tomb (Deichmann 1993, 85)

Tyre: a basilica of unknown date, destroyed in the early 4th c. persecutions, rebuilt afterwards as is known through Eusebius' description (cf. esp. Orlandos 1952-57, 31f., reconstruction in fig. 11)

Umm Idi-Djimal (Oumm el-Jimal, Syria): the so-called Julianus basilica after its founding bishop, without aisles and with laity space of ca. 21 x 75 m effectively limited by bema and pilasters to <100 persons (Lassus 1947, 26 and fig. 9, "end of the 4th c."; Nussbaum 1965, 1.44f. and 2.13 Abb. 18; White 1997, 141-51, setting the reconstruction at late 4th/ early 5th; rightly dated to 345, and the only Christian building in the south-Syria survey of Restle 1989, 374; Shereshevski 1991, 115)

Zela (Pontus): mention of an existing *ekklesia* (Basil, *Ep.* 226.2, *PG* 32.843B)

GREECE INCLUDING SALONA, AND LOWER DANUBE

Constantinople:
(1) the Constantinian cemetery Church of the Holy Apostles, known only from literary sources (Krautheimer 1983, 56; Hoddinott 1963, 43; C. and L. Pietri 1990, 208; Brandenburg 1995, 71; and above, ch. 2 n. 3)
(2) Hagia Sophia, begun 326/330, collapsed and was rebuilt and consecrated in 360; destroyed by fire in 404; and once again rebuilt to a new plan (cf. ch. 2 n. 3; Dagron 1974, 399 on the collapse).
(3) Hagia Eirene built by Constantine, a basilica still standing in 381 (Hoddinott 1963, 43)
(4) several Novatian churches in the mid-4th c., evidently in addition to non-Novatian ones (Soc., *HE* 2.38, *PG* 67.528B, and elsewhere also speaking of churches in the plural)
(5) toward the end of the 4th c., *martyria plurima*, "a good number of martyr-churches" (*Peregrinatio S. Silviae* [*Egeriae*] 23.9, *CSEL* 39.72)

Dimitrias: a basilica with side aisles, dating to ca. 400, with a laity space of ca. 15 x 10 m, taking account of an intrusive chancel (Pallas 1977, 54f., fig. 32)

Epidaurus: a basilica with two pairs of side aisles, measuring ca. 20 x 22 m, probably of the late 4th c. and with laity space, minus the intrusion of the chancel into the nave and four ranges of columns, sufficient for <300 persons (Orlandos 1952–57, 51, fig. 26; Sodini 1970, 705)

Iader (Zadar, Croatia): a church built over shops on the forum with its apse toward the east, with laity space of ca. 11 x 7 m, thus serving <65 persons, made out of a bishop's lodging in the first half of the 4th c. or toward the close (Chevalier 1996, 1.102 and pl. XVIII; 2 fig. 1; Uglesic 2002, 12f.; Vezic 2005, 18–23)

Muline (Ugljan, a little north of Iader): a small martyr-church of the second half of the 4th c., 10.5 x 6 m (Uglesic 2002, 86–89)

Narona (Vid): a church of the late 4th c. or more probably the early 5th, the city's first cathedral, with laity space of ca. 15 x 9 m, thus serving <150 (references in Carra Bonacasa and Morfino 2003–4, 27n.; Chevalier 1996, 1.436ff.; 2.pl.1.xv, fig. 2)

Philippi:
(1) in the suburbs, a basilica discovered in 1956 with ambo intruding far into the nave, leaving ca. 13 x 8 m open to the laity, and another 100 square meters in the aisles (Pelekanides 1961, 117 with plan, 173, and passim; Hoddinott 1963, 98ff., fig. 44, and 102ff.; Pilhofer 1995–2000, 2.337)

(2) foundations of "a simple hall church" ca. 29.5 x 10.5 m beneath the Octagon (Gounaris 1984, 137; White 1997, 184f.; Duval 1999, 19 fig. 23; Pilhofer 1995–2000, 2.337f.)

(3) the preceding structure was succeeded by an octagonal church (ch. 2 nn. 10f.; Pelekanides 1978, 393; Barnea 1984, 660)

Pola (Pula, Croatia):
(1) a church dating to the early decades of the 4th c. (surely post-313, since it is inside the city), built on the ruins of an earlier baths (Marusic 1978, 569)
(2) the later-named St. Thomas church built in the 390s (ibid.)

Porec (Parentum on the map, Parenzo): vestiges of a room of a private house used for worship in late 3rd c. by its owner, possibly Maurus named on a sarcophagus as bishop and *confessor*, whose cult then took root here in a meeting hall; over-built by a basilica ca. 20 x 8.5 m, with modern debate over the chronology, but pre-400 (Molajoli 1943, 10f.; Marusic 1978, 568; Cantino Wataghin 1989, 175f.; Caillet 1993, 305, fig. 214; Cuscito 1995, 96; Cuscito 1998, 186, 201; Bratoz 1999, 429f., 435f.; Terry and Maguire 2007, 3); this, joined on its south side by the much larger footing of ca. 35 x 17.5 m built after the reign of Valentinian (364–378—a coin find) and further solidified and dignified perhaps a century later to make the Eufrasian basilica (Molajoli 1943, 10ff., 17, 25; Cantino Wataghin 1989, 174ff.)

Sagvar (Pannonia = Hungary): no church pre-400, but an identifiably Christian 4th c. cemetery with two chapels (Burger 1966, 154, 162)

Salona:
(1) epigraphic evidence for a "old" church, perhaps of the 320s, which was covered over by new building toward the turn of the 5th c.; its remains, now lying under the much bigger northern one of a pair built next to each other; it once offered ca. 26 x 21 m space for the laity (Egger 1917, 80, fig. 151; 82, fig. 156; 90ff., fig. 176; 138; Rendic-Miocevic 1991, 373; Caillet 1993, 384; Marin 1994, xvi)
(2) [Manastirine cemetery-church wrongly dated to the second quarter of the 4th c., with an intrusive solea leaving ca. 15 x 20 m (earlier discussions superseded by N. Duval et al. 2000, 645f.)]
(3) Kapljuc cemetery-church of the mid-4th c. (Brønsted 1928, passim; Dyggve 1951, 79f., 83, 94, pl. 4.26f.; Marin 1986, 222; Marin 1989, 2.1231)

Serdica: a cemetery church of the 4th c. (N. Duval and Popovic 1984, 375)

Sirmium (modern Mitrovica on the Save):
(1) in a cemetery to the east, an oriented apsidal building dedicated to St. Eirenaeus, ca. 32 x 15 m containing ca. 100 burials and fragments of many round or rectangular mensae, built and in use from mid-fourth century, cf. Boskovic (1974) 627ff. and fig. 18, and Duval (1979) 82ff.—with many points doubtful

(2) in a cemetery to the west, a St. Sinerus memorium ca. 30 x 19 m with nave only and burials both inside and close in around walls from the early fourth century (Boskovic 1974, 625ff.; Duval 1979, 66, 82)

(3) across the river in the Macvanska cemetery a well-preserved oriented apse facing a building now destroyed, which may have been unroofed (in Dyggve's term, a basilic discoperta?), cf. Boskovic (1974) 629ff. and fig. 18; Duval 1979, 84ff.

Stobi (in modern Macedonia): near city center in the 2nd half of the 4th c. a small cathedral was built, with side aisles, oriented, ca. 30 x 16 m or, for the laity, ca. 22 x 14 accommodating <275, this being doubled in size around the turn of the 5th c., but with no more laity space, since the nave was now wholly reserved for the priesthood and liturgy (Wiseman 2006, 795–99)

Thasos: a small basilica on the agora, built in the 4th c. (Hoddinott 1963, 106), evidently post-313

Thebes in Thessaly: an original church, the plan now lost, underlying that of the early 5th c., and lying over the crypt of S. Demeter (Soteriou 1929, 239)

Thessalonika: a now-lost small chapel for the cult of St. Demeter, underlying the 5th c. basilica, an apsidal adaptation of rooms in a baths-building so as to enclose the Demeter-tomb (Bakirtzis 1995, 60, correcting Spieser 1984, 114, 167, who would date both this and the St. George church to the 6th c.)

Trieste:
(1) a private chapel, "oratorio" in the cemetery pre-300 (Pross Gabrielli 1969, 18–22) to which was added post-313 a rectangular hall for the community ca. 11 x 8 m with a wooden altar in the center; and at the end of the 4th c., the chapel was built over to become an apsidal martyr-shrine with a stone table, a *mensa*, in the center of the chancel; see ch. 2 at n. 9
(2) inside the city from mid-4th c. in a private residence, a chapel to family members seen as saints (Pross Gabrielli 1969, 22)

North Africa

Aïn el Ksar (a little southeast of Sétif): a chapel 27 x 16 m with a martyr-mensa, and suggestions of a 4th c. date (Y. Duval 1982, 1.346)

Aïn Ghorab: a martyr church near the edge of the city, dating to the 4th or early 5th c., with the apse, *tribunal*, dedicated to a local saint and paid for by one Sabinianus for self, wife, and children (Leschi 1957, 307–10; Y. Duval 1982, 149f.)

Altava (Ouled Mimoun, Mauretania Tingitana): an inscription refers to a *bassilica* (!) *dominica*, datable to 308–337, perhaps precisely 309 (Février 1970a, 209f.; Ferrua 1977, 227;

N. Duval 1978, 529, expressing caution about dating; Y. Duval 1982, 506f.; White 1997, 240ff.)

Ammaedara (Haïdra): a west-facing martyr-church of the second half of the 4th c. with side aisles and a second altar above a tomb, leaving a laity space of ca. 32 x 15 m, thus serving <425 persons (N. Duval and Y. Duval 1966, 2.1153f. fig. 1; N. Duval 1975, 85; N. Duval et al. 1981, 202ff.; N. Duval 1995a, 98, 107ff.)

Bou Ismail (Castiglione) in Mauretania Caesariensis: a 4th c. church with side aisles (Gui et al. 1992, 1.44ff.)

Bou Takrematen (ca. 50 miles northwest of Timgad): a church ca. 25 x 11 m, dated only by 4th c. *mensa martyrum* (Gui et al. 1992, 179, and Y. Duval 1982, 154 fig. 168 photo of the mensa)

Bourkika (ca. 10 miles southeast of Tipasa): meager ruins of a chapel with a half-dozen burials in it and an inscribed *mensa marturorum* honoring Renatus and Optata (Y. Duval 1982, 1.384ff.)

Caesarea (Cherchel): a martyr's shrine or chapel (cella) of the 4th c. known only from an inscription (Y. Duval 1982, 381f.)

Carthage:
(1) basilica Maiorum, thus celebrating the martyrs Felicitas and Perpetua, in the Mcidfa suburb close to the late great "memoria Cypriani", measuring ca. 60 x 44 with two pairs of four side aisles, built in the 320s, possibly earlier (identical with the Restituta, Meer 1961, 479; Delattre 1907, 516 and 1908, 66, 68, "basilique funéraire ou église cimitériale," distinct from the "Restituta", infra; Ennabli 1982, 7, 11; idem 1997, 9 fig. 3; 20, 129ff., 133, 147, dating it to "the beginning of the 4th c., coins of Licinius and Constantine" being the evidence; but her reference supplies no mention of coins, and the emperors indicated would rather point to the second or third decade of the 4th c.); rejection of the identity between the Mcidfa church and the *basilica maiorum* by Rebillard (1996) 182f.
(2) basilica Novarum, a huge cemetery church dating from the beginning of the 4th c. (Ennabli 1997, 20, 148)
(3) basilica Celerinae or "of the Scilli Martyrs", built near the beginning of the 4th c. (Ennabli 1997, 33ff., 147), the plan unknown;a memorial church, and mentioned in the company of cemetery churches, so presumably in the suburbs
(4) the so-called *mensa Cypriani* at the site of the martyrdom, known only from written evidence, a large building where Augustine often preached (Ennabli 1997, 24f.; unjustified identification with the ruins of fig. 5.1 by Meer and Mohrmann 1958, 117)
(5) the *memoria Cypriani*, built at the seaside on a large scale and in existence by the early 380s, where Augustine often preached and where feast-participants danced

(Aug., *Conf.* 5.8.15). Absent any discovery of another such structure, the ruin in my fig. 5.1, above, is the best candidate to be the *memoria*. It contained many burials under its floor (Ennabli 1975, 120) and was built in and over a cemetery (Ennabli 1997, 21–25, 129f.), with 3 aisles on each side, giving a total width of 35 m and, from the site of the altar at mid-nave to the façade, a length of ca. 35 m; thus laity space for >1,000.

(6) basilica Fausti, a cemetery church of the 4th c. (Ennabli 1997, 27f.)
(7) a narrow basilica, the sole place for Christian worship in the 4th c. so far found inside the city (Ennabli 1997, 65), made from a private house, with side aisles, no apse, and a laity space of ca. 16 x 9 m later, post-400, built over to become the "Restituta" so called as "given back" by Donatists to Caecilianists (Ennabli 1997, 30, 65f., 70, fig. 18)
(8) basilica Tricliarum (Ennabli 1997, 34), for memorial feasts, and thus most likely in the suburbs, dating to the 4th c.
(9) basilica "of the Tertullianists", 4th c., location and plan unknown (Ennabli 1997, 36)
(10) basilica Theodosiana (the emperor, the donor, 379–395), location and plan unknown (Ennabli 1997, 35)
(11) basilica Honoriana (emperor 395–423), location and plan unknown (Ennabli 1997, 31), of the 4th or 5th c.
(12) "at the very end of the 4th c. or the beginning of the 5th", in the seaward suburb part called Carthagenna, a narrow basilica with laity space of 14 x 8 m, for <85 persons, soon built over to form a larger basilica (Ennabli 2000, 11, 18f.)

Cirta (modern Constantine): a house-church by the end of the 3rd c., *Gesta apud Zenophilum* (*CSEL* [Leipzig 1893] 186, *cum ventum esset ad domum in qua christiani conveniebant*), where also (ibid. 187) items for liturgy and distribution, *calices* and clothing were stored; ibid. 194f., the *casa maior* also called the *sacellum*, in the suburbs; English translation in MacMullen and Lane (1992) 257f.; history of the city, Février (1989–90) 181f.

Djemila (Cuicul in Numidia):
(1) in suburbs, a north church of 390s with side aisles, a laity space of ca. 27.8 x 15 m, thus serving <400 (Février 1970a, 212; Gui et al. 1992, 92f., 96f.)
(2) in suburbs, south church of 390s with two pairs of side aisles, constructed out of a disused temple, with a laity space of ca. 32 x 28 m, thus serving <3,500 (Allais 1938, 29; Février 1970a, 212; Gui et al. 1992, 96f.)
(3) a 4th c. martyrium of the 360s (?) in a western cemetery
(4) a cemetery church of the 390s? or in any case pre-450 (Gui et al. 1992, 1.102f.)

Dougga (Thugga): a church of late 4th or early 5th with inscriptions recording the construction of an adjoining portico and chapel for martyrs (Poinssot and Lantier 1925, 238ff.; Y. Duval 1982, 39)

Henchir el Abiod (Reguibet Garres): a late-4th c. church, the ruins now lost, with laity space ca. 15.3 x 9.7 m including a pair of side aisles, thus serving <125 persons (Y. Duval 1982, 144f.; Gui et al. 1992, 1.296ff.)

Hippo Regius (Annaba, Algeria, Augustine's see):
(1) eight churches known from written evidence but only two excavated (Christern 1976, 11), e.g., a 3rd c. suburban funerary chapel to a local saint (lost); also, next
(2) a memorial basilica in the suburbs to bishop Leontius of the early 4th c. (possibly Augustine's "old church", Marec 1958, 35 fig. 2, 216—these two structures ignored by Gui et al. 1982, 347f.)
(3) the funerary "Chapel of Twenty Martyrs" (lost: Marec)
(4) built by or before the 350s, a cathedral church inside the city at first with side aisles and laity space intruded on by the sanctuary, thus ca. 23.7 x 18.5 m, serving <375, with six chapels built onto the north side, opening into the church (Marec 1958, 35ff., 216, 223, 227, fig. 2; Christern 1976, 11; Gui et al., 2.fig. 181)
(5) a church with a pair of aisles on each side, also in the city only 50 m east from the *maior* (Marec 1958, 223f.), with a laity space of ca. 12 x 6 m serving <65 persons

Kebira (Kherbet, near Sitifis): a church with side aisles built in the second half of the 4th c., a laity space of ca. 13 x 10 m thus serving <110 (Gui et al. 1992, 1.115f.)

Kelibia (near the tip of Cape Bon): a 4th c. west-facing church of about 17.5x11.5m, but with room for only <150, because of the 36 square meters taken up by an intrusive chancel; the clustering chapels around it and burials *ad sanctos* are post-400 (Cintas and Duval 1958, dating only the second phase, p. 245; Testini 1959, 123, "late 4th c. at the latest", and a post-400 date for burials and chapels, *pace* Duval; N. Duval, 1975, 85)

Kherbet El Ousfane: the church labeled the second, of the 2nd half of the 4th c., with a laity space of 15.8 x 9.8 m, thus serving <125 (Gui et al. 1992, 1.164f.)

Kherbet Guidra (ca. 15 miles west of Sitifis): a 4th c. suburban church 37 x 18 m (Gui et al. 1992, 81ff.)

Koudiat Adjala (ca. 15 miles south of Sitifis): a burial chapel known only by its lintel inscription, built in 361 for self and as memorial to two martyrs by someone apparently a priest (Y. Duval 1992, 328ff., 514)

Ksar el Kelb (Ain Touila, in Numidia north of Mascula): a 4th c. memorial chapel to the martyr Marculus, the ruins with side aisles and with laity space of ca. 11 x 11 m, with large encroachment by chancel into nave, thus serving <110 persons—noted in 1935 but since, disappeared; a mensa built in it for Saint Marculus' relics next to the apse, with those of his companions (Christofle 1938, 183, 186; Février 1970a, 212; Y. Duval 1982, 158–60, 680; Gui et al. 1992, 1.291ff.; 2.141 fig. 3)

Mactar: a civil basilica made into a Christian one, apparently, before the end of the 4th c., the laity space measuring ca. 19 x 10 m if the chancel made no intrusion into the nave; otherwise, ca. 16 x 10 m serving <150 (G.-C. Picard 1957, 50, 55, fig. 6)

Madauros: a church styled no. 2 with two side aisles and a laity space of ca. 17.6 x 12.5 m, thus serving <200 persons (Gui et al. 1992, 1.329)

Mediouna (Renault): midway between Tipasa and Oran, a chapel (memoria) erected by two fathers to their martyr-sons in 329, as known only through an inscription (Y. Duval 1982, 1.402ff.)

Orléansville (Castellum Tingitanum, modern El Asnam):
(1) a chapel, of which no trace remains, in memory of several martyrs from 329 (Y. Duval 1982, 1.402ff.)
(2) a church with an apse at each end, ca. 30 x 15 m, founded in 324 (Leschi 1940, 1.149; Gui et al. 1.1992, 11, 14; expressing doubts about the date, N. Duval 1978, 528f.; N. Duval 1999, 9)

Ptolemais (Cyrene): basilica of end of 4th c. (Romanelli 1940, 286)

Rusguniae (on the coast of Mauretania Caesariensis): a church with side aisles ca. 42 x 31.5 m, of the 4th c. or early 5th (Gui et al. 1992, 1.52ff.)—and an inscription (mid-4th c.?) records the building of a basilica by a high army officer (Y. Duval 1982, 351ff.)

Sabratha: basilica called "No. 3" by the excavators, built in the last quarter of the 4th c. (J.-C. Picard 1989, 519; Carra Bonacassa and Morfino 2003–4, 14f.)

Sbeitla (Sufetula, Africa Proconsularis): a late 4th c. church with external dimensions 36.3 x 17 m but because of intrusion of the sanctuary into the nave and intercolumniar barriers to the sides, a usable laity space of only ca. 16 x 16 m, serving <210 persons (N. Duval 1971–73, 1.17, 23f., 56f., 132, and fold-out plan II; Y. Duval 1982, 77, 144)

Sertei (Kherbet Guidra): a church of late 4th c. (?), space available to the laity ca. 32.2 x 17.5 m, therefore serving <500, but much reduced from some earlier dimensions (Gui et al. 1992, 81ff.)

Sitifis (Sétif), the provincial capital:
(1) a pre-378 funerary basilica A with side aisles outside the city's walls, laity space of ca. 19.5 x 9.5 m, thus serving <175 persons (Février 1965, 24, 39f., 55, and passim; Février 1970b, 24, 39, fig. 6; Février et al. 1970, 47ff.; Guery 1985, 313; Février 1989–90, 2.28, 31 fig. 77; Gui et al. 1992, 1.84ff.)
(2) a funerary basilica B of the 370s outside the city's walls, with laity space of 31 x 18.5 m, thus serving <550 (Février 1965; Février 1970b, 27f., 38f., 39, passim;

Février 1970a, 210f.; Févriet et al. 1970, 47ff.; Février 1986, 18; Gui et al. 1992, 1.87ff.)
(3) a martyr-shrine, church or merely a tomb, known only in an inscription of 4th or 5th c. (Y. Duval, 1982, 1.315)

Skhira (Byzacena): the great 4th c. church in the cemetery with two pairs of side aisles measuring 25 x 20 m (Nussbaum 1965, 1.204)

Tebessa (Theveste in Proconsularis): in a cemetery, a martyr-cult complex to St. Crispina, beginning with a shrine now lost of a date in the reign of, or just after, Constantius (337–361), as shown by coins, and with a dedicatory inscription by a deacon of ca. 350 in a mosaic on top, and a catacomb and reliquary beneath, the whole preserved by a tri-apsidal shrine attached to a large basilica, both of the late 4th c. into the early 5th c. The church had a pair of side aisles and and nave together measuring 20 m in width and 36 m in length from the edge of the apse to the doors; but the entirety of the nave was reserved to the clergy, apparently, leaving only the aisles for the laity, thus <300 (Février 1968, 168ff., 186, 191; Fevrier 1970a, 204ff.; Christern 1976, passim, esp. 29 fig. 8, 220-25, proposing a commencement of construction in 380s or 390s, and completion over the course of 25 years; Y. Duval 1982, 1.123–28; 2.694f.; N.Duval 1971–73, 2.36f. figs. 15f., 37, 40; N. Duval 1989, 348; Gui et al. 1992, 311ff., 315, catacomb, etc.)

Thelepte: a martyr's church of ca. 400 (Y. Duval 1982, 88f.)

Tigzirt (Iomnium on Numidia coast): ruins of a 4th or 5th c. martyr chapel (Y. Duval 1982, 350)

Timgad (Numidia):
(1) in the cemetery corner, a church with side aisles and a laity space of 18.6 x 16 m thus serving <275 persons (Gui et al. 1992, 1.264ff.)
(2) a second church of the 4th c., in the suburbs, of huge dimensions, 63 x 23 m, an inscription suggesting a date in the 390s (Marrou 1949, 193; Février 1989-90, 2.28; Gui et al. 1992, 1.274ff.)

Tipasa:
(1) a huge cathedral with a pair of aisles on each side, 52 x 45 m, probably 4th c.; minus the chancel area and the stylobate area along four lines of columns, it might accommodate <1,500 (Lancel and Bouchenaki 1971, 40, 43; Gui et al. 1992, 1.22f.)
(2) "the Chapel of Alexander", adjoining a cemetery, late 4th or early 5th c., with many burials inside; the apse at the west end; the whole, a trapezoid ca. 22 x 14 m, serving <300 persons (Christofle 1938, 82; Leschi 1950, 40–51; Leschi 1957, 371f., 378f., plan; Baradez 1966, 2.1135ff.; Février 1970a, 192f. and fig.1; N. Duval 1971, 2.12f., fig. 5; Lancel and Bouchenaki 1971, 47f.; Y. Duval 1982, 371ff., 461f.; Février 1986, 14; Gui et al. 1992, 1.34f., 2.36; Rebillard 1996, 187f.)

(3) "Eglise VII", "Peter and Paul's", so-called because of the many dedications in it, surrounded by burials, ca. 12 x 11 m with a pair of side aisles and a chancel extending ca. 8 m into the nave, the whole destroyed ca. 371, soon rebuilt, holding <100 (Gui et al. 1992, 1.30, 35-37; 2.37 plan)—referred to by an inscription of 315-320 in memory of a martyr? (Y. Duval 1982, 357f.)

(4) St. Salsa basilica measuring ca. 30.6 x 15 m, thus serving <450 persons, with side aisles, "Eglise VIII" for martyr-cult of the 2nd half of the 4th c. set in the suburbs among burials and next to an earlier little shrine ca. 12 x 11 m to the saint (Gsell 1893, 12-20; Grandidier 1902, 52, 58ff.; Leschi 1952, 182, photo of burials; Christern 1968, 199 fig. 4, 207 fig. 12, 226; Février 1970a, 196ff. and fig. 2; Février 1986, 14f.; Y. Duval 1982, 459, 463; Gui et al. 1992, 1.37f.)

Upenna (province of Byzacena): 4th c. church with side aisles, oriented, measuring ca. 23 x 12 m, the apse at the east matched by another at the west end (Raynal 1973, 34ff.)

Zoui (Vazaivi, cf. *DACL* s.v. Zoui, Numidia): laity space ca. 18 x 10 m, thus serving ca. 150 persons

Italy with Sardinia and Corsica

Albano: a Constantinian basilica known only from written mention (C. and L. Pietri 1990, 137)

Aosta: a large structure within the city taken over in the mid-4th c. to make a church measuring ca. 40 x 11 m, the laity space not clear, perhaps <400? (Glaser 1997, 194f. Abb. 96)

Aquileia:
(1) S. Ilario near city center, dating to 390s, the plan unrecoverable (Violante and Fonseca 1966, 329; Jäggi 1989, 298, 300f.)
(2) an episcopal complex, its southern hall serving as a church of ca. 36 x 18 m, thus for <600 persons, and its northern hall being expanded greatly, in the 350s, to make a second church of ca. 73 x 31 m, for 2,000 (Sotinel 2005, 44f., 217f., with plans that do not answer in dimenions); but the chronology is very confusing and the building activity may cluster around ca. 320 (Testini et al. 1989, 184; Tavano 1989b, 176; Mirabella Roberti 1995, 217; Caillet 1993, 127f., 140, preferring a construction period of 313-319; Christie 2006, 293, identifying only the "Theodore" church as of the 320-date, as was the conclusion of White 1997, 200, 206; Salzman 2007, 217-23)
(3) "Theodore" basilica, the bishop's own, in-city and small, apparently post-Constantinian and made much bigger at a disputed date, with a solea, perhaps ca. 350, the archeology being very confused (Lemarié 1989, 86f.; Cuscito 1995, 92ff.; Sotinel 2005, 41ff. and passim)

Arezzo: a diocese therefore a cathedral? first attested in 337–352 but only from literary sources (Testini et al. 1989, 19)

Benevento: a diocese therefore a cathedral? first attested in 303 but only from literary sources (Testini et al. 1989, 19)

Bologna: SS. Vitale e Agricola built in 393/4 (Testini 1980, 134f.)

Bolsena (ancient Volsinii, 100 km northeast of Rome): a civil basilica on the edge of the forum taken over for a church in the early 4th c.; but of its interior, measuring ca. 59 x 26 m, only a portion was used (Gros 1981, 49)

Canosa: a diocese therefore a cathedral? first attested in 342 but only from literary sources (Testini et al. 1989, 19)

Capua: a church built by Constantine, perhaps in 313 (the *Liber pontificalis*, in Testini et al. 1989, 19ff., 92, perhaps the three-aisled church of which traces survive; Korol 1994, 121, 127; Lehmann 2004, 46)

Chiusi: a cemetery basilica of pre-322 totally lost but inferred from written sources (Testini et al. 1989, 19ff., 81; Cipollone 2003, xxvii, xxx)

Como: diocese therefore a cathedral? attested in 386 but only from literary sources (Violante and Fonseca 1966, 314, 321; Testini et al. 1989, 19ff.)

Concordia:
(1) a *basilica apostolorum* built in the 380s, but no trace survives (Zovatto 1950, 13); a three-aisled basilica *in honorem sanctorum apostolorum* outside the city post-388, perhaps the one consecrated by bishop Chromatius, a rectangle ca. 40 x 20 m within which is a church ca. 26.5 x 20 m, thus for <500 persons (Pavan 1987, 22f.; Croce Da Villa 1989, 21; Testini et al. 1989, 190f.; Caillet 1993, 114f., 122, and fig. 92)
(2) a triconch martyr chapel of the 380s with a pair of side aisles, the whole ca. 8.7 x 7.3 m (Tavano 1989a, 174, 176; Tavano 1989b, 46, 49)

Faenza: a diocese therefore a cathedral? first attested in 313–314 but no plan recoverable (or 4th to 5th c., Testini et al. 1989, 19ff., 147; Posta 1989, 260)

Florence:
(1) a basilica of 313 but only known from literary sources (Testini et al. 1989, 19, 81)
(2) a cathedral, S. Lorenzo, consecrated by Ambrose in 386, the plan no longer recoverable (ibid. 122)

Lodi: Laus Pompeia in Lombardy, a cemetery church, S. Bassiano fuori le Mura, consecrated by Ambrose in ca. 387 (Testini et al. 1989, 216)

Luni: a cathedral with side aisles and solea, measuring ca. 8 x 18 m, thus serving <125, built in the second half of the 4th c. or ca. 400 (Lusuardi Siena and Sannazaro 1984, 37f., 39 fig. 35; Testini et al. 1989, 140f.; Caillet 1993, 31)

Milan:
(1) "*basilica vetus*", site unknown (Violante and Fonseca 1966, 327; Krautheimer 1983, 77); sometimes identified with the Portiana but cf. no. 10, below
(2) "*basilica nova*", S. Tecla, built in-city ca. 350 (Lenox-Conyngham 1982, 363; Krautheimer 1983, 73, 76f.; Fiorio 1985, 235 plan), with five aisles, the whole being ca. 45 x 43 m, and laity space for "close to 3,000" in Krautheimer's view, but I would judge less than 1,700, unless the outer side aisles were packed, and subtracting for the space taken by the solea
(3) SS. Nabore e Felice, martyrs' church of ?mid-4th c. (Sannazaro 2000-1, 45)
(4) S. Ambrogio or Ambrosiana (Krautheimer 1983, 73, 79; Fiorio 1985, 44 plan, 108; Sannazaro 2000-01, 45; Salzman 2007, 227), a cemetery church begun in 379-386, laity space of ca. 45 x 20 m, thus for <900
(5) S. Ambrogio ad Nemus (Fiorio 1985, 108), a small chapel outside the city used by Ambrose
(6) S. Dionigi (Fiorio 1985, 146), Ambrosian and small
(7) S. Lorenzo, a memorial church of the 2nd half of the 4th c. (Fiorio 1985, 324; Kleinbauer 1987, 287; Brandenburg 1995a, 53f., 67)
(8) S. Nazaro or Apostolorum (Krautheimer 1983, 77, 79, 81 plan; Fiorio 1985, 276; Brenk 1995, 82, 84 Abb. 8, plan; Salzman 2007, 227), a cemetery church with laity space ca. 44 x 15 m, thus for <500, dating to last decades of the 4th c. (Ambrosian, Krautheimer 1983, 77; looser dating, F. Cavalieri in Fiorio 1985, 276, 311 plan), where Ambrose's brother was buried (Bonamente 1988, 116)
(9) S. Simpliciano or basilica Virginum of 396/7 (Krautheimer 1983, 77, 79, 81 plan; Fiorio 1985, 125f.; Salzman 2007, 228), a cemetery church with laity space ca. 43 x 31 m, thus for <1100
(10) basilica Portiana, later S. Lorenzo (Krautheimer 1983, 88), a suburban complex of chapels complete by 380, where the saint's shrine has a centralized plan (Brandenburg 1995, 55); not likely to be what was called "the old basilica" (Lenox-Conyngham 1982, 363); or rather, identified with S. Simpliciano and of the period 320-350 (Guidobaldi 1998, 443f., 448)

Naples:
(1) the baptistery S. Giovanni built by bishop Severus (364-410) is the earliest in the West, earlier than that of the Lateran in Rome (Di Stefano 1975, 145)
(2) a Constantinian basilica only known from a written mention (C. and L. Pietri 1990, 137)

(3) S. Restituta, Constantinian, three-aisled, with inner dimensions of ca. 55 x 32 m (Di Stefano 1975, 147, plan)
(4) under Constantine a basilica, its total plan unknown (five-aisled, Testini et al. 1989, 19, 95)
(5) S. Gennaro, a basilica with two side aisles, the whole of ca. 16 x 7.5 m, thus a laity space for <125 persons (Testini 1980, 269)

Nola (Cimitile, ca. ten miles north of Pompeii): a north-facing apsidal hall for martyr-cult without side aisles, ca. 20 x 9 m, of late Constantinian date (Lehmann 1994, 284f., rejecting a later date; Brandenburg 2005–6, 246), made part of an east-facing church of basilical shape, ca. 28 x 21 m, built by the provincial governor and bishop-to-be in the 390s, the see being first attested in 398 from literary sources (Paulinus of Nola, *Poema* 20; Lehmann 2004, 35, Abb. 24ff., and passim; Christie 2006, 86, fig. 15)

Novara: a diocese therefore a cathedral? first attested in 398 but only from literary sources (Testini et al. 1989, 19ff.)

Ostia:
(1) a small martyr church of the mid-4th c. on Via Ostiense (Pergola and Barbini 1999, 223)
(2) a church discovered toward the end of the last century, identified as Constantine's and thus correcting earlier identifications with what is attested in the *Liber pontificalis* (cf. Testini et al. 1989, 19, 59f.); side aisles and a laity space measuring ca. 35 x 24 m, thus serving <775 persons (Pavolini 2006, 41, ruling out the supposed church in Ostia itself, ruling in the newly discovered one in the suburbs on the Via Laurentia, 239f.; Christie 2006, 15f.)

Palestrina: a diocese therefore a cathedral? first attested in 314 (Testini et al. 1989, 19, 91)

Pisa: a diocese, therefore a cathedral? first attested in 313 (some archeological signs, Testini et al. 1989, 19ff.)

Portus: in very center of the city, a church probably of the 4th c. (Testini et al. 1989, 19ff.; Fiocchi Nicolai 2003, 311), assembled out of private prior structures in the 4th c. but without an apse until the end of the 5th (Pavolini 2006, 290)

Ravenna: a diocese therefore a cathedral? first attested in 343 (or 4th to 5th c.); a five-aisled cathedral built in ca. 386 (Deichmann 1966, 174; Violante and Fonseca 1966, 321; Testini et al. 1989, 19ff., 142)

Rome:
(1) Callistus ca. 220 "built a basilica across the Tiber and a cemetery on the Via Appia, called the Callistan" (in A.D. 269–274, Duchesne 1955–57, 63; Luciani 2000, 136)

(2) bishop Felix (268–73) "built a basilica on the Via Aurelia" (Duchesne 1955–57, 158)

(3) ?a house-church ca. 30 x 15 m next to S. Crisogono in Trastevere, "built presumably around 310", though remains do not show a place of worship underneath the present church (Pietri 1978, 12ff.; Krautheimer 1983, 17f., 128 n. 10; 4th c., Matthiae 1962, 66, and White 1990, 132ff., fig. 26 plan)

(4) SS. Quattro Coronati, a basilica of uncertain dimensions (Krautheimer et al. 1937–77, 3.28f., 32f.); "very probably of the 4th century, by pope Melchias 311–314" (Tesei 1986, 446)

(5) S. Giovanni in Laterano, the Lateran basilica barely inside the city walls on the Caelian hill, early called the basilica Salvatoris, with a pair of aisles on each side (Krautheimer et al. 1937–77, 5.9f., 47f., 72f., pl. I; Krautheimer 1969, 250; Guyon 1977, 223; Krautheimer 1983, 18, 20; Tesei 1986, 531; Testini 1989, 16; Blaauw 1994, 113f., 127ff.; Curran 2000, 94ff.; Fiocchi Nicolai 2001, 51), "laid out" in 313 and completed in 324, ca. 100 x 56 m in its external dimensions but more like 85 x 48 m in internal dimensions, holding 3,000 persons by Krautheimer's estimate or 4,000 by Brown's (1996) 38 but in fact encroached on by various structures, especially the avenue for the solemn entry of the clergy up the center of the nave, reserved by a low barricade for the entire length from the doorway and taking up ca. 375 square meters, Brandenburg 1995, 37; Holloway 2004, 60; thus, perhaps <2500

(6) S. Sebastiano, the *basilica apostolorum*, a "circus-form" funerary church *ad Catacumbas* still in use on the Via Appia, measuring ca. 73 x 29 m, thus serving <2,000, and dated most probably under Constantine, or more cautiously, pre-350 (Krautheimer 1937–77, 3.11f., 103, 140f., fig. 127, pl. VII, pointing out that the shallow rectangular niches lining the inside of the outer wall all around held cubiculi in stacks of up to eight burials; Tolotti 1953, 220; Matthiae 1962, 50; Jastrzebowska 1981, 163, 271; Krautheimer 1983, 23; Tolotti 1984, 130, thinking it pre-dates S. Pietro, and 155; Tesei 1986, 506; Ferrua 1990, 23ff., fig. 5; Spera 1999, 228f., fig. 169; Pergola and Barbini 1999, 181ff.; Rutgers 2000, 128; Curran 2000, 97ff.; in Damasus' time, A.D. 366–384, according to Huelsen 1921, lxviii). A date before 312 has been given cautious credence by Blaauw (1995) 567 ("310?") but, in the absence of any clear supporting evidence, it seems to me quite impossible that Constantine's heathen adversary would be drawn on for the model of a place of worship (the proposal acknowledged by Cecchelli 2000, 93, but rejected, idem 2003, 27)

(7) S. Pietro (Krautheimer et al. 1937–77, 5.171, 180, fig. 148 and pl. V; Duchesne 1955–57, 79; Matthiae 1962, 44; Krautheimer 1983, 18; Tesei 1986, 540; Blaauw 1994, 452ff.; Curran 2000, 109; Fiocchi Nicolai 2001, 53, 57; Holloway 2004, 79–82), west-facing, completed in 324, perhaps later, with four side aisles, the whole without the transept offering ca. 82 x 63 m of space but with procession space down the nave excluded plus more for the columns (the two exclusions, 900 square meters?), thus room for 4,000 (so, Krautheimer 1983, 102; Brown 1996, 38) or more likely <3,000. Holloway (2004, 79f.) accepts the findings of Carpiceci

and Krautheimer in the 1990s, that the transept of the basilica was originally all that existed, a rectangular martyrium enclosing the apostle's grave, along one long side of which a long hall was bult to form a nave; and this second phase was the Constantinian church, "Old S. Pietro". It "was first and foremost a vast covered cemetery" (Holloway 2004, 182).

(8) S. Valentino, a little martyr-church on the via Flaminia where the earliest dated burials under its floor is of 318 (Pergola and Barbini 1999, 109; Fiocchi Nicolai 2000, 52f.; Fiocchi Nicolai 2001, 60)

(9) SS. Marcellino e Pietro, the ruins since the 1950s identified near the mausoleum of Helena (the later Tor Pignattara) a little more than 3 km out from the city on the Via Labicana (mod. Casilina) *inter duas lauros,* above the catacomb of the Quattro Coronati: ruins of a Constantinian "circus-form" cemetery basilica of ca. 312–324, with a laity space of ca. 48 x 28 m serving ca. 1,250 persons (Duchesne 1955–57, 1.182; Krautheimer 1937–77, 2.141, 192f., 199f., "a covered graveyard" like other circiform churches, and pl. XV; Krautheimer 1983, 6; Guyon 1984, 183ff.; Krautheimer 1992–93, 527ff.; Guyon 1994, 95, date is 320; Fiocchi Nicolai 1995–96, 119; Pergola and Barbini 1999, 164; Curran 2000, 100ff., 104; Cechelli 2003, 116; contains remains of Constantinian burials, Holloway 2004, 87–92, and fig. 3.27)

(10) S. Paolo fuori le Mura, originally a memorial church built over the tomb of S. Paolo on the Via Ostiense, dated under Constantius by Krautheimer and others, but more probably under Constantine, with dimensions uncertain before 384, probably quite modest; but with the united support of three emperors, enlarged or possibly first built then? with two pairs of side aisles and a space of ca. 90 x 65 m, therefore with space for <550 persons; destroyed by fire in 1823 (Duchesne 1955–57, 1.178; Krautheimer 1937–77, 5.97f., 149f., 154f., pl. III; Matthaei 1962, 83; Tesei 1986, 536; Fiocchi Nicolai et al. 1999, 59; Pani Ermini 2000, 2.164; Fiocchi Nicolai 2001, 91; Filippi 2005–06, 277f.; Brandenburg 1994, 230; Cecchelli 2003, 27; Brandenburg 2005–6, 239ff.)

(11) S. Lorenzo fuori le Mura, in ruins a kilometer out from the city on the Via Tiburtina, discovered in the 1950s at the so-called cemetery of Ciriaca; termed the *basilica maior* by Krautheimer, borrowing the name from an early source which distinguishes it from the small church parallel and only 25 m away; "circus-form" and measuring ca. 98 x 34 m, at first dated by Krautheimer to the 7th c. but by himself and others, later, to the second quarter of the 4th c. or built by Constantine in 314–335 as a martyr-cult church (Krautheimer et al. 1937–77, 2.6f., 11f., 18, 94, pl. II; early dismissal of Constantinian possibilities, 115f., 131f.; corrected thoughts, Krautheimer 1983, 23; Duchesne 1955–57, 81ff., 85, 181; Tesei 1986, 490; Pergola and Barbini 1999, 95; La Rocca 2000, 207, fig. 6 plan; Holloway 2004, 110f., Constantinian)

(12) S. Agnese fuori le Mura, the "circus-form" basilica the outlines of which alone are discoverable on the Via Nomentana next to S. Costanza, Constantinian in the present consensus, though 340–360 has been suggested (Krautheimer 1937–77, 1.19, pl. V; Matthiae 1962, 47; Krautheimer 1983, 6; Fiocchi Nicolai 1995–96, 119; Fiocchi Nicolai et al. 1999, 41; Fiocchi Nicolai 2001, 57; Holloway 2004, 93); mea-

suring ca. 98.3 x 40.3 m (Fiocchi Nicolai 2001, 57; La Rocca 2000, 206; Hollway 2004, 93f.) and thus accommodating <3,750 persons

(13) "basilica Marciana" on the Via Ardeatina near the mausoleum of Helena and the small "Anonima" church, the ruins discovered in 1991, a west-facing "circus-form" basilica of Constantinian date and identifiable with the mentions of the pope Marcus buried in the vicinity in 336; measuring ca. 66 x 28 m, thus laity space of ca. 56 x 23 m serving <1,250 persons (Duchesne 1955–57, 1.202; Reekmans 1995, 60f. with fig. 14, plan; Fiocchi Nicolai 1995–96, 69, 76f., 92, 98f., 129; De Santis and Biamonte 1997, 30f.; Pergola and Barbini 1999, 95f.; Spera 1999, 85ff.; Calci 2000, 408; Pani Ermini 2000, 1.17; Fiocchi Niocolai 2001, 57, 61f.). Date: in the first half of the 4th c., or possibly Damasian, i.e., A.D. 366–384 (Pergola and Barbini 1999, 98; La Rocca 2000, 207, 210) or late 4th c. (ibid. 207)

(14) Piazza Venezia church, nameless but ascribed to Pope Marcus and 336, with no aisles—a simple hall with apse and an apparent length of ca. 40 m (Cecchelli 1992–93, 308 and fig. 1)

(15) "Anonima della Via Ardeatina", a nameless small church now in ruins, perhaps originally a *titulus* or more likely built after 350 to accommodate what the pilgrim accounts call "the Greek martyrs" (Huelsen 1921, lxviii; Krautheimer 1937–77, 2.217, 227ff., 244ff., pl. XVII; Matthiae 1962, 63; Jastrzebowska 1981, 163, 271, Abb. 20; Reekmans 1989, 868; Spera 1999, 85ff.; De Santis and Biamonte 1997, 29; Fiocchi Nicolai 2001, 57; La Rocca 2000, 208, fig. 7; Holloway 2004, 111; Pani Ermini 2000, 2.116, the structure if not the cult post-400)

(16) S. Agnese fuori le Mura, on the Via Nomentana, the small basilica ca. 19x9m, of ca. 312–327, with side aisles and laity space intruded on by the chancel into the nave, thus for <180 persons (Krautheimer 1937–77, 1.16, 19, 30, 34f., pl. III, 2 and pl. IV; Duchesne 1955–57, 81; Krautheimer 1960, 22, a date under Constantius is possible)

(17) SS. Marco e Marcelliano, not far from Nereo e Achilleo, a basilica attested by literary sources between the Via Appia and Ardeatina, built by Damasus as his mother's, his sister's, and his own burial-place; but its plan conjectural, lying under the present Trappist monastery (Saint-Roch 1986, 285f., 289; De Santis and Biamonte 1997, 43; Spera 1999, 91)

(18) S. Tecla basilica of the mid-4th c., with only two aisles and its floor taken up by burials (Pergola and Barbini 1999, 222)

(19) S. Lorenzo in Damaso between the Via Ardeatina and Appia, attested but destroyed without a trace (De Santis and Biamonte 1997, 42f.)

(20) "Anonima della via Prenestina" in ruins near the Tor de'Schiavi, a west-facing "circus-form" basilica datable to Constantine's time or to the third quarter of the 4th c., measuring 65 x 28 m, but with a partition across the nave to reduce the laity space to ca. 42 x 28 m, therefore accommodating <1,000 persons (Rasch 1993, 79f., fig. 72B; La Rocca 2000, 207; Fiocchi Nicolai 2000, 48f.; Fiocchi Nicolai 2001, 57; Cecchelli 2003, 117; Holloway 2004, 104ff., "a covered cemetery"). The mausoleum just to its east may predate it. Referring to an opinion of 1979, C. and L. Pietri (1990) 774 deny any Christian character to the basilica

(21) Aequitia, a parish church (in the term of Silvester, 314–335, Duchesne 1955–57, 170; but Constantinian or later (Matthiae 1962, 61)
(22) Tigridae, a mid-4th c. parish church (Matthiae 1962, 57)
(23) Small basilicas, not surviving but attested in literary sources, built by the pope Julius (A.D. 337–352: S. Callisto and "probably" S. Felice", Fiocchi Nicolai 2000, 52f.; Fiocchi Nicolai 2001, 60; Cecchelli 2003, 28) and by Liberius under Constantius (near the Forum of Trajan, the site later to become S. Maria Maggiore: Krautheimer 1937–77, 3.5; Reekmans 1989, 868; but Luciani 2000, 132 dates this church to the year of Liberius' death, 366, identifying it with the basilica Sicinini later to be called Maria Maggiore)
(24) S. Maria in Trastevere built by Julius I (A.D. 337–52) by expanding an ancient house-church (Tesei 1986, 372)
(25) S. Croce in Gerusalemme of the mid-4th c., west-facing, measuring 28 x 22 m but intercolumniations are so small as to preclude a sense or intent of participation from the side aisles; so, effectively, a laity space of 28 x 10 m and <250 persons (Krautheimer 1937–77, 1.167; Duchesne 1955–57, 81, 179; Krautheimer 1983, 6), ca. 312–327, or post-337 (Matthiae 1962, 52; Nussbaum 1965, 1.232f.) or in the second half of the century (Tesei 1986, 440)
(26) S. Anastasia, cruciform, ca. 37 x 27 m, thus serving ca. 900 persons (?a pre-Constantinian site, Huelsen 1921, lxvii; Krautheimer 1983, 96), built "soon after the Peace" of 313 (Matthiae 1962, 65; "after the middle of the IV cent.", Krautheimer 1937–77, 1.50, 60, pl. X)
(27) basilica Juli, SS. Apostolorum, built between 337 and 352 (Duchesne 1955–57, 8; Huelsen 1921, lxviii; Matthiae 1962, 65; Reekmans 1989, 868)
(28) S. Clemente of the last third of the 4th c., perhaps 385, on the Via Labicana, west-facing, with nave and two aisles, the whole interior measuring ca. 36 x 27 m but much intruded on by a solea, thus leaving space for <600 (Krautheimer 1937–77, 1.118, 134, with conjecture of a house-church underneath; and pl. XIX showing the solea; Matthiae 1962, 70; Nussbaum 1965, 1.232f.; Krautheimer 1983, 96; Fiocchi Nicolai 2001, 95; Marino 2005, 36f.; by an old view, pre-Constantinian, Huelsen 1921, lxvii; by a recent view, late 4th to early 5th c., Roperti 2003, 47)
(29) S. Lorenzo on the Via Ardeatina; laity space of ca. 24 x 20 m, but an extended chancel which effectively reduced this to ca. 10 x 20 m, therefore for <200 persons (Duchesne 1955–57, 1.212f.; Krautheimer et al. 1937–77, 2.145f., pl. IX; Krautheimer 1983, 23 fig. 23, 96; Tesei 1986, 192; De Santis and Biamonte 1997, 43; Spera 1999, 91)
(30) Generosa basilica ca. 5 km from the city walls on the Via Portuense, a large funerary church with side aisles built by Damasus, measuring ca. 2 3x 14.3 m, thus serving <300 (Pergola 1986, 218, 224; Reekmans 1995, 66)
(31) SS. Nereo e Achilleo, a small basilica for the martyrs' cult half-sunk in the Domitilla catacombs above their cult-place, of Constantine's time or of Damasus' constructing, or of the end of the 4th c. (Testini 1980, 202; Tesei 1986, 468; Pergola and Barbini 1999, 214, 222; De Santis and Biamonte 1997, 80; Cecchelii 2003, 28); in the last decades of the 4th c., razed to build a three-aisled basilica (Krautheimer

1937–77, 3.128ff.; Testini 1980, 202; Damasus' work, Pergola 1986, 213f., 224; or a later date, Pavia 1998, 282, the construction in the 390s; Calci 2000, 411; Rutgers 2000, 75, 133)

(32) S. Sesto Vecchio (Krautheimer 1983, 96)
(33) Lucinae, a parish church built by 366 (Matthiae 1962, 64)
(34) S. Pudenzia (Krautheimer 1983, 102; Tesei 1986, 10), ca. 390 or 384
(35) S. Lorenzo in Lucina (Krautheimer 1983, 102; Tesei 1986, 104), a parish church where Damasus was elected
(36) Crescentiana, a basilica built 399–401 (Duchesne 1955–57, 218; Matthiae 1962, 55)
(37) Fasciolae, a 4th c. parish church (Matthiae 1962, 56f.)
(38) SS. Giovanni e Paolo on the Caelian hill, west-facing, its construction attributed to the friend of Jerome, Pammachius, at the end of the 4th c., over the foundations of the latter's family residence, formerly used as a house-church and *titulus*-church (Trinci Cincchelli 1978, 560, 567ff., with reminder by P.-A. Février and A. Ghetti that the evidence for Christian use before the mid- or late 4th c. is contested; Nussbaum 1965, 1.232f.)
(39) S. Vitale (Tesei 1986, 6; Fiocchi Nicolai 2001, 96) of A.D. 401 and thus not strictly belonging in this appendix; interior of ca. 35 x 28 m, hence for <900
(40) the *titulus* Sabina (Fiocchi Nicolai 2001, 98) measuring ca. 38 x 18 m, with room for <500 was not completed until the 430s. It may, however, suggest the dimensions of *tituli* earlier?

Torino: a diocese therefore a cathedral? first attested in 398 (or 4th to 5th c., with some archeological signs, Testini et al. 1989, 19ff., 225)

Vercelli: a diocese therefore a cathedral? first attested in 353/4, with some archeological signs (Testini et al. 1989, 19f.)

Verona: a diocese therefore a cathedral? first attested 343–344, and traces of a three-aisled cathedral built post-350, its external dimensions ca. 37.5 x 16.9 m, soon remodeled to a basilica with side aisles, oriented, the laity space of ca. 22 x 17.5 m diminished by an extended chancel, thus with room for <200 (Caillet 1993, 73, 83; possibly of 4th to 5th c., Testini et al. 1989, 203f.)

Vicenza: a church with apse, oriented, ca. 41 x 7.8 m traceable in ruins, datable to end of the 4th c. or beginning of the 5th (Caillet 1993, 97, 100f.)

NORTHWEST EMPIRE

Arles: an early 4th c. church, no details offered (Heijmans and Guyon 2006, 90)

Augustodunum (Autun): an early 4th c. funerary chapel in the cemetery, only ca. 8 x 4 m (Young 1988, 219f.)

Britain: in Lullingstone Villa, a chapel of mid-4th c. (Frend 1984, 564)

Cornus (Sardinia): the so-called north church in the cemetery, intended for burials, begun soon after 313, with expansion of the mid-4th c., making use of elements of a baths building and producing a laity space of ca. 35 x 17.5 m without allowance for any chancel, accommodating <450 persons (Giuntella 1999, 39 fig. 19, 42f., 79, 200f. Tav. II)

Geneva:
(1) the "Peter Church" built in mid-4th c., the northern of a pair, perhaps completed around A.D. 375 over a cult center, with external dimensions of ca. 31 x 12 m, no side aisles, expanded in ca. 400 but with interior space much split in half by a barrier and encroached on also by the chancel and solea (Bonnet 1989, 2.1409ff.; Bonnet 1993, 22–28; Glaser 1997, 178ff., Abb. 83, and on the buried "Kultraum", also Bonnet and Privati 2000, 385, and *Le Matin* of March 2005; Deuber 2002, 9f.; Bonnet 2006, 111f.; Finn 2006, 71), thus for <200 persons
(2) a basilica of ca. 25 x 11.6 m, the southern of a pair, with side aisles, built ca. A.D. 375 or 400 with a bench for clergy around the apse, an extended solea, and an extended chancel with a further barrier half-way down the nave, thus with room only for <175 (Bonnet 1986–87, 331f.; Glaser 1997, 180; Bonnet 1993, 22 Plan; Deuber 2000, 10f.; Bonnet 2006, 113 plan)
(3) Saints Gervasius and Protasius, a funerary church in the city's suburb across the Rhone, built in 5th c. with a crypt for a martyr memorial on top of a cult center identified by signs of cult meals, itself remodeled ca. 300, originating in 1st c. (Bonnet and Privati 1990, 752–64)

Lyon: the possibility that the Saint-Just basilica dates to the 4th c. is doubted by N. Duval, 1991, 198

Monferrand (a small town on the Avignon road, west-northwest of Carcassone): a cemetery church of the 4th c. (N. Duval 1995b, 26–30)

Narbo (Narbonne): a ruined house renovated for a church of the late 4th c. with dimensions ca. 17 x 13 m serving <210 persons (Duval 1995b, 32–36)

Pianottoli (village in Corsica): a church of the second half of the 4th c. measuring ca. 10 x 7 m, with space for <60 persons (N. Duval 1995b, 323)

Sagvar (Pannonia, Hungary): two chapels of the mid-4th c. in a large necropolis (Burger 1966, 154, 162)

Serdica (Sofia): a 4th c. funerary church (N. Duval and Popovic 1984, 374f.)

Vico (a village in Corsica): a church of the second half of the 4th c., the plan irrecoverable but very small (N. Duval 1995b, 329)

Notes

Preface

1. *Russica sunt; non leguntur*, were Rostovtzeff's bitter words; and in Greek, Orlandos (1952–57), naturally a bit outdated now, but still the best introduction through its hundreds of ground plans, elevations, sections, axonometrics, sketches, and photographs. His work doesn't receive mention in any standard reference work, and very rarely anywhere at all.

2. "Le culte des morts dans les communautés chrétiennes durant le IIIe siècle," *Atti del IX Congresso internazionale di archeologia cristiana, Roma 1975* (Roma 1978) 272, 273, 316; insistence on the need for "evocation" from the archeological remains, 304, 306.

3. "There was a very great deal of effort and capital poured into ecclesiastical construction of all sorts in the period I am dealing with. A story that so decisively changed the locale of greatest circulation and civic pride in literally hundreds of towns in the space of a few generations ought really to be told someday" (MacMullen 1984, 53).

Chapter 1

1. Welles (1951) 261f.; for comparison, Beloch (1886) 487 offers estimates of area in hectares for Capua, 181; Milan, 133; Naples, 106; Bononia, 83; Pompeii, 64; Aquileia, 64; Aosta, 41; Florence, 22; Pola, 16. For many of these cities there are modern estimates suggesting several hundred residents per ha; and if Carthage had 100,000 in its 300 ha (Salmon 1974, 36–38), then that would suggest a similar density. Stark (1996) 81 accepts a far larger Carthage, of 200,000, but he relies on Beloch (1886) where Salmon has the benefit of much more recent discussion; Shereshevski (1991) 123 calls 400 per ha "high density" in one mid-sized Syrian city, 300 estimated in another (Antioch: p. 237). Regarding Dura, however, I consider the number of blocks (ca. 80, cf. fig. 1 in Will 1988, 315f., better than a smaller number in an earlier dig report) and the number of separate residences per block (ca. 10 in one block, in Saliou 2004, 67, 70, fig. 4a, and in another block, cf. Allara 1988, fig. 7, here assigning at least one residence-area to the intrusive synagogue); and if there was an average of seven persons in a household on the ground floor, and half as many in the upstairs, then the density per hectare is not >300, but rather <125. Hence, for Dura, ca. 6,500? My house-occupancy figures are not out of line with those in Tacoma (2006) 41, but produce a result closer to the 6,600 of Salmon (1974) 34 and the 6,000 of Will (1988) 318.

2. Leriche and Al Mahmoud (1994) 412.

3. C. Hopkins (1979) 1, 89; Kraeling (1967) 48–72, on the paintings, not frescoes in the strict sense; a meeting area made from the usual *diwan*, the reception space (139f.) with a seating capacity of 60–70 persons on the floor on mats (109) or 65–75 (p. 19) assuming 12.6 x 5.15 m (estimates accepted by Lassus 1969, 133; but these are not the dimensions shown in Kraeling's fig. 1, by which I am guided); the attendance estimated at "60 people or so" by Lane Fox (1989) 269; apotropaic

devices and comparison with discoveries at Gerasa, Kraeling 1967, 151f.; other details, passim; and the marked predominance of Semitic names in the houses of the Christian assembly-place and its neighborhood testifying to immigration from the late 2nd c., Welles (1951) 267ff.; further, on many ethnic groups attested by names and graffiti, Cumont (1926) 1.2; Bellinger (1956) 261f.

4. Thraede (1969) 91, a *katechymenion* in the *Testamentum Domini* 1.19.

5. MacMullen (1997) 143, 240.

6. Schöllgen and Geerlings (1991) 280, the *Traditio apostolica* §26, *ne accumbant* (*non comcumbat*).

7. "Sect", the word offered by Lassus (1969) 138, cf. also 133ff. on the meaning of the five women and the connection to the 2nd c. *Diatessaron* of Tatian. Lassus seems also to favor a beginning of a Dura Christian community some generations earlier than the one favored by Kraeling, and seems to me right in his preference.

8. Beards are the rule in depictions of biblical figures, as for instance in Dura's synagogue; rarely in other art of the 3rd or 4th c.; but, in real life, warmly urged by Clement of Alexander and the *Didascalia*, as also in western texts, from Tertullian on, cf. B. Kötting, *RAC* s.v. "Haar" (1984) 196f., and seen, e.g., in Tronzo (1986) fig. 42, in the hypogeum of the Aurelii in Rome. I suppose clean-shaven was most frequent in representation partly for ease of drawing, but I have made no special search for material on the fashion.

9. Justin, I *Apol.* 67.3ff. (*PG* 6.429Bf.), "we all rise together" after the readings, *anistametha koine*, cf. Tert., *De virg. velandis* 9 (*PL* 2.902, the woman in church *illic sedet intecta*; on the flow from Jewish practice, Duchesne (1925) 47ff., allowing (p. 56) for much local variation, as does, e.g., Bradshaw et al. (2002) 60f., 69f.

10. *Didache* of Syria pre-150, Testini (1980) 4; ca. 100, Schöllgen and Geerlings (1991) 13 and Pasquato (2001) 426; 1st–2nd c., Bradshaw et al. (2002) 76; on "amateur" readers, Pallas (1984) 525f. and Markschies (2007) 147, with sections 2.3–4 passim on the locally variant wording of pre-Constantinian church services.

11. Date and region of origin: Dölger (1925) 171; Selhorst (1931) 11; Schöllgen and Geerlings (1991) 13; White (1997) 81, giving the text from Connolly (1929) §29f.

12. For women being veiled, in fact covered head to toe, *kekalyphtho ta panta*, cf. Clem., *Paed.* 3.11 (*PG* 8.628C, 652A, and 657B, "the face never uncovered", as in stricter Muslim fashion today) and the church manuals in Bradshaw et al. (2002) 99f. Traditional Greek *mores* dictated proper clothing for women in sanctuaries, with nothing "diaphanous" and no show-off jewelry or make-up, cf. Chaniotis (2006) 237, 1st c. at Andania; and for rural 4th c. Syrian *mores*, cf. below, ch. 2 n. 15; also, the Ps.-Clementine *Ep.* II *de virginitate*, Diekamp (1913) viii, 29ff.; later, such passages as Joh. Chrysos., *Homil. in Gen.* 37.5 (*PG* 53.349), *In Ps.* 48.17 *Homil.* 5 (*PG* 55.507), or his catechetical sermons, Zappella (1998) 231; concerning both *mores* and veils, MacMullen (1990) 144.

13. Men were assigned the right hand; cf. infra, n. 51 on how to determine what "right" meant.

14. Clem., *Strom.* 7.7.40 (*PG* 9.456Af.); on the idea of a conversation, see Raeder (1928–31) 2.192, a lucky worshipper at Pergamon *eis logos aphikenitai* with Asclepius; on *epekoos*, MacMullen (1981) 159.

15. Chadwick (2001) 133; Stewart-Sykes (2001) 45.

16. The bishop in Rome in the 190s, Victor, claimed to dictate the right date for Easter to his peer in Ephesus, but his advice was ignored, cf. Stewart-Sykes (2001) 13, who seems to me mistaken in adding that Victor was ignored even in Rome by other congregations; yet, p. 19, he rightly emphasizes the variety and independence among Roman church practices. Like many others, Brandenburg (1994) 209 ascribes the *Traditio apostolica* or *Apostolic Tradition* to Hippolytus and the early 3rd c.; but Bradshaw et al. (2002) 14f. argue for its being, as we have it, a compilation of instructions deriv-

ing from perhaps as early as the mid-second c. to even the mid-fourth. It was drawn on for a later manual assembled perhaps around A.D. 300 in Egypt (76, the *Apostolic Church Order*, cf. Schöllgen and Geerlings 1991, 13) and others from other dates and Eastern regions thereafter (ibid. 150f., 154). On varieties of practice in different churches well into the 4th c., cf. Bradshaw et al. (27, 52, 110f., and passim) and above, n. 2.

17. The non-Christian practice was universal, cf. a survey of regions, instances, and target-deities in MacMullen (1981) 35–39 with notes; more recently and especially relevant to Dura because of the Palmyrene connection, Veyne (2005) 326–30, who also compares the Jewish practice seen in Amos 6.7; further, Veyne (2000) 31ff. Mentions in Ignatius are many, e.g., *Ep. Ad Smyrnaeos* 8 (*PG* 5.713B); also Clem. Alex., *Paed.* 2.1 (*PG* 8.383B, 385B), warning against luxury; and Orig., *C. Cels.* 1.68 (*PG* 11.788B); H. Leclercq in *DACL* s.v. "Agape" col. 792 and passim, seeing the *agape* as unaccompanied by the Eucharist; Jewish derivation, Jungmann (1957) 179; Bobertz (1993) 171 and passim and more recently, Markschies (2007) 171ff.

18. The passage, Clem. Alex., *Paed.* 2.4 (*PG* 8.440B, section-title, and 444Bf.), is recalled in Quasten (1983) 72.

19. MacMullen (2006) offers some chapters on power exerted through early councils.

20. MacMullen (1984) 135f.; Frend (1984) 444f. with a good selection of illustrative references but conclusions (p. 988) about whole great regions more than 50% converted which seem to me quite out of the question (see below in ch. 5); and more recent estimates, including Stark (1996). Mitchell (1993) 40f. sees Christians as a majority pre-300 in a backland district ca. 175 miles south and southwest of Ancyra, on the basis of Greek inscriptions of identifiable religious affiliation—a corpus which had not (has not yet) been published. However, Levick et al. (1993) seems to supply essentially the data Mitchell had in mind. Where (at Appia and Cotiaeum) Mitchell sees 80% Christian, I find instead some 43 inscriptions identifiable as Christian out of 312, of which latter, some 200 are relevant (e.g., not milestones), therefore a population ca. 20% Christian. From the wider area covered in this whole volume, with 540 texts, I find only 17 pre-280 (which is Mitchell's preferred point of chronology), of which only 8 are Christian; Christian but undated, another 16; Christian and post-310, another 9 as against only 3 non-Christian. The indication is of a minority of Christians in an untrustworthy corpus, but an increase after the persecutions. In an adjacent area, Laodicea Combusta and its territory, perhaps 3 texts are dated pre-280, without indication of faith; 2 are post-310 (1 Christian, with another 24 not precisely datable Christian inscriptions almost all post-350); from various other nearby towns and territories (Tyriaion with 7, Hadrianopolis with 14, Kuyulu with 7, Sengen with 9, and 22 from other sites), a total of 59 Christian, all post-Nicene—these 59 plus the 24 of Laodicea Combusta totalling 83 out of some 600+ texts, cf. Calder (1956) xxxix, xli, xliii, and passim. Calder (1928) provides another 285 texts from the same site of which 68 appear to be Christian, and 16 datable to the 3rd c., four to the 4th c., the rest of uncertain date. In the tenth volume of the same series (cf. Levick et al. 1993, xxxix), among the ca. 1,000 texts from Aezani, none is early Christian and few, even in the 4th c.; in Orcistus (Calder 1956, p. xxxviii), none Christian pre-Constantine, hardly one in Nacolea (Mitchell 1993, 60); none of any date in Cilician Anemurium (Russell 1989, 1623); and in Caria, the lands lying behind Miletus, no trace of Christianity before the 4th c., cf. Serin (2004) 11. I conclude that, as Mitchell rightly emphasizes, patterns of density of Christian population are a local matter, as, e.g., in the well-known "Christians for the Christians" texts coming from an area of no more than 225km^2. The epigraphic evidence throughout these these several regions before 310 suggests a small minority of Christians and a strong increase only post-350.

21. Stark (1996) 131f., cities in categories of century, ten belonging to the 1st c., others attested only later; or sees counted, e.g., for Syria by Ulbert (1989) 431.

22. Mohrmann (1962) 159; by then and even earlier, in Latin, too, in Tertullian and Cyprian.

23. Clem., *Strom.* 7.5.1, *hiera*; Porphyry's gibe at the Christians for building temple-like structures, *Adv. Christianos* frg 76 in Macarius Magnes 4.21, quoted in Lact., *Mort. persecut.* 12.3f.; Euseb., *HE* 7.30.8f., an audience hall, *he tes ekklesias oikos*, with a speaker's platform in existence by 261.

24. Euseb., *HE* 8.1.2–5, *oikodomemata* in the 280s and 290s are succeeded by *proseukteria* "in every city", as for example in Caesarea, Eusebius, *Mart. Pal.* 11.28, where martyrs' remains were placed in "the most beautiful dwellings in temples and in sacred houses of prayer", *naon oikois perikallesin apotethenta en ierois te proseukteriois*, Winkelmann (1999) 945; *HE* 7.15.46, a *confessor*-scene in Caesarea where the victim is first led to the bishop's *ekklesia* and its altar; Lact., *Mort. persecut.* 12 (*PL* 7.213B, 214A), an imposing building in a central part of Nicomedia in 303, razed; in Çukurca (see appendix), a stone part of a church "perhaps third century"; in Oxyrhynchus in the 290s, a street named for the presence of a church, White (1990) 123 (though another mention here for Panopolis belongs probably post-310), and a second Oxyrhynchus church is mentioned for razing in 304, White (1997) 166; in Euseb., *Vita Const.* 2.2, churches plural in Amaseia in Pontus razed or closed in 311; in Euseb., *HE* 8.2.1–4, *ekklesiai* to be razed "everywhere" in 303; general razing of churches in 304, Euseb., *Mart. Pal.* 1.5.2 (short recension, Lawlor and Oulton 1927–28,336); and Euseb., *HE* 8.17.1, reference in 311 to "the houses, *oikoi*, in which they (the Christians) formerly assembled," in eastern cities generally, with confirmation in the Edict of Milan, 10.5.9.

25. References to relics-cult among the Greek-speaking Christians of the 2nd c. in Quacquarelli (1966) 243f.; and in Musurillo (1972) 16, the *Mart.* Polycarp §18, we see the collecting of the martyr's relics to be buried "in a fitting spot," and, "in joy and delight", a meeting and services on the anniversary of the martyr's death, the importance of which so early as the 180s is noted by, e.g., Février (1978) 268f., Saxer (1989) 920, or Thümmel (1994) 263. In Rev. 6.9 *hypokato tou thysiasteriou tas psychas ton esphagmenon*, "I saw under the altar the souls of those who had been slaughtered", the word "under" is so rendered by Alford (1873) 4.618, Buttrick et al. (1989) 12.568, and Morrison (1979) 22, but this translation is resisted by Barton and Muddiman (2001) 1295 as "incomprehensible". Dyggve (1951) 115 interprets the passage in the obvious sense but, with others, dates it to ca. 100; also Brandenburg (1994) 227, in passing. For the practice later, see *Peregrinatio S. Silviae* [*Egeriae*] 16.6 (CSEL 38.59), on Job's body at his shrine in Jerusalem, the *corpus ... ipsius Iob, cui in eo loco facta est ecclesia, subter altarium*, without moving his burial stone; Ephraim Syrus quoted in Egger (1926) 42; and Brandenburg 1995, martyr-relics placed under the altar of the Holy Apostles church in Constantinople, seen in Jerome's *Chronicon*.

26. Orig., *Homil. in Jer.* 4.3 (*PG* 13.288Df.).

27. Euseb., *HE* 7.13, under Gallienus "the sites of the so-called *koimeteria*"; in the suburbs of Alexandria, Orig., *Homil. in Jer.* 4.3.16; H. Leclercq, "Cimetière", in *DACL* 3 (1914) 1626, on the early usages of the Greek word; *koimeteria* in the *Apost. Const.* 6.30.2, not a structure (Metzger 1985–87, 2.391; 1992, 236) but rather an assembly (Vööbus 1979, 243; Tidner 1963, 98), and the three versions authorize the Eucharist in several circumstances: for inhumation as well as for the already entombed (Vööbus 244; Metzger locc. citt.) and for the martyrs, whether local or not. Regarding the church ownership of cemeteries, cf. the expectation by an earlier emperor, in 258, that Christians will use them for meeting-places unless forbidden, Euseb., *HE* 7.11.10.

28. Euseb., *HE* 9.2, in 311.

29. Athanas., *Apol. Ad Const.* 27 (*PG* 25.629C), in 357; *Apol. De fuga* 6f. (*PG* 25.652B).

30. I know of no excavated eastern cemeteries dating to before 300, and even those later are few and not helpful, e.g., Keil and Wilhelm (1931) 60, Diocaesarea; or Herzfeld (1930) 110; or Testini (1980) 302–11, collecting references to Antioch and other Syrian sites, as well as Cilician, Phrygian, Aegean, and mainland Greek sites.

31. The illustration draws on Orlandos (1952–57) 31f., fig. 11, who makes some use of Sepp (1879) 210.

32. On Paulinus' church, see Euseb., *HE* 10.4.26 and 36 (*PG* 20.860Bf. and 864B) on the prior tretament of the site; and 37–45 (*PG* 20.864C–865D), where I find justification for the ambo in the description that walks the reader toward the apse, reaching the lofty thrones, *ton neon epitelesas thronois te tois anotato eis ten ton proedron timen*, before arriving at the altar; see §63 for catechumens in both side aisles, *hekaterose*. Sepp (1879) 210ff. gives a good tour of the text, including (210) the clerestory-lighting; and Orlandos (1952–57) 31f. and fig. 11, gives an alternative reconstruction—my own, making use of both these predecessors. Nussbaum (1965) 2.19, reproduces Sepp's plan but (1.12, 164f.) needlessly doubts that there were in fact seats for the laity. See above, note 9, and for Paulinus' church, Eusebius (§66), *en tode to iero kai thronoi bathra te myria kai kathisteria ... en taxei kat'holon kata to prepon*. John Chrysostom refers to the seated (males) before him, *In ep. ad Heb.* 9 homil. 15.4 (*PL* 51.231); notice also, a little later, *Peregrinatio Silviae* [*Egeriae*] 31.1f. (*CSEL* 39.83) at the Eleona church, *omnis populus iubetur sedere ... levat se episcopus et omnis populus*. On the Paulinus-church, more recently, see Gamber (1976) 12, Testini (1980) 13, and White (1990) 136f.; on the term *encaenia*, see such usages as Euseb., *HE* 10.3.1, as eastern Christendom celebrates rebuilding in 313; and on the derivation of the chancel screen from the Temple, Branham (1992) 380, pointing to Euseb., *HE* 10.4 (actually 10.4.44, *PG* 20.865C—my thanks to R. Brilliant for the reference).

33. Sepp (1879) 212 rightly calls it Christendom's first known. For the dedication, see Barnes (1981) 162, "about 315"; Paulinus' advancement, p. 228; and arguing to the same effect as myself, that the plan was to some degree a known and established thing, Brandenburg (1995) 39, noting the simultaneity of the Tyre church and the similar basilica of S. Giovanni in Rome.

34. E.g., at Bosra, Butler (1929) 14, a 3rd c. basilica becomes a church; or the "Constantine basilica" in Jerusalem, cf. Coüasnon (1974) 42.

35. MacMullen (2006) 2ff.

36. *Homil. in Mt.* 85(86).4 (*PG* 58.762f.), with the interpretation of Trombley (1993) 1.110, following Harnack (1908) 2.133, regarding women and children and the congregation of "the principal church" alone, as 100,000; yet the source is tentative, saying "I suppose the number of those united here approaches a hundred thousand," *eis deka muriadon arithmon oimai tous entautha synagomenos telein*, meaning, as Harkins (1963) 244, says, "the orthodox at Antioch"; and similarly tentative, in the other text, *Homil. in Ignat.* 4 (*PG* 50.591), *demos eis eikosin ekteinomenos myriadas*. Libanius indicates 150,000, see Bernardi (1968) 141. For comparison, note that Tate (1997) 939 sets the population of both Antioch and Apamea at ca. 200,000–300,000. For the ecclesiastical archeology of Antioch, cf. Lassus (1940) 339f. and, more recently, per litteris (with my thanks), Andrea U. De Giorgi, that nothing survives save the Peter-church. If the so-called Octagon is taken to be the principal congregational church of the city, and the one so favored of Chrysostom (Kleinbauer 1987, 288; also app. s.v. Antioch no. 5), then we must reduce the estimated size of his audience to a few hundreds; but I assume that what is used is the basilica attached to the Octagon.

37. The length of services varied, and various estimates have thus been offered from reading a representative sermon; Lepelley (2001) 401 reckons 2–3 hours for a long one of Augustine; see also the diary of Egeria often specifying the length of liturgy, commonly 2–3 hours; but cf. also Lassus (1947) 216, two hours "easily" for a session of catechesis.

38. Dölger (1925) 250, hands raised for prayer (which is also the usual gesture in western wall paintings); kneeling, 327, or Funk (1905) 1.519, after prayer, *egeirometha/surgemus*; beating the breast, Aug., *Serm.* 67.1 (*PL* 38.433), prostrated, *Serm.* 311.13 (*PL* 38.1418), and Duchesne (1925) 60; these and other actions, Paverd (1970) 157, 200. As to galleries, they might be added to a basilica by

afterthought as demand grew, cf. at Tipasa the St. Salsa basilica in its building-phases as imagined by Gsell, in Christern (1968) 220 figs. 29a–b; but I lack the expertise to join in such conjectures, which excavators of all sites seem likewise to avoid.

39. MacMullen (1989) 506ff., where I quote Gregory Naz., *De paup. amore* 14 (*PG* 35.877Af.); add Joh. Chrysos., *Homil. in ep. ad Ephes.* 3.5 (*PG* 62.30), on cleaning tables, or Basil's definition of *he eschate penia*, *Ep.* 309 (*PG* 32.1057B); MacMullen (2003) 470–73; and Allen (1996) 409, on Chrysostom alone, noticing in the sermons on Hebrews (*PG* 63) the indications that the audience are rich (cols. 19, 93, 122, 145, 197—and add col. 222), compared with only a single mention of someone who was not necessarily well-to-do (but not necessarily poor, either), col. 138; most vivid, *Homil. in ep. ad Hebr.* 28.5 (*PG* 63.199f.), where Chrysostom rebukes his listeners for laughing at the very idea that a mere two slaves are enough to have with you in the streets.

40. Beggars at church doors, and "how many!" in Joh. Chrysos., *Homil.* 30 *in ep. 1 ad Cor.* 4f. (*PG* 61.255); *De verb. apost.* 3.11 (*PG* 51.300), the poor are not "us", but at our church door; by exception, acknowledgement of the really poor in festival season where the attendance was vastly different and more inclusive, cf. MacMullen (1989) 506, and the nine Lenten sermons chosen for emphasis by Maxwell (2006) 70f., 136, 159; below, at n. 66; beggars at temples, MacMullen (1990) 264.

41. In the decade since the matter was first looked at (MacMullen 1988) many special studies and an entire volume of essays have appeared, to challenge my findings (cf. Maxwell 2006, 66 notes 3f.), but without confronting the data head-on, nor defining "poverty" or "poor", or showing due regard for the proportions (references in MacMullen 2003). My words (1989, 510, "While women would be present [before Chrysostom], either they were much fewer than men, or were not ordinarily to be addressed directly")—these words, Broc 2004, 431–36, appears not to have noticed, while refuting what I don't say. Further, see ch. 5 n. 7, below, on the African evidence.

42. Cockcrow, routinely in Egeria's diary but also in manuals, cf. Bradshaw (2002) 206f.; kissing the door, Lassus (1947) 212f. and Paverd (1970) 21. Separate entrances, cf. Selhorst (1931) 11ff., Butler (1929) 29, Lassus (1947) 191f. and 212, Paverd (1970) 21, 25, and Pallas (1984) 518f.; women to be positioned apart, as the manuals say, including the *Apostolic Constititutions* 2.57.10 of just about Chrysostom's day; seeing women in the back part of the nave, Dölger (1925) 171 and Lassus (1967) 41, with this or other forms of segregation in Nussbaum (1965) 1.27 and Paverd (1970) 26f. On galleries, cf. Euseb., *Vita Const.* 3.50, Greg. Nazianzus' autobiographical poem in Bernardi (1968) 192, and Joh. Chrysos., *In ps.* 48.17 *homil.* 5 (*PG* 55.507), both in Paverd (1970) 6, 410 and 420, Soz., *HE* 7.5 (*PG* 67.1425B, *hyperoa* in Constantinople), and in Constantinople, Bernardi (1968) 186; further, a great wealth of admonitions against pretty dresses, make-up, false hair, etc., e.g., Joh. Chrysos., *Homil. in Gen.* 37.5 (*PG* 53.349), *Homil. in ep. ad Hebr.* 28.5 (*PG* 63.199f.), or in his catechetical sermons, Zapella (1998) 230f., the rules about female costumes recalling those for the traditional worship in pagan temples, e.g., Chaniotis (2006) 236f. On women veiled, above, n. 12, and examples in eastern art, Levick (1993) 87 no. 270, with references; not to sing, Quasten (1983) 78, 81ff., quoting Eusbius, Cyril, and the *Didascalia*; and women not to speak, Joh. Chrysos., *Homil. in Mt* 49.6 (*PG* 58.502), *Homil. in 1 Cor.* 37.1 (*PG* 61.316).

43. Euseb., *HE* 7.30.8, the wicked Paul found himself a huge hall and spoke from a dais, "like the rulers of the world," meaning governors and such; episcopal salary, MacMullen (2006) 9f., and an indication of a big-city bishop's treasury in Joh. Chrysos., *Homil. in Mt* 66.3 (*PG* 56.630), cited in Maxwell (2006) 69.

44. Schöllgen and Geerlings (1991) 143, dating "the definitive separation of laity and clergy" to the start of the 3rd c., clear in the Syrian-born *Apostolic Tradition*; and D. Pallas in the "Discussion" following Picard (1989) 555, on the liturgical function of court- or atrium-spaces. It is Chrysostom who terms the clergy in their entrance the King and his Angels, cf. Janeras (2000) 395ff.

45. Pallas (1984) 500f., the date between 321 and 381.

46. *Synthronon*, e.g., Butler (1929) 212 or Nussbaum (1965) 1.65f.; Gamber (1976) 12, *thronoi anotato eis ten ton proedron timen* in Eusebius' *HE* 10.4.44; elevated three steps up, in Nussbaum (1965) 1.25, something to mount, as Chrysostom says, Paverd (1970) 33f.; also Bernardi (1968) 297f., on Gregory's high throne in his church at Nazianzus; and on the intrusion of the chancel into about a third of the nave at, see, e.g., at Gerasa (appendix).

47. On the look of the chancel area including the apse, see Butler (1929) 213; Lassus (1947) 56; Tchalenko (1953–58) 1.326f.; Nussbaum (1965) 1.25, where the early-5th c. *Testamentum Domini* sets it three steps up; Paverd (1970) 42–45, 48 and 59, and 410, pointing out that, for Chrysostom, the bema is the chancel, not the mid-nave feature of North Syrian practice; so, e.g., *De beato Philogonio* 6 (*PG* 48.751), he speaks from the bema; on the curtains, see, e.g., Joh. Chrysos., *Homil. in ep. ad Ephes.* 3.5 (*PG* 62.29) and *Peregrinatio S. Silviae* [*Egeriae*] 25.8 (CSEL 39.76), with Lassus and Tchalenko (1951) 84; Nussbaum (1965) 1.26; Bernardi (1968) 366f.; Sodini et al. (1989) 351; and Janeras (2000) 396f. On the *fastigium*, the surviving structure or signs of it in various churches, e.g., Kharab Shems, see Butler (1908–30) 324 ill. 364; Tchalenko (1953–58) 1.325, a triumphal arch of mid-4th c.; Lassus (1947) 57; Taft (1968) 347; Paverd (1970) 41; Sodini et al. (1989) 351; and White (1997) 132.

48. Kitzinger (1974) passim, esp. 392f., this, the earliest dated solea, of the 370s or 380s. For singing by choirboys, in the age-old Greek tradition, see, e.g., MacMullen (1981) 22 and the index there, s.v. "Hymns" and "Music"; or Chaniotis (2003) 186; in Christian worship, with both Jewish and polytheist derivation, see Quasten (1983) 17 and 76–80; boys' choirs attested in, e.g., *Peregrinatio S. Silviae* [*Egeriae*] 24.5 (CSEL 39.72); cf. Bradshaw et al. (2002) 157, the *Testamentum Domini* of Syria (?); but Chrysostom makes it clear that the deacons also joined in the processional chanting, see Janeras (2000) 397ff. and *Homil. in ep. ad Ephes.* 3.4 (*PG* 62.29).

49. H. Leclercq, *DACL* s.v. "Ambon," 1330, from *anabainein*; referred to in the Council of Laodicea, in Mirabella Roberti (1950) 188; in 5th c. texts and later, it may be called the bema, Taft (1968) 331f.; Paverd (1970) 38f., 442, two structures that can both be called bema; north-Syrian examples, Lassus and Tchalenko (1951) passim, explaining (81ff.) the barrier or curtain across the nave at the point of the ambo, hiding all the eastern part of the church, so that (p. 84) the congregation "is wholly excluded from the ceremonies". My drawing (fig. 1.9) is based on Butler (1908–30) 324 ill. 364.

50. In the appendix, see under Kharab Shems, Kalota, Brad, Qirk Bizzeh, etc., the earliest datable site being of the 370s (Fafertin); but, out of the 32 ambones identified in northern Syria (Syria Prima: Taft 1968, 340), only a few are pre-400 (Lassus and Tchalenko 1951, 94f., naming only eight, of which one is Kaoussié; ibid. 97ff. and 104 on "the empty throne" for the Bible, cf. also N. Duval 1999, 22). On the various examples, see Butler (1929) 212ff., calling the structure an exedra and interpreting it as a place for the celebration of an agape; likewise Lassus (1940) 347–52; on functions, Grabar (1945) 130ff.; Nussbaum (1965) 1.130; Lassus (1967) 41 and N. Duval (1999) 22f., pointing out the preoccupation of the whole nave by clergy in some churches, e.g., at Fafertin and Kalota (Taft 1968, 342), a practice which Taft (p. 327) attributes more widely east and west, without any discussion or clarity.

51. Dölger (1925) 68, 147, Quacquarelli (1966) 254f., and more thoroughly, Robert (1971) 602, 615f., a pagan custom; on Robert's text from Oinoanda, also A. S. Hall (1978) 263, 265; but the custom also Jewish, Dölger (1925) 171 or Gamber (1976) 9; then in the *Didascalia*, Dölger (1925) 171; on the universality of orientation in eastern churches, see, e.g., Wilkinson (1993) 26; the direction faced by the celebrant, presenting some insoluble problems, N. Duval (1999) 24; "right-hand" determined in relation to a person facing the altar and the *Testamentum Domini* 1.19 quoted in Selhorst (1931) 12f. and 31f., Nussbaum (1965) 1.25, and Pallas (1984) 518f.; Orlandos (1952–57) 151, where "right" means "south" for an eastern church; and H. Leclercq, *DACL* s.v. "Droit (côté)," 1547ff., that

the honored side was on the right of the priest in contexts pre-6th c. Basil, *Homil.* 18 *in Gord. mart.* 1 (*PG* 31.488C), that the martyr is "to the right of the altar", is no help, because Basil doesn't indicate the viewer's position. There is a pretty good indication in the assigning of burial places to women (with a few exceptions), under the aisle that is to the left as one stands at the altar facing the nave, in the Kelibia church, Cintas and Duval (1958) 174.

52. Lassus (1947) 199; Harkins (1963) 242; Lassus (1967) 41; Taft (1968) 327; Paverd (1970) 35ff., 44; Gamber (1976) 10f.; and N. Duval (1999) 24 pointing out the perplexities.

53. Eastern prosperity surveyed with bibliography in MacMullen (2003) 468f., to which Banaji (2001) 17 adds little; with a focus on north Syria and correction offered to previous views, Tate (1997) 928-33, 935ff.

54. The rendering is shown by Sodini et al. (1989) 357 fig. 88, crediting Tchalenko (1953-59) fig. 487; also by N. Duval (1999) 23, without indication of which site he shows. In the region, the *fastigium* or triumphal arch can be traced from mid-4th c., cf. Taft (1968) 347; and the shape and placing of the ambo is easily duplicated in the other churches I have instanced in the text.

55. On increasing complications in liturgy, see Duchesne (1925) 55; Taft (1975) 12 and 51, assigning the splendor of ceremony first to the eastern practices; Bradshaw et al. (2002) 215f.; on its "theatricality" and similar terms to bring out the quality, ibid.; Pallas (1984) 519f. on eastern developments where "la liturgie, autrefois célébration enthousiaste, s'est transformée en spectacle" in the period roughly 375-450; Thraede (1969) 89ff.; and the Eucharist itself is hair-raising, *phrikodes*, in Joh. Chrysos., *Homil. in ep.* I *ad Cor.* 36.5 (*PG* 61.313), Dix (1970) 199f. on Cyril and Chrysostom, and Zapella (1998) 90.

56. For the estates that Constantine could transfer, see the rich lists in the *Liber pontificalis*, ed. Duchesne (1955-57); and Valens' various churches in Antioch mentioned by Malalas pp. 338f., in Petit (1955) 315. On Qirqbizze, see Tchalenko (1953-58) 1.319, 325f.; 2.pl. cv; other references in the appendix, el-Kefr and the rest.

57. Lassus (1947) 256, like Dölger before him, makes good use of the passage from Chrysostom's *In acta Apost.* 18 (*PG* 59.144); and epigraphic attestation well described by Chaniotis (2007) 54f.

58. Gregory's autobiography (*PG* 35.1037Af.), cited by Bernardi (1968) 129; Kitzinger (1974) 392-95, a variety of regions offering parallels to Pisidian Antioch; Arcadius, in Basil, *Ep.* 49 (*PG* 32.385C); the pious Eusebia as a martyr-chapel builder near the close of the 4th c., Delehaye (1923) 131; a bishop and his presbyter record their names as their church's builders in a Syrian town, Piccirillo (1981) 117f., toward the end of the 4th c.; post-400, Lassus (1947) 254, many more Syrian illustrations, with Haensch (2006) 48-52.

59. In the appendix, s.v. Alexandria #3; *De inani gloria* 5f., trans. MacMullen (1990) 21 with context.

60. See the appendix, s.v. Alexandria 2. Tacoma (2006) 30, the Alexandrian minimum, 200,000, maximum 600,000.

61. *In coemet. appellationem* 1 (*PG* 49.393), where he says, "Our forefathers made a rule of it to pass by the houses of prayer within the cities" (notice, John speaks of more than Antioch) "to hold our assembly outside on this day"; and he continues, §3 (*PG* 49.397), with the description of restlessness and commotion quoted in my text.

62. The differential in attendance is often noticed, e.g., by Joh. Chrysos., *Homil. in Acta apost.* 29.3 (*PG* 60.218), Easter; *Homil. in ep. ad Ephes.* 3.4 (*PG* 62.29); Bernardi (1968) 356; Allen (1996) 416f.; Maxwell (2006) 135f.—none of these authorities instancing literal overcrowding, of which, however, I think I have seen a mention in the eastern homiletic corpus.

63. Bernardi (1968) 336.

64. Euseb., *Or. ad sanctorum coetum* 12 (*PG* 20.1272B).

65. On the *agape* and its relation to holy communion and martyr's feast-days, see, e.g., Bobertz (1993) 171; Stewart-Sykes (2001) 130, 133f., 139, 143; 147 and Bradshaw et al. (2002) 152f., on the *Traditio apostolica* §29 and *Canons* of Hippolytus, reminding the faithful that Christian practice should rival the non-Christian sacred meals; above, n. 50 for the connection with *ambones*, a suggestion which has been abandoned; Jonkers (1954) 91 on *Conc. Laodicense* §28, the prohibition *en tois kyriakois e en tais ekklesias kai en to oiko tou Theou esthien kai akkoubita stronnuein*; and Kleinbauer (1973) 113 on Antioch's *klinai*, quoting Joh. Chrysos., *In Mt. homil.* 56(57).3 (*PG* 58.630) and Zach. Rhet., *HE* 7A. The church is the Octagon, cf. appendix; and, at least elsewhere in the east, the banned feasts went on for centuries, cf. sources in MacMullen (1997) 135f.

66. MacMullen (1981) 36–40, with notes, on a very large and extremely well-attested phenomenon in every corner of the eastern provinces; add an older mention, Robert (1926) 5, on the dining-area, *hestiaterion*, of Kolophon, and more recent mentions, Veyne (2000) 31 and Veyne (2005) 327ff. On Corinth, cf. MacMullen (1981) 161; there, too, more on the feasting thrown open to the whole world in the name of the deity to be honored, best known at Panamara.

67. Clem. Alex., *Paed.* 2.1 (*PG* 8.385); Orig., *C. Cels.* 1.68 (*PG* 11.788B); and below, nn. 84ff.

68. MacMullen (1981) 38ff., with similar confessional texts; Roussel (1927) 133, insistent that it is "wholly wrong" to see only a social event in meals taken with the gods; Veyne (2000) 32f., conjecturing rightly that some who attended a sacred meal cared nothing for its sacred character, while others did; further, Veyne (2005) 329; and on "faith", *pistis*, Hebrews 11.1 in the Revised Standard translation. When this "conviction" is attended by strong feelings, then it takes on the quality that is often declared to be essential to "true faith", in discussions all too familiar.

69. Wolski and Berciu (1973) 378f., libation-arrangements in sarcophagi and altars above burials; the quoted belief from Lucian, *Mourning* 9 (926 Jacobitz); non-Christian grave-side picnic inscriptions and bas-reliefs on tombstones in MacMullen (1988) 196, adding evidence from Chalcedon, in Asgari and Firatli (1978) 19f.; at Konya in Isauria, Sahin (1997) 78f. and taf. 2, 3, shown as fig. 1.11; another closely similar grave-stone relief, taf. 3, 4, both of the stones from the second half of the 3rd c.; built provision for grave-side banquets at Aphrodisias, 3rd c., in Reynolds and Tannenbaum (1987) 22, 28f.; grave-side meals and the attendant triclinia at home among the Nabataeans, seen esp. at Petra, Dalman (1908) 60ff., 89f., 202, 217, 243; a 2nd c. foundation with vineyard established for the observation of the grave-side festival, the Rosalia (Parentalia), at Miletopolis 35 km south of the coast of the Propontis in Mysia, with a grave-stone relief to accompany the inscription, showing the picnic, where women are seated, a man reclining, two servants at hand, a tripod table in front of them, in Schwertheim (1985) 83f. and pl. 15.7, noting parallels in inscriptions from Cyzicus and Nicaea; the Rosalia in 1st and 3rd c. Acmonian inscriptions, one of them Jewish, cf. Trebilco (1991) 78–81; further, in Phrygia, MacMullen (2000) 147. For John Chrysostom's "idea of death as a passing sleep while awaiting resurrection," cf. Fiocchi Nicolai (2001) 16.

70. Marinus, *Vita Procli* 36 (Saffrey and Segonds 2001) in the translation of Dillon (2007) 130, which I slightly abbreviate; ibid., on the question, were these Lycian traditions or Greek, meaning Athenian.

71. On modern ancestor cult in Greece and the Balkans, cf. MacMullen (1997) 220; ibid. 219, on the *Const. apost.* 8.44.1 (Funk 1905, 1.554), where the reminder is given, *en de tais mneiais auton meta eutaxias hestiasthe*, "in memorial dinners for them (the deceased) be sure you eat with good manners", the document being assigned to ca. 380 and ?Syria? by most scholars, e.g., Bradshaw (1992) 84, 93, or Lancel (2006) 71, and at home in some large city (Metzger 1992, 18f., with translation of the citation at 335).

72. Petzl (2005) 31f., with reference to similar texts elsewhere in the general region. The text uses *koimeterion* to mean an individual tomb, as is usual in the period.

73. Basil, *Ep.* 49 (*PG* 32.385C), "construction of a fitting *oikos* for the repose of those who loved Christ's name"; and, "where we can identify martyrs' relics, let us pray"; Calder (1920) 47, 51f., a shrine of the 340s for the cult of a bishop Severus and his successor at Laodicea Combusta; at Resafa (see in the appendix) there is one for Sergius, martyr, followed in the 5th c. by a basilica; and at Huarté, cf. Canivet (1980) passim.

74. Hier., *C. Vigil.* 4 (*PL* 23.343)—adding (*PL* 23.345) that Arcadius brought the bones of Samuel into Thrace. These mentions seem to me more likely than the contradictory ones in Hier., *Chron.* a. 359, the relics of Timothy to Constantinople, and a. 360, of Andrew and Luke (*PL* 27.687f., 689f.). Drawing on his wide knowledge of practices in both east and west, the emperor Julian, *Adv. Galil.* 335Bf., protests, "you have filled everything with tombs and memorials"—this, by the 350s.

75. The map draws on Downey (1963) fig. 5 and Lassus (1938) 215 plan 1.

76. Soz., *HE* 5.19 (*PG* 67.1273, 1276); the story known earlier, Joh. Chrysos., *In hier. Bab.* 3 (*PG* 50.532f.).

77. In the appendix, Bosra, Sardis, Damascus and Pergamum; Butler (1929) 20, several small chapels; Sodini (1989) 407, 415, undated adaptation of a baths and temples to make churches in Aezani, Sagalassos, Antioch in Pisidia, and a half-dozen other sites; Deubner (1977/78); Vaes (1984–86) 364, Selge ca. 400; and MacMullen (1997) 234.

78. Franchi de' Cavalieri (1928) 146–51, the *oikos* as it's called, also *martyrion*; two-layer burial, Downey (1963) 184.

79. For the *martyrion* in Constantinople, see Euseb, *Vita Const.* 4.58 (*PG* 20.1209), and Krautheimer (1979) 72, the structure not surviving at all; J. B. Ward-Perkins (1969) 4, "centralized", and p. 10, many variations; Kleinbauer (1987) 280, 287, "double-shell edifices"; Kaoussié described, Lassus (1938) 5f., 13ff., 38–41, 219f., plan IV; Lassus (1940) 340f., the baptistery and services from a. 401, page 342, and fig. 4, 343; Lassus (1947) 123f.; and Maraval (1985) 338. For a closely similar cruciform martyr-shrine, *martyrion*, see Greg. Nyss., *Ep.* 25 (*PG* 46.1096A), with a plan of how it would look, in Mango (1975) 26f.

80. On the role and importance of galleries, see, e.g., Coüasnon (1974) 36 or Kleinbauer (1987) 287; on the features permitting regular services, Krautheimer (1975) 76f.

81. On Gregory's parents, cf. Bernardi (1968) 110 or Bonamente (1988) 116, citing Basil (*In quadraginta mart.*, *PG* 46.784C); burials *ad sanctos* at Serjilla or Brad, cf. Lassus (1947) 230f.

82. A life of Saint Stephen popular in Nicomedia in the 360s, Saxer (2006) 42; Asterius of Amaseia (ca. 400), *Homil. in laud. S. Stephani* 11 (*PG* 40.336A), Saint Euphemia's trials are recorded seriatim on tapestry, *sindon*, in a set of illustrations, *pinakes*, for the portico of her tomb near the church at Chalcedon commissioned almost a century earlier by the local congregation as a whole, *hoi politai kai koinonoi tes threskeias*, "citizens and fellows in faith", who then honored her anniversary every year; and some of her relics removed to a shrine at the Hippodrome by Constantine, Preger (1901–7) 216f.; Greg. Nyss., *Orat. de S. Theodor. mart.* (*PG* 46.737D–744A), in the saint's shrine his relics rest and paintings show his great deeds, evidently in a narrative set of depictions; and, quoted, Basil, *Homil. in Gord. mart.* 17.3 (*PG* 31.489A).

83. Joh. Chrysos., *In S. Iulianum* 2 (*PG* 50.669f.).

84. Eulogies and big numbers, e.g., Joh. Chrysos., *De S. Droside* 1 (*PG* 50.685); *Homil. in S. Melet. mart.* 1 (*PG* 50.520), women and slaves present as well as others; *In illud, si esurierit* 2 (*PG* 51.174), many people for the occasion, *tais panegyresi*, including a working-man stratum, compared with a pitiful few at normal church attendance; *In S. Iulianum mart.* 2 (*PG* 50.669), contrast between the *trapeza* for their dining, and the altar; details from Evagrius, Sozomen, and other 5th c. sources in Maraval (1985) 215ff.; 218, processing, with, e.g., Greg. Naz., *Or.* 44 *in novum Dominicum* 12 (*PG* 36.620C), comparable to pagan processions in MacMullen (1997) 41f.; Maraval (1985) 220, "l'allure

d'un pique-nique" and constitution of a fair; the scene, *martyria*, e.g., Basil, *Homil.* 14.1 (*PG* 31.445B), and in the suburbs, idem, *Homil* 18 *in Gord. mart.* 1 (*PG* 31.489C); the poor, *penetes*, present in numbers deserving of address, Greg. Nyss., *Or.* 3 *de sacro festo Paschae* (*PG* 46.652D); the general setting in the east, Harl (1981) passim; Hier., *C. Vigil.* 4 (*PL* 23.342f.); §7 (345f.), incense and lights for *laetitia*, rebuked or denied by Jerome but universal, cf., e.g., Greg. Nyss., *In sanct. Pascha* 1 (*PG* 46.681B), with repeated invocation to *euphrosyne*; candles at his sister's funeral, *Vita Macrinae* (*PG* 46.993C); Jerome, *C. Vigil.* §13 (350), a *refrigerium*; and §9 (347C) and Joh. Chrysos., *In coemet. appelat.* 1, 3 (*PG* 49.393, 397), unruly behavior—pushing, shoving, jumping about, exchanging insults, shouting, clamor and disorder. On song, see references in the note that follows, and Chaniotis (2003) 186f., music is an offering.

85. Dancing is "our" custom in union with prayer, Clem. Alex., *Strom.* 7.4.40 (*PG* 9.456Af.); Euseb., *HE* 10.8.7 (*PG* 20.903B), in 324, dance and song in pious celebration and address to God, "in cities and the countryside, as they [the participants] had been taught"; in an anon. sermon of the 360s, "what gift shall we present to the martyr? ... We will perform our customary dances", in Quasten (1983) 175; Greg. Nyss., *In sanct. Pascha* (*PG* 46.684B), *skirtemata*, dancing in place; at another time, he hopes there will be no "choral dancing", no partying and drunkenness, *Or.* 3 *de sacro festo Paschae* (*PG* 46.656D); Greg. Naz., *Epigr.* 166, Waltz (1944) 82, "if their exertions are pleasing to the dancers, then may their good times also please the saints!"; and elsewhere he lectures his listeners on decent restraint in their manifestations of joy, *Or.* 38 *in theophania* 4 (*PG* 36.316A) and deplores fancy feasts and too much wine, Waltz (1944) 84f. (#168f.); cf. *Or.* 5 *C. Iulianum* 35 (*PG* 35.708C), warning against attention in festival times to "corporal beauty, changes of clothing and expense, partying and drinking, decorating the alleys with flowers and tables with disgraceful perfumes, and adorning one's entrances," all of which is the heathen's way, whereas we raise only our hymns and psalms without piping and clapping to show our gratitude; though, "if you must dance in festival manner and joy of the celebration, dance then, but not in a shameful Herodias-style," but decently like David (709Af.); further, on the eve before the Resurrection, Basil, *Homil. in ebriosos* 14.1f. and 6 (*PG* 31.445Bf., 448A, 453A, 456A–C, etc.); Greg. Nyss., *Or.* 3 *de sacro fest Paschae* (*PG* 46.656D), no *choroi*, cf. Harl (1981) 127f., 142; men's dance-choruses, Joh. Chrysos., *In S. Iulianum mart.* 4 (*PG* 50.673); further references in MacMullen (1981) 23ff. with notes and MacMullen (1984) 150, showing how in the traditional faith dance was seen as an offering. For the belief that the saints observed the celebrations, Joh. Chrysos., *In s. Julianum mart.* 4 (*PG* 50.673).

86. On *laetitia* (§7), see, e.g., Greg. Nyss., *In sanct. Pascha* (*PG* 46.681Df.), or the following note. *Philanthropia* was expected and besought of Zeus, in Hatzfeld (1927) 77, or of Asclepius or other gods, cf. the references in Edelstein and Edelstein (1945) 1.158 (Aristides), 220 (Lucian), 305 (Libanius).

87. *C. Vigil.* 4–7 (*PL* 23.342–346A), and other parts of the attack. For the use of candles, cf. above, n. 84.

88. On rowdy behavior, above, nn. 84f.; on dress, Greg. Nyss., *Or.* 3 *de sacro festo Paschae* (*PG* 46.652D), the poor "love festivals and even though they have no good clothes can associate with others dressed at the greatest expense" (what luck!).

89. MacMullen (1997) 121, on the scale of superhuman power desired and addressed by the common man

90. Bernardi (1968) 335f.: "In a society where the numerical predominance of the countryside was crushing and cities, rare and generally not of a great population, close to nothing of any of the sermons of these preachers [Basil, Chrysostom, Gregory of Nazianzus] was of interest to the rural resident.... All the martyrs' festivals brought a lot of rural residents to the cities' gates," and the majority of a bishop's congregation "without doubt" lay beyond the city. Since many of them lacked

Greek, the preachers' message "could reach only a limited fraction of their flock, a fraction of the population privileged by residence, culture, and wealth." To illustrate the rural attendance, I may refer to Greg. Nyss., *Or. 3 de sacro festo Paschae* (*PG* 46.657A) or Greg. Naz., *Or.* 44.12 (*in novum Dominicum*) (*PG* 36.620C), alluding to shepherds and happy at "the many thousands drawn together from every part".

Chapter 2

1. Vagueness of reference in Eusebius, Dagron (1974) 89f. or Krautheimer (1983) 56. For the quoted words, cf. Euseb., *Vita Const.* 3.48 (*PG* 20.1108C) on *eukteria*; for Constantine's burial, cf. Berger (1997) 12.

2. Soc., *HE* 2.16 (*PG* 67.217A), describes the slaughter and how "at this time" Constantius "founded, *ektizen*, the Great Church which is today called Sophia"—evidently not the one in which the slaughter took place.

3. Athanas., *Apol. ad Constantium* 15 (*PG* 25.613A), speaking of construction in Alexandria, Trier, and Aquileia.

4. The excavations described by Schneider (1941) in fact give us only a tiny glimpse of the west façade of Hagia Sophia and of the underlying structure. For the over-all plan, "shaped like a circus," *dromikes*, as we are told by the anon. [Ps.-Codinus] Πατρια Κωνσταντινουπολεως 49 in Preger (1901–7) 140, Kähler (1967) 11 compares Constantinian churches in Rome, S. Agnese and the Apostle church on the Via Appia, and sees Constantine as the builder of the Great Church; and Mathews (1971) 11 also favors Constantine as the initiator of the Great Church, but (unpersuasively) sets aside the plain meaning of *dromike*, p. 12; an ambo in mid-nave, p. 13. The fullest treatment of the literary sources is Dagron (1974) 397ff., favoring Constantius as the "founder" in the sense of dedicating in 360 what had been a-building for many years but had collapsed (p. 399—and cf. n. 3, above, showing how a church could be in use while a-building). Krautheimer (1983) 52ff. and notes, 137, offers views which seem to me, as to Dagron, confused and ill-supported. For the orientation in line with other palace-complex structures, see, e.g., Dagron (1974) 397 or Detorakis (2004) 10; on delays in construction, see Millet (1947) 598; relics, 599.

5. Krautheimer (1983) 47 hazards a guess of 90,000 for Constantinople in 337; its area was 960 ha in 447, in Stark (1996) 81; and at about that date (cf. *RE* 4.1005) there were 14 *ecclesiae*, Seeck (1876) 242.

6. Invasions of the 260s needed recovery time, and a century later, there were still more; for modest prosperity, see MacMullen (1988) 34f. and Chevalier and Mardesic (2006) 55. On Crete, Chaniotis (2004) 120, surveying some 70 sites; and compare the finding of no construction in Thessaly and "generally throughout Greece" pre-450, in Marzolff (1984) 6; most decisive, the inventory of 264 churches at 214 sites in Greece, of which only one, at Narona, is of the 4th c. or even "4th/5th c.", in Chevalier (1996) vol. 2 passim. The vast majority are 5th/6th c.

7. Bratoz (1999) 435 presents the possibility of traces of an early house church in Porec, the evidence for which is questionable.

8. Barnea (1984) 645, at Philippi, no texts pre-Peace; 646f., only five or six pre-Peace texts elsewhere.

9. Barbariga ca. 22 km north of Pola, in Marusic (1978) 569 and Bratoz (1999) 451f.; ibid. on populations estimated from both archeological and hagiographical data.

10. Pross Gabrielli (1969) 19f. and tav. II, 24ff.

11. See entry in the appendix; also Barnea (1984) 478; and on the crypt, Hoddinott (1963) 100.

12. Pelekanidis (1961) passim, plan p. 117 fig. 2; the inscriptions at 162f. ("Paul the priest", the "founder"), 164–67 and 169 (five more *presbyteroi*), 167 (*comes et tribunus notarius*); and 171 (*ex comite*); and the ambones in Gounaris (1984) 135, one datable to the last quarter of the 4th c.

13. Lemerle (1945) 1.283 assigns A to the 5th c. (other scholars, to the early part); B to the 6th c., pp. 418, 421. On barriers at Philippi, see Grabar (1945) 131; Hoddinott (1963) 102; Lassus (1967) 41; and Pallas (1984) 518ff., on the architectural custom of Philippi and other Greek sites as well.

14. On Rosalia, above, ch. 1 n. 68; Egger (1926) 78, a 4th c. inscribed gravestone in Manastirine directing anniversary celebrations for the testator, perhaps on the day of [*Parentali*]*orum*, the fines for neglect to be paid by the trustees to the church; Collart (1937) 475ff.; MacMullen (2000) 26f.; Pilhofer (1995–2000) 1.104; 2.519, 641f., 648f.; and 2.77f., on the early uses and interpretation of *koimeterion*, Joh. Chrysos., *De coemeterio* (*PG* 49.393).

15. Collart (1937) pl. 37, 2, a pre-Christian relief from Philippi showing two men and a child recumbent at their dinner, flanked on each side by a seated veiled woman, just as in fig. 1.11, above. The inscription directs that interest earned on a bequest go to "the honoring of the deceased," *ut parentaretur* on a certain day in June.

16. Pilhofer (1995–2000) 2.120ff., *heroon* (my thanks to C. Brélaz for reference to the volume).

17. Pelekanidis (1977) 396; Pelekanidis (1978) 394ff.; 397, where A. Ferrua opposes the idea of cult and the views of saints-cult expressed by E. Lucius in the 19th c.; Pelekanidis (1980) 153ff.; Bakirtzis (1998) 42–45; Koukouli-Chrysantaki (1998) 20f. and pl. IX, 2 (the pendant). As is pointed out by many, this could be no ordinary burial, since none such would be allowed inside any ancient city. The coin offerings to the holy burial is matched by those offered at the memoria in Rome's St. Peter's, from ca. 270 into the 5th c., cf. Holloway (2004) 142.

18. Barnea (1984) 661f.; Pelekanidis (1977) 396; Pelekanidis (1978) 394; Pelekanidis (1978a) 69ff. and fig. 1 p.71 showing "the Apostle Paul's basilica"; Pelekanidis (1980) 153ff.; Bakirtzis (1998) 41ff. with the Priscus-text; at fig. 6 giving a sketch of the most probable ground plan of the hall and its larger context; suggesting a date of ca. 400 for the octagon, and, 45ff., its purpose as the worship of Saint Paul; preferring an earlier date, "sometime before the middle of the 4th c." for the church built over a heroon, "and it seems all but certain that the pagan hero cult was replaced by the cult of Saint Paul," so Gregory (1986) 237; also Koukouli-Chrysantaki (1998) 21.

19. Egger (1926) 73ff. gives a number of burial inscriptions of military officers, civil officials, and imperial officials from one Salonitan cemetery (nos. 74f., 80f., 89, 93f., 106f.). I find a bare half-dozen of seventy inscriptions in Greek, but, ibid. p. 99, half of the names are of Greek origin. For the population of town and "suburbs" (of what extent, is not indicated), Dyggve (1951) 4f. imagines ca. 60,000, which appears a great overestimate (with an area of a little over 70 ha, assuming occupation of all, one might imagine 20,000 inside the walls, at the most, and another 5,000 within a half-hour's walk—on the inland side alone, of course). Compare ch. 1 n. 1 on Dura.

20. N. Duval et al. (2000) 636.

21. Duval et al. (2000) 227, the number of sarcophagi; 211, 222–25, 238, on the *hortus* with mixed burials and luxurious details, the term to be seen in a nearby cemetery, known in an inscription as the *hortus Metrodi*, cf. Chevalier and Mardesic (2006) 58 and Marin (1994) xxii; Duval et al. (2000) 369, 417–434 passim, the burial no. 82 for Primus always below floor-level; 425, for Bishop Gaianus' tomb; 367, 414–33, 441–49, on the original martyr burials, Domnius' and others, with their mensae; Orlandos (1952–57) 482, supporting Duval on the baldaquin likely to have been built; Duval et al. (2000) 634ff., 639f., on dating criteria; and older treatments in the appendix entry.

22. On dance, above, ch. 1 n. 85; at Salona, Dyggve (1951) 79; on the altar above the burial, cf. above, ch. 1 n. 25; on St. Peter's in Rome, Hier., *C. Vigil.* 8 (*PL* 23.346B), "Did that Roman bishop do wrong who offered sacrifices over the bones of the deceased, the men Peter and Paul, *qui super mor-*

tuorum hominum Petri et Pauli, secundum nos ossa veneranda ... offert Domino sacrificia, et tumulos eorum Christi arbitratur altaria?"; Blaauw (1994) 453; and J. B. Ward-Perkins (1969) 4, generalizing across the empire.

23. MacMullen (1997) 131f.

24. On the chapels, Egger (1926) 91f., 132, abb. 134, and passim on inscriptions; Dyggve (1951) 96f.; and Duval et al. (2000) 638–45.

25. Inscriptions in Egger (1926), some found inside the chapels, e.g., 76, 81f., nos. 85, 104, and 110; others elsewhere in the site.

26. The inscription quoted is Diehl (1925–31) 1.158 #838, where the ending is damaged and unclear; further, Egger (1926) 80 pointing out that there was still private land in the cemetery for sale—therefore the date is 4th c. (and not late, surely); 85, inscription #122, a *piscina* inscribed to show that the deceased *hanc piscinam ... constituerunt*, the word here being used in its ancient sense, to mean the burial, but on a slab shaped to its modern name, a *piscina*. For the origin of the term *piscina*, I have seen but am not persuaded by an alternative suggestion, that it comes from Christians being *pisciculi Christi* (Cuscito 1971, 59); other derivations in Cambi (1984) 228ff.; its meaning, a tomb or grave, 227; better derivation, N. Duval (1984a) 203f., with review of many examples generally post-400 and not *in situ*, from Sirmium and "to be found in almost all the churches of the Near East," citing, however, only Chehab (1957) 1.118, 170, on two *piscinae* at Khaldé 14 km down the coast from Beyrut, only one of which is dated (5th c.).

27. For the beliefs underlying the rites, Orlandos (1952–57) 482; and N. Duval (1984) passim.

28. The Ephesus-mensa in Keil (1930) 39 and fig. 18, the findspot being inside the oldest of the city's basilicas along with much broken pottery, lamps, and glass; Soteriou (1932/3–1933/4) 175, two similar ones at Thebes, and 177, comparing the Ephesus mensa; at a *martyrion* in a Corinth cemetery, E. Marki cited by Fasola and Fiocchi Nicolai (1989) 1181 n. 106, though G. D. R. Sanders kindly informs me that the dating may need to be moved down; in Larissa, Orlandos (1952–57) 483 and Soteriou (1932/3–1933/4) 178, a mensa with five cups, each inscribed for a different saint; many found at Sirmium in the ruins of the St. Irene church, others at Iader, cf. N. Duval (1984) 263–67 and (1984a) 193, including one "polylobée"; Duval, in Marin (1994) 121, 126, 173f.; in a chapel at Krikvine across the bay from Salona, a mensa with small relief baskets on it containing rolls, Belosevic (1998) 74 and pl. 3, 1, mid-4th c.?; general remarks on Dalmatian mensae, Jelicic-Radonic (2003) 19, the raised rim of the altar top, etc.; and a particular number at Salona's cemeteries, of which a selection is displayed on a church wall, cf. Dyggve (1951) figs. V, 21f. Chalkia (1991) catalogues over 400 marble table-tops (mensae), mostly in fragments and of several shapes, a few (myth- and hunt-scenes) identifiably non-Christian and among these, the earliest (3rd c., pp. 138f., 149); the rest, however, to be taken as Christian, as altar-tops, etc., and (123ff.) in generally Syrian and Palestinian churches, probably for meals eaten over tombs, some of them for martyrs, some for the ordinary deceased. For the Tanagra inscription, ibid., 125.

29. Walbank (2005) 272f., seeing "commemorative cult of the dead".

30. Soz., *HE* 9.2 (*PG* 67.1597Bf.), the *trapeza martyrum* for the famous Forty Martyrs in Constantinople.

31. Egger (1926) 56f. a table with three holes, and 75, in a second table, a hole in the corner bored through; Dyggve (1951) 107; Duval et al. (2000) 264f.; the inscribed mensa in the Athens museum, Soteriou (1932/3–1933/4) 173 and fig. 1 facing p. 176, "The martyrs John, Luke, Andrew, Leonides...", the earliest inscription of the sort in Greek (4th c.); also at Thessalonica, 177f., with other examples of a date perhaps too late for my purposes; and Bakirtzis (1995) 58ff., correcting the proposed chronology of Soteriou, filling in the story of construction, and emphasizing the location of the cult very close to that of Cabirus, savior of the city throughout many earlier centuries.

32. Mensae at Marusinac, cf. Dyggve and Egger (1939) 6–10, 37, 46ff., 80ff.; Dyggve (1951) 76; Marin (1989) 1236; on Asclepia, also, Deichmann (1993) 53; and a few miles to the south, Krikvine yielded many more mensae.

33. For Kapljuc, see appendix. For the basilica plan, see Dyggve (1951) fig. 4.26, which I have modified; the reconstruction is derived from Brønsted (1928) 180 fig. 240, with various comparanda of the region, e.g., Dyggve (1951) fig. 4.32; Orlandos (1952–57) 526–28, 531; Belosevic (1998) 92; and Uglesic (2002) 60.

34. The stone with the four cups was over-interpreted by Brønsted (1928) 46, 57f., 138f., 142f.; Dyggve (1951) 108; and Grabar (1975) 72 on the 4th c. date for Kapljuc and the mensa over the tomb of the four martyred soldiers; but cf. N. Duval (1984a) 222, Marin (1986) 222 offering both the earlier view and that of Duval, and P.-A. Février in the Débat, p. 229, who with Duval sees this as a privileged burial, not a martyr's (being outside the chancel).

35. Soteriou (1932/3–1933/4) 175f.; Orlandos (1952–57) 480ff.; Pross Gabrielli (1969) 28; and N. Duval (1999) 19 warning of "the extreme diversity exhibited by commentators regarding every site and feature in employment." However, Février (1970a) 208 points to Augustine's *Serm*. 310.2 which is explicit about "the practice of the eucharistic synaxary" on martyr-anniversaries at least for the province and period.

36. Dyggve (1951) 109, the *fenestella confessionis* and the *brandea* introduced through it.

37. Dyggve (1951) 102, 108; Marin (1989a) 1118; Marin (1994) xv, raising the possibility of a date for these oratories centuries later than the third.

38. Pietri (1984) 299.

39. MacMullen (1997) 121ff.

40. Dyggve (1951) 106, like the scooped-out circles I have seen in the sarcophagi at Arles.

Chapter 3

1. Frend (1984) 672; but the party of Augustine insisted on a majority, the numbers were disputed, and so we have also 286 for the Caecilianists against 285 for the Donatists—so, N. Duval (1989) 346 or Chadwick (2001) 391, and a possible total of 570 cities with bishops, Février (1989–90) 1.182. At stake was *rebaptizatio*, Jonkers (1954) 74, quoting the council of 348. For close crowding of tiny towns in Numidia having bishops in mid-3rd c., see Février (1989–90) 1.179, and increase in numbers thereafter "not solely due to the controversy" with the Caecilianists.

2. Morley (1996) 182; Lo Cascio (1999) 162f., the commonly accepted figure of 430 "cities" in Italy; and below, ch. 4 n. 82, for a total of 400; the population of all of the African provinces set at 3–4 million, and of Italy at 7–14 million, in Drexhage et al. (2002) 24.

3. Marec (1958) 42.

4. The first words are those of the general pagan populace, imagined by Tert., *Ad Scap*. 3 (*PL* 1.701A); the second, in the *Acta purgationis Felicis* §5, Maier (1987–89) 1.177 = MacMullen and Lane (1992) 243.

5. The built-up area of Cirta is naturally defined on three sides, and appears to be about 45 ha, in Gui et al. (1992) 2.pl. 101; Maier (1987–89) 1.115, 218, 220, cites the record regarding "the private house in which the Christians gathered" in the wake of confiscation of their church (their *basilica*), *Gesta apud Zenophilum* (*CSEL* 26.16, 186, 193), with mention of their *triclinium* for *agapae*; the congregation was locked up in their own martyrs' graveyard, *area martyrum* (1.234); and two houses, *casae*, are mentioned of which one was big and held the bishop's throne, ibid. (translation of passages in MacMullen and Lane 1992, 249f., 257f.). In storage were 82 women's tunics, which imply a dependent category of that size or perhaps two or three times as many. Compare, on the same scale, the 48

Christians gathered in a private house at the smaller town of Abitina in 304 (*Acta Saturni et al.* 2, *PL* 8.689), in White (1997) 87f.

6. Meer (1961) 168–76, esp. 169 with references to *Serm.* 56.8.12, 90.9, 274 ad fin., 311.3, and 324; add *Serm.* 355.2 (*PL* 39.1569); also Lepelley (2001) 401, reporting 2–3 hours to read one of Augustine's longer sermons aloud.

7. Eastern influence, cf. Lapeyre (1940) 178 and Leschi (1940) 148, 151; two-apsed churches, N. Duval (1971–73); facing east to pray, cf. Dölger (1925) 141, 331, 333, Selhorst (1931) 33, and Gamber (1976) 7 and 9, quoting Tertullian, Cyprian, and Augustine; but Augustine's "we pray turned toward the Lord" is not possible in occidented churches, N. Duval (2005) 14; N. Duval (1999) 8, 15, "occidentation of about one third" of places of worship in the 4th c., esp. in eastern parts of modern Tunisia; on liturgical conjectures, ibid. 24; and preoccupation of entire nave by clergy, pp. 11, 17.

8. Leschi (1940) 148; N. Duval (1999) 18 on a raised chancel, 16 and fig. 16 for a bishop's throne.

9. Sexes separated, Leschi (1940) 150; Dolbeau (1996) 329, separation strict under Augustine as bishop, less so in his youth; separation implied by thickness of stylobate defining the side aisles, with double columns, N. Duval (1971–73) 17, 23f.; women vowing chastity screened off by the *cancellus virginum*, Leschi (1940) 1.150 and *DACL* 2.1823; and the catechumens' view of the nave blocked off, Nussbaum (1965) 1.175.

10. Altar at mid-nave, Allais (1938) 58; Mirabella Roberti (1950) 186; Nussbaum (1965) 1.183f., 190, 197; Taft (1968) 327; Gamber (1976) 16; on the chancel-screen plus curtains at St. Salsa's, cf. Gsell (1893) 14ff.

11. Aug., *Serm.* 126 Mai, in Morin (1930) 356, a *multitudo constipata angustiis*, "compressed by the deficiencies of space" (R. Finn 2006, 143, translating "aisles", for which I find no justification) and complaining of his own weak voice which occasioned this crowding in to the side spaces around the chancel in the nave; and of this, he didn't approve.

12. Février (1965) fig 6 (fold-out plan of both churches), "basiliques funéraires" both built "toward the mid-point or the second half of the 4th c." (54f.) or "between 355 and 378," cf. also Guéry (1985) 313; 38f., "B" burials in numbers; Février (1970a) 210, on the central square enclosure, contemporaneous with the church itself; Février et al. (1970) 49, the two buildings sited outside the colony's pomerium in a suburban section opened up to new housing, enclosed by later walls; a change of the scholar's mind, and the churches supposed to have been inside the walls, Février (1989–90) 2.31 fig. 77; ibid. 2.28 explaining the square enclosure in "B", "prières privilégiées, celles du sacrifice offert au centre même de la nef" (of which I have not seen the dig-report in other publications).

13. Testini (1959) 127, "barely a few decades later" than, "at the latest, the late fourth century" (127, 123)—so, in the 420s, with (128) comparison drawn to the cemetery churches of Rome, S. Lorenzo f. l. m. and the rest; better, Cintas and Duval (1958) 161f., figs. 2f., the plan of the church in its first and second phase; 236, on the removal of the chancel in the second phase; and (238f.) dating according to mosaic styles which indicate this adaptation in the 4th c. or late 4th/early 5th c. It is worth noticing the usage at Carthage of packed-in burials under the basilica floor, in the so-called *Maiorum*, from perhaps as early as the 3rd c., cf. Delattre (1907) 63f., 66, 68.

14. See the appendix. In the fold-out plan of Tipasa (Leschi 1950 reproduced by Baradez 1966, 1136f. with some additional features), the urban area appears to contain ca. 35 ha; for the 4th c. population, cf. Lancel and Bouchenaki (1971) 16; Février (1986) 14 for the date of the basilica.

15. E.g., Krautheimer quoted in Y. Duval (1982) 2.463; Rebillard (1996) 187.

16. See the appendix; more particularly, Leschi (1950) 42 on a pre-Constantinian date for the martyr-shrine; Rogatus and Vitalis, in Y. Duval (1982) 1.371f.; the *martyre professus*, Y. Duval (1982) 1.371, most likely dated to 310 or 315; Leschi (1957) 382 on the coin, with other pages and details, N.

Duval (1995c) 194 on the sequence, martyr-portico first and then Alexander-church; and Rebillard (1996) 187 on the three identifiable martyrs in the six chambers.

17. On "culte", see the exchange of Février (1978), in the "Discussion", with L. Reekmans, pp. 320f.; for "worship" used where others might say "veneration", see Dyggve at n. 36 of ch. 2, above, and ch. 5 n. 20 (Brown); further, MacMullen (1997) 123, 227.

18. Grandidier (1902) 52 fig. 1, the plan, and 62 fig. 20, the reconstruction, with the mensa, coins for dating, and the lintel-inscription, at 58ff., 65; for the position of the St. Salsa tomb in the basilica nave, Y. Duval (1982) 360f.

19. Février (1970a) 201f.; the *fratres* mensa in Y. Duval (1982) 1.377–80; another at Koudiat Adjala (see in appendix); a rectangular mensa set up by one Felix to himself and wife, "in honor of the blessed martyrs" at Mopth(…) a little south of Djemila, Y. Duval (1982) 1.288f.; dedicants' families associated with martyr-shrines built at Sitifis, Haidra, Thelepte, and Rusguniae, ibid. 2.588; detached *mensae martyrum* from two further sites "offered by the faithful for the celebration of commemorative ceremonies dedicated to the martyrs", ibid. 1.337; an enclosed burial area bequeathed to his church by someone, likely a member of the clergy, for his own burial, along with a *cella* as a martyr's *memoria* which he paid for (appendix s.v. Caesarea; a similar gift at Aïn Ghorab, ibid.); a chapel for two martyrs near Tipasa, with its own mensa in place (appendix sv. Bourkika); and, as an inscribed plaque says, a portico built next to (or, since the plaque was found in the church, opening off?) the Dougga church "in the name of the martyrrs," Poinssot and Lantier (1925) 238. As in other provinces, in Africa also the construction of and in churches was generally in the gift of the clergy, cf. Y. Duval (1982) 2.592.

20. Février (1970a) 209ff.; Y. Duval (1982) 1.413f.; White (1987) 240ff. The date is beginning of the 4th c., perhaps 309 if there was a single digit "X" lost at the edge of the indicated provincial date. Subsequent text introduces a construction project, *bassilica dominica*. "Mensa" here means the tablet, not a building, Y. Duval 1.414; and *pie zeses*, transcribed Greek, is/was a universal salutation.

21. Bradshaw et al. (2002) 221, with illustrations of later 4th c. from Africa, Syria, and Italy.

22. Aug., *Conf.* 6.2 (*PL* 42.719f.), Monica attending at *memoriae martyrum, cum solemnibus epulis praegustandis atque largiendis,* these seen as objectionable *quasi parentalia*; Y. Duval (1982) 654f. quoting Paulinus Milan., *Vita S. Ambros.* 14 (*PL* 14.31), Nabor and Felix in their church *celeberrime frequentabantur*, special favorites of Ambrose where he received a vision revealing the burials of Gervasius and Protasius under the floor of the Nabor-and-Felix church (*Ep.* 22, *PL* 16.1619), and whom he calls *martyres nostri*.

23. A stone in the chancel of a church at Bou Tekrematen inscribed *mensa marturorum*, with four cups in its surface, Gui et al. (1992) 179; a mensa in the sacristy at Ksar el Kelb with a saint's tomb in the chancel and eight burials in the apse, ibid. 141; quantities of lamps, vases, jugs, amphorae, and cups of the 5th c. in the St. Salsa shrine, Grandidier (1902) 60; for wells and channels cut into mensae, a common element, see, e.g., Février (1970a) 194, Bouchenaki (1975) 113, 170, or Y. Duval (1982) 2.525; also the latter's general conclusion, accepting for some mensae "la pratique effective des banquets autour de la table commémorative", with guests, which would be *agapai*, 541f.; and Aug., *Serm.* 273.8 (*PL* 38.251), *lagenae, saginae,* and *ebrietates* inside the church, "wine jugs, heavy eating and drinking" (E. Hill's translation of *saginas*, "roasting pans," I think is not justified). For earlier times, cf. the testimony of Tertullian in A.D. 211, *De corona* 3.3 (*PL* 2.79), describing general Christian practice of the time: *oblationes pro defunctis, pro natalitiis, annua die facimus,* "we make offerings for the dead on their anniversary to celebrate their birthday" (trans. E. A. Quain in the series Fathers of the Church), where some readers would take *oblationes* to be eucharistic; but the passage is "not at all clear," Y. Duval (1982) 2.456. Cf. Rossi (1864–77) 3.497f. and the *Thesaurus Linguae Latinae* s.v. for the range of the word *oblatio*. On real eating and drinking in eastern churches, see above, ch. 1 n. 65.

24. Aug., *Civ. dei* 1.35 (*PL* 41.46), in 411: *perplexae quippe sunt istae duae civitates in hoc seculo invicemque permixtae.*

25. Above, ch. 1 at n. 69; ch. 2 at n. 15; and Scheid (2005) 162, looking only at western provinces.

26. For one's deceased kin, the *parentalia, cara cognatio,* and *rosalia.*

27. At Aïn Kebira = Satifis, *CIL* 8.20277 = Diehl (1925–31) 1.301 no. 1570; among many mentions, cf. Iosi (1924) 105f. In the inscription "mensa" is taken in the sense of a building, whereas, as I've explained, the alternative and older meaning of "table" is what I favor.

28. *Serm.* 361.6 (*PL* 39.1602) with the comments of Rebillard (1999) 1043; *Ep.* 22.6 (*PL* 33.92) distinguishing between drunken excess in the cemeteries and the quite permissible and usual celebrations by Christians as *solacia mortuorum*, cf. n. 29, below.

29. Aug., *Ep.* 22.3ff. (*PL* 33.91f.), *convivia ... cotidie celebrentur ... labes domestica* as if *privatis parietibus...*, *in cimiteriis, loca sacramentorum* and *domus orationum...; convivia ... non solum honores martyrum a carnali et inperita plebe credi solent, sed etiam solacia mortuorum*, though celebration with properly restrained rites is allowed, so that *nec deserere memorias suorum ... et id celebrabitur in ecclesia quod pie et honeste celebratur.* Further, *Contra Faustum* 21 (*PL* 42.384), referring to the martyrs that you Christians (says the critic) *votis colitis, defunctorum umbras vino placatis et dapibus.* For the belief that the dead slept, seen in the terms for "graveyard" (*koimeterion*, e.g., Joh. Chrysos., *Coemet.* 1, *PG* 49.393f., in Fiocchi Nicolai 2001, 16, and Lat. *dormitorium*, in Y. Duval 1982, 1.288), there is the canon of the early 4th c. forbidding candles at graveside ceremonies lest they wake the dead, *C. Elvira* §34 in Jonkers (1954) 13 and, for the date pre-325, Sotomayor (1996) 264; earlier, Tert., *De test. animae* 4 (*PL* 1.614B); *De anima* 51 (*PL* 2.737A), a part of the spirit survives in the remains of the dead and may be "refreshed", *refrigerasset* (738A); and Février (1984) 163–66, 179. Later in a 4th c. source, the dead only seem to have died and "it is for this reason that we set up memorial shrines to the saints and celebrate memorial days of our deceased kinfolk and friends in the faith, rejoicing as much in their enjoyment, *refrigerium,* as petitioning a pious outcome in the faith for ourselves" (I translate the text quoted by Testini 1980, 144).

30. Summing up and giving point to much earlier discussion, as he generously emphasizes, Marrou (1949) put the phenomenon on the map, so to speak. Cf. 193f., Timgad, and (195) pagan practice at Carthage; Y. Duval (1982) 288ff. on the *dormitorium*, the tomb, of Felix and Rogata and their mensa, from the Sitifis area; a similar combining of a mensa for the saints and the burial of the dedicant, ibid. 303 (where the difference from the Felix mensa, drawn by Duval, is not persuasive); more recently, e.g., libation tubes into non-Christian sarcophagi of the 3rd c. at Leptiminus, Ben Lazreg et al. (2006) 352; also at Tipasa, non-Christian, Bouchenaki (1975) 43f., along with facilities for food; ch. 2 at nn. 31f.; ch. 1 at n. 69; and ch. 4 n. 33.

31. Marrou (1949) 197, 200; Testini (1980) 144; carven dishes, etc., Y. Duval (1982) 253f.; and Lancel and Bouchenaki (1971) 48, on Tipasa's "Alexander" church and its mensa in the right-hand aisle, so as "to dine in honor of the deceased and to share with them a meal that had nothing of the symbolic about it"; 96, similarly on the St. Salsa church emphasizing the reality of the meals, though also a ritual; and the plan of the excavated area (reproduced as my fig. 3.6), see Leschi (1941–42) 356, shown again in later publications by Leschi and others.

32. Tipasa sarcophagi in Leschi (1957) 366; non-Christian cooking utensils, e.g., in Leveau (1978) 130 or Bouchenaki (1975) 43f., at Tipasa, quoting Février; and dining equipment is shown carved on pagan altars and gravestones at various 3rd and 4th c. sites, Stirling (2004) 433.

33. Tertullian, above, n. 22, and *De test. animae* 4.4 (*PL* 1.614), the *convivia* of the *conrecumbentes* are accepted as normal; "snacks and stews", *obsonia et mattea,* for the dead, *De anima* 4.4; and in *Exhortatio. cast.* 12.3 in Saxer (1980) 12.3, accepting of *parentare* among the survivors (though cf. *De*

spect. 13.4); witness the remains of animal bones, nuts, figs, etc., at burial sites, along with uneaten offerings to the dead themselves, in Stirling (2004) 436f.; and Bouchenaki (1975) 192, counting 46 Christian mensae in Tipasa cemeteries, with (194) five newly discovered in the so-called "Matares" cemetery.

34. Noisy, Aug., *Ep.* 29.11 (*PL* 33.119); all-night *vigilia*, Aug., *Enarr. in ps.* 32.5 (*PL* 36.279) and *Serm.* 311.5 (*PL* 38.415), "Awful songs they sang the whole night through and danced to their singings", just as was the custom also in the Restituta basilica, cf. Ennabli (1997) 23; on instruments, never the kithara but always the psalter (I have no idea what the actual difference was), see Aug., *Enarr. in ps.* 32.1.5 (*PL* 36.279), and Quasten (1983) 176 (showing there were exceptions); on dance, Aug., *Ep.* 29.11 (*PL* 33.119) of 395, on the Donatists' celebrations, and *Ep.* 22, cf. Jastrzebowska (1979) 85; ibid. 86 and passim on the derivation of martyr-cult from non-Christian practices.

35. Munier (1974) 41 on the Hippo council of 393, against clerics' dining inside churches, forbidding the laity also to join them at these *convivia* "so far as it can be forbidden"; ibid. 185 on the Council of Carthage of 397 §42, "that no bishops or clergy should have parties in churches, and, so far as is possible, the people also should be barred from such parties, *convivia*"; of 401, §60 (pp. 196f.) against Christians being "forced" (! *cogantur*) to join pagan *convivia*; Van Bavel (1995) 352 on Augustine's campaign; and the reasonable conjecture that "at most, the customs of church dinners did not disappear but were displaced to annexes adjoining, as close as possible to the saints", says Y. Duval (1982) 1.39.

36. *Tumultuarii* within the very church walls, *intra ecclesiae parietes*, wickedly cling to their so-called *laetitia*, their *solemnitas* which only hides their love of drink, *nomine religionis*, Aug., *Ep.* 29.2 (*PL* 33.115); Dolbeau 26.9, of the partying pagans in *vigilia*, *stultum est et irreligiosum inde velle placere martyribus*, in Dolbeau (1996) 373; and notice, much later, Caesarius of Arles deploring the feasting practices, the singing, and "the custom of dance at the very doors of the saints," *ballationes et saltationes ante ipsas basilicas sanctorum*, and "if they [the worshippers] are Christians when they come in, they're heathens when they leave; for this custom of dancing lingers on as a heathen rite" (*Sermo* 13.4, in *Sources chrétiennes* 175.424), cited by Belayche (2007) 45f., where "the festival expression could thus be by itself a form of religious expression, independently of specific rites of sacrifice"; and, against the idea of masses of people perpetuating traditional gestures of veneration brainlessly, without meaning, see the most interesting remarks of Marcel Le Glay (1966) 160f., on the rationality and independence of mind of Saturn-worshippers even of quite humble classes. But of course such humble classes don't express their thoughts in literary form.

37. For the characterization, cf. above, nn. 22 and 31, and *Ep.* 29.10 (*PL* 33.119), regarding the *magna carnalium multitudo* in Rome; "joy" as in *laetitia*, quoted, or in the non-Christian roots of such tributes to the dead, e.g., *hilaritas animorum* quoted in Jastrzebowska (1981) 181. The church authorities' argument can be seen early in Cypr., *Ep.* 67.6, *gentilium turpia et lutulenta convivia*.

38. A familiar passage, *Ep.* 29.9, in the translation I offered in (1997) 114f.; for comparison, Dolbeau (1996) 288, the sermon Dolbeau 21 §15, "only a few years ago you were pagans, you are just barely Christians, your family used to worship the demons".

39. Jonkers (1954) 75 or Munier (1974) 4, where the bishops deride the dead whom they accuse of insane self-murder; ibid. 204 or the trusty old Héfélé (1869) 2.262 on the council of 401, *de falsis memoriis*; also Y. Duval (1982) 457, with the comment which I go on to quote.

40. To Février (1989–90) 2.37 and Ennabli (1997) 24f., add (with help from the Maurist editors) *Serm.* 261 (*PL* 38.1202), 260 (1201), 262 (1207), 280 (1280) in Carthage; the Basilica Tricliarum, Aug., *Enarr. in ps.* 32.2.29 (*PL* 36.300); in Hippo, Aug., *Serm.* 273 (*PL* 38.1248) and 1251, Theognis'; further, the basilica Restituta of Saint Vincentius, 277 (1257); and sermons for other saints like Castus and Aemilius in Carthage, Marianus and Jacobus, and "the Twenty Martyrs" in Hippo, 325 (1447).

41. Ennabli (1997) 65f., 70, "a meeting hall in a private home turned into a church," which in its later, built-over, grand shape, she believes was the Restituta. The original space was ca. 16 x 9 m. For the population, closer to 300,000 than to 100,000, see Le Bohec (2005) 220.

42. See the appendix.

43. Aug., *Ep.* 78.3, quoted in Meer (1961) 478; quoted also, 482.

44. Leschi (1950) 46, "hundreds of sarcophagi" with "the agape-room"; Lancel and Bouchenaki (1971) 94 fig. 4, 96.

45. At various sites: Février (1986) 20; N. Duval (1986) 29; Ennabli (1997) 133, burial-shroud with gold thread; Cintas and Duval (1958) 174; a good illustration of the care to be buried *ad sanctos* in a certain Januaria of a site near Sitifis who "built for herself a *sanctorum mensa*" in 324, cf. Février (1970a) 202 and Y. Duval (1982) 302ff., 528; ibid. 522 on domination of clergy among *ad sanctos* burials from before the 5th c.

46. Quoted, Y. Duval (1982) 2.516f.; on ecclesiastical misgivings and anti-cult legislation, see below, ch. 5 nn. 23-26; at Carthage, on numbers of days set aside for martyr-anniversaries, I count 79 at a date not long past Augustine's death (*PL* 13.1219-30, the *Kalendarium antiquissimum ecclesiae carthaginensis*—11 of them, bishops); and notice also Morin (1930) 714 (Wilmart 13.5), where Augustine describes the number of saints recognized in a certain Carthaginian church as far greater than 153.

47. *De miraculis S. Steph.* 1-2 (*PL* 41.855-58 passim), of the opening 5th c.; the sickbed vision of the saint *qui sanare venerat, Serm.* 286.7 (*PL* 38.1300).

48. Aug., *Serm.* 286.2 (*PL* 38.1298); 354.5 (*PL* 39.1565); *De sanct. virg.* 44 (*CSEL* 41.290); *Ennarr. in ps.* 120.13 (*PL* 37.1616f.), addressing *fratres* on the saint *cuius hodie natalitia celebramus ... clarissima enim fuit, nobilis genere, abundans divitiis*; 137.3 (1775), *Crispina cuius hodie solemnitas celebratur.* Recognition of Augustine's enthusiasm, Y. Duval (1982) 2.694; on the targeting of men not women by bishops in sermons, see MacMullen (1989) 510 and above, ch. 1 n. 41.

49. Christern (1976) 26 indicates a bounded town of ca. 550 m to 700 m x 450 m = 25-50 ha, translating (see ch. 1 n. 1) into 3,000 to 6,000. A church holding <300 would then be right for some 6% of the population.

50. Water provision, Christern (1976) 171, 244 (quoted).

51. Tebessan mensae in Kadra (1989) 266, 268ff., 271; for discussion of the Crispina-cult in combination with that of her seven companion martyrs, and the succession of layers in the south apse of the triconch and the removal of her reliquary to the center of the triconch, see Christern (1976) 111-21 (pages which serve as a reminder to me—one among many—that archeological exploration and interpretation can be a beautiful art).

52. The "catacomb", so-called, in Christern (1976) 30, 105f. The north-south initial part of the gallery predates the complex above-ground, of which the water-induction would have drowned the passage; the east-turning branch of the gallery may be later. Underground burial corridors or networks of chambers are rare in Africa, but cf. Carra Bonacasa and Morfino (2003-4) 17f. on Sabratha, and Ben Lazreg et al. (2006) 348f., 357ff., on Leptiminus.

Chapter 4

1. *Puticuli* in MacMullen (1993) 53.

2. Shown, the Novatian catacomb, Fiocchi Nicolai (2001) Tav. IVb; the average width of the galleries, about three feet, cf. Pergola and Barbini (1999) 66; the S. Callisto Catacomb (perhaps the earliest?) extending 40 m down, Brandenburg (1994) 213; levels of galleries beneath levels, to a fourth, e.g., under SS. Marcellino e Pietro, Fasola (1989) 2176, or a fifth in the S. Ippolito catacomb, Pergola

and Barbini (1999) 154; in the first two centuries of the church (i.e., to ca. 240) Christians too poor to leave any trace of themselves in funeral art or inscriptions, Lampe (1989) 114f.; *loculi* of a representative catacomb averaging 1 x 2 m, Guyon (1987) 99.

3. *Aen.* 2.755f., translation by David Ferry, by permission and with thanks; the passage, Hier., *In Ezech.* 12.40 (*PL* 25.375), is often quoted, e.g., by Armellini (1893) 125, Brandenburg (1994) 206, or Fiocchi Nicolai (2001) 80.

4. The derivation of our term (as Americans would say, "at the Sink-holes") in, e.g., Armellini (1893) 46 or Testini (1980) 93, *ad catacumbas, kata kymbas (-en)*, from the second half of the 3rd c., on, for the original location; but the general application is centuries later.

5. A calculation of slave numbers, in MacMullen (1990) 327; slave origins, MacMullen (1993) 50; and the wreckage of successive Jewish revolts over a seventy-five-year period in the first and second centuries insured that many slaves imported into Rome, and freedmen in due course, would be Jews, for whom also Greek would be the lingua franca. For a recent, minimalist estimate of the Jewish community in Rome (well under 10,000), cf. Rutgers (2006) 353ff.

6. For the city's total, cf. MacMullen (1993) 48f.; but there is a range of estimates, with 650,000 being the choice of Stark (1996) 81; 700,000, the choice of T. M. Finn (2000) 296, in ca. 250; 750,000, of Christie (2006) 321; 600,000 "not counting slaves and foreigners" (!), of Lo Cascio (1999) 166; 800,000 the choice of Krautheimer (1983) 109 and Rutgers (2000) 72, for the year 400; 850,000, of Morley (1996) 38 for the earlier Empire; a million in the early Empire, counting some suburbs, the choice of Purcell (1987) 32f., as also Gatto (1998) 148f., dropping to 400,000 in the 5th c. Supposing the 1,300 ha within the Aurelian walls did not constitute the whole of the truly urban area in 300 and that high-rise housing produced density of population to several hundreds per hectare (cf. ch. 1 n. 1), an estimate of 500,000 seems to me the most easily defended for ca. 300, with 10–20% more, earlier, and less, later.

7. Manuals in Greek, cf. ch. 1 n. 16; cf. transliterated terminology like *papas, episcopus, diaconus, ecclesia, coemeterium, catechumen, exorcizatus, apoforetus*; general usage in 2nd/3rd c., Lampe (1989) 117; ibid. 13 and Abb. 3, showing Christian clustering in the west, Trastevere, and southern precincts of the city, where also the poorest immigrants clustered, cf. MacMullen (1993) 53–58.

8. Bilingualism (as is well known among the elite of the city, most strikingly illustrated by Caesar's dying words, "You too, Brutus!" in that language); but more relevant, the 8.2% of Roman Christian inscriptions that are in Greek in the Domitilla catacomb, in Rossi et al. (1922–) 3 nos. 7157–7278 and 8036–90, plus scattered others, though the percentage is a little less in other volumes; e.g., in the catacomb of SS. Pietro e Marcellino, vol. 6, cf. common phrases there in Guyon (1987) 348f., where the texts are further down in date; Guyon (1974) 561 on the proportion of Greek names among *fossores* in the S. Callisto catacombs, 20% pre-337 but only 10% post-337; roughly the same, i.e., 30% Greek among the inscriptions pre-Constantine throughout the catacombs, but 3.18% in the S. Sebastiano post-350, 4.8% in the Commodilla of the same late period, cf. Carletti (2003) 82f.; more on the S. Sebastiano mix, post-250, of Latin, Greek and both together among the votive graffiti, cf. Jastrzebowska (1981) 194. The title in Greek, *papas*, had been long in use for the bishop in Carthage and of course Alexandria, cf. V. Saxer in C.and L. Pietri (1990) 58.

9. A few random indications: in Naples, Liccardo (1992) 262f.; in Concordia, Pavan (1987) 24; rare in Ostia, cf. Calza (1940) 47.

10. Quoted, Rutgers (2006) 352, continuing in explanation, "an environment in which population growth was minimal or non-existent"; ibid. 349ff. on 26% infant mortality, and expectancy of 39 years.

11. Rutgers (2006) 352f. suggests 40–45% per thousand for the empire over-all, while citing the estimate of Guyon for Rome, at 45–50%; Egypt offers the best evidence (cf. Parkin 1999, 157ff.), in

which Bruce Frier suggests 42.1% (per litteris—with my thanks). Morley (1996) 53 works with a birth rate of 42% which would be (p. 39) .8% above the death rate (the latter therefore 41.2%), while emphasizing the terrible health conditions in Rome. I adjust my estimate to suit the circumstances of Rome, as does Purcell (1987) 32; and he also indicates (pp. 37ff.) how extremely expensive burial-space became in the Roman suburbs.

12. Of symbols, words, or paintings indicative of one's trade, a clustering in gallery-sections nearest access-points, e.g., in the Callisto catacomb, Bisconti (2000) plan VI or the *coemeterium maius*, plan XXI; Baruffa (1992) 77f., early 3rd c. *loculus*-lid symbols; varieties of trade declared, in Bisconti (2000) 21, 24, 31–60 passim; and comparative material from the Greek-speaking East and Africa in MacMullen (1974) 105, 202, and (1990) 257, 277, 386f.

13. Seventy catacombs, Speier et al. (2007) 6, but the Jewish also included; the cemetery *ad catacumbas* with 12 km, De Santis and Biamonte (1997) 45; cubic footage excavated, some figures for the catacomb *inter duos lauras*, Guyon (1987) 99, 2 million square meters for 500 m of gallery.

14. *Copiatae*, "toilers" in Greek, cf. *hoi kopiontai* in Ignatius, quoted in Conde Guerri (1979) 166; representative texts on dealings with *fossores*, ICUR nos. 8328, 8428, and passim to 9580a; Bellarmino Bagatti (1936) 123, 127; Guyon (1987) 344; back-fill dumped in a pre-existing gallery, Testini (1980) 103 and Saint-Roch (1986a) 189; humidity, Pergola and Barbini (1999) 16; a *fossores*' union in early 4th c., Guyon (1974) 575f. or Pani Ermini (2000) 2.51. For the tomb-prices, see the *Apostolic Tradition* §40, in Bradshaw et al. (2002) 192, and the epigraphic material gathered, e.g., by Armellinii (1893) 121f., Bellarmino Bagatti (1936) 123, 127, or Guyon (1974) 550, where 13% of catacomb inscriptions indicate sales, from a. 338 on; a *cubiculum* would take 10 days' work (p. 568); and clerical status for *fossores* attested in Rome in the 2nd c. (above, Ignatius), Africa from early 300s, and in Italy from 350s (Guyon 1974, 574f.). *Pace* Conde Guerri (1979) 171, 180, there is no substantiation or likelihood for *fossores* laying down their picks and taking up the brush to glorify themselves in tomb-paintings, a suggestion unwarily adopted by Charles-Murray (2007) 55—a *fossor* in court calling himself an *artifex* is in fact only claiming status as an "artisan", cf. the context in MacMullen and Lane (1992) 255—, nor, *pace* Bisconti (2000) 98, that visitors to the catacombs believed in a Great Digger, a superhuman *fossor* who presided there as a *genius loci*.

15. First catacombs in 2nd c. by church-*community* purchase with donors coming in 3rd c. and later, Testini (1980) 79, 112f., 156, the principal source being the *Liber pontificalis*, ed. Duchesne (1955–57) 1.4, showing Fabius a. 236–50 "made the division of the urban precincts, *regiones*, among the deacons, and directed many assembly halls, *fabricas*, to be erected in the cemeteries" (for the translation of the word, cf. Armellini 1893, 78); ibid. 63, Callistus a. 220 *fecit ... cimiterium via Appia*; the Callistus catacomb in use from ca. 200, cf. Lampe (1989) 14, and disciplined use of space from at least an early decade, Spera (1999) 379 and (2003a) 24; a strong increase in catacomb use from the turn of the 3rd c., cf. Février (1960) 13 or Fasola and Testini (1978) 106, 110f., 113f., 119; corresponding with the take-over of administration of Christian burials by the hierarchy, in at least one catacomb, Février (1960) 13 or Fiocchi Nicolai (2001) 16; "direct intervention" on a broad scale from the second half of the 3rd c., in Pergola and Barbini (1999) 74 or Fiocchi Nicolai (2001) 37f.; heyday of the catacombs in the 4th c., ibid. 49f., Deichmann (1993) 53, or Spera (2003a) 29; but for the poorest who are identifiable as such., i.e., lowly trades people, burial might be many miles out of town, cf. Spera (2003) 309–15.

16. In the Priscilla catacomb, the so-called *coemeterium maius*, often reproduced, e.g., by Marinone (2000) 76 fig. 4 or by sketches, Iniguez Herrero (2000) 47 pl. II, 11, 1; 158 pl. VI-12.

17. The richer catacomb burials, as shown by frescoes, of course represent "a minute minority", Guyon (1987) 192; for the range in favor, ibid. 158 and the comparative table, fig. 93; for the Callisto catacomb being the premier, Spera (1999) 379, 407ff., Pergola and Barbini (1999) 196ff., Fiocchi

Nicolai (1999) 42ff. and (2001) 64, 70; also below SS. Marco e Marcellino, ibid. 68f.; *inter duas lauros*, Guyon (1986) 173f. and Fiocchi Nicolai et al. (1999) 41; in the Damasus catacomb, Saint-Roch (1986a) 189; in the Pretestato, Spera (1992) 299f.; in the *coemeterium maius*, Fiocchi Nicolai (2001) 70; a hierarchy of catacombs recognized by Damasus' time, Guyon (1987) 411f.; and the rise in wealth evidenced from the closing 3rd c. on, Fiocchi Nicolai (2001) 44f. From literary evidence the same phenomenon of rising wealth among Rome's Christians is well known, cf., e.g., good pages in Salzman (2002) 203f.

18. Guyon (1987) 99ff. assumes 5.5 burials (*loculi*) per meter of gallery, thus, 5,500 per km in a 2 km stretch that has ca. 30 *cubicula*; so the rich would represent about .5% or, if each cubiculum held five burials, then 2.5%. Rutgers (2006) 354 uses 3.8 tombs per meter as a working figure, which would increase the 2.5% considerably. In Pergola and Barbini (1999) 189, the Pretestato catacomb appears to have ca. 2,100 m of galleries (with 4 burials per meter), thus 8,400 *loculi*, and 45 *cubicula* with ?225 burials, representing <3%; and by the same assumptions, in the Panfilo catacomb (p. 113), 550 m of galleries = 2,200 *loculi* and 8 *cubicula* with 40 burials representing <2%. For apparently similar ratios in the Commodilla catacomb, the Ippolito, SS. Pietro e Marcellino, and so forth, see the plans, fig. 25 p. 219, fig. 12 p. 155, fig. 15 p. 163, etc.

19. From the hypogeum of Trebius Iustus in the Vibia catacomb, Wilpert (1903) Tav. 132 ("a Eucharist supper") and 157 ("a heavenly feast", S. Marcellino e Pietro catacomb), both of second half of the 4th c.; other such scenes, Tav. 15, 2 and 41, 2-3 from the Callisto catacomb; and 1.260-83 on the interpretation of *refrigeria*-scenes as eucharistic; Ferrua (1970) 23ff., 33ff., and idem (1971) 61. They're called "picnics," Zanker and Ewald (2004) 35 or De Santis and Biamonte (1997) 46.

20. Mixed burials in many of Rome's catacombs, Bowder (1978) 182f., 211f.; Testini (1980) 79ff.; Jastrzebowska (1981) 198; Fasola and Fiocchi Nicolai (1989) 1154; Rutgers (1998) 83; Pergola and Barbini (1999) 92, 210ff.; and the Vibia *refrigerium*, De Santis and Biamonte (1997) 63-66.

21. Fiocchi Niciolai et al. (1999) 46, "a real explosion of offerings of all sorts, libations, food," in catacomb chambers in the second and third quarters of the 4th c., accompanying a very marked rise in general use of the catacombs, Reekmans (1989) 872f.; the shift from only poor, to rich, underground, Carletti (2000) 84 quoting A. Ferrua; carven furniture, e.g., in Jastrzebowska (1981) 148-53 (chairs or thrones), Fasola (1989) 2165ff. and fig. 15, Pergola and Barbini (1999) 78, Pani Ermini (2000) 2.64f., or Fiocchi Nicolai (2001) 44f., 69; small articles pleasing to the dead, perfume or the like, Iosi (1926) 76f., 129, 147, 192, etc.

22. Ritual Christian suppers supposed actually in *cubicula*, Rossi (1864-77) 3.474, 496, or Iosi (1924) 104f.; but the underground unsuited to them, Février (1978) 216, 240, and meal facilities and paintings more often "an evocation", 254f.; cf. esp. the remarks at 321ff., where other scholars at the conference defend traditional views in a valuable and interesting exchange; the modern consensus, finding only "symbolic" or "evocative" purpose in the furnishings, Guyon (1987) 334f., Spera (1992) 300, Pani Ermini (2000) 2.68, Marinone (2000) 1.76, 78, or Fiocchi Nicolai (2001) 72.

23. Above, ch. 1 n. 69; ch. 2 nn. 28ff., with n. 14 on John Chrysostom's seeing the deceased as sleeping, as Augustine does also, *dormientes*, *Ep*. 22.6; and ch. 3 n. 28; in the west (Italy esp.), Testini (1980) 147f., on the belief inspiring the stone chairs in *cubicula*; Février (1978) 259, a prayer of a. 291 inscribed in the Callisto catacomb to the deceased, *bene refrigera* (*ICUR* 9913) and idem (1984) 164, quoting Tert., *De monogamia* 10.4, on the *interim* in which the *anima* exists, where we may pray for its *refrigerium*; Guyon (1987) 200, 347ff.; Carletti (1989) 2191 on the common address to the deceased, *in bono refrigeres*; other uses of the same term in catacomb epigraphy, Marinone (2000) 71ff., Rutgers (2000) 74, Fiocchi Nicolai (2001) 16, and Dunbabin (2003) 108ff.; but these beliefs about the dead asleep are dismissed as "superstition", Ferrua (1941) 373ff., and "unfounded ... archaizing", Ratzinger (1988) 131.

24. In Ambrose's own church in Milan, Diehl (1925–31) 2.422, the two letters "DM" flanking a chrism; other texts in Milan, Giuntella et al. (1985) 47f.; registering distress at the letters on Christian stones, Ferrua (1984) 75, among many commentators of the past; instances or discussion in Delattre (1907) 525, 531, from the Carthage basilica; Nordberg (1963) passim, from Rome, pointing out with emphasis the reality beyond mere rhetoric of the "concept of the *manes* in the Christian *carmina cantica* at Rome", p. 218; Y. Duval (1982) 1.202ff., 734, a 4th c. African reliquary for martyr-relics, inscribed to the "gods and *manes*" of the saints named; at Greek sites, E. Marki's report in Février (1984) 168; MacMullen (1997) 218 with bibliography, esp. for western provinces and into the Middle Ages, but also in the east; Carletti (2000a) 324f.; Guyon (2001) 59, the letters/words meaning "les 'dieux Bienveillants'"; and the hope "may the Manes be good to you" (the deceased), expressed by the family, Février (1984) 169; coins for Charon, D'Angela (1983) 82 or Fiocchi Nicolai (1995–96) 169; and fragments of glass or coins in the plaster-closing of graves, e.g., Fiocchi Nicolai (1999) 46 or Pergola and Barbini (1999) 67.

25. Rebillard (1999) 1029f. on Cypr., *Ep.* 67.6, and Tert., *De idol.* 14.5.

26. For the assumption that Christians utterly rejected burial alongside non-Christians, cf., e.g., Armellini (1893) 42; but cf. sites in Africa, G.-C. Picard (1957) 48; Ben Lazreg et al. (2006) 348f.; in Salona, Dyggve (1951) 75 and Marin (1989) 1231 and idem (1994) xxiiif.; in many eastern sites, Fasola and Fiocchi Nicolai (1989) 1154f., 1181; in Aquileia, Sotinel (2005) 70f.; in Concordia, Zovatto (1950) 48; in Sicily, Agnello (1957) 237f., 241; in Rome's cemeteries, Lampe (1989) 18f., 22; Pergola and Barbini (1999) 171ff.; Rutgers (2000) 55; Fiocchi Nicolai (2001) 8, 32; in Gaul (Arles), Fasola and Fiocchi Nicolai (1989) 1158; and debate in the discussion growing out of Fasola and Fiocchi Nicolai (1989) 1207ff.

27. On days for remembrance, ch. 1 n. 66; ch. 2 n. 15; Scheid (2005) 177f.; Testini (1980) 140f.; Jastrzebowska (1981) 180, on Jan. 1, and 196f., on the Cara Cognatio transformed for Christians into the *natale Petri de cathedra*, referring to and detoxifying those empty thrones for the deceased in *cubicula*; further, Baldovin (2006) 113; on *hilaritas animorum*, Jastrzebowska (1981) 181 quoting Valerius Maximus; 147, 197, the often-cited graffito dated a. 375 in the Priscilla catacomb, "it's the Ides of February, we've come for the wine-glass"; and Pani Ermini (2000) 2.74.

28. On pagan Roman meal customs, see, e.g., Dunbabin (2003) passim; on the Christian, it is enough to cite Jastrzebowska (1979) passim, idem (1981), and idem (2001).

29. Ovid, *Fasti* 3.537f., the rites of Anna Perenna; and the *tripudium* was still the men's dance who were priests of another deity. For the condemnation of the demons' dinner-party, *mensa daemoniorum*, and *cantilenae turpes* of February 15, see Pomares (1959) 140, 164, 168, 176.

30. "We know nothing of of the cemeteries above-ground," so, Février (1978) 215, and similarly Reekmans (1968) 176 or Fiocchi Nicolai (2001) 76.

31. Calza (1940) passim, the burial grounds in use into Constantine's reign but providing only one Christian inscription, p. 41; walled *areae*, 44; 58 fig. 16, a good view of a built mensa, a "biclini" as opposed to a normal *triclinium* with three couches, and similar to my fig. 4.7 from Février (1978) 221 fig. 3; and otherwise similar but proper three-sided couches, e.g., in ibid. 221, Pompeii, or Gerlach (2001) 24 Abb. 25, Herculaneum. Libation-tubes or holes were a common feature of sarcophagi, Calza (1940) 78 or, in a Roman cemetery, Lissi Caronna (1970) 357f. and figs. 19f., dated ca. 100; under St. Peter's, a burial Christian or pagan, the question disputed, Holloway (2004) 142; from the first half of the 1st c., tubes aligned with ashes of a cremation at Pompeii, in Van Andringa and Lepetz (2006) 1144f. with fig. 8, 1146f. Frogs unluckily lost their lives exploring the tubes.

32. *Areae* of the 3rd c., in Spera (1999) 109, 113, 192, or Pani Eermini (2000) 2.16, 19; Mielsch and Hesberg (1986) 11, 16, non-Christian; in Pompeii, Tolotti (1953) 150; and mausolea once lining a road in the Vatican necropolis under S. Pietro, Pani Ermini (2000) 2.6f.; also under S. Sebas-

tiano, cf. Tolotti (1953) 55 and Tav. II; idem (1984) 126 fig. 1, 137 fig. 4; De Santis and Biamonte (1997) 46.

33. Under St. Peter's, the later-second-century mausolea in a double line are described by Apollonj Ghetti et al. (1951) 1.23–135 passim; libation-tubes at 74 and 111; and note (134f.) that one of these burials, called gamma, of the first century, was evidently venerated next to the Memoria Apostolica, along with a third burial, also unidentified; a good photo, 26, and a good plan, 24 fig. 8 and vol. 2 Tav. CV, or in Hesberg (1987) 46 and fold-out Abb. 2–3; further, Mielsch and Hesberg (1986) 11 Taf. 8–9; for the *memoria* under San Sebastiano, see Tolotti (1984) 127f.; Kjaergaard (1984) 59, 67ff., who also speaks of the animal remains from *vigilia* for St. Peter, p. 70; Deichmann (1993) 61; Pergola and Barbini (1999) 183; Fiocchi Nicolai (2001) 36 fig. 21; and the graffiti referring to the veneration of the saints by the devout who visited their shrine as a *refrigerium*, Tolotti (1984) 150, ICUR 13,003. The mention in Commodian is hard to place in date, but a significant indication of a general phenomenon seen in the west, "You want to chill out? Off to the martyrs!" (*refrigerare cupis animam, ad martyres i, Instruct.* 2.17 line 19, CSEL 15.82).

34. Février (1978) 254.

35. Minimal inhumation by *tegulae* lining the bottom and sides of the cavity is to be seen in Carthage, for example, and Greek sites; also, closer to Rome, well illustrated by Manniez (2007) 92f.

36. Duchesne (1955–57) 1.172, the silver statues, and 178, *S. Paolo ex suggestione Silvestri*.

37. Krautheimer speaks in Italian, in the Discussion after N. Duval (1978) 572; cf. Euseb., *Vita Const.* 3.32, Constantine tells Jerusalem bishop Macarius to work with and advise church architects.

38. Chastagnol (1966) 436 calls attention to the text from the *Coll. Avellana* 3, to Sallustius prefect of Rome. N. Duval (1999) 28 rightly pooh-poohs the notion that Constantine imposed his own ideas from the model of an imperial audience-hall, rather than the more obvious civil basilicas.

39. For the 150 in S. Sebastiano, see Pani Ermini (2000) 2.122. The Ardeatina basilica is discussed with a photo in Spera (1999) 78ff. or La Rocca (2000) 208–12; for the stacking of bodies and the inclusion of coins in many burials here by which the use of the church floor may be dated, into the 6th c., see Spera 161, 165f., and 174 fig. 53; for the semi-attached mausolea on the outside walls of S. Sebastiano and SS. Marcellino e Pietro, see Guyon (1984) 190f.

40. In Milan, burial next to Gervasius and Protasius for Ambrose and the sister of the praetorian prefect, and for Ambrose's brother next to Nazarus, Bonamente (1988) 116; parallels in the east, ch. 1 n. 82 (Gregory of Nyssa's parents, etc.); the inscription, Rossi et al. (1922–) 1 no. 3127 of a. 382.

41. Access to confessions restricted to the elite, Jerome quoted in Brenk (1995) 76; in Rome, debate about the donors of *tituli*-churches, e.g., Lampe (1989) 304ff.; on papal construction, see Duchesne (1955–57) passim, e.g., 202, 208, and Matthiae (1962) 74, on financing of S. Sabina; besides Milan construction by Ambrose, some in Aquileia by its bishop, Sotinel (2005) 43ff., 179, 217; but a cemetery given to Velitrae by an heiress, Fiocchi Nicolai et al. (1999) 23. Wealth-distribution in the capital had a unique shape, given that the average senator at the turn of the 2nd c. would have an income enough to support 2,000 families (K. Hopkins 1998, 208). For the pre-eminence of the clergy, see above, ch. 1 n. 58 (a mixed picture), ch. 3 n. 45, MacMullen (2006) 9f. on the socioeconomic position of bishops; and, broadly, Pietri (1984) 306f.

42. Ferrua (1990) 26.

43. The Six all of Constantinian date except the Ardeatina, Pani Ermini (2000) 1.17 and 2.115f., but cf. alternatives in the appendix; slanted end of many circuses, Humphrey (1986) 23, 335, 340, 346, 352, 363, 377, 403, 563, 578 and 588 (Maxentian); Krautheimer et al. (1937–77) 2.141f. with the first correct discussion; further, 3.134, 141, and Curran (2000) 104 and Cechelli (2003) 113, on the several layers of burials in S. Lorenzo and elsewhere; accepting of the funerary purpose, De Santis and Biamonte (1997) 50f.; Spera (1999) 387; La Rocca (2000) 209; Fiocchi Nicolai (2001)

58; on the sarcophagus from a mausoleum adjoining S. Sebastiano with a libation-tube in it, Pani Ermini (2000) 2.71; on the mensa in the Ardeatina basilica, ibid. 113; on possible processional uses, Jastrzebowska (1981) 162, and dining, 164 (quoted); Ferrua (1990) 25 fig. 5 on the crypt-stairs down to the memorial of the apostles; on an altar in place for saints'-day services, Deichmann (1970) 146, quoting the *Vita S. Melaniae,* and 160, citing the gift of a silver altar recorded in the *Liber pontificalis.*

44. C. R. Galvao-Sobrinho in an unpublished paper points to civic banquets that would serve as models (at his nn. 388f.), e.g., Lact., *De mort. persecut.* 11.1f. or *Syll. inscr. Graec.,* ed. 3, no. 1009; further on the custom, Donahue (2004) 143f.; for the grand gesture of the senator Pammachius in 397, see Paulinus Nolensis, *Ep.* 13.11ff. (*PL* 61.213Bff.), the text in Skeb (1998) 1.322-26, where the host directed the *pauperes* to be arranged *distincte per accubitus, in terra,* to receive their *sportae*; noted of course by Jastrezebowska (1979) 84; also by Brandenburg (1995a) 45, where "in the transept, as we may assume, *refrigeria* (Totenmahlerfeiern) were quite the normal thing next to the tomb" of St. Peter. For large crowds, obviously the transept would not suffice.

45. *Civ. dei* 8.27, "who among the faithful ever heard of a priest standing at an altar, even over the holy body of some martyr, that" prayed to them not God; for "at their *memoriae* the offering is made to God." For altars directly above martyr burials, see, e.g., Hier., *Contra Vigil.* 8 (*PL* 23.346B), indicating a Rome setting; Paulinus of Nola, *Ep.* 32.6 (*PL* 61.333Bf.), remains beneath a private chapel altar, for veneration; Ward-Perkins (1969) 4; various examples in archeology in my earlier chapters (ch. 1 n. 25; ch. 2 nn. 1, 10f., 22, 34), and Brandenburg (1995) 73f.; emphatically denied as ever a possibility by Deichmann (1993) 64f.

46. Libation-tubes to martyr-burials, Jastrzebowska (1981) 206; Matthiae (1962) 83, S. Paolo f.l.m.; the tube given a late date by Curran (2000) 106ff. or Filippi (2004) 201, 210, 214 and idem (2005-6) 280. For martyr-mensae, notice the built one next to the tomb of Callisto in the catacomb of S. Calepodio, Pergola and Barbini (1999) 237; or see the inscription cited by Krautheimer (1960) 15, marking a burial site bought *ad me(n)sa Laurenti descintibus in cripta parte dextera,* with another similar text also in S. Lorenzo, and one from S. Paolo (p. 29). Compare the *mensa Cypriani,* ch. 3 at n. 34. The most recent report on the Paul-sarcophagus and the basilica "beyond the Walls" is Filippi (2005-6) passim, esp. the explanation (289f.) that, whatever the liturgy for saints' days, the same altar-mensa would be used for the Eucharist and *refrigeria* (the Eucharist at martyrs' tombs had been authorized at Rome by Felix, A.D. 269-274, cf. Duchesne 1955-57, 1.158).

47. Pietri (1976) 604 draws attention to the text and customs indicated in Paulinus Nolensis, *Carm.* 27.569 (*PL* 61.661A), *mensa Petri recipit, quod Petri dogma refutat* (with reference to I Peter 4.5, which excoriates drunkenness); and for pot-sherds showing what went on at the sites of the Six, cf. Krautheimer (1937-77) 2.142.

48. MacMullen (1981) 63f.

49. *Votum solvit* in Rome's epigraphy is the most common; also as obvious terminology, *vot(um) sol(vit) dibus, CIL* 6.98; *Bonae Deae ex voto fecit,* 57; *Soli Invicto ex voto promisso donum donavit,* 729; *Iovi Optimo Maximo de voto fecit,* 2818; *voto suscepto posuit* or *redidit,* 697; *voti compos dedit,* 3723; *quod promiserat,* 9422.

50. Diehl (1925-31) conveniently supplies *peto, vel sim.,* nos. 2320, 2324, 2330, 2332-37; *votum promisit/solvit/obtulit/reddit,* 1906, 1906A-B, 1907, 1909; *voto fecit/dedit,* 1929-30; *de donis dei fecit,* 1935A; *refrigeri Ianuarius Agatopus Felicissimus martyres,* in the Pretestato catacomb, 2318; *mensa marturum Felicis Naboris in mente habete,* 2331, near Sitifis in Africa.

51. Most frequent, *in mente habete, vel sim.,* Carletti (2000) 82f., e.g., conveniently in Rossi et al. (1922-) no. 12973, for safe sailing; or "we ask" a safe sail, 12959; the petitioners "offered a *refrigerium* so bear us in mind," 12942; or "promised a *refrigerium* as a vow," 12932, 12993-94, 13003, 13030,

13048; "the *refrigerium* he promised he did offer," 12907; or simply "he fulfilled his vow," 13032; many prayers for victory for a choice of chariots, 13088a–c, 13089a–d and Eck (1995) 217f.; below, ch. 5 n. 6; and on the declaration of having offered a *refrigerium*, Marinone (2000) 74; on the setting, Jasrezebowska (1981) ch. 5.

52. Guyon (1987) 362–71, Deichmann (1993) 60, and Pergola and Barbini (1999) 164, dating the expansion to the 340s; Reekmans (1995) on Urban and Quirinus in the Praetextatus catacomb, from the mid-third century; Pietri (1984) 298 on the cult and graffiti offered to a revered priest; and compare the archeological record lying behind the cult of the martyr Valentinus and its expression in expanded facilities, from catacomb to basilica, by 318, ibid. 109ff.; and, emphasizing the simplicity and poverty of pre-Constantinian martyr-burials in the catacombs, Deichmann (1993) 61 or Spera (2003a) 28.

53. Martyr-numbers, Fiocchi Nicolai (2001) 79; Jastrezebowska (1981) 210. Compare in Carthage, ch. 3 n. 46.

54. Consensus sees all the Six as memorial churches, even if the martyr celebrated in the "Anonima della via Prenestina" is not identifiable, cf., e.g., Brandenburg (1995a) 44 and Fiocchi Nicolai (2001) 88 (they are the so-called "Greek martyrs"?).

55. The count of the bodies is given twice (137 in Amm. 27.3.12, or 160 in Faustinus, *Adv. Damasum* 2, *PL* 13.82Af., or *Coll. Avellana* 1.7, *CSEL* 35.3); the site, S. Sebastiano, Frutaz (1969) 28; or perhaps, by rather complicated reasoning, S. Maria Maggiore, Luciani (2000) 132; Damasus' role and strategy, Fiocchi Nicolai (2001) 79 and Ferrua (1985) 4f.

56. As an example of the less-critical suggestions of the past, Kirsch (1940) 120f.; some good pages in Matthiae (1962) 16–24; no *domus ecclesiae* so far identified, Pietri (1978) 10, Reekmans (1989) 864, or Fiocchi Nicolai (2001) 8, 49, in agreement with Krautheimer, earlier, and Cechelli (2003) 8 or Snyder (2003) 128; proposals disposed of by Kraeling (1967) 130ff., another by Trinci Cecchelli (1978) 560, with Discussion from other scholars, 567f.

57. On *tituli* pre-313, numbering 15–23 (Lampe 1989, 303) or 18 identifiable at least by name, and seven more in the course of the 4th c., see Puza (2001) 54; doubtful that any *tituli*-remains of today served worship pre-313, Snyder (2003) 142; further, including surviving fabric, see, e.g., Matthiae (1962) 19ff., Reekmans (1989) 866, and Fiocchi Nicolai (2001) 93ff., and in the appendix below, "Rome" nos. 14–34 passim, where some dimensions of churches are supplied.

58. Quoted, Krautheimer (1983) 94 and 102. His estimates of space inside his churches cannot, in my opinion, be supported, and he seems to have made no realistic calculation of crowds; but he sees the problem, and remarks on the total of available space even under Constantine, with the Lateran and St. Peter's included, not to be estimated at a total exceeding 10,000, "amazingly small when set against the probable size of the total Roman congregation." For more on papal *tituli*, ibid. 96ff. or Tesei (1986) passim.

59. The estimate is that of Optatus, *Adv. Donat*. 2.4 (*CSEL* 26.39), probably well informed whether for the work's first or second edition, ca. 375 or 385.

60. In the mid-3rd c. the church supported 1,500 widows and orphans, and the assumption has been made that these were the survivors from ordinary mortality within some larger group, the Christian population. But how large a group? Lampe (1989) 116f. quoted estimates of 10,000 to 30,000; Trombley (2006) suggested 40,000 which he took to be 5-10 per cent of the city; Edwards (2006) 155 suggested 40,000, Matthiae (1962) 26 suggested 40,000 to 50,000 in the mid-3rd c.; 30,000 was the estimate of Stark (1996) 105; Guyon (1987) 101 split the difference (30,000 to 50,000). But these assumptions seem to me out of the question. Readiness by the church to offer support surely drew in the indigent from the general non-Christian population, just as did Pammachius' public banquet. Once on the lists as saved from starvation, being instructed also, the indigent might well

become Christian. But their numbers say nothing about the host group. And there is also the physical impossibility of fitting such numbers into the conjectured total of the so-called *tituli*-churches of the time, twenty of them able to accommodate, let us say, 300 each, and thus a total for the city of 6,000.

61. Christie (2006) 98 with 321 suggests "up to approximately 250,000 Christians in the early fourth c.", working from Rome's 25 parish churches at the turn of the fourth century on the undefended assumption of 10,000 congregants per *titulus*; and "a few hundred thousand" in Constantine's time, says Krautheimer (1983) 102. Reekmans (1989) 873 supposes "a great majority" of the population was Christian by the mid-4th c. (= ?300,000). If, however, we take only the largest buildings, we have (in round figures) 2,000 Christians in S. Giovanni plus 10,000 or 20,000 at most in the Six and another 3,500 in St. Peter's, plus another 8,000 in the remaining 30 churches, almost all of them quite small, making the grand total I suggest, of <35,000 or <7% at the turn of the 5th c.

62. Ample solea among smaller basilicas, e.g., about half of the area of the nave in S. Clemente, cf. Krautheimer et al. (1937–77) 1.pl. XIX; the solea in S. Giovanni, Blaauw (1994) 127f., 141, or Brandenburg (1995a) 62 Abb. 1 and pp. 37 and 41, a feature ca. 3 m wide and of the early 4th c.; and a processional passage marked by sockets for posts in St. Peter's, cf. the references in the appendix.

63. E.g., at S. Marco, Krautheimer et al. (1937–77) 2.245; in a number of other churches, Brandenburg (1995a) 46; also, however, in a martyr church, St. Peter's, ibid., or S. Sebastiano, Tolotti (1953) 228 or Brandenburg (1995) 72f.

64. Matthiae (1962) 124.

65. Dölger (1925) 3, the date being mid-4th c.

66. Selhorst (1931) 33–35 passim; on the casket, Angiolini (1970) 22 and passim, Brenk (1995) 75f. and pls. 3a–b, and Speier et al. (2007) 117; but correcting and adding to all other accounts, Longhi (2006) identifies the three more visible panels with the three major churches (56f., 66f., 71f., 127) and (76, 94ff.) supplies a persuasive date.

67. Fiocchi Nicolai (1995–96) 71 fig. 2 conveniently collects the plans of the Six, from which my fig. 4.8 draws. The date at which two of the Six basilicas passed out of active service is unknown (one on the via Ardeatina, "Marciana", and the other on the via Prenestina, the "Anonima"); SS. Pietro and Marcellino was abandoned by the 9th c., cf. Krautheimer et al. (1937–77) 2.197, 203; S. Agnese wholly reconstructed to other purposes, *a solo* says the source, by Pope Honorius in the 7th c., ibid. 1.17, 34; S. Sebastiano in the same century subject to major alterations and then taken over as a monastery in the 12th c., ibid. 4.105, 110f., 143, 146; and S. Lorenzo made into "an entirely new church" in the late 6th c. and in the 8th, re-dedicated to St. Mary, it lapses into disuse, ibid. 2.10, 138.

68. Milan a capital from 286, Stein (1959) 66, 68, 202ff.; population, Krautheimer (1983) 71, including suburbs, 130,000 to 150,000, repeated by Salzman (2007) 225.

69. Quoted Markus (1990) 143, with Ambros., *Ep.* 22.1ff.

70. Sannazaro (2000–1) 51–56 on the very large cemetery, some burials of the fourth century with coins for Charon, libation tubes, and the ashes of meals cooked there.

71. See the appendix s.v. Milan.

72. *De Elia et ieiunio* 17 (*PL* 14.719).

73. Zeno, *Tract.* 1.25.6 (10f.), in Löfstedt (1987) 12, noted by Jastrezebowska (1979) 84.

74. *De laude sanctorum* 5 (*PL* 20.447), writing ca. 396: *psallite, psallite, et choreis tramites quibus ad coelum ascenditur et pede pulsate.*

75. *In Lk* 6.5 (*PL* 15.167A).

76. On Paulinus' career, Cantino Wataghin and Pani Ermini (1995) 142f.; ibid. 142, burials in the basilica floor; on the evolution of the basilica, Ferrua (1977a) 106; in excellent detail, Lehman (1994) 284ff. and idem (2004) pls. 19f. Abb. 24–27 and fold-out pl. 1, on which my fig. 4.13 is based; size of

Nola at Abb. 34–36, ca. 35 ha; discussion, ibid. 33–60; the deputation, p. 146; the date of the project, p. 156 (begun in a. 400) and Christie (2006) 86f.; its reception, Brandenburg (1995) 77ff.; and relics received from high friends, Paulinus, *Carm.* 27.410ff. (*PL* 61.661).

77. On St. Clarus, see the *Bibliotheca Sanctorum* (Rome 1961–70) 3.1231, with a day for celebration in November; and Paulin. Nol., *Ep.* 32.6 (*PL* 61.333Bf.).

78. Exorcism, Saxer (1995) 50; slaughtering, MacMullen (1997) 113, with similar cook-outs on saints' days in eastern settings, 117, 135; Grottanelli (2005) 387ff., with considerable apologetic, 392–95; 389, on the formulae of gifts to the saint, *votum solvit* or the like, cf. Paulinus, *Carm.* 20.64f. (*PL* 61.553C) or *Ep.* 13.11 (*PL* 61.562Bf., 565Bf.); the same in graffiti *in situ*, Ferrua (1963) 18f.; pouring in of liquids, Paulinus, *Carm.* 18.38f. (*PL* 61.491) and 21.588ff., and MacMullen (1997) 114; *vigilia* and song, ibid.; the quotation, Paulin., *Carm.* 27.563ff.; and attendance from afar, Saxer (1995) 4.

79. Terrier (2003) 22.

80. On the funerary church of Saints Gervasius and Protasius, see Bonnet and Privati (1990) 752–57. For the construction history inside the city, see the appendix; and for further details, including his estimate of the population of town and suburbs (2,000–3,000, and another 2,000–3,000), I draw on a tour of the site guided by the chief excavator, Charles Bonnet, with my thanks to him also for advice per litteris.

81. Remains of funerary meals in south Gaul show the sacrificial meat to have been all or mostly burnt up, not eaten, Bats (2002) 287f. (but these, pre-Roman only?); funerary altars with carved receptacles for food and drink offerings in their tops in the museums of Vaison and Arles, I have seen, but they are undated; for a banquet scene of the first half of the 4th c. on a sarcophagus at Arles, similar to figs. 4.4–5, above, see Jastrzebowska (2001) 57, the reference thanks to P. De Michèle; Young (1988) 219 notices with surprise church construction at Autun for funerary purposes in the first half of the 4th c. (which is what one would expect), with evidence of Greeks among the Christian community; and at Narbo, another funerary church, i.e., with 46 burials under its floor, of the latter quarter of the 4th c., cf. N. Duval (1995b) 32–38. At Vaison, Christians show up in a cemetery mixed among pagan burials, cf. Goudineau and Kisch (1991) 127. Regarding the rate of spread of Christianity, there is some control offered by the Congressi internazionali di archeologia cristiana, meeting every five or six years since 1894 except as interrupted by wars and the Depression. In their Proceedings, the periodic regional surveys are very helpful, without, I think, pointing to more sites than I have listed in the appendix; but more might well be found in local archeological publications of the last couple of decades. For the third century, at least, we have an authoritative denial of any Christian presence at all, attested archeologically, throughout Istria, Noricum, and western Pannonia, in Sotinel (2005) 66.

82. Tacoma (2006) 33; on the number of sees, C. and L. Pietri (1990) 135f., identifying 25 in A.D. 312 with some unknown number, but not vastly greater, later in the century. Most of the sees overlap with sites known archeologically.

83. Cf. above, n. 59 (Optatus).

Chapter 5

1. Illustrations in MacMullen (1984) 8 or Nongbri (2008) ch. 4. Underlying most discussion of what "religion" really *is,* is the irritating error (realist as opposed to nominalist) that because we have the word, therefore a corresponding thing must exist—if we could only agree on it (!).

2. Cf. North (1992) 187f., and for the contrast drawn between religion and ritual, see further, below, n. 40. Echoing North on the necessity of "an organized system," etc., Rebillard (2003) 9 would reject "the totality of beliefs and practices of Christians" in defining Christianity, and would include

only what belongs in "the organized" (evidently meaning, authorized by clergy); but he gives only a glance at certain older studies of Rome's catacombs, otherwise ignoring archeological evidence, and this explains his definition.

3. Ambrose, above in ch. 4 at n. 72; Augustine in ch. 3 nn. 36f. and in *De cura pro mort.* 1.2 (*PL* 40.593), that rites for the dead fulfill the purposes or nature of *religio*; again, *Sermo* 361.6 (*PL* 39.1602), defending rites at the tombs of the dead, *ista fideles faciant religiose erga memorias suorum*, including the Eucharist; Symm., *Relatio* 6 in *PL* 16.967B (Barrow 1973, 38, *Relatio* 3.7), *cumque alias religiones ipse* (the Christian emperor Constantius) *sequeretur, has servavit imperio*; and, against the idea of masses of people perpetuating traditional gestures of veneration brainlessly, without meaning, see the very interesting remarks of Marcel Le Glay (1966) 160f., on the rationality and independence of mind of Saturn-worshippers even of quite humble classes.

4. E.g., ch. 3 at n. 47; ch. 4 at nn. 69 and 78. The most striking testimony lies in the beliefs underlying instruction of catechumens and baptism, throughout punctuated by exorcism (ch. 1 at nn. 3–6), on which a great deal more could be said; on the visible results, such statements as Origen's, "We see the foul spirits being flogged, for by such means many are brought round to God," *Homil. in Sam.* 1.10 (Nautin 1977, 134) with many other texts in the east matched also in the west by Justin or Tertullian or later writers, cf. MacMullen (1984) 26f.; much that I don't like to reiterate, e.g., on interventions by saints, texts in MacMullen (1997) 121ff., 166, and passim; and many more references to show all such ideas about causation ubiquitous, in MacMullen (2006) 42–51.

5. Above, ch. 2 nn. 14f.; ch. 3 nn. 28, 30; ch. 4 nn. 22f.; and in Rome, the last line of a versified epitaph, *ossibus infundam quae nuncquam* [!] *vina bibisti*, *CIL* 6.23472.

6. For the quid-pro-quo quality in prayers to the saints, a clearer example than most is the cleric's dedication of the church to St. Salsa, "an answering gift", *reciprocum munus*, *CIL* 8.20914 in Christern (1968) 236 or Y. Duval (1982) 2.588 (notice, the dedicator was answered in mid-life, so the prayer was not for his soul); or again, the gift of construction to the church at Aphrodisias pledged to the resident saint in return for healing. As to the Tertullian quotation, see *Apol.* 21.31 (*PL* 1.404A).

7. Dolbeau (1996) 281–90, Dolbeau 21.3ff. passim, *fratres*, etc.; quoted, pp. 281f. §4; and Hill (1990–2007) 3, 1.165, "Augustine never addresses brothers and sisters; it's *fratres* throughout.... it's quite clear, again and again, that he is in fact addressing himself to the men of the congregation, to whom he will occasionally talk about women in the third person. Not only in fact is he almost always addressing himself to the men, he is addressing himself to the upper class men in the congregation." In Dolbeau, cit., insolence, p. 288 §7; significance and ubiquity of references to slave-owning in sermons, MacMullen (1989) 507ff., idem (2003) 470f.; and amply attested as the assumption of the usual situation, that everyone had a slave, often more than one, and indeed in the parlance of the preacher's audience and stratum, counted as *pauper* if restricted only to a few slaves, cf. Morin (1930) 264 §13 at Hippo (*PL Suppl.* 2.434, Caillau and Saint-Yves 2.11) and 630 §5 (Morin 11), Aug., *Serm.* 21.5f. (*PL* 38.145) and 61.9 (412), both at Hippo, 72.5 (469), 345.3 (1519), 357.5 (1585) at Carthage, and 356.6 (1576) at Hippo, still a *homo pauper* although owning *aliqui servuli* (Augustine minimizing the wealth indicated by the use of the diminutive, "just a few little slaves").

8. Ennabli (1997) 21ff. gathers the references to Augustine's preaching in the basilica ten times or more, and the later description of its mensa and the *vigiliae*, songs, and dances, the latter in the 5th c. forbidden; the anniversary, on September 19.

9. Ch. 4 n. 17.

10. Caillet (1993) 432f., 445ff.; above, ch. 3 n. 19 and 4 at n. 41; on elections, MacMullen (2006) 20f. and 124 with the sources. They show the old ways to be still the forms of record for a time, as e.g. in Soc., *HE* 5.8.12, election "by the people" still in 381 in Constantinople or Philostorgius, *HE* 9.10

(ordination in a. 370); a choice between the new procedures and the old, Council of Hippo a. 393, canon 20 (*Corp. Christianorum series latina* 149 [1974], p. 39); and thereafter especially in Italy and the west, the populace becoming merely a spectator to approve a decision of the elite and clergy. For the obsession with precedence and seniority, cf. MacMullen (2006) 22 and notes 35f.

11. MacMullen (1981) 24–28 provides illustrations from many eastern cities.

12. The date, 370s or early 380s, Hier., *C. Joannen. Hieros.* 8 (*PL* 23.377C), often cited; good remarks on the setting (with a slip in the citation) in Salzman (2002) 61f., 67, 203f., 332, regarding the striving for *gloria* in any path or post that was held in honor, in priesthoods such as Vettius Agorius Praetextatus had held (*pontifex Solis, pontifex Vestae,* etc., cf. *PLRE* 1.722) or in the church, increasingly acceptable. A little later, Augustine explains and defends how a local notable professed a change from his heathen ways in order to qualify for Hippo's municipal council or mayoralty, Morin (1930) 591f. (Morin 1.2f.).

13. MacMullen (1984) 154.

14. Above, ch. 1 n. 41 and ch. 5, above, n. 7.

15. Tert., *Ad Scap.* 2.10, *pars paene maior civitatis cuiusque*, "almost a majority everywhere" (*civitas*, for Tertullian as for Augustine, meaning both *urbs* and *territorium*, not just a conurbation), a statement taken to be the literal truth by Quacquarelli (1957) 91 but rightly dismissed by W. Elliger as "laughable," *RAC* 20 (2001) 250; Harnack (1908) 2.133 on Chrysostom's figure of 200,000 for the *demos* of the city (thus, excluding slaves, children, and transients, and requiring a total quite out of the question), and the total congregants of the chief church being 100,000 (the round figures amounting to an apology for a guess, and wildly at odds with the possible space available for worship); further, *CT* 16.10.22, doubting there are any non-Christians left, where the opinion is meant as off-hand and derisory rather than a statistic. Notice also Augustine's term for the Christian population, constituting the *orbis terrarum*, "the whole globe" in *Serm.* 62.4 (*PL* 38.416).

16. On the two statistical items, see ch. 1 at n. 36; ch. 4 at n. 60.

17. For Harnack as the starting point for attempts at statistical modelling, see, e.g., Hopkins (1998) 192 or Stark (1996) 14, 132. The latter starts with several assumptions which I think are mistaken (no need to say here, why), e.g., that Constantine was in part induced to become a Christian because Christians "were so numerous" (p. 50), giving us a clue to their great numbers, or that Christianity "accorded higher status" and "was unusually appealing" to women (p. 95) compared to non-Christian religious groups.

18. For a date around A.D. 300, Drake (2005) 2 finds "almost everyone" in agreement with what Harnack "guessed", i.e,. 7–10% Christian—e.g. myself (1984) 32, proposing five million out of 60 = 8% or (1997, 72) 10%; cf. also Lane Fox (1989) 592, 4–5%; Stark (1996) 5–7.5 million = 8–12%; Brown (1996) 24, 10%; Hopkins (1998) 6 million = 12%. But no one attempts to justify his guess.

19. Salamito (1995) 678.

20. Hopkins (1998) 223 (36 million are Christians out of 60 million); Stark (1996) 7, 10 (in A.D. 350, 33,882,008 are Christians = 56.5%); graphs and tables, e.g., ibid. 13; parametrics, Hopkins 213; various historical developments posited to explain the rapid rate, Stark p. 5 (*re* Constantine); Hopkins on "continuous rapid growth" or the like words (pp. 205, 210, 219, 223) requiring historical conjectures; more cautious estimates in Baus and Ewig (1973) 4, Christians "a considerable minority" in 324 and (434) "a majority" in 450; but no attempt at an estimate in C. and L. Pietri (1990) or Chadwick (2001).

21. Frend (1984) 988, with little justification at 444f. besides Harnack's work, and with no allusion to archeological evidence.

22. On the two glimpses, see MacMullen (1997) 66f., 69, 199.

23. On the cult of the saints, Brown (1982), esp. 13–21 and 27f., offers assertions and polemic,

much of the latter directed at other scholars from centuries ago, without supplying evidence for his views; and the pages (37f., 40f., "new foci of worship") where he includes some archeological evidence rather weaken his argument since he confuses Tipasa with Tebessa. General correction was offered by a scholar entirely at home in the period and subject matter: cf. Pietri (1984), pointing out the large errors of vision, especially the slighting of the story pre-375 and of archeology in general. In illustration of Pietri's criticisms, it is archeology that shows us the cult of the saints originating in private initiatives at least from the mid-third century (above, at Trieste: at Salona's Manastirine and Marusinac cemeteries; in Eusebia's religious practices in Constantinople; and in Rome, the examples gathered at n. 52 of ch. 4). Lancel and Mattei (2003) 94 conclude rightly that, in regard to martyr-cult, later, Augustine's was an effort, "a new approach to the divine, by which the ecclesiastical institution (the episcopacy) tries (and successfully) to get the upper hand in the 'question'".

24. See, for example, Marin (1989a) 1127ff. on the east; also in the same volume of *Actes du XIe congrès international d'archéologie chrétienne* (1989) some 350 pages of survey of the east (pp. 1562–1908: Oriens, Egypt included)) in which only two or three sites of construction pre-date 451; similarly, construction only 5th c. or later in Greece and Illyricum, Marzolff (1984) 6 and Ulbert (1984) 20; on the other hand, even in the 5th c. there were areas showing hardly a touch of Christian construction, cf., e.g., Elton (2006) 306. But it would have been too much for me to include the empire's churches known in the fifth century alone, a number half again as great as I have found for my appendix.

25. For example, non-Christian in Edelstein and Edelstein (1945) 1.220, 320, *edeito, deomenos, supplico*; Christian in Caillet (1993) 407 #49, *contra votum fecerunt* or, in numberless building-inscriptions, *ex voto, hyper euches*.

26. MacMullen (1997) 121.

27. *Acta S. Cypriani* 11.4 in Musurillo (1972) 175; at the martyr's tomb, from the dramatic date of ca. 315 forward, *magna quotidie signa fiunt*, by the account in Hier., *Vita Hilarionis* 47 (*PL* 23.54A); martyr's miracles depicted on martyr-church walls, Basil, *Homil. 17 in Gord. mart.* (*PG* 31.489A); Bernardi (1968) 164, Gregory Nazianzenus' report of miracles of healing in Cple by Cyprian's relics.

28. On Lucilla, cf. Optatus, *De schismate Donat.* 1.12 (*CSEL* 26.18), to which Dölger (1932) draws attention: the martyr is *nescius qui*, twice, *si tamen martyr, nescio quis homo*, a mere man, who has not even been *vindicatus*, i.e., approved for worship; Joh. Chrysos., *In S. Julianum mart.* 2 (*PG* 50.669), relics expel demons whenever they are applied; *DACL* 10.2438 or 2451, Basil sends relics to a fellow-bishop; Ambros., *Ep.* 22.17 (*PL* 16.1020A); further, Vigilantius, in Hier., *C. Vigil.* 4 (*PL* 23.342); and Bradshaw et al. (2002) 221, collecting various references to the Christians in both east and west who carry relics or the eucharistic bread in amulets on their person. An instance is Paulinus' carrying bits of the Cross on his person, to be kissed in moments of danger, *Carm.* 28.116. On miracles of healing from the tomb celebrated in sermons, see Basil, *Orat. in S. Mamantem* 26 (*PG* 31.589C), Greg. Nyss., *Laudat. in SS XL* (*PG* 46.784) or Greg. Naz., *Homil. in SS. XL* (*PG* 46.784C).

29. Above, ch. 1 at n. 87; ch. 3 at n. 38; a slightly different target of disapproval in Cyprian, Saxer (1969) 298f. and (1980) 100f.; and above, ch. 4 at n. 76.

30. Jonkers (1954) 13, whose date (305) for the Council of Elvira is too early, cf. Chadwick (2001) 181, whom I follow (MacMullen 2006, 2), but there is room for still later dates, cf. Sotomayor (1996) 256, 264; and on candles at sepulchres, cf., e.g., Ferrua (1941) 377; a non-Christian example, *CIL* 8.9052.

31. Cf. illustrative passages above, ch. 1 at nn. 71 and 85; ch. 4 at n. 78; also references in MacMullen (1997) 220 n. 27.

32. E.g., Joh. Chrysos., *Homil. in Hebr.* 15; Bradshaw et al. (2002) 219.

33. On the *Peregrinatio Egeriae*, cf. ch. 1 n. 25 and elsewhere.

34. Illustrations in MacMullen (1997) 211.

35. Aug., *Serm.* 310.2.2 (*PL* 38.1415).

36. Bernardi (1968) 306, 80ff. (Gordius the martyr), 216 (procession).

37. "Counterfeiting the name of Christians" is how Eusebius describes the flow into the church already in the 330s, *Vita Const.* 4.54 (*PG* 20.1205A); *nec christiani nec pagani* is a pope's description of those who indulge in cult banquets, much later, cf. Pomarès (1959) 168, 176, §§9 and 19; yet Bernardi (1968) 69f., from the trio Basil, Gregory and Gregory, concludes that the name "Christian" would be freely given to "anyone who took a responsive part in services", with an illustration or explanation in delay of baptism, ibid. and 299, with Bradshaw et al. (2002) 219 referring to the "half-converted", and neglect of Eucharist even among the baptized, this, a frequent complaint from John Chrysostom, *Homil. in 2 Cor.* 2 (*PG* 61.401) or *Homil. in ep. ad Ephes.* 3.4f. (*PG* 62.29), and *Homil.-in-Hebr.* passages in Allen (1996) 416f. For the fuzzy boundaries, cf. references in MacMullen (1990) 152 and a good reading of Zeno Veronensis et al. in Daut (1971) 178ff. and passim (his essay provoking a furious critique); also Markus (2005) 8, on "the flood of the half converted".

38. Aug., *C. Iulianum* 2.14 (*PL* 45.1147); *De cat. rud.* 22.40 (*PL* 40.339), *carnalis populus*; and many other illustrations of the class sense in the later Empire, MacMullen (1974) 192 and (1990) 264f.

39. Brooks (1923) 234; Aug., *En. in ps.* 78 *sermo* 2.14 (*PL* 37.1140).

40. As a small instance: G. J. Johnson (1984) 119 on "an easy and unthinking co-existence of Christianity and traditional culture" in Bithynian inscriptions, a phenomenon amply attested in other contexts and a favorite for philologists to write about, quoting Jerome and dozens of others on the temptations of heathen literature. Cf. some references in MacMullen (1997) 241f. On A. D. Nock, MacMullen (1985–86) 74f.; and on the essential role of the "spiritual" as opposed to the ritual in religion (cf. above at n. 2), notice the interesting pages in Corinne Bonnet (2007), esp. 4 on the hugely influential Franz Cumont: "the almost unknowing inheritor of a Judeo-Christian view of life, he made something holy out of the inner life, belief, conscience, spirituality, while rejecting the ritual in the pagan sphere". For modern authors, quoted, cf. MacMullen (1997) 184, 217 (R. A. Markus, A. Gurevich, and others noticed by S. R. F. Price). Recently, Scheid (2005) at the end of his very substantial book indicates that, finding nothing else in his written sources regarding the cult of the dead, he concludes that its only meaning or (in French) "sens" was to make explicit the higher rank of the Beings addressed, compared with mortals, and his "surprise that this should be the unique obsession of the ritual" (276f.). "Did it deserve to be called 'religion'?" Were there no spiritual or mystic currents?—for surely religion is unimaginable without a true mystery, something un-knowable, at its heart as defined and dictated by a priesthood. In contrast, Roman ritual was "empty" (279–82, without defining "spirit" or "spiritual"). Each worshipper could make up his own "sens". Scheid's reasoning is very like supposing we all pay our taxes each for a different reason, and it is therefore a mere rite, since we do not explain in our surviving sources why we all do it. In fact, however, had Scheid looked beyond literary texts to inscriptions, he would have found plenty of indications of just what people thought they were doing in the cult of the dead.

41. Bernardi (1968) 69 on the reach of the term "a Christian" in Basil's world; as to the mocker, cf. the words from an exchange in Milan in mid-century, Aug., *Conf.* 8.2.4 (*PL* 32.750).

42. Comment on attendance in Chrysostom, e.g., *Homil. in ep. ad Ephes.* 3.4 (*PG* 62.29); other texts in Allen (1996) 410, 413, 416f.

43. Ch. 4 n. 24.

44. Some estimating in ch. 4 n. 61, above. Rome's in-city accommodations were quite limited (chiefly S. Giovanni) as against St. Peter's and the Six in the suburbs, to name only those large ones. Constantinople was an anomaly, equipped with a new religion and new walls and new or at

least sharply increased population, all at once. Carthage's churches were, on the other hand, almost entirely suburban; Milan's, apparently in the middle of the range.

45. Above, ch. 1 n. 20, on conversion in Asia Minor; MacMullen (1997) 158f. on pagan survivals in France, Greece, and elsewhere, randomly and casually noticed.

46. The point I make is banal, but historians of the ancient world, unlike students of other periods, may not see quite large possibilities, as, e.g., in MacMullen (2008).

47. Some indications above, chap. 1 n. 58; chap. 2 n. 6; chap. 4 n. 81; and above, nn. 15, 24.

Bibliography of Works Cited

Agnello (1957) – Agnello, S. L., "Paganesimo e cristianesimo nelle cataccombe di S. Lucia a Siracusa," *Actes du Ve Congrès international d'archéologie chrétienne ... 1954* (Roma) 235–43

Alford (1873) – Alford, H., *The Greek Testament*, 4 vols. (Boston)

Allais (1938) – Allais, Y., *Djemila* (Paris)

Allara (1988) – Allara, A., "Les maisons de Doura-Europos. Les données du terrain," *Syria* 65 (1988) 323–42

Allen (1996) – Allen, P., "The homilist and the congregation: Chrysostom," *Augustinianum* 36 (1996) 397–421

Angiolini (1970) – Angiolini, A., *La capsella eburnean di Pola* (Bologna)

Apollonj Ghetti et al. (1951) – Apollonj Ghetti, B. M., et al., *Esplorazioni sotto la Confessione di San Pietro in Vaticano ... 1940–1949*, 2 vols. (Roma)

Armellini (1893) – Aremellini, M., *Gli antichi cimiteri cristiani di Roma e d'Italia* (Roma) (reprint 1978)

Asgari and Firatli (1978) – Asgari, N., and N. Firatli, "Die Nekropole von Kalchedon," *Studien zur Religion und Kultur Kleinasiens*, eds. S. Sahin et al. (Leiden) 1–92

Bakirtzis (1995) – Bakirtzis, C., "Le culte de Saint Démétrius," *Akten des XII Kongresses für christliche Archäologie ... 1991* (Münster) 58–68

Bakirtzis (1998) – Bakirtzis, C., "Paul and Philippi: the archaeological evidence," *Philippi at the Time of Paul and after His Death*, eds. C. Bakirtzis and H. Koester (Harrisburg PA) 37–48

Baldovin (2006) – Baldovin, J. F., "The empire baptized," *The Oxford History of Christian Worship*, eds. G. Wainwright and K. B. Westerfield Tucker (Oxford) 77–130

Banaji (2001) – Banaji, J., *Agrarian Change in Late Antiquity. Gold, Labour, and Aristocratic Dominance* (Oxford)

Baradez (1966) – Baradez, J., "L'enceinte de Tipasa et ses portes," *Mélanges d'archéologie et d'histoire offerts à André Piganiol*, ed. R. Chevallier (Paris) 2.1133–52

Barnea (1984) – Barnea, I., "L'épigraphie chrétienne de l'Illyricum oriental," *Rapports présenté au Xe Congrès international d'archéologie chrétienne ... 1980* (Thessalonika) 631–78

Barnes (1981) – Barnes, T. D., *Constantine and Eusebius* (Cambridge)

Barrow (1973) – Barrow, R. H., *Prefect and Emperor. The Relationes of Symmachus AD 384* (Oxford)

Barton and Muddiman (2001) – Barton, J., and J. Muddiman, eds., *The Oxford Bible Commentary* (Oxford)

Baruffa (1992) – Baruffa, A., *Le catacombe di San Callisto. Storia – Archeologia – Fede* (Roma)
Bats (2002) – Bats, M., "Mythe et réalités des consummations funéraires en Gaule méridionale (IVe s.–Ier s. av. J.-C.)," *Mémoire de la Société archéologique champeroise* 16 (2002) 285–93
Baus and Ewig (1973) – Baus, K., and E. Ewig, *Die Reichskirche nach Konstantin dem Grossen*, 1: *Die Kirche von Nikaia bis Chalkedon* (Freiburg) (*Handbuch der Kirchengeschichte* II)
Baynes (1972) – Baynes, N. H., *Constantine the Great and the Christian Church*, ed. 2 (London)
Bellarmino Bagatti (1936) – Bellarmino Bagatti, P., *Il cimitero di Commodilla* (Roma)
Bellinger (1956) – Bellinger, A. R., et al., *The Excavations at Dura-Europos ... Final Report* VIII Part 1 (New Haven)
Belayche (2007) – Belayche, N., "Des lieux pour le 'profane' dans l'Empire tardo-antique? Les fêtes entre koinonia sociale et espaces de rivalités religieuses," *Antiquité tardive* 15 (2007) 35–46
Beloch (1886) – Beloch, J., *Die Bevölkerung der griechisch-römischen Welt* (Leipzig)
Belosevic (1998) – Belosevic, J., "Il complesso dell'architettura paleocristiana a Crkvina di Galovac nei pressi di Zadar," *Acta XIII congressus internationalis archaeologiae christianae, Split-Porec ... 1994* (Rome) 3.69–102
Ben Lazreg et al. (2006) – Ben Lazreg, N., et al., "Roman and early Christian burial complex at Leptiminus," *Journal of Roman Archeology* (2006) 347–69
Berger (1997) – Berger, A., "Die Hagia Sophia in Geschichte und Legende," *Die Hagia Sophia in Istanbul. Akten des Berner Kolloquiums ... 1994* (Bern) 11–27
Bernardi (1968) – Bernardi, J., *La predication des pères cappadociens. Le prédicateur et son auditoire* (Paris 1968)
Bisconti (2000) – Bisconti, F., *Mestieri nelle catacombe. Appunti sul declino dell'iconografi del reale nei cimiteri cristiani* (Roma)
Blaauw (1994) – Blaauw, S. de, *Cultus et Decor. Liturgia e architettura nella Roman tardoantica e medievale*, 2 vols. (Roma)
Blaauw (1995) – S. L. de Blaauw, "Die Krypta in stadtrömischen Kirchen: Abbild eines Pilgerziels," *Akten des XII Kongresses für christliche Archäologie ... 1991* (Münster) 559–67
Bobertz (1993) – Bobertz, C. A., "The role of patron in the *cena dominica* of Hippolytus' Apostolic Tradition," *Journal of Theological Studies* 44 (1993) 170–84
Bonamente (1988) – Bonamente, G., "Apoteosi e imperatori cristiani," *I cristiani e l'impero nel IV secolo. Colloquio sul Cristianesimo ... Atti del Convegno ... 1987* (Macerata) 107–42
Bonnet (1986–87) – Bonnet, C., "The archaeological site of the cathedral of Saint Peter (Saint-Pierre), Geneva," *World Archaeology* 18 (1986–87) 330–40
Bonnet (1989) – Bonnet, C., "Baptistères et groupes épiscopaux d'Aoste et de Genève," *Actes du XI Congrès international d'archéologie chrétienne ... Lyon ... 1986* (Roma) 2.1407–26
Bonnet (1993) – Bonnet, C., *Les fouilles de l'ancien groupe épiscopal de Genève (1976–1993)* (Genéve)

Bonnet (2006) – Bonnet, C., "Eléments de topographie chrétienne à Genève (Suisse)," *Gallia* 63 (2006) 111–15
Corinne Bonnet (2007) – Bonnet, Corinne, "'L'histoire séculière et profane des religions' (F. Cumont): observations sur l'articulation entre rite et croyance dans l'historiographie des religions," *Entretiens sur l'Antiquité classique, Fondation Hardt* 53 (2007) 1–27
Bonnet and Privati (1990) – Bonnet., C., and B. Privati, "Les origines de Saint-Gervais à Genève," *Comptes rendus de l'Académie des inscriptions et belles-lettres* (1990) 747–64
Bonnet and Privati (2000) – Bonnet, C., and B. Privati, "De la ville antique à la ville chrétienne. Les chantiers archéologiques de Genève," *Romanité et cité chrétienne. Permanences et mutations, intégrations et exclsuion du Ier au VIe siècle. Mélanges ... Y. Duval* (Paris) 381–90
Boskovic (1974) – Boskovic, N., "Recherches archéologiques à Sirmium. Campagne franco-yugoslavie de 1973," *Mélanges d'archéologie et d'histoire de l'Ecole française à Rome, Antiquité* 86 (1974) 597–656
Bouchenaki (1975) – Bouchenaki, M., *Fouilles de la nécropole occidentale de Tipasa (Matarès) (1968-1972)* (Alger)
Bowder (1978) – Bowder, D., *The Age of Constantine and Julian* (London)
Bradshaw (1992) –Bradshaw, P. F., *The Search for the Origins of Christian Worship. Sources and Methods for the Study of Early Liturgy* (New York)
Bradshaw et al. (2002) – Bradshaw, P. F., et al., *The Search for the Origins of Christian Worship*, ed. 2 (Oxford)
Bratoz (1999) – Bratoz, R., trans. M. Rener, *Il cristianesimo aquileiese prima di Costantino fra Aquileia et Poetovio* (Udine)
Brandenburg (1994) – Brandenburg, H., "Coemeterium. Der Wandel des Bestattungswesens als Zeichen des Kultumbruchs der Spätantike," *Laverna* 5 (1994) 206–32
Brandenburg (1995) – Brandenburg, H., "Altar und Grab," *Martyrium in Multidisciplinary Perspective*, eds. M. Lamberigts and P. Van Deum (Leuven) 71–98
Brandenburg (1995a) – Brandenburg, H., "Kirchenbau und Liturgie. Überlegungen zum Verhältnis von architektonischer Gestalt und Zweckbestimmungen des frühchristlichen Kultbaues," *Divitiae Aegypti. Koptologische und verwandte Studien zu Ehren von Martin Krause*, eds. C. Fluck et al. (Wiesbaden) 36–69
Brandenburg (1998) – Brandenburg, H., *Die Kirche S. Stefano Rotondo in Rom. Bautypologie und Architektursymbolik* (Berlin)
Brandenburg (2005-6) – Brandenburg, H., "Die Architektur der Basilika San Paolo fuori le mura," *Mitteilungen des deutschen archäologischen Instituts, Römische Abteilung* 112 (2005-6) 237–73
Branham (1992) – Branham, J. R., "Sacred space under erasure in ancient synagogues and early churches," *Art Bulletin* 74 (1992) 375–94
Bratoz (1999) –Bratoz, R., *Il cristianesimo aquileiese prima di Costantino fra Aquileia e Poetovio* (Udine)
Brenk (1995) – Brenk, B., "Der Kultort, seine Zugänglichkeit und seine Besucher," *Akten des XII internationalen Kongresses für christliche Archäologie ... 1991* (Münster) 1.69–122
Broc (2004) Broc, C., "Y avait-il toujours des femmes lorsque Jean Chrysostoime prêchait à Antioche?" *Topoi. Orient-occident. Supplément* 5 (2004) 427–38

Brønsted (1928) – Brønsted, J., "La basilique des cinque martyrs à Kapljuc," *Recherches à Salone* 1 (Copenhague) 33-186
Brooks (1923) – Brooks, E. W., *John of Ephesus. Lives of the Eastern Saints* (Paris) (*Patrologia Orientalis* 17.1-307)
Brown (1981) – Brown, P., *The Cult of the Saints. Its Rise and Function in Latin Christianity* (Chicago)
Brown (1996) – Brown, P., *The Rise of Western Christendom. Triumph and Diversity AD 200-1000* (Oxford)
Budde (1987) – Budde, L., *St. Pantaleon von Aphrodisias in Kilikien* (Recklingshausen)
Burger (1966) – Burger, A. S., "The late Roman cemetery at Sagvar," *Acta archaeological academiae scientiarum Hungaricae* 18 (1966) 99-234
Butler (1929) – Butler, H. C., *Early Churches in Syria. Fourth to Seventh Centuries* (Princeton)
Butler (1908-30) – Butler, H. C., *Syria. Publications of the Princeton University Archaeological Expeditions to Syria in 1904-5 and 1909* II: *Ancient Architecture in Syria*, Section B, 6 (Leyden)
Butler et al. (1930) – Butler, H. C., et al., *Syria. Publications of the Princeton University Archaeological Expeditions to Syria in 1904-5 and 1909* (Leyden): *Division* I: *Geography and Itinerary*
Buttrick et al. (1989) – Buttrick, G. A., et al., *The Interpreter's Bible* (Nashville)
Caillet (1993) – Caillet, J.-P., *L'évergétisme monumental Chrétien en Italie et à ses marges* (Rome)
Calci (2000) – Calci, C., *Roma archeologica. Le scoperte piu recenti della città antica e della sua area suburbana* (Roma)
Calder (1920) – Calder, W. M., "Studies in early Christian epigraphy," *Journal of Roman Studies* 10 (1920) 42-59
Calder (1928) – Calder, W. M., ed., *Monumenta Asiae Minoris Antiqua* 1 (Manchester)
Calder (1956) – Calder, W. M., ed., *Monumenta Asiae Minoris Antiqua* 7: *Monuments from Eastern Phrygia* (Manchester)
Calza (1940) – Calza, G., *La necropoli del Porto di Roma nell'Isola Sacra* (Roma)
Cambi (1984) – Cambi, N., "Salonitan piscinae," *Vjesnik za arheologiju i historiju delmatinsku* 77 (1984) 227-41
Canivet (1980) – Canivet, P., "Le *Michaelion* de Huarte (Ve s.) et le culte syrien des anges," *Byzantion* 50 (1980) 85-117
Cantino Wataghin (1989) – Cantino Wataghin, E. L., "Parenzo," *Actes du XIe Congrès international d'archéologie chrétienne. Lyon ... 1986* (Rome) 1.174-77
Cantino Wataghin and Pani Ermini (1995) – Cantino Wataghin, G., and L. Pani Eermini, "Santuari martiriali e centri di pellegrinaggio in Italia," *Akten des XII Kongresses für christliche Archäologie ... 1991* (Münster) 123-51
Carletti (1989) – Carletti, C., "Nuove scoperte di epigrafia cristiana a Roma (1975-1985)," *Actes du XIe Congrès international d'archéologie chrétienne ... 1986* (Roma) 2149-76
Carletti (2000) – Carletti, C., "Spazio e parola: l'epigrafia dei Cristiani a Roma tra tradizione e innovazione," *Christiana loca. Lo spazio cristiano nella Roma del primo millennio*, ed. L. Pani Ermini (Roma) 1.81-88

Carletti (2000a) – Carletti, C., "L'epigrafia dei cristiani: prassi e ideologia tra tradizione e innovazione," *Aurea Roma. Dalla città pagana alla città cristiana*, eds. S. Ensoli and E. La Rocca (Roma) 323–29

Carletti (2003) – Carletti, C., "Nuove iscrizioni della regione di S. Eutichio nel cimitero di S. Sebastiano," *Rivista di archeologia cristiana* 79 (2003) 45–89

Carra Bonacasa and Morfino (2003-4) – Carra Bonacasa, R. M., and D. Morfino, "Il cristianesimo a Sabratha alla luce delle piu recente indagini," *Rendiconti della Pontificia Accademia Romana di Archaeologia* 76 (2003-4) 3–77

Cecchelli (1992-93) – Cecchelli, M., "S. Marco a Piazza Venezia: una basilica romana del periodo costantiniano," *Costantino il Grande. Dall'Antichità all'Umanesimo. Colloquio ... 1990*, 2 vols., eds. G. Bonamente and F. Fusco (Macerata) 1.299–310

Cecchelli (2000) – Cecchelli, M., "I luoghi di Pietro e Paolo," *Christiana loca. Lo spazio cristiano nella Roma del primo millennio*, ed. L. Pani Ermini (Roma) 1.89–97

Cecchelli (2003) – Cecchelli, M., ed., "Il cristianesimo a Roma: le incidenze nello spazio urbano e suburbano," *Roma archeologica* 16-17 (2003) 2–122

Chadwick (1985) – Chadwick, H., "The many into the one," *Times Literary Supplement* (1985) 379–80

Chadwick (2001) – Chadwick, H., *The Church in Ancient Society from Galilee to Gregory the Great* (Oxford)

Chalkia (1991) – Chalkia, E., *Le mense paleocristiane. Tipologia e funzioni delle mense secondarie nel culto paleocristiana* (Roma)

Chaniotis (2003) – Chaniotis, A., "Negotiating religion in the cities of the eastern Roman empire," *Kernos* 16 (2003) 177–90

Chaniotis (2004) – Chaniotis, A., *Das Antike Kreta* (München)

Chaniotis (2006) – Chaniotis, A., "Rituals between norms and emotions: rituals as shared experience and memory," *Ritual and Communication in the Graeco-Roman World*, ed. E. Stavrianopoulos (Liège) 211–38

Chaniotis (2007) – Chaniotis, A., "Murphy's law of ritual disasters—or, why rituals require staging," *The Greek Theatre and Festivals. Documentary Studies*, ed. P. Wilson (Oxford) 48–66

Charles-Murray (2007) – Charles-Murray, M., "The emergence of Christian art," *Picturing the Bible. The Earliest Christian Art*, eds. J. Speier et al. (New Haven) 51–63

Chastagnol (1966) – Chastagnol, A., "Sur quelques documents relatifs à la basilique de Saint-Paul-hors-les-murs," *Mélanges d'archéologie et d'histoire offerts à André Piganiol*, ed. R. Chevalier (Paris) 421–37

Chéhab (1957) – Chéhab, M. H., *Mosaïques du Liban*, 2 vols. (Paris) (*Bulletin du Musée de Beyrouth* 14)

Chevalier (1996) – Chevalier, P., *Ecclesiae Dalmatiae. L'architecture paléochrétienne de la province romaine de Dalmatie (IV - VII s.)*, 2 vols. (*Salona* II) (Rome)

Chevalier and Mardesic (2006) – Chevalier, P., and J. Maresic, "La ville de Salone dans l'Antiquité tardive," *Hortus artium medievalium* 9 (2006) 55–68

Christern (1968) – Christern, J., "Basilika und Memorie der heiligen Salsa in Tipasa," *Bulletin d'archéologie algérienne* 3 (1968) 193–256

Christern (1976) – Christern, J., *Das frühchristliche Pilgerheiligtum von Tebessa* (Wiesbaden)
Christie (2006) – Christie, N., *From Constantine to Charlemagne. An Archeology of Italy, AD 300–800* (Aldershot UK)
Christofle (1938) – Christofle, M., *Rapports sur les travaux de fouilles ... 1933–1936 par le Service des Monuments Historiques d'Algérie* (Alger)
Cintas and Duval (1958) – Cintas, J., and N. Duval, "L'église du prêtre Félix (région de Kélibia)," *Karthago* 9 (1958) 55–269
Cipollone (2003) – Cipollone, V., ed., *Inscriptiones christianae Italiae*, ed. 2, XI: *Regio VII. Clusium* (Bari)
Collart (1930) – Collart, P., "Inscription de Sélian-Mésoréma," *Bulletin de correspondance héllénique* 54 (1930) 376–91
Collart (1937) – Collart, P., *Philippes ville de Macédoine depuis ses origins jusqu'à la fin de l'époque romaine*, 2 vols. (Paris)
Conde Guerri (1979) – Conde Guerri, E., *Los 'fossores' de Roma paleocristiana* (Roma)
Connolly (1929) – Connolly, R. H., ed., *Didache Apostolorum* (Oxford)
Corbett (1959) – Corbett, [G. U.] S., "Santo Stefano Rotondo," *Rivista di archeologia cristiana* 35 (1959) 249–61
Corbo (1981) – Corbo, V. C., *Il Santo Sepolcro di Gerusalemme. Aspetti archeologici*, 3 vols. (Jerusalem)
Corbo (1993) – Corbo, V., "The church of the house of St. Peter at Capernaum," *Ancient Churches Revealed*, ed. Y. Tsafrir (Jerusalem) 71–76
Coüasnon (1974) – Coüasnon, C., *The Church of the Holy Sepulchre in Jerusalem* (London)
Croce Da Villa (1989) – Croce Da Villa, P., "Concordia romana e tardo-antica," *La chiesa concordiese 389–1989* (Fiume Veneto 1989) 17–39
Crowfoot (1940) – Crowfoot, J. W., "The Christian basilica in Palestine," *Atti del IV Congresso internazionale di archeologia cristiana ... 1938* (Roma) 1.321–33
Crowfoot (1941) – Crowfoot, J. W., *Early Churches in Palestine* (London)
Cumont (1926) – Cumont, F., *Fouilles de Doura-Europos (1922–1923)*, 2 vols. (Paris)
Curran (2000) – Curran, J. C., *Pagan City and Christian Capital. Rome in the Fourth Century* (Oxford)
Cuscito (1971) – Cuscito, G., "Depositus in hanc piscinam. Morte e resurrezione nell'antico cristianesimo aquileiense," *Aquileia nostra* 42 (1971) 58–62
Cuscito (1995) – Cuscito, G., "Lo spazio sacro negli edifici cultuali paleocristiani dell'Alto Adriatico," *Hortus artium medievalium* 1 (1995) 90–109
Cuscito (1998) – Cuscito, G., "Ancora su Mauro *episcopus et confessor* e sul *locus duplicatus* de Parenzo," *Domum tuam dilexi. Miscellanea in onore de Aldo Nestori* (Roma) 185–210
Dagron (1974) – Dagron, G., *Naissance d'une capitale. Constantinople et ses institutions de 330 à 451* (Paris)
Dalman (1908) – Dalman, G., *Petra und seine Felsheiligtümer* (Leipzig)
D'Angela (1983) – D'Angela, C., "L'obolo a Caronte. Usi funerary medievali tra paganesimo e Cristianesimo," *Quaderni medievali* 15 (1983) 82–91

Daut (1971) – Daut, W., "Die 'halben-christen' unter den Konvertiten und Gebildeten des 4. und 5. Jahrhunderts," *Zeitschrift für Missionswissenschaft und Religionswissenschaft* 55 (1971) 171–88
Deichmann (1939) – Deichmann, F. W., "Frühchristliche Kirchen in antiken Heiligtümern," *Jahrbuch des deutschen archäologischen Instituts* 54 (1939) 105–36
Deichmann (1966) – Deichmann, F. W., "Zum ältesten Geschichte des Christentums in Ravenna," *Rivista di archeologia cristiana* 42 (1966) 167–75
Deichmann (1970) – Deichmann, F. W., "Märtyrerbasilika, Martyrium, Memoria und Altargrab," *Mitteilungen des deutschen archäologischen Instituts, Römische Abteilung* 77 (1970) 144–69
Deichmann (1993) – Deichmann, F. W., *Archeologia cristiana* (Roma)
Delattre (1907) – Delattre, A. L., "La basilica majorum. Tombeau des saintes Perpétue et Félicité," *Comptes rendus de l'Académie des inscriptions et belles letters* (1907) 516–31
Delattre (1908) – Delattre, A. L., "La basilica majorum. Puits rempli de squelettes," *Comptes rendus de l'Académie des inscriptions et belles letters* (1908) 59–68
Delehaye (1923) – Delehaye, H., "Euchaïta et la légende de S. Théodore," *Anatolian Studies Presented to Sir William Mitchell Ramsay*, eds. W. H. Buckler and W. M. Calder (Manchester) 129–34
De Santis and Biamonte (1997) – De Santis, L., and G. Biamonte, *Le catacombe di Roma* (Roma)
Detorakis (2004) – Detorakis, T., Αγια Σοφια. Ο ναος της αγιας του Θεου Σοφιας. (Athens)
Deuber (2002) – Deuber, G., *St. Peter's Cathedral Geneva* (Bern)
Deubner (1977–78) – Deubner, O., "Das Heiligtum der alexandrinischen Gottheiten in Pergamon," *Mitteilungen des deutschen archäologischen Instituts, Istanbuler Abt.* 27/28 (1977–78) 227–50
Diehl (1925–31) – Diehl, E., *Inscriptiones latinae christianae veteres*, 3 vols. (Berlin)
Di Stefano (1975) – Di Stefano, R., *La cattedrale di Napoli* (Napoli)
Diekamp (1913) – Diekamp, F., *Clementis Romani epistulae De Virginitate* ... (Tübingen) (*Patres Apostolici*, ed. F. X. Funk, II)
Dillon (2007) – Dillon, J. M., "The religion of the last Hellenes," *Entretiens sur l'Antiquité classique, Fondation Hardt* 53 (2007) 117–38
Dix (1970) – Dix, G., *The Shape of the Liturgy*, ed. 2 (London)
Dolbeau (1996) – Dolbeau, F., ed., *Augustin d'Hippone, Vingt-six sermons au peuple d'Afrique* (Paris)
Dölger (1925) – Dölger, F. J., *Sol Salutis. Gebet und Gesang im christlichen Altertum*, ed. 3 (Münster)
Dölger (1932) – Dölger, F., "Das Kultvergehen der Donatistin Lucilla von Karthago. Reliquienkuss vor dem Kuss der Eucharistie," *Antike und Christentum* 3 (1932) 245–52
Donahue (2004) – Donahue, J. F., *The Roman Community at Table during the Principate* (Ann Arbor)
Downey (1963) – Downey, G., *Ancient Antioch* (Princeton)
Drake (2005) – Drake, H. A., "Models of Christian expansion," *The Spread of Christianity in the First Four Centuries. Essays in Explanation* (Leiden) 1–13

Drexhage et al. (2002) – Drexhage, H.-J., et al., *Die Wirtschaft des römischen Reiches (1.–3. Jahrhundert)* (Berlin)

Duchesne (1925) – Duchesne, L., *Origines du culte Chrétien. Etude sur la liturgie latine avant Charlemagne*, ed. 5 (Paris)

Duchesne (1955–57) – Duchesne, L., *Le Liber pontificalis*, 3 vols. (Paris)

Dunbabin (2003) – Dunbabin, K. M. D., *The Roman Banquet. Images of Conviviality* (Cambridge UK)

N. Duval (1971–73) – Duval, N., *Les églises africaines à deux absides ... Recherches archéologiques à Sbeitla*, I: *Les basiliques de Sbeitla à deux sanctuaires opposés*; II: *Inventaire des monuments – interprétation* (Paris)

N. Duval (1975) – Duval, N., "Réflexions sur l'architecture à plan rayonnant et ses rapports avec le culte des martyrs," *Disputationes Salonitanae 1970* (Split 1975) 83–90

N. Duval (1978) – Duval, N., "Les édifices de culte des origins à lépoque constantinienne," *Atti del Congresso internazionale di archeologia cristiana*, 1: *I monumenti cristiani precostantiniani ... 1975* (Roma) 513–37

N. Duval (1979) – Duval, N., "Sirmium 'ville impériale' ou 'capitale'," *XXVI Corso di cultura sull'arte ravennate e bizantine* (1979) 53–90

N. Duval (1984) – Duval, N., "Brèves observations sur l'usage des *mensae* funéraires dans l'Illyricum," *Rivista di archeologia cristiana* 60 (1984) 259–75

N. Duval (1984a) – Duval, N., "Mensae funéraires," *Vjesnik za arheologiju i historiju delmatinsku* 77 (1984) 187–226

N. Duval (1986) – Duval, N., "L'inhumation privilégiée en Tunisie et en Tripolitaine," *L'inhumation privilégiée du IVe au VIIIe siècle en Occident. Actes du colloque ... 1984*, eds. Y. Duval and J.-C. Picard (Paris) 25–34

N. Duval (1989) – Duval, N., "L'évêque et la cathédrale en Afrique du Nord," *Actes du XI Congrès international d'archéologie chrétienne ... Lyon ... 1986* (Roma) 1.345–99

N. Duval (1991) – Duval, N., "L'architecture cultuelle," *Naissance des arts chrétiens. Atlas des monuments paléochrétiens de la France* (Paris), 186–219

N. Duval (1995a) – Duval, N., "Les martyrs de la persécution de Dioclétien à Haïdra (Tunisie)," *Martyrium in Multidisciplinary Perspective*, eds. M. Lamberigts and P. Van Deum (Leuven) 99–124

N. Duval (1995b) – Duval, N., ed., *Les premiers monuments chrétiens de la France* I: *Sud-Est et Corse* (Paris)

N. Duval (1995c) – Duval, N., "Les nécropoles chrétiennes d'Afrique du Nord," *L'Afrique du nord antique et médiévale. VIe colloque international ... 1993*, ed. P. Trousset (Nancy) 187–205

N. Duval (1999) – Duval, N., "Les installations liturgiques dans les églises paléochrétiennes," *Hortus artium mediaevalium* 5 (1999) 7–28

N. Duval (2005) – Duval, N., "L'autel paléochrétien: les progrès depuis le livre de Braun (1924)," *Hortus artium medievalium* 11 (2005) 7–18

N. Duval and Y. Duval (1966) – Duval, N., and Y. Duval, "L'église dite de Candidus à Haïdra (Tunisie) et l'inscription des Martyrs," *Mélanges d'archéologie et d'histoire offerts à André Piganiol*, ed. R. Chevallier (Paris) 2.1153–89

N. Duval et al. (1972) – Duval, N., et al., "Groupes épiscopaux de Syrie et d'Afrique du Nord," *Apamée de Syrie. Bilan de recherches archéologiques 1969-1971. Actes du Colloque ... 1972*, eds. J. and J. C. Balty (Bruxelles) 214–45

N. Duval et al. (1981) – Duval, N., et al., *Recherches archéologiques à Haïdra II. La basilique I dite de Melléus ou de Saint-Cyprien* (Rome)

N. Duval et al. (2000) – Duval, N., et al., *Manastirine. Etablissement préromain, nécropole et basilique paleochrétienne* (*Salona* III) (Rome)

N. Duval and Popovic (1984) – Duval, N., and V. Popovic, "Urbanisme et topographie chrétienne dans les provinces septentrionales de l'Illyricum," *Rapports présenté au Xe Congrès international d'archéologie chrétienne ... 1980* (Thessalonika) 369–402

Y. Duval (1982) – Duval, Y., *Loca sanctorum Africae. Le culte des martyrs en Afrique du IVe au VIIe siècle*, 2 vols. (Rome)

Dyggve (1951) – Dyggve, E., *History of Salonitan Christianity* (Oslo)

Dyggve and Egger (1939) – Dyggve, E., and R. Egger, *Der altchristliche Friedhof Marusinac* (*Forschungen in Salona* III) (Wien)

Eck (1995) – Eck, W., "Graffiti an Pilgerorten im spätrömischen Reich," *Akten des XII Kongresses für christliche Archäologie ... 1991* (Münster) 206–22

Edelstein and Edelstein (1945) – Edelstein, E. J., and L. Edelstein, *Asclepius. A Collection and Interpretation of the Testimonies*, 2 vols. (Baltimore)

Edwards (2006) – Edwards, M., "The beginnings of Christianization," *Cambridge Companion to the Age of Constantine*, ed. N. Lenski (Cambridge) 137–58

Egger (1917) – Egger, R., "Zur Entstehungsgeschichte und Bedeutung der Kirchen von Salona," *Die Bauten im nordwestlichen Teile der Neustadt von Salona*, ed. W. Gerber (*Forschungen in Salona* I) (Wien) 89–138

Egger (1926) – Egger, R., *Der altchristliche Friedhof Manastirine bearbeitet nach dem Materiale Fr. Bulic* (*Forschungen in Salona* II) (Wien)

Elton (2006) – Elton, H., "A new Late-Roman urban centre in Isauria," *Journal of Roman Archeology* 19 (2006) 300–312

Ennabli (1975) – Ennabli, L., *Les inscriptions funéraires chrétiennes de la basilique dite de Sainte-Monique à Carthage* (Paris)

Ennabli (1982) – Ennabli, L., *Les inscriptions funéraires 2: La basilique de Mcidfa* (Rome)

Ennabli (1997) – Ennabli, L., *Carthage. Une métropole chrétienne du IVe à la fin du VIIe siècle* (Paris)

Ennabli (2000) – Ennabli, L., *La basilique de Carthagenna et le locus des Sept Moines de Gafsa. Nouveaux édifices chrétiens de Carthage* (Paris)

Fasola (1989) – Fasola, U. M., "Le ricerche di archeologia cristiana a Roma fuori le mura," *Actes du XIe Congrès international d'archéologie chrétienne ... 1986* (Roma) 2149–76

Fasola and Testini (1978) – Fasola, U. M., and P. Testini, "I cimiteri cristiani," *Atti del IX congresso internazionale di archeologia cristiana ... 1975* (Roma) 105–57

Fasola and Fiocchi Nicolai (1989) – Fasola, U. M., and V. Fiocchi Nicolai, "Le necropolis durante la formazione della città cristiana," *Actes du XI Congrès international d'archéologie chrétienne ... Lyon ... 1986* (Roma) 2.1153–1205

Ferrua (1941) – Ferrua, A., "Il refrigerio dentro la tomba," *La civiltà cattolica* 92 (1941) 373–78

Ferrua (1963) – Ferrua, A., "Graffiti di pellegrini alla tomba di San Felice," *Palladio* 13 (1963) 17–19
Ferrua (1970) – Ferrua, A., "Una nuova regione della catacomba dei SS. Marcellino e Pietro," *Rivista archeologia cristiana* 46 (1970) 7–83
Ferrua (1971) – Ferrua, A., "La catacomba di Vibia," *Rivista di archeologia cristiana* 47 (1971) 7–62
Ferrua (1977) – Ferrua, A., "Due iscrizioni della Mauritania," *Rivista di archeologia cristiana* 53 (1977) 225–29
Ferrua (1977a) – Ferrua, A., "Le iscrizioni paleocristiane di Cimitile," *Rivista di archeologia cristiana* 53 (1977) 105–36
Ferrua (1984) – Ferrua, A., "Documenti sullo scavo e pubblicazione della catacomba di S. Caterina di Chiusi," *Rivista di archeologia cristiana* 60 (1984) 63–99
Ferrua (1985) – Ferrua, A., *Damaso e i martiri di Roma* (Roma)
Ferrua (1990) – Ferrua, A., *La basilica e la catacomba di S. Sebastiano*, ed. 2 (Roma)
Février (1960) – Février, P.-A., "Etudes sur les catacombes romaines," *Cahiers archéologiques* 11 (1960) 1–14
Février (1965) – Février, P.-A., *Les fouilles de Sétif. Les basiliques chrétiennes du quartier nord-ouest* (Paris)
Février (1968) – Février, P.-A., "Nouvelles recherches dans la sale tréflée de la basilique de Tébessa," *Bulletin d'archéologie algérienne* 3 (1968) 167–91
Février (1970a) – Février, P.-A., "Le culte des martyrs en Afrique et ses plus anciens monuments," *Corsi di cultura sull'arte ravennate e bizantina* 17 (1970) 191–215
Février (1970b) – Février, P.-A., *Les fouilles de Sétif. Les basiliques chrétiennes du quartier nord-ouest* (Paris)
Février (1978) – Février, P.-A., "Le culte des morts dans les communautés chrétiennes durant le III siècle," *Atti del IX Congresso internazionale di archeologia cristiana ... 1975* (Roma) 211–74
Février (1984) – Février, P.-A., "La tombe chrétienne et l'au-delà," *Le temps chrétien de la fin de l'Antiquité au Moyen Age IIIe-XIII siècles ... 1981* (Paris) (*Colloques internationaux du CNRS* no. 604) 163–83
Février (1986) – Février, P.-A., "Tombes privilégiées en Maurétanie et Numide," *L'inhumation privilégiée du IVe au VIIIe siècle en Occident. Actes du Colloque ... 1984*, eds. Y. Duval and J.-C. Picard (Paris) 13–23
Février (1989–90) – Février, P.-A., *Approches du Maghreb romain*, 2 vols. (Aix-en-Provence)
Février et al. (1970) – Février, P.-A., et al., *Fouilles de Sétif (1959–1966). Quartier nord-ouest, rempart et cirque* (Alger)
Filippi (2004) – Filippi, G., "La tomba di San Paolo e le fase della basilica tra il IV e VII secolo," *Bollettino dei monumenti musei e gallerie pontificie* 24 (2004) 187–224
Filippi (2005–6) – Filippi, G., "Die Ergebnisse der neuen Ausgrabungen am Grab des Apostels Paulus," *Mitteilungen des deutschen archäologischen Instituts, Römische Abteilung* 112 (2005–6) 277–92
R. Finn (2006) – Finn, R., *Almsgiving in the Later Roman Empire. Christian Promotion and Practice (313–450)* (Oxford)

T. M. Finn (2000) – Finn, T. M., "Mission and expansion," *The Early Christian World*, ed. P. Eslar 1 (London) ch. 11
Fiocchi Nicolai (1995-96) – Fiocchi Nicolai, V., "La nuova basilica circiforme della Via Ardeatina," *Rendiconti della Pontificia Accademia Romana di archeologia*, Ser. 3, 68 (1995-96) 69-233 [1999]
Fiocchi Nicolai (1999) – Fiocchi Nicolai, V., *Les catacombes chrétiennes de Rome. Origine, développment, décor, inscriptions*, trans. J. Guyon (Turnhout)
Fiocchi Nicolai (2000) – Fiocchi Nicolai, V., "L'organizzazione dello spazio funerario," *Christiana loca. Lo spazio cristiano nella Roma del primo millennio*, ed. L. Pani Eermini (Roma) 1.43-58
Fiocchi Nicolai (2001) – Fiocchi Nicolai, V., *Strutture funerari ed edifici di culto paleocristiani di Roma dal IV al VI secolo* (Roma)
Fiocchi Nicolai (2003) – Fiocchi Nicolai, V., "Scavi e scoperte di archeologia cristiana nel Lazio dal 1983 al 1993," *Atti del VII Congresso nazionale di archeologia cristiana … 1993* (Cassino) 309-31
Fiocchi Nicolai et al. (1999) – Fiocchi Nicolai et al., *Les catacombes chrétiennes de Rome. Origine, développement, décor, inscriptions*, trans. J. Guyon (Turnhout)
Fiorio (1985) – Fiorio, M. T., ed., *Le chiese di Milano* (Milano)
Franchi de' Cavalieri (1928) – Franchi De' Cavalieri, P., "Il κοιμητηριον di Antiochia," in idem, *Note agiografiche* 7 (Roma) (*Studi e Testi* 49) 146-53
Frend (1984) – Frend, W. H. C., *The Rise of Christianity* (London)
Frutaz (1969) – Frutaz, A. P., *Il complesso monumentale di Sant'Agnese* (Roma)
Funk (1905) – Funk, F. X., ed., *Didascalia et Constitutiones apostolicae*, 2 vols. (Paderborn)
Galvao-Sobrinho (2009) – Galvao-Sobrinho, C., "Doctrine and Power. Theological Controversy and Christian Leadership in the Later Roman Empire, A.D. 318-64" (publication pending)
Galvao (2010) – "Poverty, compassion, and social change" (publication pending)
Gamber (1976) – Gamber, K., *Liturgie und Kirchenbau. Studien zur Geschichte der Messfeier und des Gotteshauses in der Frühzeit* (Regensburg)
Gatto (1998) – Gatto, L., "Riflettando sulla consistenza demografica della Roma altomedievale," *Roma mediovale: Agiornamento*, ed. P. Delogu (Roma) 143-57
Giuntella (1999) – Giuntella, A. M., *Cornus I: L'area cimiteriale orientale* (Oristana)
Gerlach (2001) – Gerlach, G., *Zu Tisch bei den alter Römern* (Stuttgart)
Giuntella et al. (1985) – Giuntella, A. M., et al., *Mensae e riti funerary in Sardegna. La testimonianza di Cornus* (Taranto)
Glaser (1997) – Glaser, F., *Frühes Christentum im Alpenraum* (Regensburg)
Gounaris (1984) – Gounaris, G., "Le problème de l'existence de deux ambons dans l'Octogone de Philippes," *Actes du Xe Congrès international d'archéologie chrétienne … 1980* (Rome) 2.133-40
Goudineau and Kisch (1991) – Goudineau, C., and Y. de Kisch, *Vaison-la-Romaine* (Paris)
Grabar (1945) – Grabar, A., "Les ambons syriens et la fonction liturgique de la nef dans les églises antiques," *Cahiers archéologiques* 1 (1945) 129-33
Grabar (1975) – Grabar, A., "Les monuments paléochrétiens de Salone et les débuts du culte des martyrs," *Disputationes Salonitanae 1970* (Split 1975) 69-74

Grandidier (1902) – Grandidier, O., "Deux monuments funéraires à Tipasa (Algérie: Maurétanie Césarienne)," *Atti del IIo Congresso internazionale di archeologia cristiana ... Roma ... 1900* (1902) 51–77

Gregory (1986) – Gregory, T. E., "The survival of paganism in Christian Greece," *American Journal of Philology* 107 (1986) 229–42

Gros (1981) – Gros, P., *Bolsena. Guides des fouilles* (Rome)

Grossman (1989) – Grossman, P., "Neue frühchristliche Funde aus Agypten," *Actes du XI Congrès international d'archéologie chrétienne ... Lyon ... 1986* (Roma) 2.1843–1908

Grottanelli (2005) – Grottanelli, C., "Tuer des animaux pour la fête de Saint Félix," *La cuisine et l'autel. Les sacrifices en questions dans les sociétés de la Méditerranée* (Turnhout) 387–407

Gsell (1893) – Gsell, S., *Recherches archéologiques en Algérie* (Paris)

Guéry (1985) – Guéry, R., *La nécropole orientale de Sitifis (Sétif, Algérie). Fouilles de 1966–1967* (Paris)

Gui et al. (1992) – Gui, I., et al., *Basiliques chrétiennes d'Afrique du Nord* (Paris)

Guidobaldi (1998) – Guidobaldi, F., "Per una cronologia preambrosiana del S. Simpliciano di Milano," *Domum tuam dilexi. Miscellanea in onore de Aldo Nestori* (Roma) 423–50

Guidoni (2003) – Guidoni, G., "Scavi e scoperte di archeologia cristiana in Toscana dal 1983 al 1993," *Atti del VII Congresso nazionale di archeologia cristiana ... 1993* (Cassino) 249–66

Guignebert (1923) – Guignebert, C., "Les demi-chrétiens et l'Église antique," *Revue de l'histoire des religions* 83 (1923) 65–102

Guyon (1974) – Guyon, J., "La vente des tombes à travers l'épigraphie de la Rome chrétienne," *Mélanges de l'école française de Rome. Antiquité* 86 (1974) 549–96

Guyon (1977) – Guyon, J., "Stèles funéraires d'equites singulares," *Rivista di archeologia cristiana* 53 (1977) 208–24

Guyon (1984) – Guyon, J., "Recherches sur les bâtiments constantiniens du site *inter duas lauros*, via Labicana à Rome," *Actes du Xe Congrès international d'archéologie chrétienne ... 1980* (Rome) 2.183–96

Guyon (1986) – Guyon, J., "L'inhumation privilégiée dans un cimetière romain au IVe siècle," *L'inhumation privilégiée du IVe au VIII siècle en Occident. Actes du Colloque ... 1984*, eds. Y. Duval and J.-C. Picard (Paris) 173–78

Guyon (1987) – Guyon, J., *Le cimetière aux deux lauriers. Recherches sur les catacombes romaines* (Rome)

Guyon (1994) – Guyon, J., "Peut-on vraiment dater une catacombe?" *Boreas. Münstersche Beiträge zur Archäologie* 19 (1994) 89–103

Guyon (2001) – Guyon, J., "Le culte des martyrs," *D'un monde à l'autre. Naissance d'une Chrétienté en Provence IVe – VIe siècle*, eds. idem and M. Heijmans (Arles) 58–61

Haensch (2006) – Haensch, R., "Le financement de la construction des églises pendant l'Antiquité tardive," *Antiquité tardive* 14 (2006) 47–58

A. S. Hall (1978) – Hall, A. S., "The Klarian oracle at Oinoanda," *Zeitschrift für Papyrologie und Epigraphik* 32 (1978) 263–67

L. J. Hall (2004) – Hall, L. J., *Roman Berytus. Beirut in Late Antiquity* (London)

Harkins (1963) – Harkins, P. W., trans., *St. John Chrysostom: Baptismal Instructions* (London)

Harl (1981) – Harl, M., "La dénonciation des festivities profanes dans le discours épisciopal et monastique," *La fête, pratique et discours d'Alexandrie hellénistique à la fin du IVe siècle* (Paris) 123–47

Harnack (1908) – Harnack, A., *The Mission and Expansion of Christianity in the First Three Centuries*, 2 vols., trans. J. Moffat, ed. 2 (London)

Hatzfeld (1927) – Hatzfeld, J., "Inscriptions de Panamara," *Bulletin de correspondance hellénique* 51 (1927) 57–122

Héfélé (1869) – Héfélé, C.-J., *Histoire des conciles d'après les documentaux originaux*, trans. Goschler and Delarc (Paris)

Heijmans and Guyon (2006) – Heijmans, M., and J. Guyon, "Archéologie de la France antique: antoquité tardive, haut Moyen Age et premiers temps chrétiens en Gaule méridionale," *Gallia* 63 (2006) 1–170

Herzfeld (1930) – Herzfeld, E., *Meriamlik und Korykos. Zwei christliche Ruinenstädten des rauhen Kilikiens* (Manchester) (*Monumenta Asiae Minoris Antiqua* 2)

Hesberg (1987) – Hesberg, H. von, "Planung und Ausgestaltung der Nekropolen Roms im 2. Jh. n. Chr.," *Römische Gräberstrassen. Selbstdarstellung – Status – Standard. Kolloquium ... 1985* (München) 25–41

Hill (1990–2007) – Hill, E., trans., *Works of Saint Augustine : A Translation for the 21st Century* (New York)

Hoddinott (1963) – Hoddinott, R. F., *Early Byzantine Churches in Macedonia and Southern Serbia* (London)

Holloway (2004) – Holloway, R. R., *Constantine and Rome* (New Haven)

C. Hopkins (1979) – Hopkins, C., *The Discovery of Dura-Europus* (New Haven)

K. Hopkins (1998) – Hopkins, K., "Christian number and its implications," *Journal of Early Christian Studies* 6 (1998) 184–226

Huelsen (1921) – Huelsen, C., *Le chiese di Roma nel Medio Evo* (Firenze)

Humphrey (1986) – Humphrey, J. H., *Roman Circuses. Arenas for Chariot Racing* (Berkeley)

Iniguez Herrero (2000) – Iniguez Herrero, J. A., *Arqueologia cristiana* (Pamplona)

Iosi (1924) – Iosi, E., "Il cimitero di Panfilo e i martiri in esso venerati," *Rivista di archeologia cristiana* 1 (1924) 42–119

Iosi (1926) – Iosi [spelt Josi], E., "Il cimitero di Panfilo," *Rivista di archeologia cristiana* 3 (1926) 51–211

Jäggi (1989) – Jäggi, C., "S. Ilario in Aquileia," *Aquileia nostra* 60 (1989) 298–302

Janeras (2000) – Janeras, S., "Saint Jean Chrysostome et la 'Grande Entrée'," *Crossroad of Cultures. Studies in Liturgy and Patristics in Honor of Gabriele Winkler*, eds. H.-J. Feulner et al. (Rome) 395–403

Jastrzebowska (1979) – Jastrzebowska, E., "Les scènes de banquet dans les peintures et sculptures chrétiennes des IIIe et IV siècles," *Recherches augustiniennes* 14 (1979) 30–90

Jastrzebowska (1981) – Jastrzebowska, E., *Untersuchungen zum christlichen Totenmahl aufgrund der Monumente der 3. und 4. Jahrhunderts unter Basilika des Hl. Sebastian in Rom* (Frankfurt)

Jastrzebowska (2001) – Jastrzebowska, E., "Les rituels des banquets funéraires," *D'un monde à l'autre. Naissance d'une Chrétienté en Provence IVe – VI siècle*, eds. J. Guyon and M. Heijmans (Arles) 56–57

Jelicic-Radonic (2003) – Jelicic-Radonic, J., "Altar types in early Christian churches in the province of Dalmatia," *Hortus atrium medievalium* 9 (2003) 19–28

G. J. Johnson (1984) – Johnson, G. J., "Roman Bithynia and Christianity to the Mid-fourth Century" (Diss. University of Michigan)

M. E. Johnson (2000) – Johnson, M. E., "Worship, practice and belief," *The Early Christian World*, ed. P. F. Esler (London 2000) 1.475–99

Jonkers (1954) – Jonkers, E. J., ed., *Acta et symbola conciliorum quae saeculo quarto habita sunt* (Leiden)

Jungmann (1957) – Jungmann, J. A., "Agape," *Lexikon für Theologie und Kirche* 1 (Freiburg) 178–81

Kadra (1989) – Kadra, K. F., "Nécropoles tardives de l'antique Théveste: mosaïques funéraires et *mensae*," *Africa romana. Atti del VI convegno ... 1988*, ed. A. Mastino (Sassari, Sardinia) 265–82

Kähler (1967) – Kähler, H., *Hagia Sophia*, trans. E. Childs (New York)

Karwiese (1989) – Karwiese, S., *Erster vorläufiger Gesamtbericht über ... die Marienkirche in Ephesos* (Wien)

Keil (1930) – Keil, J., "XV vorläufiger Bericht über die Ausgrabungen in Ephesos," *Jahreshefte des oesterreichischen archäologischen Institutes in Wien* 26 (1930) Beiblatt 6–66

Keil and Wilhelm 1931 – Keil, J., and A. Wilhelm, *Denkmäler aus dem rauhen Kilikien* (Manchester) (*Monumenta Asiae Minoris Antiqua* 3)

Kirsch (1940) – Kirsch, G. P., "La basilica cristiana nell'antichità," *Atti del IV Congresso internazionale di archeologia cristiana ... 1938* (Roma) 1.113–26

Kitzinger (1974) – Kitzinger, E., "A fourth century mosaic floor in Pisidian Antioch," *Mansel'e Armagan. Mélanges Mansel* (Ankara) (*Türk Tarih Kurumu Yayinlari* 7, 6) 385–95

Kjaergaard (1984) – Kjaergaard, J., "From 'Memoria Apostolorum' to Basilica Apostolorum. On the early Christian cult-center on the Via Appia," *Analecta Romana Instituti Danici* 13 (1984) 59–76

Kleinbauer (1973) – Kleinbauer, W. E., "The origin and functions of the aisled tetraconch churches in Syria and northern Mesopotamia," *Dumbarton Oaks Papers* 27 (1973) 89–114

Kleinbauer (1987) – Kleinbauer, W. E., "The double-shell tetraconch building at Perge in Pamphylia and the origin of the architectural genus," *Dumbarton Oaks Papers* 41 (1987) 277–93

Korol (1994) – Korol, D., "Zum frühchristlichen Apsismosaik der Bischofskirche von 'Capua Vetere'," *Boreas. Münstersche Bieträge zur Archäologie* 17 (1994) 121–48

Koukouli-Chrysantaki (1998) – Koukouli-Chrysantaki, C., "Colonia Iulia Augusta Philippensis," *Philippi at the Time of Paul and after His Death*, eds. C. Bakirtzis and H. Koester (Harrisburg PA) 5–35

Kraeling (1967) – Kraeling, C. H., *The Christian Building* (in: *The Excavations at Dura-Europos ... Final Report*, ed. C. B. Welles, 8, 2, New Haven)

Krautheimer (1960) – Krautheimer, R., "Mensa-coemeterium-martyrium," *Cahiers archéologiques* 11 (1960) 15–40
Krautheimer (1969) – Krautheimer, R., "Constantine's church foundations," *Akten des VII. internationalen Kongresses für christliche Archäologie ... 1965* (Roma) 237–53
Krautheimer (1979) – Krautheimer, R., *Early Christian and Byzantine Architecture*, ed. 3 (Harmondsworth, UK)
Krautheimer (1983) – Krautheimer, R., *Three Christian Capitals. Topography and Politics* (Berkeley)
Krautheimer (1992–93) – Krautheimer, R., "The ecclesiastical building policy of Constantine," *Costantino il Grande. Dall'Antichità all'Umanesimo. Colloquio ...1990*, 2 vols., eds. G. Bonamente and F. Fusco (Macerata) 2.509–52
Krautheimer et al. (1937–77) – Krautheimer, R., et al., *Corpus basilicarum christianarum Romae. The Early Christian Basilicas of Rome (IV-IX Cent.)*, 5 vols. (Rome)
Lampe (1989) – Lampe, P., *Die stadtrömischen Christen in der ersten beiden Jahrhunderten*, ed. 2 (Tübingen)
Lancel (2006) – Lancel, S., "Saint Augustin et le miracle," *Les miracles de saint Etienne. Recherches sur le recueil pseudo-augustinien*, ed. J. Myers (Turnhout) 69–77
Lancel and Bouchenaki (1971) – Lancel, S., and M. Bouchenaki, *Tipasa de Maurétanie* (Alger)
Lancel and Mattei (2003) – Lancel, S., and P. Mattei, *Pax et Concordia. Chrétiens des premiers siècles en Afrique (IIIe – VIIe siècles)* (Alger)
Lane Fox (1989) – Lane Fox, R., *Pagans and Christians* (New York)
Lapeyre (1940) – Lapeyre, P. G., "La basilique chrétienne de Tunisie," *Atti del IV Congresso internazionale di archeologia cristiana ... 1938* (Roma) 1.169–244
La Rocca (2000) – La Rocca, E., "Le basiliche cristiane 'a deambulatorio,'" *Aurea Roma. Dalla città pagana alla città cristiana*, eds. S. Ensoli and E. La Rocca (Roma) 204–20
Lassus (1938) – Lassus, J., "L'église cruciforme. Antioche-Kaoussié," *Antioch-on-the-Orontes II. The Excavations 1933–1936*, ed. R. Stillwell (Princeton) 1–220
Lassus (1940) —Lassus, L., "Remarques sur l'adoption en Syrie de la forme basilicale pour les églises chrétiennes," *Atti del IV Congresso internazionale di archeologia cristiana ... 1938* (Roma) 1.335–53
Lassus (1947) – Lassus, J., *Sanctuaires chrétiens de Syrie* (Paris)
Lassus (1967) – Lassus, J., *The Early Byzantine World* (New York)
Lassus (1969) – Lassus, J., "La maison des chrétiens de Dura-Europos," *Revue archéologique* (1969) 129–40
Lassus and Tchalenko (1951) – Lassus, J., and G. Tchalenko, "Ambons syriens," *Cahiers archéologiques* 5 (1951) 75–122
Lawlor and Oulton (1927–28) – Lawlor, H. J., and J. E. L. Oulton, *Eusebius, The Ecclesiastical History and the Martyrs of Palestine*, translated with introduction and notes (New York)
Le Bohec (2005) – Le Bohec, Y., *Histoire de l'Afrique romaine (146 avant J.-C.–439 après J.-C.)* (Paris)
Le Glay (1966) – Le Glay, M. *Saturne africain. Histoire* (Paris)

Lehmann (1994) – Lehmann, T., "Anmerkungen zum jüngsten erschienen EAM-Artikeln 'Cimitile'," *Boreas. Münstersche Beiträge zur Archäologie* 17 (1994) 279–92

Lehmann (2004) – Lehmann, T., *Paulinus Nolanus und die Basilica Nova in Cimitile/Nola* (Wiesbaden)

Lemarié (1989) – Lemarié, J., "Il sermone XXVI di Cromazio d'Aquileia per la dedicazione della Basilica Apostolorum," *La chiesa concordiesa 389-1989* (Fiume Veneto) 81–112

Lemerle (1945) – Lemerle, P., *Philippes et la Macédoine orientale à l'époque chrétienne et Byzantine*, 2 vols. (Paris)

Lenox-Conyngham (1982) – Lenox-Conyngham, A., "The topography of the Basilica conflict of A. D. 385/6 in Milan," *Historia* 31 (1982) 353–63

Lepelley (2001) – Lepelley, C., *Aspects de l'Afrique romaine. Les cités, la vie rurale, le christianisme* (Bari)

Leriche and Al Mahmoud (1994) – Leriche, P., and A. Al Mahmoud, "Doura-Europos. Bilan des recherches récentes," *Comptes rendus de l'Académie des inscriptions et belles letters* 1994, 395–420

Leschi (1940) – Leschi, L., "La basilique chrétienne en Algérie," *Atti del IV Congresso internazionale di archeologia cristiana ... 1938* (Roma) 1.145–67

Leschi (1941-42) – Leschi, L. "Fouilles à Tipasa dans l'église d'Alexandre," *Bulletin archéologique du Comité des travaux historiques* (1941–42) 355–70

Leschi (1950) – Leschi, L., *Tipasa de Maurétanie* (Alger)

Leschi (1952) – Leschi, L., *Algérie antique* (Paris)

Leschi (1957) – Leschi, L., *Etudes d'épigraphie, d'archéologie et d'histoire africaines* (Paris)

Leveau (1978) – Leveau, P., "Une mensa de la nécropole occidentale de Cherchel," *Karthago* 18 (1978) 127–31

Levick et al. (1993) – Levick, B., et al., eds., *Monuments from the Upper Tembris Valley, Cotiaeum ...* (London) (*Monumenta Asiae Minoris Antiqua* X)

Liccardo (1992) – Liccardo, G., "Lineamenti di epigrafia cristiana napoletana," *Rivista di archeologia cristiana* 68 (1992) 259–70

Lissi Caronna (1970) – Lissi Caronna, E., "Resti di sepolcri e di alcune strutture romana nel parco della villa Dorio-Pamphili al Gianicolo," *Notizie degli scavi di antiochità*, Ser. 8, 24 (1970) 345–61

Littmann et al. (1921) – Littmann, E., et al., *Syria. Publications of the Princeton University Archaeological Expeditions to Syria in 1904-5 and 1909*, III (Leyden)

Lo Cascio (1999) – Lo Cascio, E., "The population of Roman Italy in town and country," *Reconstructing Past Population Trends in Mediterranean Europe*, eds. J. Bintliff and K. Sbonias (Oxford) 161–71

Löfstedt (1987) – Löfstedt, B., ed., *Zenonis Veronensis tractatus* (Milan)

Longhi (2006) – Longhi, D., *La capsella eburnea di Samagher. Iconografia e committenze* (Ravenna)

Luciani (2000) – Luciani, R., "Le chiese Mariane," *Christiana loca. Lo spazio cristiano nella Roma del primo millennio*, ed. L. Pani Ermini (Roma) 1.131–45

Lusuardi Siena and Sannazaro (1984) – Lusuardi Siena, S., and M. Sannazaro, "Gli scavi della cattedrale di S. Maria," *Archeologia in Liguria* II: *Scavi e scoperti 1976-81* (Genova) 36–48

MacMullen (1981) – MacMullen, R., *Paganism in the Roman Empire* (New Haven)
MacMullen (1984) – MacMullen, R., *Christianizing the Roman Empire (A. D. 100–400)* (New Haven)
MacMullen (1985–86) – MacMullen, R., "Conversion: a historian's view," *The Second Century* 5 (1985–86) 67–81
MacMullen (1988) – MacMullen, R., *Corruption and the Decline of Rome* (New Haven)
MacMullen (1989) – MacMullen, R., "The preacher's audience (AD 350–400)," *Journal of Theological Studies* 40 (1989) 503–11
MacMullen (1993) – MacMullen, R., "The unromanized in Rome," *Diasporas in Antiquity*, eds. S. J. D. Cohen and E. S. Frerichs (Atlanta) 47–64
MacMullen (1990) – MacMullen, R., *Changes in the Roman Empire. Essays in the Ordinary* (New Haven)
MacMullen (1997) – MacMullen, R., *Christianity and Paganism in the Fourth to Eighth Centuries* (New Haven)
MacMullen (2000) – MacMullen, R., *Romanization in the Time of Augustus* (New Haven)
MacMullen (2003) – MacMullen, R., "Cultural and political changes in the 4th and 5th centuries," *Historia* 52 (2003) 465–95
MacMullen (2006) – MacMullen, R., *Voting about God in Early Church Councils* (New Haven)
MacMullen (2008) – MacMullen, R., "The problem of fanaticism," *Sécurité collective et ordre public dans les sociétés anciennes. Fondation Hardt, Entretiens sur l'Antiquité classique ... 2007* (54, 2008) 226–60
MacMullen and Lane (1992) – MacMullen, R., and E. N. Lane, *Paganism and Christianity 100–425 C. E. A Sourcebook* (Minneapolis)
Maier (1987–89) – Maier, J.- L., *Le dossier du Donatisme*, 2 vols. (Berlin)
Mango (1975) – Mango, C., *Byzantine Architecture* (New York)
Manniez (2007) – Manniez, Y., "Les pratiques funéraires à Nîmes dans l'Antiquité Tardive," *Mémoire du geste. Bulletin de l'Ecole antique de Nîmes*, Nîmes, Ecole Antique de Nîmes, no. 27 (2007) 92–99
Maraval (1985) – Maraval, P., *Lieux saints et pèlerinages d'Orient. Histoire et géographie des origines à la conquête arabe* (Paris)
Marec (1958) – Marec, E., *Monuments chrétiens d'Hippone ville épiscopale de Saint Augustin* (Paris)
Marin (1986) – Marin, E., "L'inhumation privilégiée à Salone," *L'inhumation privilégiée du IVe au VIIIe siècle en Occident. Actes du Colloque ... 1984*, eds. Y. Duval and J.-C. Picard (Paris) 221–32
Marin (1989) – Marin, E., "Les nécropoles de Salone," *Actes du XI Congrès international d'archéologie chrétienne ... Lyon ... 1986* (Roma) 2.1227–39
Marin (1989a) – Marin, E., "La topographie chrétienne de Salone," *Actes du XI Congrès international d'archéologie chrétienne ... Lyon ... 1986* (Roma) 2.1117–31
Marin (1994) – Marin, E., "Le contexte archéologique de la sculpture architecturale de Salone," *Catalogue de la sculpture architecturale paléochrétienne de Salone*, eds. N. Duval et al. (*Salona* II) (Rome) xv–xxv
Marino (2005) – Marino, E., "San Clemente," *Roma sacra* 11 (2005) 35–74

Marinone (2000) – Marinone, M., "I riti funerari," *Christiana loca. Lo spazio cristiano nella Roma del primo millennio*, ed. L. Pani Ermini (Roma) 1.71–80

Markschies (2007) – Markschies, C., *Kaiserzeitliche christliche Theologie und ihre Institutionen. Prolegomena zu einer Geschichte der antiken christlichen Theologie* (Tübingen)

Markus (1990) – Markus, R. A., *The End of Ancient Christianity* (Cambridge)

Markus (2005) – Markus, R. A., "Church reform and society in Late Antiquity," *Reforming the Church before Modernity. Patterns, Problems and Approaches*, eds. C. M. Bellitto and L. J. Hamilton (Aldershot UK) 3–19

Marrou (1949) – Marrou, H.-I., "Survivances païennes dans les rites funéraires des donatistes," *Hommages à Joseph Bidez et Franz Cumont* (Bruxelles) 193–203

Martin (1996) – Martin, A., *Athanase d'Alexandrie et l'église d'Egypte au IVe siècle (328–373)* (Paris)

Marusic (1978) – Marusic, B., "Le christianisme et le paganisme sur le sol de l'Istrie aux IVe et Ve siècles," *Arheoloski vestnik* 29 (1978) 567–72

Marzolff (1984) – Marfzolff, P., "Die religiöse Architektur im östlichen Illyrikum," *Rapports présentés au Xe Congrès international d'archéologie chrétienne … 1980* (Thessalonika) 1–17

Mathews (1971) – Mathews, T. F., *The Early Churches of Constantinople: Architecture and Liturgy* (University Park PA)

Matthiae (1962) – Matthiae, G., *Le chiese di Roma dal IV al X secolo* (Bologna)

Maxwell (2006) – Maxwell, J. L., *Christianization and Communication in Late Antiquity. John Chrysostom and his Congregation in Antioch* (Cambridge UK)

Meer (1961) – Meer, F. van der, *Augustine the Bishop. The Life and Work of a Father of the Church*, trans. B. Battershaw and G. R. Lamb (London)

Meer and Mohrmann (1958) – Meer, F. van der, and C. Mohrmann, *Atlas of the Early Christian World* (London)

Metzger (1985–87) – Metzger, M., *Les constitutions apostoliques*, 3 vols. (Paris) (*Sources chrétiennes* 320, 329, 336)

Metzger (1992) – Metzger, M., *Les Constitutions Apostoliques. Introduction, traduction et notes* (Paris)

Mielsch and Hesberg (1986) – Mielsch, H., and H. von Hesberg, *Die heidnische Nekropole unter St. Peter in Rom. Die Mausoleen A   D* (Roma)

Migeon (2006) – Migeon, W., "Le groupe épiscopal de Bordeaux," *Gallia* 63 (2006) 117–19

Millet (1947) – Millet, G., "Sainte-Sophie avant Justinien," *Orientalia Christiana periodica* 13 (1947) 597–612

Mirabella Roberti (1950) – Mirabella Roberti, M., "La posizione dell'altare nelle piu antiche basiliche di Aquileia e di Parenzo," *Rivista di archeologia cristiana* 26 (1950) 181–94

Mirabella Roberti (1995) – Mirabella Roberti, M., "Le basiliche teodoriane di Aquileia e gli 'oratori'," *Splendida civitas nostra. Studi archeologici in onore di Antonio Frova* (Roma) 217–21

Mitchell (1993) – Mitchell, S., *Anatolia. Land, Men, and Gods in Asia Minor* II. *The Rise of the Church* (Oxford)

Mohrmann (1962) – Mohrmann, C., "Les dénominations de l'église en tant qu'édifice en grec et latin," *Revue des sciences religieuses* 36 (1962) 155–74

Molajoli (1943) – Molajoli, B., *La basilica eufrasiana di Porenzo* (Padova)
Morin (1930) – Morin, G., ed., *Sancti Augustini sermones post Maurinos reperti* (Roma) (*Miscellanea Agostiniana. Testi e studi* 1)
Morley (1996) – Morley, N., *Metropolis and Hinterland. The City of Rome and the Italian Economy 200 B. C.– A. D. 200* (Cambridge UK)
Morrison (1979) – Morrison, C., *An Analytical Concordance to the Revised Standard Version of the New Testament* (1979)
Munier (1974) – Munier, C., ed., *Concilia Africae A. 345–A. 525* (Turnhout) (*CCSL* 149)
Musurillo (1972) – Musurillo, H., *The Acts of the Christian Martyrs. Introduction, Texts and Translation* (Oxford)
Nautin (1977) – Nautin, P., ed., *Origène: homélies sur Jérémie Xii–XX et homélies latines* (Paris) (*Sources chrétiennes* 328)
Nongbri (2008) – Nongbri, B., "Paul Without 'Religion': The Creation of a Category and the Search for an Apostle Beyond the New Perspective" (Diss. Yale University)
Nordberg (1963) – Nordberg, H., "Elements païens dans les tituli chrétiens de Rome, 1: Le sigle DM(s) dans les tituli de la ville de Rome," *Sylloge inscriptionum christianarum Musei Vaticani*, ed. H. Zilliacus (Helsinki) 2.211–29
North (1992) – North, J. "The development of religious pluralism," *The Jews among Pagans and Christians in the Roman Empire*, eds. J. Lieu et al. (London) 174–93
Nussbaum (1965) – Nussbaum, O., *Der Standort des Liturgen am christlichen Altar vor dem Jahre 1000*, 2 vols. (Bonn)
Orlandos (1952–57) – Orlandos, A. K., Η ξυλοστεγος παλαιοχριστιανικη βασιλικη της Μεσογειακης λεκανης : μελετη περι της γενεσης της καταγωγης, της αρχιτεκτονικης μορφης, και της διακοσμησεως των χριστιανικων οικων λατρειας αποτων αποστολικων χρονον μεχρις Ιουστινιανου, 3 vols. in 1 (Athens)
Pallas (1977) – Pallas, D., *Les monuments paleochrétiens de Grèce découverts de 1959 à 1973* (Roma)
Pallas (1984) – Pallas, D., "L'édifice cultuel chrétien et la liturgie dans l'Illyricum oriental," *Rapports présentés au Xe Congrès international d'archéologie chrétienne ... 1980* (Thessalonika) 497–570
Pani Ermini (2000) – Pani Ermini, L., ed., *Christiana loca. Lo spazio cristiano nella Roma del primo millennio*, 2 vols. (Roma)
Parkin (1999) – Parkin, T., "Clearing away the cobwebs: a critical perspective on historical sources for Roman population history," *Reconstructing Past Population Trends in Mediterranean Europe*, eds. J. Bintliff and K. Sbonias (Oxford) 153–60
Pasquato (2001) – Pasquato, O., "Katechese," *Reallexikon für Antike und Christentum*, eds. F. J. Dölger et al., 20 (Stuttgart) 423–94
Pavan (1987) – Pavan, M., "Concordia tra IV a V secolo," *Rufino di Concordia e il suo tempo* (*Antichità Altoadriatiche* 31) 2 (Udine) 7–28
Paverd (1970) – Paverd, F. van de, *Zur Geschichte der Messliturgie in Antiocheia und Konstantinopel gegen Enden des vierten Jahrhunderts* (Roma)
Pavia (1998) – Pavia, C., *Guida di Roma sotteranea* (Roma)
Pavolini (2006) – Pavolini, C., *Ostia*, ed. 3 (Roma)

Pelekanidis (1961) – Pelekanidis, S., "Η εξω των τειχων παλαιοχριστιανικη βασιλικη των Φιλιππων," Αρχαιολογικη εφημερις 1955 [1961] 114–179
Pelekanidis (1977) – Pelekanidis, S., Μελετης παλαιοχριστιανικης και Βυζαντινης αρχαιολογιας (Athens)
Pelekanidis (1978) – Pelekanidis, S., "Kultprobleme in Apostel-Paulus-Oktagon von Philippi in Zusammenhang mit einem älteren Heroenkult," Atti del IX Congresso internazionale di archeologia cristiana … 1975 (Roma) 2.393–97
Pelekanidis (1978a) – Pelekanidis, S., "Ανασκαφη Φιλιππων," Πρακτικα της αρχαιλογικης εταιρειας (1978) 65–72
Pelekanidis (1980) – Pelekanidis, S., "Συμπερασματα απο την ανασκαφη του Οκταγωνου των Φιλιππων," Η Καβαλα και η περιοχη της του Συμποσιο αυτο (Καβαλα … 1977) (Thessalonica) 149–58
Pergola (1986) – Pergola, P., "Nereus et Achilleus martyres: l'intervention de Damase à Domitilla," Saecularia Damasiana. Atti del Convegno internazionale … 1984 (Roma) 203–24
Pergola and Barbini (1999) – Pergola, P., and P. M. Barbini, Le catacombe romane. Storia e topografia, ed. 2 (Roma)
Petit (1955) – Petit, P., Libanius et la vie municipale à Antioche au IVe siècle après J.-C. (Paris)
Petzl (2005) – Petzl, G., "Neue Inschriften aus Lydien," Epigraphica Anatolica 38 (2005) 21–36
G.-C. Picard (1957) – Picard, G.-C., "L'archéologie chrétienne en Afrique 1938–1953," Actes du Ve Congrès international d'archéologie chrétienne … 1954 (Rome) 45–59
J.-C. Picard (1989) – Picard, J.-C., "L'atrium dans les églises paléochrétiennes d'Occident," Actes du XIe Congrès international d'archéologie chrétienne. Lyon … 1986 (Rome) 505–53
Piccirillo (1981) – Piccirillo, M., "Note di viaggio in Alta Siria nei villaggi di Qubbet es-Shih e Hawwa," Rivista di archeologia cristiana 57 (1981) 113–25
Pietri (1976) – Pietri, C., Roma Christiana. Recherches sur l'Eglise de Rome, son organisation, sa politique, son idéologie de Miltiade à Sixte III (311–440) (Rome)
Pietri (1978) – Pietri, C., "Recherches sur le domus ecclesiae," Revue des études augustiniennes 24 (1978) 3–21
Pietri (1984) – Pietri, C., "Les origines du culte des martyrs (d'après un ouvrage recent)," Rivista di archeologia cristiana 60 (1984) 293–319
C. and L. Pietri (1990) – Pietri, C., and L. Pietri, eds., Histoire du christianisme des origines à nos jours II. Naissance d'une chrétienté (230–430) (Paris)
Pilhofer (1995–2000) – Pilhofer, P., Philippi, 2 vols. (Tübingen)
Poinssot and Lantier (1925) – Poinssot, L., and R. Lantier, "L'église de Thugga," Revue archéologique 22 (1925) 228–47
Pomares (1959) – Pomares, G., ed., Gélase Ier. Lettre contre les Lupercales (Paris) (Sources chrétiennes 65)
Posta (1989) – Posta, P., "La cattedrale paleocristiana di Faenza," Actes du XI Congrès international d'archéologie chrétienne. Lyon … 1986 (Roma) 1. 257–71
Preger (1901–7) – Preger, T., Scriptores originum Constantinopolitanarum (Leipzig) (one-volume reprint, New York 1975)

Pross Gabrielli (1969) – Pross Gabrielli, G., *L'oratorio e la basilica paleocristiana di Trieste (via Madonna de Mare)* (Bologna)
Purcell (1987) – Purcell, N., "Tomb and suburb," *Römische Gräberstrassen. Selbstdarstellung – Status – Standard. Kolloquium … 1985* (München) 25–41
Puza (2001) – Puza, R., "Titelkirchen, römische Tituli," *Lexikon fü Theologie und Kirche*, ed. 3 (Freiburg) 10.54–56
Quacquarelli (1957) – Quacqarelli, A., ed., *Q. S. F. Tertulliani, Ad Scapulam* (Roma)
Quacquarelli (1966) – Quacqarelli, A., "I luoghi di culto e il linguaggio simbolica nei primi due secoli cristiani," *Rivista di archeologia cristiana* 42 (1966) 237–66
Quasten (1983) – Quasten, J., *Music and Worship in Pagan and Christian Antiquity*, trans. B. Ramsay (Washington)
Raeder (1928–31) – Raeder, J., *Oribasii collectionum medicarum reliquiae* (Leipzig)
Rasch (1993) – Rasch, J. J., *Das Mausoleum bei Tor de' Schiavi in Rom* (Mainz)
Ratzinger (1988) – Ratzinger, J., *Eschatology: Death and Eternal Life*, trans. M. Waldstein (Washington DC)
Raynal (1973) – Raynal, D., "Culte des martyrs et propagande donatiste à Uppena," *Cahiers de Tunisie* 21 (1973) 33–72
Rebillard (1996) – Rebillard, E., "Les *areae* carthaginoises (Tertullien, Ad Scapulam 3, 1). Cimetières communitaires ou enclos funéraires de Chrétiens," *Mélanges d'archéologie et d'histoire de l'Ecole française de Rome, Antiquité* 108 (1996) 175–89
Rebillard (1999) – Rebillard, E., "Eglise et sepulture dans l'antiquité tardive (Occident latin, 3e–6e siècles)," *Annales. Histoire Sciences Sociales* (1999) 1027–46
Rebillard (2003) – Rebillard, E., *Religion et sépulture: l'église, les vivants et les morts dans l'antiquité tardive* (Paris)
Reekmans (1968) – Reekmans, L., "L'implantation monumentale chrétienne dans la zone suburbaine de Rome du IVe au IXe siècle," *Rivista di archeologia cristiana* 44 (1968) 173–207
Reekmans (1989) – Reekmans, L., "L'implantation munumentale chrétienne dans le paysage urbain de Rome de 300 à 850," *Actes du XI Congrès international d'archéologie chrétienne. Lyon … 1986* (Roma) 2.861–915
Reekmans (1995) – Reekmans, L., "Recherches récentes dans les cryptes des martyrs romains," *Martyrium in Multidisciplinary Perspective*, eds. M. Lamberigts and P. Van Deum (Leuven) 31–70
Rendic-Miocevic (1991) – Rendic-Miocevic, D., "Pitanje kronologije razvoja salonitanskih gemina," *Anticka Salona*, ed. N. Cambi (Split) 367–77
Restle (1989) – Restle, M., "Les monuments chrétiens de la Syrie du Sud," *Archéologie et histoire de la Syrie* II. *La Syrie de l'époque achéménide à l'avènement de l'Islam*, ed. J.-M. Dentzer and W. Orthmann (Saarbrück) 373–84
Reynolds and Tannenbaum (1987) – Reynolds, J. M., and R. Tannenbaum, *Jews and Godfearers at Aphrodisias* (Cambridge UK)
Robert (1926) – Robert, L., "Décret des Asklépiastes de Kolophon," *Revue des études anciennes* 28 (1926) 3–9
Robert (1971) – Robert, L., "Un oracle grave à Oinoanada," *Comptes rendus de l'Académie des inscriptions et belles lettres* (1971) 597–619

Romanelli (1940) – Romanelli, P., "La basilica cristiana nell'Africa settentrionale italiana," *Atti del IV Congresso internazionale di archeologia cristiana ... 1938* (Roma) 245-89

Roperti (2003) – Roperti, A., "San Clemente," *Roma Archeologica* 16-17 (2003) 46-48

Rossi (1864-77) – Rossi, G. B. de, *La Roma sotterranea cristiana* (Roma)

Rossi et al. (1922-) – Rossi, G. B. de, et al., eds., *Inscriptiones Christianae urbis Romae septimo saeculo antiquiores* (Roma)

Rott (1908) – Rott, H., *Kleinasiatische Denkmäler aus Pisidien, Pamphylien, Kappadokien und Lykien* (Leipzig)

Roussel (1927) – Roussel, P., "Les mystères de Panamara," *Bulletin de correspondance hellénique* 51 (1927) 123-37

Russell (1989) – Russell, J., "Christianity at Anemurium (Cilicia)," *Actes du XIe Congrès international d'archéologie chrétienne ... Lyon 1986* (Roma) 1621-37

Rutgers (1998) – Rutgers, L. V., *The Hidden Heritage of Diaspora Judaism*, ed. 2 (Leuven)

Rutgers (2000) – Rutgers, L. V., *Subterranean Rome. In Search of the Roots of Christianity in the Catacombs of the Eternal City* (Leuven)

Rutgers (2006) – Rutgers, L. V., "Reflections on the demography of the Jewish community of ancient Rome," *Les cités de l'Italie tardo-antique (IVe-VIe siècle)*, eds. M. Ghilardi et al. (Roma) 345-58

Saffrey and Segonds (2001) – Saffrey, H. D., and A.-P. Segonds, *Marinus, Proclus ou sur le bonheur* (Paris)

Sahin (1997) – Sahin, M., "Grabdenkmäler aus Isaurien und ihre Künstler," *Epigraphica anatolica* 27 (1997) 75-81

Saint-Roch (1986) – Saint-Roch, P., "Sur la tombe du pape Damase," *Saecularia Damasiana. Atti del Convegno internazionale ... 1984* (Roma) 285-90

Saint-Roch (1986a) – Saint-Roch, P., "Un cubicule important dans le cimetière de Damase," *L'inhumation privilégiée du IVe au VIIIe siècle en Occident. Actes du colloque ... 1984*, eds. Y. Duval and J.-C. Picard (Paris) 189-91

Salamito (1995) – Salamito, J.-M., "Chapitre IV. La christianisation et les nouvelles règles de la vie sociale," *Histoire du christianisme des origines à nos jours* II. *Naissance d'une chrétienté (230-430)*, ed. C. and L. Pietri (Paris) 675-717

Saliou (2004) – Saliou, C., "La forme d'un îlot de Doura-Europos. L'îlot C7 revisité," *Doura-Europos. Etudes* V *(1994-1997)* (Paris) 65-78

Salmon (1974) – Salmon, P., *Population et dépopulation dans l'Empire romain* (Bruxelles)

Salzman (2002) – Salzman, M. R., *The Making of a Christian Aristocracy. Social and Religious Change in the Western Roman Empire* (Cambridge)

Salzman (2007) – Salzman, M. R., "Christianity and paganism, III: Italy," *The Cambridge History of Christianity 2: Constantine to c. 600*, eds. A. Casiday and F. W. Norris (Cambridge UK) 210-30

Sannazaro (2000-1) – Sannazaro, M., "L'area si S. Ambrogio a Milano tra tarda antichità e altomedioevo," *Rendiconti della Pontificia Accademia Romana di Archaeologia* 73 (2000-1) 43-61

Saxer (1969) – Saxer, V., *Vie liturgique et quotidienne à Carthage vers le milieu du IIIe siècle* (Rome)

Saxer (1980) – Saxer, V., *Morts martyrs reliques en Afrique chrétienne aux premiers siècles* (Paris)

Saxer (1989) – Saxer, V., "L'utilisation par la liturgie de l'espace urbain et suburbain," *Actes du XIe Congrès international d'archéologie chrétienne. Lyon ... 1986* (Rome) 917–1033

Saxer (1995) – Saxer, V., "Pilgerwesen in Italien und Rom im späten Altertum und Frühmittelalter," *Akten des XII. internationalen Kongresses für christliche Archäologie ... 1991* (Münster) 1.35–57

Saxer (2006) – Saxer, V., "Aux origines du culte de saint Etienne protomartyr. La préhistoire de la révélation de ses reliques," *Les miracles de saint Etienne. Recherches sur le receuil pseudo-augustinien*, ed. J. Myers (Turnhout) 37–46

Scheid (2005) – Scheid, J., *Quand faire, c'est croire. Les rites sacrificiels des Romains* (Aubier)

Schneider (1941) – Schneider, A. M., "Die Grabungen im Westhof der Sophienkirche zu Istanbul," *Istanbuler Forschungen* 12 (1941) 1–47

Schöllgen and Geerlings (1991) – Schöllgen, G., and W. Geerlings, eds., *Didache. Zwölf-Apostel-Lehre, Traditio Apostolica, Apostolische Uberlieferung* (Freiburg)

Schwertheim (1985) – Schwertheim, F., "Neue Inschriften aus Miletopolis," *Epigraphica anatolica* (5 (1985) 77–87

Seeck (1876) – Seeck, O., ed., *Notitia dignitatum* (Berlin)

Selhorst (1931) – Selhorst, H., *Die Platzordnung im Gläubigenraum der altchristlichen Kirche* (Münster)

Sepp (1879) – Sepp, C. S. N., *Meerfahrt nach Tyrus zur Ausgrabung der Kathedrale mit Barbarossa's Grab* (Leipzig)

Serin (2004) – Serin, U., *Early Christian asnd Byzantine Churches in Caria: An Architectural Survey* (Roma)

Shereshevski (1991) – Shereshevski, J., *Byzantine Urban Settlements in the Negev Desert* (Jerusalem)

Skeb (1998) – Skeb, M., ed., *Paulinus von Nola. Epistulae* (Wien)

Snyder (2003) – Snyder, G., *Ante Pacem. Archaeological Evidence of Church Life before Constantine*, 2nd edition (Macon GA)

Sodini (1970) – Sodini, J.-P., "Mosaïques paleochrétiennes de Grèce," *Bulletin de correspondance hellénique* 94 (1970) 699–753

Sodini (1989) – Sodini, J.-P., "Les groupes épiscopaux de Turquie," *Actes du XI Congrès international d'archéologie chrétienne. Lyon ... 1986* (Roma) 1.405–26

Sodini et al. (1989) – Sodini, J.-P., "Les églises du Nord," *Archéologie et histoire de la Syrie II. La Syrie de l'époque achéménide à l'avènement de l'Islam*, ed. J.-M. Dentzer and W. Orthmann (Saarbrücken) 347–72

Soteriou (1929) – Soteriou, G. A., "Αι Χριστιανικαι Θηβαι της Θεσσαλιας," Αρχαιολογικη εφημερις (1929) 1–248

Soteriou (1932/3–1933/4) – Soteriou, G. A., "Τραπεζα μαρτυρων του βυζαντινου Μουσειου Αθηνων," *Byzantinisch-Neugriechische Jahrbücher* 10 (1932/3–1933/4) 173–82

Sotinel (2005) – Sotinel, C., *Identité civique et christianisme. Aquilée du IIIe au VI siècle* (Rome)

Sotomayor (1996) – Sotomayor, M., "Las actas del concilio de Elvira. Estado de la cuestion," *Spania. Estudis d'Antiquitat Tardana oferts ... al professor Pere de Palol I Salallas* (Barcelona) 251–66

Speier et al. (2007) – Speier, J., et al., *Picturing the Bible. The Earliest Christian Art* (New Haven)

Spera (1992) – Spera, L., "Un cubicolo monumentale nella catacomba di Pretestat," *Rivista di archeologia cristiana* 68 (1992) 271–307

Spera (1999) – Spera, L., *Il paesaggio suburbano di Roma dall'Antichità al Medioevo. Il comprensorio tra le vie Latina e Ardeatina dalle Mura Aureliane al III miglio* (Roma)

Spera (2003) – Spera, L., "Il territorio della Via Appia. Forme trasformative del paesaggio," *Suburbium. Il suburbio di Roma dalla crisi del sistema delle ville a Gregorio Magno. Atti ... 2000* (Roma) 266–330

Spera (2003a) – Spera, L., "The Christianization of space along the Via Appia: changing landscape in the suburbs of Rome," *American Journal of Archaeology* 107 (2003) 23–43

Spieser (1984) – Spieser, J.-M., *Thessalonique et ses monuments du IVe au VIe siècle. Contribution à l'étude d'une ville paléochrétienne* (Paris)

Stark (1996) – Stark, R., *The Rise of Christianity. A Sociologist Reconsiders History* (Princeton)

Stein (1959) – Stein, E., *Histoire du Bas-Empire* (Paris)

Stewart-Sykes (2001) – Stewart-Sykes, A., *Hippolytus. On the Apostolic Tradition* (Crestwood NY)

Stirling (2004) – Stirling, L., "Archaeological evidence for food offerings in the graves of Roman North Africa," *Daimonopylai. Essays in Classics and the Classical Tradition Presented to E. G. Berry* (Winnipeg, Canada) 427–52

Tacoma (2006) – Tacoma, L., *Fragile Hierarchies. The Urban Elites of Third-Century Roman Egypt* (Leiden)

Taft (1968) – Taft, R. F., "Some notes on the bema in the East and West Syrian traditions," *Orientalia Christiana periodica* 34 (1968) 326–59

Taft (1975) – Taft, R. F., *The Great Entrance. A History of the Transfer of Gifts and Other Preanaphoral Rites of the Liturgy of St. John Chrysostom* (Rome)

Tate (1997) – Tate, G., "Expansion d'une société riche et égalitaire: les paysans de Syrie du nord du IIe au VIIe siècle," *Comptes rendus de l'Académie des inscriptions et belles lettres* (1997) 913–40

Tavano (1989a) – "I monumenti paleocristiani di Concoria," *La chiesa concordiese 389–1989* (Fiume Veneto 1989) 167–90

Tavano (1989b) – Tavano, S., "Origini cristiani di Concordia," *La chiesa concordiese 389–1989* (Fiume Veneto 1989) 41–52

Tchalenko (1953–58) – Tchalenko, G., *Villages antiques de la Syria du Nord*, 3 vols. (Paris)

Terrier (2003) – Terrier, J., "Approche archéologique des églises rurales edifiées au voisinage de la ville de Genève," *Hortus atrium medievalium* 9 (2003) 21–32

Terry and Maguire (2007) – Terry, A., and H. Maguire, *Dynamic Splendor. The Wall Mosaics in the Cathedral of Eufrasius at Porec*, 2 vols. (University Park PA)

Tesei (1986) – Tesei, G. P., *Le chiese di Roma* (Roma)

Testini (1959) – Testini, P., "Il complesso cultuale scoperto nella regione di Kelibia (Capo Bon)," *Rivista di archeologia cristiana* 35 (1959) 123–44
Testini (1980) – Testini, P., *Archeologia cristiana. Nozioni generali dalle origini alla fine del sec. VI*, ed. 2 (Bari)
Testini et al. (1989) – Testini, P., et al., "La cattedrale in Italia," *Actes du XIe Congrès international d'archéologie chrétienne. Lyon ... 1986* (Rome) 5–229
Thraede (1969) – Thraede, K., "Exorzismus," *Reallexikon für Antike und Christentum*, ed. F. J. Dölger et al., 7 (Stuttgart) 44–117
Thümmel (1994) – Thümmel, H. G., "Tertullians Hirtenbecher, die Goldgläser, und die Frühgeschichte der christlichen Bestattung," *Boreas. Münsterche Beiträge zur Archäologie* 17 (1994) 257–65
Tidner (1963) – Tidner, E., ed., *Didascaliae apostolorum canonum ecclestiasticorum traditionis apostolicae versiones latinae* (Berlin)
Tolotti (1953) – Tolotti, F., *Memorie degli apostoli in Catacumbas* (Roma)
Tolotti (1984) – Tolotti, F., "Sguardo d'insieme al monumento sotto S. Sebastiano," *Rivista di archeologia cristiana* 60 (1977) 123–61
Trebilco (1991) – Trebilco, P. R., *Jewish Communities in Asia Minor* (Cambridge)
Trinci Cecchelli (1978) – Trinci Cecchelli, M., "Osservazioni sul complesso della 'domus' celimontana dei SS. Giovanni e Paolo," *Atti del IX Congresso internazionale di archeologia cristiana ... 1975* (Roma 1978) 551–62
Trombley (1993) – Trombley, F. R., *Hellenic Religion and Christianization c. 370–529*, 2 vols. (Leiden)
Trombley (2006) – Trombley, F., "Overview: the geographical spread of Christianity," *Cambridge History of Christianity* 1 (2006) 302–13
Tronzo (1986) – Tronzo, W., *The Via Latina Catacomb: Imitation and Discontinuity in Fourth-Century Painting* (University Park PA)
Tsafrir (1993) – Tsafrir, Y., "The development of ecclesiastical architecture in Palestine," *Ancient Churches Revealed*, ed. idem (Jerusalem)
Uglesic (2002) – Uglesic, A., *Ranokrscanska arhitektura na podrucju danasnje Zadarske nadbiskupije* (Zadar)
Ulbert (1984) – Ulbert, T., "Die religiöse Architektur im östlichen Illyricum," *Rapports présentés au Xe Congrès international d'archéologie chrétienne ... 1980* (Thessalonika) 19–30
Ulbert (1989) – Ulbert, T., "Bischof und Kathdrale (4.- 7 Jh.): archäologische Zeugnisse in Syrien," *Actes du XIe Congrès international d'archéologie chrétienne. Lyon ... 1986* (Rome) 429–57
Vaes (1984–86) – Vaes, J., "Christliche Wiederverwendung antiker Bauten," *Ancient Society* 15–17 (1984–86) 305–443
Van Andringa and Lepetz (2006) – Van Andringa, W., and S. Lepetz, "Pour une archéologie de la mort à l'époque romaine: fouille de la nécropole de Porta Nocera à Pompei," *Comptes rendus de l'Académie des inscriptions et belles-lettres* (2006) 1131–61
Van Bavel (1995) – Van Bavel, T. J., "The cult of the martyrs in St. Augustine," *Martyrium in Multidisciplinary Perspectives*, eds. M. Lamberigts and P. Van Deum (Leuven) 351–62

Vezic (2005) – Vezic, P., *Zadar na Pragu krscanstva. Arhitektura ranoga krscanstva Zadru* (Zadar)
Veyne (2000) – Veyne, P., "Inviter les dieux, banqueter. Quelques nuances de la religiosité gréco-romaine," *Annales. Histoire, sciences, sociétés* 55 (2000) 3–42
Veyne (2005) – Veyne, P., *L'empire gréco-romain* (Paris)
Violante and Fonseca (1966) – Violante, C., and C. D. Fonseca, "Ubicazione e dedicazione delle cattedrali dalle origini al periodo romanico nelle città dell'Italia centro-settentrionale," *Il romanico pistoiese nei suoi rapporti con l'arte romanica dell'Occidente. Atti del I Convegno internazionale ... 1964* (Pistoia) 303–46
Vööbus (1979) – Vööbus, A., trans., *The Didascalia apostolorum in Syriac*, II: *Chapters XI–XXVI* (Louvain) (*Corpus scriptorum christianorum orientalium, Scriptores Syri* 180)
Walbank (2005) – Walbank, M. E. H., "Unquiet graves: burial practices of the Roman Corinthians," *Urban Religion in Roman Corinth. Interdisciplinary Appraoches*, eds. D. N. Schowalter and S. J. Friesen (Cambridge)
Waltz (1944) – Waltz, P., ed., *Anthologie Palatine* VIII (*Anthologie grecque* VI) (Paris)
B. Ward-Perkins (1998) – Ward-Perkins, B., "The cities," *Cambridge Ancient History* 13 (Cambridge UK) 371–410
J. B. Ward-Perkins (1969) – Ward-Perkins, J. B., "Memoria, martyr's tomb and martyr's church," *Akten des VII. internationalen Kongresses für christliche Archäologie ... 1965* (Roma) 3–24
Welles (1951) – Welles, C. B., "The population of Roman Dura," *Studies in Roman Economic and Social History in Honor of Allan Chester Johnson*, eds. P. R. Coleman-Norton et al. (Princeton) 252–74
White (1990) – White, L. M., *Building God's House in the Roman World. Architectural Adaptation among Pagans, Jews, and Christians* 1: *The Social Origins of Christian Architecture* (Valley Forge PA)
White (1997) – White, L. M., *Building God's House in the Roman World*. 2: *Texts and Monuments for the Domus Ecclesiae* (Valley Forge PA)
Wilkinson (1993) – Wilkinson, J., "Constantinian churches in Palestine," *Ancient Churches Revealed*, ed. Y. Tsafrir (Jerusalem) 23–27
Will (1988) – Will, E., "La population de Doura-Europos: une evaluation," *Syria* 65 (1988) 315–21
Wilpert (1903) – Wilpert, G., *Roma sotterranea. Le pitture delle catacombe romane*, 2 vols. (Roma)
Winkelmann (1999) – Winkelmann, F., *Eusebius Werke. Die Kirchengeschichte* (Berlin) (*Griechische-christliche Schriftsteller* 6)
Wiseman (2006) – Wiseman, J., "The early churches and the Christian community in Stobi, Macedonia," *Akten des XIV internationalen Kongresses für christliche Archäologie ... 1999*, ed. R. Harreither (Roma) 795–803
Wolski and Berciu (1973) – Wolski, W., and I. Berciu, "Contribution au problème des tombes romaines à dispositif pour les libations funéraires," *Latomus* 32 (1973) 370–79
Young (1988) – Young, B. K., "Sacred topography and early Christian churches in Late Antique Gaul," *The First Millennium Papers. Western Europe in the First Millennium* AD (Oxford) 219–40

Zanker and Ewald (2004) – Zanker, P., and B. C. Ewald, *Mit Mythen Leben. Die Bilderwelt der römischen Sarkophage* (München)

Zapella (1998) – Zapella, L., trans., *Giovanni Crisostomo. Le catechesi battesimali* (Milano)

Zovatto (1950) – Zovatto, P. L., *Antichi monumenti cristiani di Iulia Concordia Sagittaria* (Roma)

Index

Aelia Secundula 58
agapai, see suppers
Agnese, S. 80
Alexander bishop 55
Alexandria, churches 22
altars, Christian, position
    above tomb 9, 26, 33, 35, 37, 42–43, 48,
        50 62, 82, 93, 109, 127, 146, 168
    in nave 35, 53, 89
ambo 17, 33, 36, 53, 89, 94, 146–47
Ambrose 57–58, 82, 89–90, 91, 93, 96
Anastasis church 13, 28
Anastasius 47
Andrew relics 26, 91
Anna Perenna 77
Antioch in Pisidia 16–17
Antioch in Syria
    churches in 25–26
    population of 12, 14, 102
Apamea 25
Aphrodisias in Caria 151
Apostles, Instructions of the, see *Didascalia*
Apostolic Tradition 7–8
Aquileia 94
Arcadius bishop 21
arch over chancel 16, 20, 48, 80
arcosolia 67, 73
Ardeatina, anonima della via, see *Marciana*
area enclosed for burials 35, 43, 46, 55, 78
Asclepia 47, 50, 107
Asia Minor, western 8, 22
Asterius bishop of Amaseia quoted 14, 28
Asterius priest 48–49
attendance at Christian service 3, 14–15, 23, 107
Augustine
    opposes cemetery rites 60–61
    preaches 53, 65, 97, 99
    quoted 58–59, 61, 63, 65, 85, 108–9

Augustine
    sends representatives to Nola 92
Aurelius bishop 60
Babylas 26
baptisteries 3ff.
Baris 21
Basil quoted 14, 29, 104
basilica, civil, as model 12, 53
beards 6, 144
bema, see chancel
Bernardi, Jean 23
Bible, quoted 7ff., 24–25, 30, 97, 100, 102
bishops 15–16, 21, 44
Bosio, Antonio xi
Brad 20, 28
burial
    ad sanctos 28, 42, 44, 64, 82, 93
    in cities forbidden 9
    mixed pagan-Christian 25, 43, 74–77
    plots sold for 40, 43
    under church floor 28, 33, 44, 53–54, 59,
        65, 82ff., 93, 110, 125
Caecilianists 51–52, 56, 62, 106
Caesarea 9
Calama 65
Callisto catacomb 74, 97, 168
candles in cult 30, 107, 160
Cappadocia 21, 28
Cara Cognatio 85, 166
Carthage 53, 61, 63, 65
Castellum Tingitanum 57
catacombs, worship in
    in Africa 67
    in Rome ix, xi, 72, 88
catechumens 3–4, 9, 38, 96
    meaning of term 4
    separation of 3–4, 10, 13, 20, 53, 98
cathedra 16, 28, 53
Celsus 31

cemeteries as places for Christian worship   3, 9–10, 52, 63, 104, 164
Chalcedon   28
chancel
   elevated/marked off   10, 17, 36, 53
   extent down nave   10, 14, 16, 49, 53–54, 83, 89, 94
Christian conduct at services   13–14, 53, 108, 110
Christianizing, see conversion
Cirta   52
Clarus   93
class, social
   elite/rich   xi–xii, 6, 14, 20, 37, 44, 47, 62–63, 73–74, 80, 94, 98
   lower   15, 22, 31, 62, 74, 80, 94, 109
   middle   15, 72
Claudian   100
Clement of Alexandria quoted   7, 9
coins as offerings   37, 39–40, 76, 167
Commodilla catacomb   71
Constantine
   and martyr-cult   26, 33, 106
   conversion   ix, 103
   funds church-building   ix, 10, 13, 28, 33, 80–81
Constantinople's churches   15, 28, 33–34
construction of churches post-400   34, 44, 106, 125
conversion
   degree in eastern empire   8, 12, 22, 34
   degree in western empire   94, 104, 112
   historical process   30, 58, 62, 95, 103–4, 112–13
Corinth   23, 45–46
councils ecclesiastical   xii, 12, 16–17, 29, 40, 61–62, 76, 94, 102, 107
Crete   34
Crispina   65ff.
cubicula   69, 73ff.
curtains close off chancel   16, 53
Cyprian
   his mensa and memoria   61, 63, 99, 109
   his relics   106
   quoted   77
Damasus pope   86–87, 90, 100, 104
dancing at worship   29, 44, 61, 77, 91
Daphne   26

deacons   6, 12, 15, 103
death as sleep   24, 37, 58–59, 76, 97
death rate   72
Demeter   46–47
demons/*daimones*
   exorcized   4, 29
   said to be pagan gods   30
   ubiquitous   96
Didache   6
Didascalia   6
diggers, see *fossores*
dining rooms, see triklinia
"DM" *dis manibus*   76, 110
Diocletian   40
diptychs   100
Domnius bishop   41, 43
Donatists   51–52, 56
Drosis   26
Dura
   Christians   2–10
   discovery   xi, 2
   non-Christian religion in   2
Duval, Noël   53, 105
Duval, Yvette   51, 62
Dyggve, Einar   49
East end of churches, see orientation
economy of churches, see finances
Egeria   15
Egypt   163–64
ekklesiai   x, 9, 12
Ennabli, Liliane   63
Ephesus   23, 45
Eucharist
   at anniversaries of decease   9, 59
   at saints' day anniversaries   23, 48, 60, 85
   at synaxary   5
   rites and atmosphere   31, 106
Eufemia/Euphemia   28, 91, 105–6
Eusebia   46
Eusebius quoted   9–10, 16, 33
evergetism, see finances
exorcism/exorcists   4–5, 12, 93, 96
Fafertin   17, 20
fastigium, see arch
Faustus   63
Felix
   Minucius   51
   of Kelibia   55

Felix
    of Nola   91, 93
Février, Paul-Albert   xii, 56, 80, 105
fideles defined   13
finances of churches   20ff., 36, 40, 119, 122
Flavian bishop   28
fossores   72
Frend, W. H. C.   103
frescoes, religious   3, 5, 28–29, 49, 74, 93
funerary meals, see picnics
funerary churches, see burial
Gaianus bishop   43
Geneva   93
Gervasius and Protasius   65, 90–91, 93, 159
Giovanni, S.   80, 89
Gordius   29
Greek language
    use in Dura   6
    use in Rome   x, 7, 70–71
    use in Salona   42
Gregory of Nazianzus quoted   14
    his father   21
Gregory of Nyssa   28
Guyon, Jean   74
Harnack, Adolf von   102
heroes
    heroon   37–40, 93–94
    in the Greek sense   9, 39, 93–94
hippodrome/circus
    in Antioch   118
    in Constantinople   33
Hippo Regius   52, 65
Hippolytus   7
honorabiliores/honoratiores   6, 100
hortus, graveside garden   43, 47
house-churches
    Capernaum   119
    Cirta   157
    Dura   2–5
    Greece   117, 154
    Hippo Regius   52
    Porec   34
    Rome   87
Huarté   25–26
hypogea   25–26, 37
Iader   36, 45
Ignatius of Antioch   8, 26
Irenaeus   x

Isaac bishop of Geneva   94
Isola Sacra   78–79
Italy's cities   51, 94
Januarius   57
Jastrzebowska, Elisabeth   105
Jeradé   19, 98
Jerome quoted   29–30, 70
Jerusalem shrines   10, 13, 167
Jews, Judaism, synagogues   3, 143ff., 163–64
John Apostle   91
John Chrysostom
    at Antioch   12, 26
    at Constantinople   17
    quoted   21ff., 37
Judgment, Last   58, 111
Julian emperor   26
Julian saint   27
Julianus   20
Justin   6
Justus   35
Kalota   17, 20
Kaoussié   26ff.
Kapljuc   47ff.
Kefr, el-   20
Kelibia   54–55
Kharab Shems   21
koimeterion, see death as sleep
Konya   25
Kraeling, Carl   3–4
Krautheimer, Richard   80–81, 87–88
laetitia, see picnic
Laodicea Combusta (Kekaumene)   21, 23
Larissa   45
Lassus, Jean   28
Lateran basilica, see S. Giovanni
Lebaba   20
left position, see right
Libanius   14
libations
    at tombs   24–25, 44ff., 78, 93, 97, 120, 171
    tubes for   24, 37, 59, 79, 85, 93
loculi   67, 72ff., 84
Lorenzo, S.   80
Lucilla   106
Luke relics   26, 91
Lycia   25
Macarius   167
Manastirine   41ff.

manuals, church 4, 6
Marcellino e Pietro, SS.
　basilica 80, 92
　cult 82, 86
Marcellinus pope 71
Marciana basilica 80, 82, 138
Marrou, Henri-Irénée 59, 105
martyr cult
　clergy's attempts to control 57, 60ff., 65, 82, 91, 174
　develops from private act or shrine 35–36, 44, 46–47, 49–50, 57, 60, 86, 91, 93, 107, 130
　in Africa 55–61, 63, 65
　in Asia 25, 29
　in Greece 35ff., 40–41, 46–47
　in Rome 80ff.
　in Syria 25, 29
　includes clergy as such 26, 28, 37, 43–44, 55, 91, 93, 99–100
　saints-days 29, 43, 46, 65, 85–86, 93
　saints' relics treasured 29–30, 33, 46, 49, 57, 91, 93, 106–7
Marusinac 47, 50
mausolea
　in Africa 63
　in and near Rome 69, 78–79, 80
　in Greece 44
　in Nola 91
　in Salona 44, 82
Maxentius 82
Meer, Frederik van der 63
Melania 93
Meletius bishop 26
mensa
　built as a *triklinium* 43, 45–46, 55–56, 63ff., 67, 78–79
　meaning table-top 43, 45–46, 50, 59, 73, 83, 125, 127
　serving as altar 35, 43, 47, 50, 109
Milan
　churches 89ff.
　Edict ix, 10
　saints' cult at 57, 82
Miltiades pope 80
miracles 29, 65, 90, 93, 97, 100, 106, 108, 119–20
mneia, see refrigerium

Monica 57–58
music, see singing
Nabor and Felix 57, 90
nave
　encroachments on 66
　screened 37
Nazarius 93
Nicene council 22
Nicomedia church 9
Nock, Arthur Darby 110
Nola 90ff.
orientation and "occidentation" 17, 37, 53, 89
Origen quoted 8–9
Orlandos, Anastasios K. xi, 48
Ossius 105
Ostia 78
Ovid quoted 77
Oxyrhynchus 23
paganism
　beliefs 24, 85–86, 96
　rites and customs of 23–24, 30, 96, 107
　social structure 100
Palmyra 23
Pammachius 85
Paolo, S. 80, 85
Parentalia and ancestors' anniversary-days 25, 37, 44, 58, 60, 72, 77, 80
patronage, see finances
Paul Apostle
　memorial 37–38, 79ff., 85
　quoted 7, 15
Paul presbyter 37
Paulinus bishop of Nola 91ff., 104, 106
　quoted 85, 93
Paulinus bishop of Tyre 11
peasants, see rural population
Perpetua and Felicitas 63
persecutions
　Decius' 26
　"Great" (A.D. 303–) 8–9, 40–41, 47–48, 56
Peter Saint 79
Peter's, St., church 59, 79–80, 85, 88–89
Philippi 36ff.
Phrygia 25
picnics grave-side (*refrigeria, mneiai*) 24–25, 29, 31, 46, 61, 77
　and remains of food, dishes, ashes 25, 45, 59, 77, 79, 83, 85

pilgrim(age)   15, 44, 49, 93, 108
piscina   45
Pola   34
Polycarp   9
popes   70–71, 82
population, urban
    of Alexandria   22
    of Antioch   12
    of Carthage   63
    of Cirta   52
    of Constantinople   34
    of Dura   9
    of Geneva   94
    of Milan   90
    of Nola   92
    of Oxyrhynchus   122
    of Rome   70
    of Tebessa   65
    of Tipasa   55
Porec   34
Porphyry quoted   9
Porphyrius bishop   40
poverty and beggars   15, 23, 53, 69–70, 85–86, 93
Praetextatus   100
prayer
    intent and reciprocal 30–31, 63, 65, 85–86, 97, 106
    manner of 6–7, 14, 17, 53, 85, 89, 91
Prenestina, basilica "anonima" of the via   80
Primus bishop   43
Provence   104, 112
puticuli   69
Qirqbizze   20
Ravenna   94
race-track-shaped basilicas   34, 81–82
refrigerium, see picnics
relics, see martyr-cult
"religion" defined   25, 30, 55–56, 61–62, 95ff.
reuse of secular or pagan buildings by Christians   26, 39, 93
right-hand position and left   5, 7
ritual, empty   25, 95–96
Rogatus and Vitalis   55
Rosalia "Roses" festival   37
Rossi, G. B. de   xi
Rostovtzeff, Michael   xi
Rouen   91

rural population   12, 17, 21, 31, 93, 102
Sabazius cult   74
Salamito, Jean-Marie   102
Salona   40, 49
Salsa   55–56, 64
salvation   5, 28, 44, 64, 86
Sarapis   24
Satafis   58
seating in churches
    for bishop   28, 53
    for clergy   5, 11–12, 17
    for laity   6–7, 11, 13–14
Sebastiano, S., basilica   79–80, 82ff., 86
sects and heresies
    in Africa   51, 55–56
    in Constantinople   33
    in Dura   5
    in Rome   86
Serjilla   28
Silvester pope   80
singing and instrumental music
    in African churches   61
    in eastern churches   8, 16, 23, 29–30
    in Greek churches   44
    in Italy's churches   93
    in Rome's worship   77
Sirmium   45
Sitifis   53–54, 57
Six, the circiform churches   81–82, 84, 86–87, 105
slaves
    domestic servants   14ff., 20, 74, 98
    numbers in Rome   x, 70
    ownership of   14
Smyrna   9
Socrates Scholasticus quoted   33
solaia/solea   16–17, 35, 44, 84, 94
Sozomen   26
Sperantus   56
Stephen   65
Sulpicius Severus   93
suppers, church
    at Antioch   9
    at Rome   7, 75
    manners at   6, 8, 23
Symmachus   96
synaxary   5, 49, 89
Synesius bishop   100

synthronon 16
    in African churches 53
    in Philippi churches 36
    in Salona churches 48
    in Tyre church 53
Syria churches 15, 17–21
Syriac language 6–7, 20
Tanagra 46
Tebessa 65ff., 106
Tertullian quoted 97, 102
Thebes 45
Theodosius emperor 102
Thessalonica 34, 46–47
Thomas 91
Thignica 98
Tiber (a god) 77
Timgad 54, 59
Timothy, relics of 26
Tipasa 55–61
tituli 87
Trieste 34ff.
triklinia, "dining rooms" 23–24, 45, 63, 79
"Triumph" (clerical procession) 14, 16, 35
Turkey, see Asia Minor
Twenty Martyrs 65, 129

Tyre, basilica of 10–11, 16
Urbanus bishop 86
Uzala 65
Valens emperor 20
Valentinian martyr 47
Velitrae 82
Vibia tomb in Rome 74
Victricius bishop 91, 104
Vigilantius quoted 29–30
vigilia 23, 29, 79, 91, 93
vows/*vota* 63, 86, 97, 168, 171, 174
wells for picnics 55, 58, 77, 79
women
    at picnics 74
    attending church 15
    dancing 29, 44, 77
    indigent 23, 157, 169
    separation from men 5, 7, 13, 20, 24, 53, 89, 97
    veiled 7, 15, 29
    virgins 15, 23
    widows 15, 23
"worship" or "venerate" defined 30, 159
Zeno bishop 108

www.ingramcontent.com/pod-product-compliance
Lightning Source LLC
Chambersburg PA
CBHW062128160426
43191CB00013B/2229

DE LA LOIRE
AUX PYRÉNÉES.